Lachlan Shaw, James Frederick Skinner Gordon

The History of the Province of Moray

Lachlan Shaw, James Frederick Skinner Gordon

The History of the Province of Moray

ISBN/EAN: 9783337326166

Printed in Europe, USA, Canada, Australia, Japan

Cover: Foto ©ninafisch / pixelio.de

More available books at **www.hansebooks.com**

The History

of the

Province of Moray.

Comprising the Counties of Elgin and Nairn, the greater part of the County of Inverness, and a portion of the County of Banff,—all called the Province of Moray before there was a division into Counties.

By LACHLAN SHAW.

NEW EDITION.—IN THREE VOLUMES.

Enlarged and brought down to the Present Time

By J. F. S. GORDON,

Author of "Scotichronicon," "Monasticon," &c.

VOLUME I.

GLASGOW:
Printed at the University Press,
And Published by
HAMILTON, ADAMS, & CO., LONDON,
And
THOMAS D. MORISON, GLASGOW.
1882.

CONTENTS OF VOLUME I.

	PAGE
Author's Preface,	vii.
Editor's Preface,	ix.

INTRODUCTION.

Hector Boece and old Roman Writers,	1
Early Inhabitants of the Province,	7
Origin of the Druids and Celts,	9
Languages of Ancient Britain,	11
Names in the Cartulary of Moray,	16
Marcheta Mulierum,	17
Roman Progress,	19
Buchanan's and Gordon's Descriptions,	28
Possessions of the Celts and Picts,	30
New Families Imported,	32
Culdees and Religious Houses,	33
Land Cultivation,	34
Primitive Dress,	37

PART I.

Name, Extent, and Division of Moray,	40

PART II.

The Geography of Moray,	48
The River Spey,	49
The Parish of Bellie,	50
Family of GORDON,	52
The Parish of Dundurcoss,	76
The Parish of Rothes,	80
The Parish of Knockando,	87
Family of GRANT,	89
The Parish of Boharm,	123

	PAGE
The Parish of Mortlich,	126
Family of DUFF,	156
The Parish of Aberlour,	170
The Parish of Inveravon,	190
The Parish of Kirkmichael,	215
The Parish of Cromdale,	225
The Parish of Abernethy,	240
The Parish of Duthel,	250
The Parish of Rothemurchus,	260
GRANT of Rothemurchus,	261
SHAW of Rothemurchus,	262
FARQUHARSON of Invercauld,	265
Family of MACINTOSH.	268
Family of MACPHERSON,	272
The Parish of Alvie,	277
The Parish of Kingussie and Inch,	284
The Parish of Laggan,	293
The Parish of Speymouth,	300
The Parish of Urquhart,	312
Family of INNES,	313
The Parish of Lhanbryde,	326
The Parish and Royal Burgh of Elgin,	346

AUTHOR'S PREFACE.

THE Author of this undertaking collected the materials of it at different times, and wrote them for his own amusement, without any design of offering them to the public. He perused descriptions of several counties, but had not the good fortune to meet with any tolerable account of the Province of Moray; whereof, mindful of the observation,

> Nescio qua natale solum dulcedine captos
> Tenet, et immemores non sinit esse sui,

he has arranged his collections into the order in which they now appear.

The Geographical Part would be less entertaining if it was not intermixed with a Genealogical Account of several families of eminence and distinction. In this his chief view was to give the true origin and antiquity of those families. It is generally agreed that we had not fixed surnames in Scotland earlier than the eleventh century. Before that period our Kings were named patronymically—as Malcolm MacKenneth, Kenneth MacAlpine, &c. The Author has in his hands manuscript accounts of the families treated of, from which entertaining anecdotes might have been extracted. But this he was afraid, would too much swell the work. He has added the Armorial Bearings of Families. The Romans preserved the distinction of families by the *Jus Imaginis*. They divided the people into *Nobiles, Novi, et Ignobiles*. He that had the Images or Statues of his ancestors, who bore eminent offices, as Prætor, Edile, Consul, &c., was called *Noble;* he that had only his own Image or Statue was *Novus*, or an *Upstart;* and he that had no Statue was *Ignoble*. Those little statues of wood, marble, brass, &c., were carefully preserved and exposed at funerals and other solemn occasions, and possibly from this came our coats of arms. (Vide Suet. in *Octav. et* Diocles and Nisbet's *Use of Armories*.)

In the Geographical and some other parts of this work, the Author has given the names of places in the Gaelic language, which is a dialect of the Celtic. In this he has generally observed the proper orthography, which often differs from the common pronunciation in this kingdom. This he has done to make the etymology of these names of places the more intelligible.

The Natural History, although it contains little to gratify the curiosity of those who are much versant in such reading, yet valuable authors have given an account of natural productions of countries such as they write of, and the peculiar product of this Province ought not to be omitted, and may be entertaining to many.

In the Civil Part there is such variety as cannot but be agreeable to some readers. In the Roll of Barons there are several alterations since the 1760—in some, sons have come into the place of their fathers, in others, collaterals have succeeded; and in 1774 the King and Parliament granted to Major General Fraser the lands and estate of the late Lord Lovate, his father. But the Roll as it now stands is so well known that it is unnecessary to write it.

The Military History is drawn up from the best writers the Author has met with.

The Ecclesiastic Part may appear to some readers too long; the length, however, may be excused, considering the great variety of matter it contains. The Author has used a style so laconic and brief that he could not express his thoughts intelligibly in fewer words; and it may be agreeable to some to find the succession of Ministers in parishes and the changes in ecclesiastical government since the Reformation.

In a Collection of this nature there cannot but be mistakes and errors, which the Author hopes the candid reader will correct rather than condemn.

EDITORIAL PREFACE.

Lachlan Shaw was the son of Donald Shaw, a respectable farmer at Rothiemurchus, in the county of Inverness, and supposed to be a descendant of the ancient family of the Shaws who were long settled at, and proprietors of, the estate of Rothiemurchus. He was an exception to the majority who fill the Scottish pulpits who rise from lowly birth and reach the pinnacle of their meritorious ambition by being schoolmasters or tutors (rarely) in county families. The family of Shaw of Rothiemurchus originally came from the south of Scotland, but was settled in the Highlands at an early period; and as early as the year 1226 they held the lands of Rothiemurchus as tenants from the Bishops of Moray. The Historian was evidently proud of his connections with the ancient family of the Shaws of Rothiemurchus.

His birth must have taken place between the years 1685 and 1690. He probably received the rudiments of his education at Ruthven, in Badenoch, then the only school of any importance (as he states himself) on the whole course of the river Spey; and it is likely he studied philosophy at the University of Old Aberdeen, to which Highland students then, as now, generally resorted. In 1712 he was parochial teacher at Abernethy. In that year the Presbytery of Abernethy presented him to a divinity bursary (see *Synod Records*, v., 314), and he is noted in that capacity in the *Synod Records* of 1712 and 1713. In 1714 (see *Synod Records*, vi., 14) he passed a Synod examination, having previously produced a favourable certificate from Professor Hamilton of Edinburgh.

Having completed his divinity studies at the University of Edinburgh, the Synod recommended their commissioners to send him north to their bounds for active duty. On the 20th September, 1716, he was settled as minister of the parish of Kingussie, and appears on the roll of members of the Synod of Moray on the 30th October that year. (*Synod Records*, vi., 35.) He continued minister at Kingussie until 19th November, 1719, when he was translated to the parish of Calder, and on the 9th May, 1734, he was settled at Elgin, where he continued during the remainder of his life.

Mr. Shaw seems early to have turned his attention to collecting statistics for his History, perhaps for his own personal information, and with no view to after publication. So early as 1726 he had made a tour through the remote parts of the Highlands of the Province of Moray, particularly Glengarry, then almost inaccessible, and he gives a deplorable account of the state of religion, and of the gross ignorance of the inhabitants. It is supposed that his History was written and completed many years before it was published, and that at, or even previous to, the year 1760, it was ready for the press. He speaks of the Rebellion of 1715 as fresh in the memory of persons then living, of the Rebellion of 1745 as a matter of yesterday, and he gives a roll of the freeholders in the different counties connected with the Province for the year 1760. All his facts point to a period much antecedent to the year 1775, when the History was published, except that he brings down the settlement of parochial clergymen and some other necessary details to the period of publication. Mr. Shaw had many facilities for writing a History of the Province of Moray. Born and brought up on the banks of the Spey, and minister of Kingussie until the year 1719, he had thus an opportunity of acquiring the most accurate information as to the families of Grant, Gordon, Macpherson, Macintosh, and others, then the leading proprietors in that district. Removed next to Calder, he remained for fifteen years among the Campbells of Calder, Roses of Kilravock, Brodies, Frasers, &c., to whose charter-chests he had no doubt free access. Translated to Elgin, where he remained for 43 years, till the close of his long life, he had doubtless the best opportunities of examining all the County Records, Registers of Synods and Presbyteries, titles of the families of Dunbars, Innes, Duff, and other proprietors. These advantages, coupled with unwearied diligence and very considerable talents, enabled him to complete the best local history of any district in Scotland, and to embody in wonderful small space a mass of most accurate information, which, except for his industry, would have been in a great measure entirely lost. His pages are not encumbered with *talk*. A few words communicate the fact, backed with his authority—without a particle of humour or wit to sharpen or enliven the assertion. All throughout, the patient reader has to wade through the slough of historic drudgery which the footsteps of the industrious author long ago imprinted. Every line is a study and draft on the attention; for a "popular" work (in modern acceptation) it is not. In the year 1769, Pennant visited Elgin on the occasion of his first tour in Scotland, and he mentions having then visited Shaw, whom he states to be 90 years of age. (This is evidently a mistake, for Shaw could not have been then above 84 at the utmost.) He furnished Pennant with a great many details and statistics relative to the Province of Moray, evidently extracted from his History, not then published, and which are printed in the Appendix to the first volume of his Tour. (See *Pennant*, vol. i., edition 1790, p. 163, and Appendix to that volume, pp. 280-314.)

Lauchlan Shaw was twice married. His first wife was a Miss Stewart, daughter of Collector Stewart (of the Customs), at Inverness, by whom he had a son and daughter, David and Anne. David went to New York and there married a Miss Day, by whom he had two sons and two daughters. Janet, one of the daughters of David, married a Mr. Wilkies, nephew of the famous John Wilkies, and by him had a daughter married to the late Lord Jeffrey of Edinburgh. Anne married Bailie John Copland, of Aberdeen, and had a daughter, Helen, married to Dr. Patrick Forbes, minister of Boharm, afterwards Professor of Humanity at Aberdeen. Mr. Shaw's first wife did not live long, and he married again on 14th March, 1727, Ann Grant, daughter of Duncan Grant, one of the Bailies of Inverness. By her he had a large family, of whom grew up Duncan, Lachlan, and Donald, Mary, Isabella Marjory, and Sarah. Duncan was minister at Rafford from 1753 to 1783, whence he was translated to Aberdeen. He was eminent in his day as a divine and a scholar, was made a Doctor of Divinity, and Moderator of the General Assembly. He married Jean Gordon, daughter of the Rev. George Gordon, minister of Alves, and had three sons and four daughters, all of whom seem to have died without issue. Lachlan, the second son, went to Jamaica, was there seventeen years, and died in London on his return to England. David died at the age of eighteen, when preparing to set out to join his brother Lachlan in Jamaica. Mary and Isabella both died unmarried. Marjory married the Rev. William Peterkin, one of the ministers of Elgin. Sarah married a son of William Donaldson, at Morriston, near Elgin, and had a large family, of whom was Lachlan Donaldson, St. John, New Brunswick, and some time Mayor of that city, who compiled this sketch.

Shaw resigned his charge as one of the ministers of Elgin on 5th April, 1774, and died at Elgin, 23rd February, 1777, and must have been then at least 90 years of age. (See separate *Register of Presbytery of Elgin*, p. 149.) He was survived by his wife, Ann Grant.

He was evidently a hard student, and kept up his knowledge of the literature of his country to the close of his long life, and he was the centre of the literary society of this part of the country at the time. He was on intimate terms with many of the proprietors of the county, particularly the families of Brodies and Dunbar of Northfield, with whom he communicated on the literature of the day, and exchanged new publications. He seems also to have been a Gaelic scholar. He corresponded with Lord Hailes and others on historical, literary, and antiquarian subjects.

During his life the most important events in the history of his country, both in Church and State, took place, and these he has recorded in his interesting Work. He was probably alive at the time of the Revolution in 1688, when the sceptre for ever passed away from the male line of the House of Stuart. He was approaching the years of manhood when the Union between Scotland and England took place in 1707. He witnessed the Rebellions of 1715 and 1745, and the breaking up of the Highland Clans by the abolition of the heritable jurisdictions in 1748; and he lived to see the commerce, agriculture, and manufactures of the country raised from the state of depression succeeding the Union to one of much comparative progress and prosperity, and the foundations of national wealth placed on a sure and firm basis. In regard to the Church, he was alive when, by the Act 1690, Episcopacy and lay patronage were abolished, and Presbyterianism was restored. He was only grown to manhood when lay patronage was again introduced by the Act 1712; and he was a minister of the Church during the famous Marrow controversy, the Secession of 1732, and the commencement of the Relief Church in 1752. A contemporary of Wodrow, Boston, Willison, and the Erskines, as well as of Robertson, Blair, and Carlyle, he saw the decline of the "Evangelical" party, and the beginning, progress, and final triumph of the "Moderate" party in the Church. With reference to national literature, he saw it, from a period of the deepest depression, raised to the full blaze of glory by the publications of Robertson, Hume, Adam Smith, Blair, Smollet, and others.

Cosmo Innes writes in his Preface to the *Registrum Episcopatus Moraviense:*—"The Bishoprick of Moray has been more fortunate than the other districts of Scotland in forming the subject of the labours of a diligent and zealous local historian. Shaw's *History of the Province of Moray*, though awkwardly arranged and defective in many particulars, may yet boast of being the best district history of Scotland. He derived his information in general from authentic sources, and, among other materials, made use of the Chartulary of the Bishoprick. It seems now indeed wonderful that the access to such sources of knowledge, and the acknowledged care and industry of the author, did not produce a more learned and satisfactory Work. But it must be remembered that the study of historical antiquities was in his time in its infancy, and that in Scotland the Reformation produced such a revolution in laws, customs, manners, and even language, that it is still like venturing to talk in a foreign tongue for a Scotchman to enter upon the field of ancient ecclesiastical institutions."

Within the latter half of this century, Historical subjects have gradually been rewritten. Evidence, not before possessed by the writers of a previous generation, is now freely laid open and diligently explored. Our National documents and State papers are no longer excluded from the research of the student, whilst our landed gentry are doing their best to further this spirit of inquiry by permitting their Papers to be examined by the Historical MSS. Commission. The result of these advantages is now apparent. Events which, with their dates, we learned (by *taws*) in the days of our youth in School books, puerile in all conscience, are proved never to have taken place; while the characters of prominent persons, *e. g.*, Mary Queen of Scots, assume now altogether a different phase.

In addition to his *History of the Province of Moray*, Shaw is the author of the continuation of Rose's *Genealogy of the Family of Kilravock*, published by the Spalding Club in 1848. He also edited the Rev. Dr. Macpherson's *Critical Dissertations*, with Notes and Additions: London, 1768. Mr. Robert Young states that he left a good many MSS. on scientific subjects, which he saw in the possession of Mrs. Grant, his granddaughter, at whose decease they were lost.

In 1827 a second Edition of Shaw's *Province of Moray* was published by John Grant, bookseller in Elgin; but the original text cannot be distinguished from the extraneous additions and partizan observations. In the present Edition the whole of the original *Shaw* is given in prominent large type, at once distinguishable from the bracketed Corrections and Addenda, with the authorities. Even the *tilts* for his and Shaw's idea of ecclesiastical polity are allowed to pass unchallenged, the field being left to themselves, where they have their own play in their own way. A common transgression of Historians is to foist their idiosyncrasies, leaving an evanescent offensive odour.

In a verbose Note of small type, extending from page 325 to page 327, in Grant's Edition, occurs this intolerant episode :—
. . . . "The foolish maintenance of all the variety of vagabond Gospellers, Seceders, Reliefs, Methodists, Haldonites, Independents, &c., who prey upon their people by substituting their respective kinds of sanctimonious scrupulosities for the simple apostolic worship of the Presbyterian [Established] Church, unvarnished by prelatic pomp, and purified from sectarian cant and hypocritical grimace. The first Bishops of our nation . . . . were similar to the modern sectarian vagabonds, and performed their prelatic functions in all places without distinction." The most befitting ejaculation, in the way of rejoinder, to this editorial specimen can be supplied by the appreciative reader. It is not fit for the home circle nor out of doors.

In translating some of the Charters (mutilated in the Appendix), Grant renders Bricius "*Bruce*" / At page 421 Ranulph, Earl of Moray, is called "*Randolph,*" which is much the same as calling rain *drain.* At page 455, line 3, *fratri* is translated "*gentlemen.*" At page 456, line 1, *gentes* is translated "*blackguards.*" It should be people, followers, or vassals—certainly not "*blackguards.*" Since the Issue of both Editions of *Shaw,* the *Registrum Episcopatus Moraviense* has been published, which utterly negatives the re-issue here of the fragmentary and incorrect Charts given in the former Appendix or Appendices.

In 1798, " A Survey of the Province of Moray : Historical, Geographical, and Political, was printed at Aberdeen for Isaac Forsyth, bookseller, Elgin." This was the conjoint labour of the Rev. John Grant, Minister of Dundurcas, and latterly of Elgin, and of the Rev. William Leslie, Minister of St. Andrews-Lhanbryd, whose eccentricities and beneficence in granting original certificates of character, to all and sundry, are still in remembrance. Mr. Grant prepared Chapters I. and II., and Mr. Leslie the III. and IV. It is now very scarce, and has in consequence been printed *in extenso* in this Edition, as a valuable auxiliary to *Shaw*. It got the soubriquet of " Little Isaac."

"*Sketches of the Past and Present State of Moray*" came before the public in 1839, by William Rhind, illustrated with beautiful etchings by Donald Alexander. The former was born at Inverlochty in 1797. He had the misfortune to be deformed in the ankles, but was a genius in mind, being a surgeon and the author of many volumes and treatises on Natural history, geology, zoology, &c. He died at Woodhaven, near Newport, Fifeshire, in 1874.

In 1842 appeared "*Sketch of the Geology of Moray,*" by Patrick Duff. I bought the Presentation Copy "To Mr. Oswald Brodie, with best wishes from the Author.—July, 1844." This thin 8vo is illustrated with eleven plates, and its contents were first published in a series of twelve articles in *The Elgin Courant.*

In 1851, from the *Gazette* office, Forres, came "*The Lintie o' Moray,*" being a Collection of Poems, chiefly composed for and sung at the Anniversaries of the Edinburgh Morayshire Society from 1829 to 1841. This thin volume contains for the most part the compositions of William Hay, who was born in the White Horse Inn Close, Elgin, about 1794. In 1860 appeared a Lecture on the Antiquities of Moray by Professor Cosmo Innes. In 1866 John Camden Holden, of London, published " Elgin and the Lantern of the North." In 1868 " Morayshire Described " was issued by Russell & Watson, Elgin.

At a meeting of the Edinburgh Geological Society in 1881, a Paper was read by Thomas D. Wallace, Inverness, on "Recent Geological Changes on the Moray Firth." He gave an elaborate description of the changes in question, and remarked that there could be no doubt but the waters of the Moray Firth from Buckie to Covesea, a distance of over 20 miles, were receding from the land. This was not caused by the mass of land rising, but by the sea banking itself out with the aid of the wind. From Lossiemouth to Kingston, at the mouth of the Spey, great changes might be seen taking place daily. The changes at the mouth of the Spey were very remarkable, although they had proved most disastrous to the inhabitants of this interesting little village. In summarising the results brought out in the course of his paper, Mr. Wallace said that all the rivers which he had mentioned at no great distant date entered the Firth at points considerably to the west of their present outlets, and they were again tending in that direction; that some of the rivers had not only changed their mouths, but their channels for considerable distances; that all around the shore of the Firth there were beaches or terraces of different origins and of different dimensions; that in some places the sea was gaining upon the land, while in others the very reverse was taking place; and that the accumulation of sand, gravel, and pebbles were almost entirely confined to the south shore.

Mr. James Fraser, C.E., Inverness, also contributed a Paper on "The Recent Formations and Glacial Phenomena of Strathnairn." It was stated that Strathnairn had been found to be remarkably rich in traces of the great Ice Age, and an account was given of the boulder clay and other superficial deposits found overlying the silurian and old red sandstone rocks of the district, and of the traces of ice in connection with the rocks and boulders. All the recent formations, in their various forms, the writer was disposed to ascribe almost entirely to the operation of ancient glaciers. The Nairn valley runs in a north-easterly direction, and is 30 miles long, by from 2 to $7\frac{1}{2}$ miles wide. Its eastern watershed is formed by a high range of hills, composed of gneiss, rising to a maximum height of 2,637 feet, all giving evidence of glacial denudation in their smooth-rounded tops and ice scratchings. The western watershed is formed in great part of a low ridge of old red sandstone, the extreme south end of this watershed being a series of hills and gaps. In discussing the boulder clay and the overlying gravelly till and sand, Mr. Fraser indicated the opinion that the large accumulations of sand found at, and for some distance above, Daviot and Craggie originated in great measure from floods diverted from the Findhorn to the Nairn by way of Loch Moy and Craggie. Travelled boulders of granite, gneiss, red porphyry, conglomerate, and sandstone, of all shapes and sizes, up to 500 or 600 tons, are found in great numbers over the district, and, with a few unaccounted-for exceptions, are found in a north-easterly direction from the parent rocks.

The Paper was illustrated by carefully-prepared diagrams.

The Corrections, Emendations, and Addenda "to the Ministers of the Protestant Church" have been laborious, and this Compartment, *per se*, much needed, was worth republishing. The trustworthy *Fasti Ecclesiæ Scoticaniæ* of the late Rev. Dr. Hew Scott, Anstruther Wester, has been consulted and collated, parish after parish.

Some idea of the labour and continuous research involved in preparing the *Fasti* may be formed, when the author states that he has "visited all the Presbyteries in the Church and above 760 different parishes, for the purpose of examining the existing records. In this way he has had an opportunity of searching 860 volumes of Presbytery and 100 volumes of Synod records, besides those of the General Assembly, along with the early Registers of Assignations and Presentations to Benefices, and about 430 volumes of the Testament Registers in the different Commissariats."

"*Annals of the Parish and Burgh of Elgin*," &c., by Robert Young, solicitor, appeared a few months after his death in January, 1879. Although inconvenient and bulky in form, yet the volume is well executed by the industrious author, who for many years was preparing so large a mass of reliable history. A very limited impression of his first literary labours was printed in 1868, titled "*Notes on Burghead:* Ancient and Modern, with Appendix, containing Notices of Families connected with the place at different periods, and other information. (For private circulation)," pp. 106. Captain Dunbar Dunbar sent as a contribution to the thin volume an Inventory of the furniture, plate, and effects which belonged to James, second Lord Duffus, at the period of his death in 1705, in his houses at Elgin and Duffus. The apartments show the size of "The Lodgeing Att Elgin":—Hall, dyning room, drawing room, moy-hair room, my lady's room, back room, green room, laigh or east room, blew room, oratry chamber, oratry, second table room, dressing room, brew house. In "The Lodgeing Att Duffus":—Low parlour, parlour chamber, my lady's room, second table room, dyning room, my lord's closet, my lady's closet, east room, nurcery room, gentleman's room, liggatter room, green closet, painted room, the oratry, fyre closet, woman-house, stables, garden chamber, plate, &c., horses, &c., kitchin and fyre vessel.

In 1870 Mr. Young published a small Edition of 250 copies of a "*History of Spynie*," compiled with his usual accuracy.

HISTORY OF THE
PROVINCE OF MORAY.

INTRODUCTION.

IN vain shall one expect to find a rational account of the ancient state of Scotland or North Britain, unless he consult the Roman writers. Geoffrey of Monmouth [born 1110, died 1154] will have North Britain called Albania, from Albanactus, son of Brutus, the grandson of Æneas the Trojan. And Hector Boece* calleth the same country Scotia, from Scota, the daughter of one of the Pharaohs, kings of Egypt. These, and the like, are fables below the dignity of history, and fit only for venal bards.

* Hector Boece, Boyce, or Boethius, was born at Dundee in 1470. He was appointed Principal of King's College, Aberdeen, about 1500. He wrote *Lives of the Bishops of Aberdeen*, but his great production is the *History of Scotland* (*Scotorum Historia ab illius gentis origine*), 1526, which has been alternately abused and complimented, especially by Lloyd and Stillingfleet, both Bishops of Worcester. His *Scottish History* is indeed full of natural eloquence, although tinctured with fanciful miracles pretended to signalise every public revolution. He died about 1550.—(ED.)

In describing the ancient state of the southern provinces of this kingdom, the Roman writers are sure guides that may be relied on. Tacitus' account of the expeditions of Julius Agricola, Herodian, Dion Cassius, Ammianus Marcellinus, Claudian,* and others, throw much light upon our history, give an account of the actions of the Romans in Britain during 400 years, describe their colonies, forts, camps, prætentures, naval stations, and military ways; and give some

---

* 1. *Caius Cornelius Tacitus* was born about 61, at Interamna (now Terni), and died about 117. He was successively Prætor and Consul, and was on intimate friendship with Pliny. His principal works are his "Annals," containing the History of Rome, from the death of Augustus to that of Nero; a History, embracing a period of 28 years, from 69 to 96; a Life of his father-in-law, Cn. Julius Agricola; and his Treatise on the manners of the Germans.

2. *Cneius Julius Agricola* was born about 37, and died in 93. His father, Julius Græcinus, was put to death by Caligula, and his mother afterwards was murdered in a piratical excursion by the fleet of Otho. The Romans had never been able to conquer Britain; hence this charge was committed to Agricola, who arrived in Britain in 78, and extended his inroads as far as the Tay. He crossed the Forth in 84 at Queensferry, and subjected whole regions unknown to the Romans. Domitian, the Roman emperor, gets the credit of having poisoned him.

3. *Herodian* was a Greek historian of the Roman empire about 236.

4. *Dion Cassius* was born about 155, and died about 229.

5. *Ammianus Marcellinus* was born at Antioch. At an early age he became a soldier. Although a Greek, he wrote his *History* at Rome, embracing a period from the reign of Nerva to the death of Valens. He died about 390.

6. *Claudian* or *Claudius Claudianus* flourished in the fourth century. Authors differ in his birth-place, mentioning Florence, Gaul, Spain, and Alexandria in Egypt. No poet has approached nearer to Virgil. He died about 404.—(ED.)

account of the natives with whom the Romans had any intercourse, and whom they call in the general, Britanni, Britones, and Caledonii; and more particularly Scoti, Picti, Altacoti, Vecturiones, Dicalidones, Vacomagi, Ladeni, &c. But it was the misfortune of the northern parts of Scotland that the Romans (from Julius Cæsar's first descent into Britain to about A.D. 426, that they abandoned the island) never, that I have found, penetrated into them, excepting once in the reign of the Emperor Septimius Severus, in the beginning of the third century, of whom Xiphilinus writeth, that he marched into the northmost extremity of the island. "Ingressus est in Caledoniam, eamque dum pertransiret, habuit maxima negotia, quod sylvas cæderet, et loca alta perfoderet, quodque paludes obruerit aggere, et pontes in fluminibus faceret: Nec ab inceptis desiit, quousque ad extremam partem insulæ venit; ubi diversum, quam apud nos sit, cursum solis, itemque noctium et dierum, tam æstivorum quam hybernorum, magnitudinem diligentissime cognovit."* In this expedition Severus lost 50,000 of his army, without once fighting

---

* *Translation.*—He invaded Caledonia, and in his progress endured the heaviest labour in cutting his passage through woods, levelling obstructions, in raising mounds through marshes, and in making bridges on rivers. He did not relinquish his undertaking, until he came to the farthest end of the island, where he most studiously remarked the difference in the course of the sun, and also the greater length both of the summer days and of the winter nights than it is with us.—(ED.)

the Caledonians, being overcome by cold, hunger, and fatigue. And after him no Roman marched so far into the north.

I have said it was the misfortune of the northern countries that the Romans were so little acquainted with them; for wherever they settled they softened the rough temper and civilised the rude manners of the natives. They introduced letters, arts, and sciences. They taught agriculture, and laid the foundations of cities and towns, navigation and commerce. Hence the many towns and villages on both sides of the Frith of Forth had their rise from the Roman colonies, forts, and naval stations. And the foundation of the culture and fertility of the Lothians was laid by their industry; while the western coast, from the Clyde northward, into which the Romans never entered (though better furnished by nature with bays, harbours, and creeks), remained long uncivilised, without towns, trade, or commerce.

It is true, Julius Agricola sent a fleet of ships to sail round the island, of which Tacitus says— "Hanc oram novissimi maris tunc primum Romana classis circumvecta, insulam esse Britanniam affirmavit, ac simul incognitar ad id tempus insulas, quas Orcades vocant, invenit, domuitque; dispecta est et Thyle."* To this navigation, I

---

* Tacit. *Vita Agricolæ*, cap. 10 sect. 5.—*Translation*—The Roman fleet then first sailed round the coast of this wholly unknown sea, ascertained that Britain was an island, and at

question not, we owe the geographical Tables of Ptolemy in the second century; which tables, as Gerard Mercator observeth, are pretty exact, if what he placeth towards the east is turned to the north. In their descents the captains of these ships described the coasts, discovered the people inhabiting them, and gave them the names we have in Ptolemy's Tables—not new Latin names (the Romans seldom, if ever, gave such to any place or people they discovered or conquered), but the names the natives gave them in their own language, and to which these sailors, or perhaps Ptolemy, gave a new termination, and softened some British words, by the change of one or more letters. Such names are—*Vernicones*, or the inhabitants of the Mearns; *Morini*, of Mar; *Tazali*, of Buchan; *Cantini*, of Ross; *Cantæ*, of Caithness; *Cornavii*, of Strathnaver; and *Æsturium Vararis*, the Frith of Moray. All these are British words, with Latin inflexions; and, let me add, that as these navigators could only discover the coasts, so Ptolemy only describeth the coasts, and not the inland parts.

In the middle ages of our nation we have mention, and little more than mention, of Moray and the inhabitants thereof. A manuscript, *De Situ Albaniæ* (a trifling performance in the twelfth

the same time discovered and subdued the unknown islands, which they call the Orkneys; and even Thule was descried.— (ED.)

century), speaking of the ancient division of Albania into seven kingdoms, says—" Sexto divisio est Muref et Ros." *Excerpta ex veteri chronico Regum Scotorum* beareth—" Donevaldus, filius Constantini, apud oppidum Fother occisus est a gentibus." " Malcolmus filius Domnail cum exercitu perexit in Moreb." *Nomina Regum Scotorum ex Registro Prioratus St. Andreæ*, says— " Dovenal Mac Constantin mortuus est in Fores." " Malcolmus Mac Dovenald interfectus est in Ulurn (forte Aldern) a Moraviensibus." " Duff Mac Malcolm interfectus est in Fores, et absconditus sub ponte de Kinlos, et sol non apparuit quamdiu ibi latuit."* After the tenth century we have so frequent accounts of Moray that I shall not descend to particulars.

There are few countries in Scotland (except Moray) but descriptions of them may be met with in print or in manuscript. Even in the northern parts, Dr. Nicolson, in his *Scottish Historical Library*, mentions descriptions of Shetland, Orkney, Caithness, Sutherland, Buchan,

* Innes' *Critical Essay*, vol. ii., Appendix.—*Translation*— " The sixth division is Moray and Ross. *Extracts from the old chronicle of the Kings of Scotland* beareth—" That Donald, the son of Constantine, was murdered near the town of Forres by the savages." " Malcolm, the son of Domnail, proceeded with an army to Moray." *The Names of the Kings of Scotland from the Register of the Priory of St. Andrews*—" Dovnal Mac Constantin died in Forres." " Malcolm Mac Dovenald was slain by the people of Moray in Ulurn (probably Auldearn)." " Duff Mac Malcolm was murdered in Forres, and concealed under the bridge of Kinloss; and the sun did not shine as long as he lay hidden there."—(ED.)

Mearns, and others. But I have not been so
fortunate as to have read or heard of a description
of the country of Moray. This renders the
task I have cut out for myself the more difficult.
I walk on untrodden ground, having no author,
ancient or modern, to conduct me; and I must
rest contented with what materials my sphere of
reading, and the testimony of credible persons,
have furnished me.

THE sequel is drawn from Ptolemy of Alexandria, Richard of Cirencester, The Chartulary of Moray, Fordun, Ferrerius, History of the Abbey of Kinloss, and the writings of Sir James and Sir David Dalrymple, and Sir William Jones.

THE EARLY INHABITANTS OF THE PROVINCE.

The wandering tribes and barbarous clans who occupied the country in remote times gave little attention to their own history, and had few advantages for preserving accounts of their state and actions. This limits the knowledge of the Aborigines of our country in early periods to a few facts conveyed to us, through the medium of foreign language and manners, from a lettered people, who, by trade or conquest, had acquired some acquaintance with them; or to conjecture and reasoning, founded on a few public monuments, with remains of their language, and some ancient usages that were observed, until history became established on positive evidence.

The conjectural part of our history is highly uncertain, if not in many particulars fabulous. Before the use of letters, neither the names nor the actions of men could be preserved little more than a century after their death. Our insular situation exposed us to every invading foe, and colonies of various nations were established among us. This weakens the evidence of our national traditions: it gives us an unstable heterogeneous mass of circumstances, to which we neither can assign original or date; nor can we often separate them so as with an absolute degree of precision to determinate what part of these indigested materials belong to the Aborigines or to the colonies who at different periods settled in the island. After every degree of selection and accuracy, darkness and uncertainty attend the conclusions, that by no means banish doubt from the human mind.

But, amidst all this obscurity in which our antiquities are involved, a dawn appears that throws a portion of light on even the ancient part of our history. By this we can ascertain in a certain degree from the local situation of the neighbouring countries, from the present evidence of language, and from ancient authors, who were the original inhabitants of Britain, and the distinguished colonies that established themselves in it at different periods. It is impossible to ascertain the eras of these events exactly: it can be only asserted that they were.

It is evident to a demonstration that the west was peopled from the east. Modern researches have in a great measure established it, that Iran, or Persia in its largest extent, was the centre of population, knowledge, languages, and arts, which, from the earliest antiquity, spread out in all directions to all the regions of the world. From that country Hindoos, Arabs, Tartars issued; as did, in the direction from north-east to south-west, those myriads that at first peopled the wilds of Europe and afterwards at different times invaded it. They are descended of an older nation, from whom the Hindoos, Goths, &c., had a common origin, as the similarity of language and religion fully evinces, and from whom they also received their arts and sciences.

This might be proved by analytical investigation, in as convincing a manner as historical facts of so high antiquity are capable of receiving, was this the proper place. Suffice it to mention that the Hindoos, Greeks, Tuscans, Scythians, or Goths, Celts, Chinese, and Japanese, proceeded from one central country—Iran at large. There is great affinity between the primeval languages of Asia and those spoken in Europe, particularly in the British isles. The language of the first Persian empire was the mother of the Sanscrit as well as of the Gothic, Greek, and Latin. Pliny observed that the British religious ceremonies were similar to those of Persia. Strabo mentions that the Samothracian institutions were practised in Britain.

It is more than probable that the Druids of this island were the immediate descendants of a tribe of Brahmins who emigrated from Thibet into Tartary, and there uniting with the Celto-Scythians introduced the Bramin religion, which, mingling with the tenets of the Celto-Scythians, spread over Europe.

The Brahmanic original of the Druids appears from their doctrine of transmigration, their knowledge of astronomy, their abstinence from certain kinds of food as unclean, and belief of the destruction of the world by fire, &c. The Druid circles were solar temples, of which Stonehenge was the most distinguished. These circles were also employed for public deliberation and the distribution of justice. In Norway and Iceland they are named *Dom Thing*, *Ting*, or *judicial circles*. They were used for these different purposes, as the ancients always opened their meetings for civil affairs with acts of religion. From this eastern source we are to derive those hieroglyphical representations of serpents, elephants, and other figures on the obelisks in Angus-shire. Similar figures are carved on obelisks in Japan.

The most ancient inhabitants that can be traced in Europe are the Celts who, in remote antiquity, occupied all the Continent from the mouth of the Oby to Cape Finisterre. They were the Aborigines of Gaul, which was early and powerfully peopled, and from Gaul they penetrated into Britain. It is uncertain how long they preserved the undisturbed possession of Europe; but, in time, another immense body, called Scythians, came from Iran, and making an irruption, drove the Celts before them and occupied a great part of the Continent. At length they penetrated into Britain, which produced the first mixture of inhabitants in that island. But, independent of this general evidence that the Celtæ and Scythians came from the east, there is also evidence in the antiquities of Britain and Ireland that establishes it with a high degree of probability. The worship of the sun, with many other practices, proves this, as do the names of hills, rivers, and promontories, which last long, and can only be deciphered on the principles of Bryant's Analysis of ancient Mythology. These Scythians, and the tribes afterwards called Teutons and Goths, were the same people, and early established themselves in Germany and penetrated into Gaul. They gradually confined the ancient Celtæ into a corner of Gaul, and, under the name of Belgæ, took possession of the opposite shores of Britain, and pushed the Celtæ to the northern parts of the island. Yet, so low as Augustus Cæsar's time, the Celtæ, at large, were a powerful people in Europe, and are never to be confounded with the Scythians, though both came originally from the east.

These Scythians also established themselves in Scandinavia, on the Baltic, and becoming bold adventurers at sea, settled many colonies on the coasts of Europe, particularly on the north and east of Britain, from the Orkneys to the mouth of the Humber.

The Phœnicians early carried on trade with Britain and Ireland, where they spread their religion and communicated some of their arts to the inhabitants. They also, for the benefit of their commerce, colonised some of the southern maritime parts of these islands. They came from Spain, as did the Iberians, and in conjunction with them occupied a considerable part of Ireland, as appears from the remains of their language and many other particulars.

This emigration of Phœnicians and Iberians from Spain probably happened when the Chaldeans, under Nebuchadnezzar, conquered part of Africa and Spain, about the year 571 before Christ. The irruption of the Chaldeans is mentioned by Strabo, who names their king Nauocodrosorum. It is also related by Josephus. There is the more probability in this expedition, as it happened after the Chaldeans had taken Tyre and subdued Egypt, who at that period carried on an extensive commerce with Spain and Africa, and had founded Leptis, Utica, Carthage, Gades, and other cities. Pliny gives an account from Varro that Persians, Phœnicians, Iberians, and Celts had settled in Spain.

The great mass of the ancient population of Britain and Ireland originated from these races of men. This appears by comparing the various languages and their structure which as yet prevail in these countries. The Celtic and Gothic are radically different, even in their modern dialects, Erse, Welch, English, and broad Scotch.

The Iberno-Scythian, or Irish language differs from these in many particulars, and abounds with Punic words, introduced by the Iberians and Phœnicians; and in Ireland they once used the eastern Boustrophedon manner of writing. The Irish call one of their dialects *berla fene*, the Phœnician speech.

Tacitus informs us that in the age of Agricola, our island was inhabited by the people of Caledonia, the Silures and Cumbri. He estimated the Caledonians to be of German extraction from their appearance and size; the Silures, he judged, came from Spain, and therefore were Iberians and Phœnicians, and that the Cumbrians were of Gallic extract, from their similarity in language and religious institutions. The Caledonians probably spoke one of the Gothic dialects, mingled with the language of the Celtæ, who retreated northward on the irruption of the Belgæ and Romans, and relinquishing their Sylva Caledonia, on the banks of the Thames, preserved that name in Caledonia, afterwards Scotland.

The united body of these Celtæ and the Scandinavian colonies formed that nation afterwards called Picti by the Romans. The Cumbrians spoke a dialect of the Celtic and Gothic languages, and were those Celtæ, Belgæ, Picti, and other Britons who, after the Saxon invasion, occupied the western coast, from Antoninus' Wall to Land's-End.

Bede, who died in 735, informs us that, in his age, there were five languages used in Britain,—the Saxon, British, Scottish, Pictish, and Roman. The Saxon and Pictish were dialects of the Gothic, being spoken by people of the same origin. The British language was composed of the Celtic and Gothic dialects, introduced by the Belgæ. The Scottish was partly Celtic and partly Irish, the Scots and Irish being one and the same people. When the Romans conquered a nation, they introduced their language among them; but, before Bede's time, it had ceased to be in common use in this island, and was only adopted in religious services, and as a learned language.

From the intercourse between these races of men, and the confusion of language that must necessarily arise, we cannot imagine that their language could be preserved pure and unmixed to modern times. A medley would be formed that makes it now difficult, if not impossible, to define, with accuracy and precision, the boundaries between these different languages, and decidedly say to which of them innumerable words, both ancient and modern, belong.

This proves how fundamentally many fail in their etymological enquiries. In this there is a fashion as in other branches of research. It is the mode with many at present to derive all the names of places in Scotland from the modern Gaelic—a mass of Gothic, British, Celtic, and Iberish words, yet dignified with the character of ancient Celtic. There can be no doubt that many of these can be derived from no other source, but this cannot with propriety be universally done. This puts one in mind of the ancient Greeks, who adopted a similar plan, which created the utmost confusion in history, and, instead of truth, made it a tissue of fable. That the Erse is a dialect in general of the Celtic, combined with the Iberish, admits of no doubt, but it is a dialect abounding with innumerable Gothic words. Besides, from the lapse of time and the want of written standards, it must materially vary from what it originally was when these names were appropriated. We should never make use of a language which is modern, or comparatively modern, to deduce the etymology of ancient words; more particularly, as the moderns in general implicitly copy the ancients in being guided by the ear, which renders all their conceptions on that subject precarious and uncertain, as appears in etymologists so widely differing from each other.

This appears to be a probable account of the ancient inhabitants of Britain:—The Celts and Belgæ from Gaul; the Scythians or Goths from Germany, who in time were called Caledonians and Picts, with Phœnicians and Iberians from Ireland; besides these, in more modern times, many straggling colonies came into Scotland from Denmark, Norway, and Ireland. Among these were the Scots, who, originally possessing a small part of the island in Argyle, gradually spread abroad. At length they conquered the Picts and Cumbrians, and as the Angles gave their name to England, so they imposed the name of Scotland on the other part of the island.

There has been much ingenuity, not a little learning, with a considerable share of acrimony, employed by the Irish and Scots in determining the original of the latter and the rise of the appellation. It appears highly probable that they both at first were one and the same people, as the north of Ireland might have been partially colonised from the neighbouring parts of Caledonia. This circumstance, and their vicinity, would keep up frequent communications between both islands and a frequent interchange of colonies. At length, two or three centuries after the Christian era, a colony from Ireland, under Fergus, or Riada, or some other unknown leader, was established in Caledonia, and the appellation Scots first used within Britain. Bede, who lived at no great distance of time from that period, fixes this colony on the northern banks of the Clyde. They gradually pushed their conquests on the western shores till they reached Caithness; and in time all to the north of the River Forth was called Scotland, and the Firth of Forth was named Mare Scoticum. The Picts, or Caledonians, occupied the eastern shores and low countries. This distinction between the boundaries of the Picts and Scots was preserved long in even the Province of Moray. It can be traced in the names and hills throughout the whole of the Province.

Among the charters of Dunbar of Grange there is one granted in 1221 by King Alexander II. to the Abbacy of Kinloss, of the lands of Burgy, in which a boundary is "Rune Pictorum"—the Picts' Cairn. In another charter from Richard, Bishop of Moray, after the year 1187, to the same abbacy, is mentioned "Scoticum molendinum"; and to this day a road from the Highlands to the low districts of the Province is called "the Scots Road." It is through the hills to the east of Dollas.

After a variety of fortune and much bloodshed the Scots, Picts, and Caledonians, in the 9th century, united themselves under one sovereign, and took the single name of Scots, though that of Picts also remained in some parts of the kingdom many years after this.

It is difficult to give a satisfactory account of the origin of the appellation Scots. Probability leads us to judge that Scot and Scythi are the same names, and that Scot was afterwards applied to them as a term of reproach on account of their plundering and rapacious manners. One particular is certain, that it was imported from Ireland, which was the ancient Scotia, and its inhabitants were called Scots after the year 1400.

Tradition is silent with regard to the time when the first colonies came into the north of Scotland from Scandinavia and Germany. We learn from Claudian that the Saxons were in the Orkneys before the year 390 and the Picts in Thule, by which he means the north of Scotland. Torfeus informs us that about 927 the Norwegians, under the command of Sigurd, Earl of Orkney, conquered Moray, where probably they built Elgin. At that period, or rather before it, the Picts occupied a Roman station on the Moray Firth called Ptoroton, which they named *the Burgh*, and established themselves under its protection in great numbers, as appears by the ruins of houses that extend along the sea shore to the east almost two miles. This, and more ancient colonies of the same people, mingling with the British, impelled northwards by the invasions of the Belgæ, Iberians, Romans, and Saxons, peopled the Province of Moray.

We are entirely ignorant of their internal state and partial revolutions, but we have every reason to believe that they were a necessitous, turbulent, unsettled people. This is confirmed by their killing King Malcolm I. at Ulrin, which, by the Chartulary of Moray, is the Castle of Forres. They also murdered King Duffus at Forres about 966, when he came to punish them for their crimes. They rebelled in the reign of Malcolm IV., who, about 1160, led an army against them. They submitted, but, to break their future licentiousness, in 1161 he transplanted all those engaged in the insurrection into the other counties of Scotland, from Caithness to Galloway. In 1171 there was an insurrection of the inhabitants of Moray, so that Malcolm's policy had not all the effects he expected from it.

In conformity to the practice some time before introduced into Scotland of surnames being taken from names of places, their general surname was Murref, after their country, but many altered this into that of the place where they were established. Those called Sutherland, Earls of Sutherland, were originally Murrefs; as appears from a Protection granted by Edward, King of England, to William de Murref, son of the Earl of Sutherland. It is dated 28th Jan., 1367. The first of the family of

ALL DARK BEFORE MALCOLM CANMORE.

Sutherland in record is Hugo Freskyn, between 1186 and 1214. When this transportation of the inhabitants of Moray took place, it is highly probable that the King granted their lands to others, who founded new families, of whom many of the present inhabitants are descended.

Malcolm III. and his successors received with open arms many exiles and discontented persons of rank from England, of Saxon and Norman extraction. They also received adventurers from the Continent, so that imperceptibly the greatest part of the property in Scotland belonged to these strangers. At this day most of the nobility of Scotland and many commoners of ancient families are of their blood.

Before the reign of Malcolm Canmore all is darkness in the history of Scotland at large; and still less can we expect any authentic documents of what regards the province of Moray. The most ancient one is the Chartulary of Moray, which contains a series of charters from about the 1200 to 1529, in which a variety of names are mentioned of Pictish, Saxon, Irish, and Low Country origin. The names are numerous; some local, some patronymics, some from occupation, and others from causes now inexplicable. The modern practice of Clan names does not appear to have prevailed in any great degree in these days; but afterwards, many people uniting for their joint defence, assumed the name of their common chieftain, or of the most powerful body of the association. It is proper to mention some of the names in the Chartulary of Moray and other charters in these different periods.

From A.D. 1200 to 1400 appear the following:—

Bricius Malcolm.	Patrick.	Stephen.
Robert Gilmakel.	Gillesbred.	Symon.
Macbeth.	Walter.	

all clergymen, with the names of their livings annexed.

Hugh son of Freskyn.	Dugal.	Thomas Rolland.
Walter of Moray.	Alexander Black.	Thomas de Dalton.
William de Rist.	John Cambron.	John Tullois.
William Agnus (Lamb) Malice.	Malcungy Mallinack Macbeth.	John Bully. James Suter.
Archibald Lambert.	Macferchar.	Walter Thorald.
Gillemere.	Walter Crawford.	Faucounere of Lethinbar.
John de Hedon.	Murin.	
Morgund Ranold.	William Noreys.	Ross.

NAMES IN THE CARTULARY OF MORAY.

Gillemallovock Macknakingelle.
Sythak Mackmallon.
Robert Hado.
Archibald de Dufphus miles.
Hugh Douglass.
Augustine of Elgin.
William Wiseman.
Walter Innes.
Adam Gurmund miles.
Gyllimaked Macgillipatrick.
Gilcrist Grathack.
Marynus.
Sumerlet of Bucharyn.
John Byseth.
William Stephen.
Hugh Corbet.
Wadyn Gamell.
Hutyng Marshall.
John Prat.
Thomas Syband.
Hugh Lormac.
Gilmalnoc MacThomas.
Regunald de Chin.
⌐MacCrather Macquoin.
Duncan Fraser.
John Corbeth.
Robert de Joniston.

William de Fenton.
Dominus Barth.
Flamang
Laurence and Robert Grant.
Thomas Man.
Bredan son of Fergus
Martin More.
Maldowney Beg.
Maldowney MacMartin.
Bredan Breach.
Martin McColy.
Donymore.
Michael Mulswayn.
Maldowney MacRobe.
Colin MacGilbride.
Alexander Mencrys.
John de Forbes.
Michael Schapmar.
William Vaus.
Henry Portar.
Falconar.
Husband.
Muil.
Wood.
Orlet.
Elias Sister.
John de Killour.

Vylgus.
William Pope.
William Soreys.
Henery Scypard.
Robert Mykel.
Malin Glaud.
Hugh Grene.
Lulack McIman.
John Scott.
William Walkere.
Stephen Skinner.
Alexander Irynpins.
William Tavernire.
John Gray.
Adam Flemynges.
Thomas Urchard.
John Sibbald.
William de Dun.
Christian McKinnach Gartned.
Robert Curry.
Donald Rogerston.
Ninynus de Achors.
Eva Murtach.
Murriel Pollock.
Morgund.
Alexander Chisholm
Hugh Fraser de Loveth.

From A.D. 1400—Fotheringhams, Dunbars, Gordons, Winchesters, Stewarts, Cummings, Carrowe, Clerk, Hill, Tait, Quorsque, Wilson, Ogilvie, Flemyng, Duffs, &c., are the most numerous names. After A.D. 1529 there are no accounts of any great change of the inhabitants or names, but what might naturally happen during the lapse of years, from the change of property and the rise and fall of different families and names.

After this general account of the inhabitants of the Province, a short detail is to be given of the principal families, beginning with those nobilitated, according to their antiquity in Moray; but previous to considering those vested with modern titles, it may not be improper to inquire into the import and dignity of *Thane*, which was the appellation of persons of rank and consequence in Scotland before the days of Malcolm III. They were the nobility and gentry of those days, and the title long remained after those of Earl and Baron were introduced by Malcolm Canmore, who began to reign in 1057. There were many Thanes in Ross and the other counties in Scotland, in the reign of William the Lion: they existed in the Province of Moray till about 1500.

Scotland was divided into Thanedoms, and the title was originally borrowed from the Danes or Norwegians and the Saxons in England. It signifies the King's Minister. There is great uncertainty as to their privileges and rank, as these can only be learned by record, and few records remain of these ancient days. It appears by "the Regiam Magistatem" that the marchet of the daughter of a Thane was two cows, or twelve shillings; but that of an Earl's daughter was twelve cows; and that of a freeman's daughter, not lord of the village, one cow.* To this Marcheta Mulierum was the pertinent of the first night of concubinage with the wife of the villain or serf. Many extant charters in Scotland refer to this strange right or rite. The Cro of an Earl was 140 cows; of an Earl's son, and a Thane, was 100 cows; and that of a husbandman was 16 cows. At this period, therefore, there was a middle rank between the nobility and freemen.

This is also confirmed by an Assize, mentioned in the Chartulary of Moray, of William the Lion, at Perth, in which the rank is Bishops, Abbots, Earls, Barons, Thanes,

---

* The administrator of the Crown lands, the collector of rents, the magistrate and head man of a little district, known among his Celtic neighbours as the Toshach, took a charter of the whole district from the Sovereign, whereby he became, under the Saxon name of Thane, hereditary tenant; paying the sum at which the land stood in the King's rental, and preserving all his ancient authority now strengthened and legalised. In this manner it fell that the Saxon title of Thane became common, chiefly in the north, and in the least Saxon part of Scotland; but it does not follow that the title expressed exactly the same rank and dignity with the English title of Thane. This is the opinion of the erudite Cosmo Innes.

One of our ancient codes of customary law, which was specially abrogated by the famous ordinance of Edward I., A.D. 1305, had for its object that which was common to all the northern codes—to estimate the grades of society and the penalties to be paid for injuring each. There, after the King comes the Earl. The Thane ranks equal with the Earl's son. —(ED.)

and all the Community. In the same Chartulary there is a charter of Alexander II., about 1232, where Thani Regis and Firmarii, or King's Thanes and Tenants, are classed together, whose lands might be changed as he pleased.

The same King had also rents paid him by his "feodi firmarii" in Moythas, Brothyn, and Dyke, which were Thanedoms. In a Submission between Andrew, Bishop of Moray, and Hugh Rose, Baron of Kilravock, in 1492, written in Latin, among the arbiters are William Calder of Calder and John Brodie of Brodie. In this deed they are promiscuously called Thane, or *de eodem*, of that ilk; but in the decreet arbitral, written in English, the designation is Thani. From this it appears that Thane, or Gentleman, the head of the name, are the same.

The Thanedoms, or grants of lands, were probably at first during pleasure, then for a certain number of years, and at length were for life and hereditary. About A.D. 1200, there were several Thanes of different families in a short space of time over a Thanedom in the Mearns, now a part of the estate of Arbuthnot.

In 1206, there was a dispute between William, Bishop of St. Andrews, and Duncan of Arbuthnot, ancestor of the present Viscount of Arbuthnot, concerning the property of the Kirktown of Arbuthnot in the Mearns. It was determined by a synod met at Perth that year. One of the witnesses declares on oath that he had known thirteen Thanes in his lifetime to have the lands in question, to whom the Bishops paid tribute. From this it appears that Thanes were collectors of the King's revenue and received perquisites of office.

They conducted their followers to the field, as it was an essential part of their dress to go abroad with a spear in their hands. It appears by the laws of King David that Thanes held of the King and also of Earls; as Thanes of both descriptions were subjected to certain penalties if they were absent from the loyal army, and are distinguished from Barons and Milites.

They, no doubt, paid out of their lands a certain yearly revenue, in kind, to those from whom they had their grants. It is uncertain what jurisdiction they had in their domains, or if they appeared before the King's or Earl's judges. By an order of William the Lion, in the Chartulary of Moray, when the Villanus or Rusticus refuses to pay tithes, his Thane, or Dominus, if he has a Dominus, shall seize them from him; but if the Thane or Lord neglect this, then the Vice-Comes, or Sheriff, and failing him, the King's Justiciar, shall seize the tithes and the penalty for neglect of payment.

A thanedom was less than a sheriffdom or county, as there were several thanedoms in Moray. In Banffshire there were also many of them, as the thanedom of Boyne, of Conwath, of Aberkirdor, Nathdole, &c. And in the foundation charter of the Bishoprick of Aberdeen by Malcolm IV. he endows it, among other revenues, with the tithes of his thancages in the counties of Aberdeen and Banff.

§ 1. *Roman Progress.*

The idea of Caledonian independence long influenced the opinions of our historians and antiquaries. It prevented their judging with candour of the proofs that the Romans penetrated to the northern part of Scotland. These prejudices now begin to subside, and Scotsmen allow equal weight to the same degree of evidence of the Roman progress in their native country, as they do with regard to Germany, or any other province of that empire which they are not particularly interested in.

This evidence and information is not to be derived from the legendary tales of our historians, or the crude theories of our antiquarians, founded in fiction and supported by credulity. The genuine sources they are to be drawn from, are the Roman and Greek writers. The history they give us of the Roman progress in this island, is confirmed by those stupendous monuments of their power and industry that remain—as walls, stations, military roads, and ruins of towns.

It is from Tacitus' life of Agricola, that we obtain the first correct information of the success of the Roman arms in Scotland. He commanded their troops for nine years, and penetrated into Scotland as far as the foot of the Grampian mountains. Had Tacitus' account of Agricola's eight campaigns been attended to, the field of his battle with the Caledonian chief, Galgacus, could never be conjectured to have been in Strathearn, near the kirk of Comrie, nor at Fortingal Camp, a place somewhat farther on the other side of the Tay. These places are too inland, as that campaign was near the sea coast. The land army and fleet co-operated in attacking the enemy and supporting each other. The sailors often were in the Roman camps, and detailed the dangers they encountered by sea to the legions, who related the hardships they were exposed to in their marches through hills and forests. This was also the case in Agricola's sixth and seventh campaigns; and remains of his fortified camps are yet to be seen from Camelon, near Falkirk, to his camp at Stonehaven, and the extensive works on Finlaystone hill, near to Ury, where the battle with Galgacus was fought.

Though it is a little foreign to the present inquiry, yet it throws light on the Roman progress at large, to mention the series of Agricola's camps, during the three years he employed in his progress northward, after his crossing the Bodotria, or Forth. They are taken from a map that General Roy published several years ago, and have all been verified:—Camelon, Kier, Ardoch, Camp Castle, Strageth, Perth, Grassywalls, Burghtay, Lintrose, Coupar in Angus, Kirkboddo, Battle Dykes, Kiethick, Fordun, Stonehaven. This chain of posts, not far distant from the sea shore, preserved the communication with his fleet and secured both his conquests and retreat. The remains of a Roman camp were, some years ago, to be seen near the shore at Stonehaven, but are now effaced. It was the station Agricola occupied, before his battle with Galgacus. The extensive works on Finlaystone hill, about two miles to the west of Stonehaven, contain within the entrenchments about 120 Scots acres. There the Caledonians encamped, who learned this art of fortification from the Romans, and had it so large as to contain their flocks and herds. The face of the ground between Stonehaven and Finlaystone hill corresponds to Tacitus' description, particularly at Campstone hill, a mile to the north-east, and near to the sea shore, where was the field of battle, as there are the remains of many small cairns and some single-stone obelisks.

It was Agricola's plan, according to Tacitus, to have penetrated to the extremities of Britain. With this view, his fleet sailed round the island, and, as Juvenal informs, conquered the Orkney Islands. So enterprising and steady a general would have completed his plan, had not Domitian's jealousy recalled him. His successor was

Lucullus, who also appears to have been eminent in the military line; and there is every degree of probability that he pushed his conquests at least to Inverness. This opinion is combated by national vanity and prejudice; but if the evidence it is supported by is carefully examined, and impartially weighed, it will be found strong, if not decisive.

Ptolemy of Alexandria flourished about the year 140 of the? Christian era. He wrote a System of Geography, which is yet extant, and gives not only the longitude and latitude of the sea coasts of Scotland, but that of some of the northern and inland places of it. He names the towns of Tuessis, Ptoroton, Banatia, Tamea, and the different clans of inhabitants who occupied the whole country. This information he could only obtain from the Romans; and making some allowances for the inaccuracy of the observations communicated to him, or from perhaps the errors in the manuscripts of his work, there is more exactness in the relative situation he gives of places, than at first could be supposed. The east in modern maps is the west in his. Notwithstanding this, and that he makes the coasts of Scotland trend to the east instead of running north or so, yet he lays down the places agreeable to their real situation on the respective sides of the island.

His Tables have been often misrepresented and tortured to support hypothesis and opinion. This arose from not delineating a map agreeable to the degrees he assigns. Had this been done, Ptoroton, or Castra Alata, would never have been placed at Cramond or Edinburgh, but where Ptolemy places it, on the Sinus Vararis, the Moray Firth. But allowing Ptolemy's geography to be more inaccurate than it is, it decidedly proves that, when he wrote, the Romans were well acquainted with the interior country of the north of Scotland, as well as the sea coasts.

The inhabitants of the Province of Moray he names Vacomagi and Caledonij. Among them, on the Sinus Vararis, or Moray Firth, he places Tuessis, which answers to much about where Gordon Castle is. An English mile to the north of Gordon Castle, are the remains of an Encampment which, from its square figure, and ditch, and ramparts, and ports, has every appearance of being Roman. It no doubt was originally intended to cover the ford on the river Tuessis, or Spey, which at that period ran at the foot of the bank on which the station was placed.

Ptolemy mentions Ptoroton Stratopedon, or Castra Alata, in the country of the Vacomagi, which, from the situation which he assigns to it on the Moray Firth, and its relative position to Tuessis, can be no other than what is now called "the Burgh," a fisher-town in the parish of Duffus.

In the same country of the Vacomagi, or Province of Moray, the Alexandrian geographer mentions Banatia as in the neighbourhood of Tuessis and Ptoreton. When the river Ness issues from the loch it runs about five or six hundred yards and falls into another small loch, which is bent into a semicircular figure, and with the river forms a peninsula. On this slip of ground there has been a military station of two small forts. The outer fort is a square of fifty paces by fifty-three, which on the one side is protected by the river and on the other by the small loch; and next the field is a rampart and a ditch, fourteen feet wide: on the inner side is another ditch and rampart of the former breadth. The inner fort is built of rather modern masonry, and is also a square of twenty-four paces on each side. These forts cover the only ford on the Ness, which is called Bona, or Buness; but in Erse, the ancient dialect of the country, it is called Bana. From this similarity of name, and being in the country of the Vacomagi, it probably is the Banatia of Ptolemy.

Dio Cassius, whom some conjecture to have been the Emperor Severus' private secretary in his British expeditions, wrote his history by that Prince's particular desire. The information he gives may be considered authentic in what regards Severus' operation in North Britain; as he relates events that either passed under his own eyes, or were reported to him by those who were principally engaged in them. His testimony is express that Severus lost 50,000 men in the expedition, but penetrated by land to the utmost northern bounds of Scotland. This he confirms by the astronomical observations that were made on the different lengths of the days and nights in these regions from what they were in Italy.

Captain Shand, who some years ago commanded the detachment of the Royal Artillery at Perth, employed himself in exploring the Roman geography from Camelon to Stonehaven, the limits of Agricola's progress. He conjectured that the Romans had penetrated further into the country; and, on a survey, found the great camp at Glen-mailen on Ythan, in Buchan, perhaps the Statio ad Itunam, as also the remarkable prefidium near Old Meldrum, and a number of similar works of the same character with those on the other side of the Grampians, though not executed with such accuracy.

Besides these historical accounts of the Roman conquests to the north of the Grampian chain of mountains and the remains of fortifications that, from geography and their form, have every appearance of being erected by that warlike and industrious people, there have been urns, medals, and weapons discovered that also afford additional evidence of their progress. Two urns were lately found in Findlater, at the farm of Brankanentham, in two large heaps of stone. They were full of ashes. One of them had a cover, with the figure of something like a pine apple on the top of the cover, but was broken in digging it out. The other urn had no cover but a flat stone, and was ornamented with a variety of rude carvings. In the same neighbourhood, several years ago, were discovered some medals, which Gordon mentions in his *Itinerarium Septentrionale.*

Another urn, likewise full of ashes, was discovered near Gordonstown, and is in excellent preservation. Two more were dug out of a tumulus near to Lethen, but, from the precipitancy of the labourers, were broke to pieces.

These urns may be considered as Roman, as there is no evidence that our ancestors burned their dead. They buried them in stone coffins, or under small arches of half-burnt clay, as in the muir at the Kirk of Alvie in Badenoch.

The heads of "pilums" of different figures, for foot and horse soldiers, have been also discovered in Moray and Nairn-shires. It is true they are of that species of copper or brass which Pliny names "caldarium," and it is said they are the weapons of the natives and not Roman. To this it may be replied, that Herodian asserts, that in his time the natives of Britain knew the use of iron, and therefore might employ it for their weapons as well as the Romans. Livy says that the arms of the first class of Servius were all of copper. Cæsar used the same metal in refitting his ships, and Dio Cassius informs that sometimes the point of the Roman dagger was steel, or iron, which implies that the remainder of the blade was of another metal, copper. It is also said that all the extant arms and tools of that illustrious people are copper, which they had the art to temper and harden in a very high degree.

Thus the Roman progress is traced to Inverness, by ancient geography and history, encampments, weapons, coins, and urns. The proofs arising from each of these sources, taken single and unconnected, might give a certain degree of credibility to the opinion; but united, they have such accumulated evidence on the whole, that establishes it as fact we may depend on. They receive additional weight from the geographical Treatise, *De Situ Britanniæ*, and the map that accompanied it.

The manuscript was discovered and published by Charles Bertram, at Copenhagen in 1757. The author is supposed to be Richard of Cirencester, a monk of Westminster, who made the history of Britain the object of his studies. He lived under the reign of Edward III. Whoever was the author, the work has merit, and claims attention, as it illustrates the geography and history of the island, and though wrote by a monk of the fourteenth century, is not to be classed among the futile productions of that age. It is the composition of one conversant with the best writers of antiquity, and who had the discernment to select what was valuable and adapted to the nature of his dissertation. Cæsar and Tacitus, Lucan and Claudian, were familiar to him. He also appears to have had other sources of information, equally important, that are now lost. From all these he acquired an accurate knowledge of the history and geography of even the interior and northern parts of Scotland.

By his map he places Banatia to the west of Ptoroton, and both on the Sinus Vararis, in the country of the Vacomagi, or Province of Moray. He delineates the Tuessis, or river Spey, with accuracy, and has the station of Tuessis at the mouth of the river. He also inserts in his treatise an itinerary of a Roman officer, from which he gives a variety of routes different from those of Antoninus, and describes two from Ptoroton, on the Moray Firth—one along the sea coast to Luguballium, or Carlisle, and the other by Varris, or Forres, and Tamea, or Braemar Castle, to Isca Damnoniorum, or Exeter. The distances were effaced in the manuscript between many places, but in so far as regards the Province of Moray they are—between Selinam, or Banff, and the station of Tuessis, xxviii m. p., from that to Ptoroton the number is wanting. By the inland route Ptoroton is viii m. p. from Varis, from Varis to the river Tuessis are xviii m. p., from that to Tamea are xxvii m. p.

There can be no doubt that Richard's "Varis" is Forres. It appears by the direction and distance. The provincial mode of pronouncing the name at this day is Farris; and everyone knows that F and V are synonymous letters.

The map is singular. What stamps it with value and authenticity, and demonstrates that Richard had his materials from the purest sources, is that the places he has laid down as Roman stations in Scotland, not only correspond with Ptolemy, but have been verified by Roman works at or near them. He mentions some not taken notice of by Ptolemy, as that one near Stonehaven, and calls it *immane castrum*. Nay, his map has discovered a Roman station near the Cairns of Tarbet-Ness, in Ross-shire, which he calls *arœ finium imperij Romani;* and which, before its publication, was not considered in that light, but now, upon investigation, indicates the labours of a foreign people—the Romans.

Though these cairns and that station are not within the limits of the Province of Moray it is not improper to give a short description of them.

There are two cairns. The western one is raised about five or six feet, on a base of seventy-two feet in circumference, and upon that is built a small pyramid, six feet broad at the bottom, and elevated a few feet. This cairn is called Ulli-vacum. The other is east from the first cairn about two hundred paces and is of a similar shape, on a base of only half the circumference, but rises to much about the same height. It is called Spadie-lingum. They are both constructed, without any art, of earth and the common muir stones.

A mile to the north-west of them is a place on the sea shore called Port-a-chaistel, where there is an excellent small harbour; and on the rising ground that commands it are the vestiges of a military station, surrounded with two ditches twenty feet asunder, and each of them twelve feet wide. The circumference of the area enclosed by the inner ditch is about an hundred feet, from which runs southward a rampart about a quarter of a mile in length, with many curves and angles in it.

Near the outer ditch, and not far from the point of the rock, and above the harbour, is a square fortification about one hundred paces of a side. Through the muir, near a mile round, are scattered many circular figures, about forty feet in circumference, with ramparts running from them southwards in the same style as in the one mentioned before. This square has every appearance of a Prætorium and camp. The other works have probably been barracks for hutting the troops, or constructed by an opposing enemy.

He mentions in his map and description of Caledonia, a Province which the Romans occupied for a short time that extended from Agricola's "prætentura," between the Forth and Clyde, to the *aræ finium imperij Romani*. It had the name of Vespasiana from the imperial family, and was probably conquered in the reign of Domitian. Under the Emperor Theodosius it was named Thule. Richard is singular in mentioning this Province, as no ancient writer, nor any of the middle ages that have been published, mention it.

Though Richard's testimony of this fact stands alone, instead of being disregarded, it ought to have great weight, as in every other particular he is well informed, and has been faithful to such of his authorities as are published, which we have an opportunity of examining. But independently of this, partiality may be indulged to his relation, when we recollect the remains of the Romans that have been discovered within the limits of the "Provincia Vespasiana." They demonstrate their progress through the whole of its extent, however short time they maintained possession of it. This Richard allows was the case only from Domitian's reign to near the end of Marcus Aurelius's, when the Romans finally lost it, till it was recovered for a short period by Severus.

May it not be conjectured that Agricola's fleet, in circumnavigating the island, touched at Ptoroton, Banatia, and Tarbet-Ness; that Lucullus fortified them and Tamea, and so carried the Roman arms by land from

Finlaystone hill to the northern limits of the "Provincia Vespasiana"?

The Romans soon relinquished the possession of this Province, as, in its uncultivated state, and exposed to the vigorous attacks of the Caledonians then crowded among the hills, it was not worth holding. This accounts for the only remains they left in it, and the Province of Moray being of the military kind. Inscriptions, baths, and military roads are the works of peaceable times and permanent settlement.] (*Survey of Province of Moray.*)

[The ancient Province of Moray extended from the mouth of the River Spey on the east, to the River Beauly on the west. A line stretching from Loch Lochy on the south-west, through Lochaber, and following nearly the course of the River Spey along the base of Cairngorm and Benrinnes, formed its southern boundary; while the Moray Firth terminated it on the north, and separated it from the Peninsula of Ross. Moray thus included the whole district of country stretching along the sea coast; and hence, probably, the Gaelic derivation of the name *Murar* or *Morar*, the sea-side, from *Mor*, the sea, and *Taobh* or *Tav*, the side. (*Shaw.*)

The present boundaries of the county are much more circumscribed—Nairnshire occupying the western, and part of Inverness-shire the south and south-western portions of the ancient Province. Its greatest length is about 40 miles; and its breadth varies from 8 to 15 and 23 miles. The northern range of the Grampian Mountains terminating in Benrinnes, which has an elevation of 2,300 feet, forms the southern boundary and most elevated part of the county; from whence there is a gradual descent to the sea level by a series of parallel hills intersecting the county from west to east, with valleys between. The hills to the south consist of primary rocks, and are of considerable height, while those towards the north are composed of sandstones and newer formations, and gradually decrease in elevation as they approach the sea. Hence the streams and rivers which water the county take their rise to the south and south-west, and flow north and north-eastward to the sea. These are the Spey, with its tributaries, forming the south-eastern boundary; the Findhorn on the west, and the Lossie in the centre.

The plain of Moray consists generally of a light arenaceous soil, interspersed with valleys and tracts of rich alluvium and loam. In the lower district there is a deep clay. From the position of the county along the shores of an estuary, from its slight elevation above the sea level, and from the dry and porous nature of the sub-soil, the climate is genial, and superior to that of the neighbouring shires. The elevated hills to the south carry off much of the atmospheric moisture which would otherwise fall; and the level of the firth, extending to the northward, still farther prevents an excess of rain; while the porous surface readily absorbs, and as readily gives off by evaporation, that moisture which, stagnating in less favoured localities, renders the surrounding air chill and ungenial. The average annual fall of rain at Elgin for the last three years (1836-39) is 25·355 inches. The average temperature for the same period is 48°.33. Both these results do not differ much from those of the localities on the eastern coast of Scotland generally, at or near the sea level; but, as compared to the mountainous districts, the difference, had we sufficient data, must be very considerable.

Buchanan extols Moray as superior to any other part of Scotland for the mildness of its climate, the richness of its pastures, and the abundance of its fruits; and Bishop Leslie, with all the enthusiastic partiality of a son of the soil, reiterates these praises. Sir Robert Gordon of Straloch, describing it in 1640, says, "that in salubrity of climate Moray is not inferior to any, and in richness and fertility of soil it much exceeds our other northern provinces. The air is so temperate that, when all around is bound up in the rigour of winter there are neither lasting snows nor such frosts as damage fruits or trees; proving the truth of that boast of the natives, that they have forty days more of fine weather in every year than the neighbouring districts. There is no product of this kingdom which does not thrive there perfectly; or, if any fail, it is to be attributed to the sloth of the inhabitants, not to the fault of the soil or climate. Corn the earth pours forth in wonderful and never-failing abundance. Fruits of all sorts, herbs, flowers, pulse, are in the greatest plenty, and all early. While harvest has scarcely begun in surrounding districts, there all is ripe and cut down, and carried into open barn-yards, as is the custom of the country; and, in comparison with other districts, winter is hardly felt. The earth is almost always open, the sea navigable, and the roads never stopped. So much of the soil is occupied by crops of corn, however, that pasture is scarce; for this whole district is devoted to corn and tillage. But pasture is found at no great distance, and is abundant in the upland country and a few miles inland, and thither the oxen are sent to graze in summer, when the labour of the season is over. Nowhere is there better meat, nor cheaper corn, not from scarcity of money, but from the abundance of the soil."

There are few lakes or marshes of any extent in the shire. *Lochindorb*, in the upper part of the county, is the most considerable. *Loch-na-bo*, in the neighbourhood of Elgin, is celebrated for its picturesque beauty. *Loch Spynie* was of considerable extent, but it is now almost entirely drained. It is highly probable that, in ancient times, a large portion of the low country of Duffus and Drainie was under water. There are evident proofs in the remains of marine shells that the sea extended farther southwards, perhaps to join the eastern part of Loch Spynie, near Pitgaveny, and that it approached much nearer Kinnedar than it does at present.* The hollow land

* " In 1368, on the 7th day of June, while Lord Alexander, Bishop of Moray, was passing from his Castle of Kyneder, towards the Priory of Urchard (Urquhart), by his water of Lossy, through the ford, which is called *Krannokysford*, he found a small ship (*navicula*), viz., *farcost*, lying in his said water, near the sea. To which coming, he asked of a person who was called —— ——, who was the only one found in the vessel, whose vessel that was, and by whose license it entered that water; who answered, that the vessel, that is *farcost*, belonged to John de Lany, and that he had come there by order of the Burgesses of Elgyn. To whom the Bishop replied, 'that neither the burgesses, nor any other person whatever, had the power to grant this authority or license, since the water, at the time being, flowed in its proper channel within his diocese of Moray, and his it was, and no one's else;' and on this account, he demanded of him to give a pledge in name of the arrestment of the said vessel. The man put into the hands of the said Bishop a small axe, which, in name of his master, he begged to give him as a concession, which the said

extending from the Castle of Old Duffus to Roseisle, was also most likely partially or entirely covered with water. In former times a stream flowed past Unthank which drove a mill, and in a chart of the county laid down by Sir Robert Gordon of Straloch, dated 1640, a Loch of some extent is marked extending south of the village of Roseisle, from which a stream appears to issue to join the sea, near Burghead.

That such an inviting district of Scotland should have been among the first to have been taken possession of, is not at all to be wondered at. Yet, so imperfect is tradition, that we are left almost entirely in the dark regarding the particular race who first peopled it. Of those migrating swarms who came from the neighbouring continents to occupy our islands, two distinct races have been recognised—the Celts and the Picts. While the Gaels or Celts took possession of the more central and mountainous parts of our island, it has been supposed that the Picts settled along our shores, and that thus the northern and eastern districts of Scotland skirting the sea were peopled by tribes of Scandinavian origin. It is easily to be supposed

Bishop received, to be restored again when it should be asked of him."

It is farther added, that the Bishop, returning the same day by the same way, found in the said vessel certain Burgesses of Elgin, viz., Philip Byset and Henry Porter, dragging out of the vessel certain barrels of beer, and certain sacks of tallow and flour, together with a horse and sledge, &c.; and so on the Bishop goes to arrest the vessel with its anchor," &c., &c. —(*Regis. Episc. Morav.*)

We leave to the curious to trace the Bishop's route from the above extract; but one thing seems apparent, that the Lossie, at its junction with the sea, formed a wider estuary southwards than it does at present, else a vessel so loaded could not have sailed up so far. The remains of recent periwinkles (*turbo littoralis*), and of oyster shells found in the clay at Pitgaveny, will thus be satisfactorily accounted for. It will show, too, that the jolly ecclesiastics of those days must have feasted on oysters, while their Presbyterian successors are deprived of that luxury. An ingenious Paper read before the Morayshire Scientific Association, by Patrick Duff, Esq., attributes the large accumulations of gravel and sand in this district to the action of the littoral tidal current carrying the matter brought down by the Spey and Lossie to the westward.

that, during those early migratory and unsettled periods, many changes and admixtures may have taken place. We learn from the Norse authorities, or rather legends, that Moray, as well as a considerable part of the North of Scotland, was frequently under Norwegian rule, and at one time for nearly two centuries in succession. Thorstein the Red, Sigurd, and Thorfin, held an independent sway, or with a slight acknowledgment of the sovereignty of the Scottish monarchs, from the beginning of the tenth to the middle of the eleventh century. An ancient Charter still extant, describing the boundaries of the lands of Burgie, is curious, from an incidental allusion to the Picts. Beginning at the great oak marked with a cross, the boundary ran by a place or object, named *Rune Pictorum*, which, in the Charter, is translated, "the Carne of the Pethis, or the Pecht's fieldis." This is, perhaps, the only allusion to the Pictish people to be found in any Scottish charter; and if it shall be found, in tracing the boundary, that the expression has reference to the sculptured Pillar situated at the east end of the town of Forres, an authority so ancient as the time of Alexander II. for ascribing that extraordinary monument to the ancient Pictish inhabitants, must be regarded as an important hint for the elucidation of this subject.

After the decline of the Pictish power, we find the country convulsed by the rebellions of its native chiefs against the sovereign. Of these *Maormors*, or Earls, as they now first began to be styled, we know little more than the names. They seem to have been connected with the reigning family, and aspired themselves to the throne. These insurrections became so frequent that at length, effectually to quell them, Malcolm IV. transported all those concerned in these rebellions, including the greater part of the population, to the southern provinces of the kingdom, and introduced other families to supply their places. It is from this circumstance that the rarity of the name of Murray in the Province has been accounted for, while it is by no means uncommon in the counties south of the Grampians. After this, the county appears to have been the frequent residence of King Malcolm and his successor, William the Lion, for several Charters granted by them are dated from Elgin, Inverness, and other places in Moray.

That an importation of families at this time took place there is little doubt. Among these, it is supposed that the once great names of Comyn, Byset, Ostiarii, and the powerful Earls of Fife and Strathearn, were the principal. It is as likely, on the other hand, that many of the original families remained, among whom were the Inneses, Calders, &c. The powerful family of De Moravia, of whom Freskinus, Lord of Duffus, is the first mentioned, now also appears as holding extensive possessions, and exercising great influence in the country. On the whole, after all these changes, the district seems to have preserved the characteristics of its Scandinavian origin; and this is evident, even in the present day, from the traces of ancient architecture still extant, and from the pronunciation peculiar to the counties of Moray, Banff, and Aberdeen, which resembles in a remarkable degree that of the German and Danish, especially in converting the double *o* into *ee*, as *meen*, *sheen*, &c. For the lapse of many centuries, too, the people seem to have kept apart from their Celtic neighbours. We find the district, whether from its superior richness or from the more civilized and less warlike state of its inhabitants, frequently the prey of thievish marauders. Indeed, Moray-land was proverbial as a region where every Highland kateran sought his prey. In the Rental of the church lands in the year 1565 we find no admixture of Highland names,* but, on

* Names from the *Rental of the Bishoprick of Moray*, 1565, in the Baronies of Spynie, Kinedar, Birney, Rafford.

Adam	Dunbar	Lumisden	Rynd	*The following Names seem*
Allan	Duncan	Malies	Sandeson	*now uncommon or dis-*
Alves	Forsyth	Man	Schiphird	*used.*
Andersoun	Forbes	Michell	Simsoune	Genot Lesk
Barroun	Fraser	Moreis	Smyth	Yeman Puggat
Brodye	Fyndlay	Moncreif	Stronoch	Brabanere (Bremner)
Brown	Geddes	Murdocht	Stevin	Glaiswrycht Muldonycht
Cant	Gardin	Mylne	Talyour	Gillemichell Weland
Cowey	Hay	Nicol	Trowpe	Mawcie
Cowper	Hendry	Ogilvye	Umfray	
Crystie	Hossoke	Paul	Urquhard	In the baronies of Arclauch,
Cummyng	Huchone	Peterkyn	Wilson	the few names are Ross and
Dik	Innes	Rob	Winchester	Rose; in Keith, Ogilvie, Gor-
Duff	Junkin	Runsiman	Wisman	don, and Huntly; in Kilmyles,
Duffus	Kay	Russel	Wyat	Fraser; in Strathspey, Grant.

The ancient names of places remain much the same to the present time, notwithstanding the change of spelling and slight change in pronunciation. Tullibarden is a name which frequently occurs in the Charters; the situation is described as lying south-east of the Lossie, and is no doubt the Barden of the contrary, such as are purely of Lowland origin, and common around Elgin at the present day. It was not till comparatively recent times that the declining feuds of inveterate warfare and the prejudices of clanship permitted of an admixture with the neighbouring Gordons, Grants, or M'Phersons.

The Lowland situation of Moray, joined to the amenity of its soil and climate, must have pointed it out as a desirable locality for our first religious establishments. It was early visited by the Culdees. Subsequently, about the beginning of the 11th century, numerous religious establishments from Italy planted the Roman religion in the Province, and, from that period till *the Reformation*, the Church engrossed the chief sway, and held extensive possessions in the district. A bishoprick was established about the year 1100. The Abbey of Kinloss, and the Priories of Urquhart, Pluscarden, and Kingussie, besides several other religious houses and hospitals, quickly followed, and the Province was regularly subdivided into parishes, and churches or chapels were erected in each.

But, if our records of the early history of the Province be meagre and unsatisfactory, it may not be uninteresting to look back upon the state of the county a century ago; and, by drawing a picture, for which materials are not wanting, set it in contrast with the existing state of things. In this way, the rapid progress of recent improvement will be brought more vividly under view.

At a remote period the greater part of the plain of Moray was covered with ancient forests of native growth, and these were dense and luxuriant in proportion to the fertility of the valleys. We have proof of this in the large trunks of oaks and pines still imbedded in our mosses, and in the channels of many of our streams. In the Black Burn or Lochty, near its junction with the Lossie, many large oak trunks may still be seen lodged

the present farm so called. These lands belonged to an offset from the ancient family of De Moravia, conjectured to be of Flemish origin, and either gave to, or derived the name from, the Tullibardens of Perthshire. The Morays of Abercairney are also a branch of the same family, from which stock also sprung the noble family of Sutherland, and, in all probability, the famed Douglas, which afterwards, transported to the south of Scotland, became so conspicuous in its warlike annals.

in the mud of its channel, and these undoubtedly had belonged to the "*Sylvæ Caledoniæ*," of ancient historians. When cultivation began, it was on the upper slopes of our hills, in the most accessible and securest positions, when as yet wolves and other wild animals possessed the valleys. Ridges indicating this early cultivation are still visible, but such unproductive spots were gradually forsaken, as the lower grounds were burned and cleared of their thickets. At first, no doubt, pasturage was more practised than tillage, but latterly a comparatively larger quantity of grain was raised in proportion to the number or wants of the inhabitants; but a mere fraction in respect to what the art and enterprise of modern times can produce from the soil. Wheat is mentioned by the early historians as not uncommon in the county; but, we suspect, it became less plentiful at a subsequent period, oats and barley being the chief grains raised. The land was formerly portioned out into mailens, crofts, and small farms, and leases to any extent were by no means general. There was neither capital nor enterprise among the tenants to carry on the extensive farming concerns now so common. A number of those small tenants congregated together in villages, such as those of Urquhart, Duffus, the Keam, Alves, &c. The arable land around these was portioned out into small strips or ridges, of which each one shared alternately. Their respective flocks and cattle all pastured together on their commons; and when their crops were taken off the fields the whole range of country was laid open to the community. This arrangement, which still prevails on some parts of the Continent, was, no doubt, first adopted on a principle of self-protection, as well as sociability, during a rude and turbulent state of society; but it was the worst possible for the purposes of an active and efficient agriculture. In those periods green crops, artificial grasses, and all those provisions for winter sustenance, were almost entirely unknown. The animals destined for winter food were slaughtered in the end of the year and used as salt provisions; while, in severe winters, it was with considerable difficulty that the remaining stock was kept alive. In spring they were so lean and exhausted that they had frequently to be lifted up from the ground and led to the pastures. Hence a general phrase for lean and poor animals was that they were "at the lifting." The agricultural implements were of the most rude and primitive description. A simple ploughshare, with a very inartificial adjustment of its parts, to which were yoked four, and often six, cattle, with one or two drivers, and a ploughman to guide the whole, creeped like a snail through the field, and did little more than scratch up the weed-bound surface. The immatured and unmixed manure was scattered about very sparingly; the seed, without much regard to selection, was deposited, and a few scrapes of a light harrow finished the process. The simple pannier, borne on the horse's back, began to give way, as roads improved, to the *slede*, or sledge, and the *kelloch*. The former was a rudely constructed frame of wood, dragged without wheels on the ground; the latter was a similar frame mounted on wheels, which were often composed of two semicircles of solid board, joined in the middle, and fixed into an axle which revolved in two hoops of wood attached to the bottom of the frame. Upon this mounted framework was fixed a conical wicker basket, capable of holding about a third of a modern cart load. The accompanying harness, which was generally of home manufacture, consisted of hemp or horse hair ropes, thongs of half tanned hides, and twisted straw— the whole knotted together and tied to wooden pins. The exertions of man and beast were much in accordance with the primitive nature of their adjustments. The labours of the field were pursued with much coolness and deliberation. A few hours of work in the summer morning (for they allowed the spring almost to elapse before they commenced), and a hearty breakfast, prepared them for a long sleep during the hottest part of the day, when their work was again resumed in the evening, if nothing more interesting came in the way. Yet, with all this freedom from hard work, the daily comforts of the general population were not upon that sumptuous scale which would excite the envy of the present day. They had heavy contributions to pay out of their scanty incomings. The lords of the soil and the claims of the Church were both to be satisfied. Notwithstanding the fertility of the Province, famines from inclement seasons were by no means unfrequent. The year 1743, or the "dear year," is memorable in Moray, as well as over all Scotland. In the summer of that year, in consequence of the failure of the previous harvest, thousands of destitute beings wandered among the fields in search of whatever could satiate the famishing demands of hunger, devouring sorrel and other wild plants, and the leaves and stems of the yet unfilled peas and beans. Many perished from absolute want, and more from consequent disease and debility. A grievous scarcity occurred even so late as 1782, the memorable year of the "frosty har'st." The food of the peasantry was of the most simple nature. Wheaten bread, except among the gentry in towns, was a rarity seldom seen. Oat, rye, barley, and pease bread were the chief staples of existence. Cultivated vegetables were also rare throughout the county. As yet the inestimable potato had not become a general article of culture. This root was introduced into Scotland about the year 1728, but only began to be generally cultivated in Morayshire about the middle of last century. It is a common tradition that kail and cabbage were introduced into the north of Scotland by the soldiers of Cromwell, and Dr. Johnson shrewdly remarks that, supposing this to be true, it is difficult to conceive what the people had to eat before this time. But, besides that the kail plant (*Brassica*) is indigenous to Scotland, we suspect that the Saxon emigrants were long before that period acquainted with the culture and use of a vegetable so much prized in their native country. It is quite true, however, that even kail-yards were a rarity among our peasantry so late as half a century ago. A farmer then, and even long afterwards, deemed it below his notice to cultivate a garden. A variety of weeds and herbs from the fields, among which were the savoury mugwort and nettle, were usually collected to add a relish to their oatmeal soups. Unskinned peas boiled into a soup were also a favourite dish in some parts of the county. Sowins, or oatmeal bran fermented to a slight degree of acidity, formed then a universal dish, and is peculiar as a regular article of food to the northern parts of Scotland. Sour cakes of a similar composition as sowins, with aromatic seeds, were also an essential luxury at Christmas feasts.

Bees must have been cultivated to some extent in the county, especially in the neighbourhood of towns, for we find "ane stane of wax" as the entry fee of a burgess of

Elgin in 1540, and "ane pund of wax to St. Giles' wake" as a fine imposed on a common culprit. Meal-mills were not so general, or so cheap, or convenient, as on all occasions to allow the ancient *quern* to be altogether dispensed with. Pot-barley was prepared by first softening it in water and then beating off the husks in a hollow stone, using for this purpose a wooden mallet. This was generally the operation of a Saturday night, as the delicacy was one peculiar to a Sunday dinner. As rents and Church contributions were paid in kind, we suspect few of the live stock or their productions were consumed at home. Milk, even, was a rarity, except for a few months in summer. Home-made beer among the more wealthy supplied its place. Fish were an occasional luxury. But shoals of herrings were as yet permitted to swarm around the coasts without being turned to any account. Dried fish were eaten with home-grown mustard, bruised by the revolution of a stone bullet in a wooden box. After the county was denuded of its woods, peat became the chief article of fuel, the importation of coal being of rare occurrence. From the low countries of Duffus and Drainie an annual expedition was made to the hills, consisting of all the youth of the district, with their horses and conveyances, in order to bring home heather for winter fuel; and few families considered their domestic arrangements complete, without a snug stock of this article laid up for the season. In return for this visit, the natives of the hills made an annual pilgrimage to the seaside at the period of Lammas-tide, when the waters of the ocean were supposed to possess a peculiar medicinal efficacy. Almost all the clothing of the country people was the product of their own flocks and fields. Wool was spun and manufactured at home, and dyed mostly with the roots and herbs of the district. And flax was raised in their fields and converted into linen. The dress of the people was very simple and unvaried. A light blue or gray cloth, or "hodden grey," was the universal material. Short knee-breeches and long stockings, in cold weather surmounted by boot-hose, a long or short coat, according to circumstances, and a broad flat blue bonnet, with a red "tap," formed the equipment. The long dress coats were of an ample size and unvaried cut, with huge round brass buttons curiously ornamented. Such a coat lasted sometimes for two or three generations, and a "well-hained" one of this description may even yet be seen occasionally at kirk or market, forming a singular contrast to the modern fashions. The females also dressed plainly in home manufacture, and wore the high muslin *mutch*, or the flat *toy*, the originals of both of which are still common among the Norman and Flemish peasantry. The modern sub-divisions of labour were then much less practised than at present. The first pair of bellows introduced into the Keam of Duffus was looked on as a rarity, and often, on loan, made the round of the whole village. A long wooden tube, with a bore through the centre, by which the fire was blown upon from the mouth, had long previously been applied by the more ingenious part of the population as a substitute. On the whole, if there was not the unceasing activity, and intelligence, and bustle of the present day, there was a simplicity, and an undisturbed uniformity of existence, the actual amount of enjoyment between which two conditions we leave philosophers to determine.

In their seasons of festivity, the stated periods of which were at Christmas, the New Year, Halloween, and at their weddings, baptisms, and, however incongruous, even at funerals, they held formal feasts, and gave themselves up to the pleasures of eating and drinking. In winter, matches of football were favourite amusements.

Sir Robert Gordon writes as if, in his time, they were rather addicted to the pleasures of the bottle; this, perhaps, they may have inherited along with their Scandinavian descent: but it was the fault of former times, not, we hope of the present. "In the low lands," says this author, "along the coast, the natives suffer inconvenience from the want of turf or fuel, which is the only hardship experienced by that happy region, and that is only felt in a few places. It must be owned that they generally counteract the cold by hard drinking, but those who exert themselves industriously in the labours of agriculture little feel or care for it." And again he remarks—"The drink of these provinces is beer, either with hops, or more commonly without hops, after the old manner. There is plenty of foreign wine, and cheap enough, in all the towns. I remember when I was a boy, on my way home from Paris, finding wine at Rouen

much dearer than it sold, a few months afterwards, on
the Moray coast. Both had been brought from Bordeaux,
but the difference was caused by the lowness of our duty.
But besides wine they have their native liquor, called
aqua vitæ, and when that is to be had, which is seldom
wanting, they reject even the most generous wines.
This liquor is distilled from beer mixed with aromatic
plants. It is made almost everywhere, and in such
abundance that there is plenty for all. They swallow
it in great draughts, to the astonishment of strangers,
for it is excessively strong. Even the better classes are
intemperate, and the women are not free from this dis-
grace. Travelling in the depth of winter, in the severest
cold, fortified with a jug of this liquor, and a few small
cheeses—for they care little about meat and bread—they
perform immense journeys on foot without inconvenience."

In later times illicit distillation became a great nuisance
in the county and a source of demoralization to thousands
of the lower orders. A change in the excise laws, however, put an entire stop to this traffic, and the consequence has been that the attention of these smugglers
was diverted from their unlawful and precarious traffic
to the honest culture of the soil, and thus many hitherto
neglected wastes are now smiling in all the richness of
fertile cultivation. The glen of Rothes, the sloping hills
of Kellas, and the upper vale of Pluscarden, are pleasing
examples of this circumstance.

We have no means of ascertaining the population of
the county previous to the census of recent dates. Like
the rest of Scotland, it probably remained long nearly
stationary, or sometimes retrograded. In recent times it
has progressively and greatly increased, notwithstanding
the declamations against new improvements and the
extravagance and enervating luxury of the times.]
(*Rhind's Sketches of Moray.*)

PART I.

THE NAME, EXTENT, SITUATION, AND DIVISION OF MORAY.

THE NAME OF THE COUNTY OF MORAY.

PTOLEMY, speaking of Caledonia (or rather of *Sylva Caledonia*), says that it extended "A Lelalonio Lacu usque ad Æstuarium Vararis."* It is generally allowed that, by the *Æstuarium Vararis*, is meant *the Firth of Moray*, and hence some have conjectured that Moray was anciently called *Varara*. But it is of the Firth, not of the country, that Ptolemy speaketh, and firths were denominated from the rivers that emptied into them—as *Æstuarium Tai, Bodotriæ, Glotæ*, the Firths of Tay, Forth, Clyde. *Varar*, therefore, must be the name of a river that falleth into the Firth of Moray, and a river of that name there is, which enters into the very head of that Firth. It is now commonly called *the River of Beauly*, and the Highlanders call it *Avon na*

* *Translation*—From Loch Fyne as far as to the Firth of Beauly. (Ed.)

Manach, i.e., *the Monk's River*, because the Priory of Beauly stood on the bank of it; but the true name of it is *Farar*. It floweth out of Loch *Monar*, in the hills of Ross, and the valley through which it runneth is called *Strathfarar*. Now, the Romans did, and we do, often change the digamma F into V, as in knife, knives; shelf, shelves, &c. Agricola's fleet coasting along would search every firth and bay, into the head of it, to know if it communicated with the Western Sea or not; and having come to the head of this firth, and finding a river falling into it called by the natives *Farar*, they changed the F into V and called it *Varar*, and from it they named the Firth *Æstuarium Vararis*, but this gave no name at all to the country.

The only name by which I have found the country called is *Moravia* or *Moray*. Hector Boece writes, that, in the 1st century, a colony from Moravia in Germany settled in this country, and gave it the name of the country from which they came. But he did not consider that at that time the country called *Moravia* was called *Marcomania*, and the inhabitants *Marcomani* and *Quadi* (*Tacit. de Mor. Germ.* cap. 42). Others, finding the word *Mureff* in some ancient manuscripts, and *Rief*, signifying *Bent*, will have it called *Mureff*, from the abundance of that grass growing on the sea shore. But, in my opinion, those have changed the V into F, and made it *Mureff*, instead of *Murev* or *Murav*. The Highlanders call it *Murav* or *Morav*, from the Celtic words *Mur* or *Mor*, the sea, and *Taobb* or *Tav* the side, and in construction *Mor'av*, i.e., *the sea side*. This, I think, is the true notation of the name, answering to the situation of the country, by *the side of the sea*.

THE EXTENT OF THE COUNTRY OF MORAY.

Ptolemy doth not touch this point, nor doth any ancient writer that I know. I cannot be of opinion that *Moravia* comprehended no more than the plain and champaign ground by the sea side, which is all that is strictly called *Moray* in our day. But I include within the province or country, as it was before the division of it into counties or shires, all the plain country by the sea side, from the mouth of the River Spey to the River of Farar or Beauly, at the head of the Firth; and all the valleys, glens, and straths situated betwixt the Grampian Mountains south of Badenoch and the Firth of Moray, and which discharge rivers into that Firth. And I incline to give the country this large extent for the reasons following :—

The plain country by the sea side, from Spey to Ness, is always called *Moray*, and I see no reason for extending it eastward beyond the mouth of Spey; but that it extended westward to the River of Beauly is probable, from the notation of the word *Morav;* for so far the Firth extends, and the country taking its name from the Firth, it is reasonable to extend the one as far as the other. This is much strengthened by what we find in *Dalrymple's Collection*, p. 199— "That King Alexander I. pursued the Moraymen that conspired against him from Innergoury over Spey into Murray-land, and at the Stockford above Beauly passed over to Ross." This fixes the boundaries both to the east and west, viz., the Rivers of Spey and Beauly. The situation of the country of Ross, northward from Moray, confirms this. Its name *Ross* signifieth a peninsula, or a head or point of land jutting out between rivers or firths; and it is the Firth of Moray with that of Tain that form this peninsula, or Ross.

The bounds by the sea side being thus fixed, Moray extended towards S.S.W. to the head of Loch Lochy, on the borders of Lochaber. This one observation throweth abundant light on this assertion.

Our historians agree that the castle of Urquhart in Moray held out bravely for King David Bruce against Edward Baliol. This castle did not stand in Urquhart, near Elgin; for there are no vestiges of a fort or castle there nor any tradition that there ever was such a fort. But on the west bank of Loch Ness there was a strong fort, the walls whereof do still remain.* This

* This ancient Stronghold, the ruins of which now form so

showeth that Loch Ness, with the glens around it, was in the country of Moray. And that the whole course of the River Spey, even to Lochaber, was in the province or country of Moray may be gathered from King Robert Bruce's charter of the *Comitatus Moraviensis* to Thomas Randulph Earl of Moray. To all which, let me add, that the Highlanders always did, and as yet do, march and bound the countries by the hills and rivers.

picturesque an object on the south side of Loch Ness, about two miles from Drumnadrochet, is supposed, from the designation of "King's House," which was given to it in the 13th century, to have been originally a royal castle, and to have formed one of a chain of forts which extended along the Caledonian valley from the German Ocean to the Atlantic. It stands upon a peninsulated rock, jutting out into the loch, at the extremity of the western promontory of the Bay of Urquhart, and is separated from the mainland by a deep fosse. The lofty massive walls, now greatly dilapidated, which surrounded it inclosed an area of about 5 acres in extent, and had a *terre plein* inside, upon which the engines used for its defence were worked.

The keep, or square tower, which had three storeys, was 50 feet high and 30 feet broad. It had a crenellated battlement and watch-towers at the four corners. The walls were 9 feet thick. The gateway leading into the court was approached by a drawbridge across the moat. It was machicolated, and had its portcullis flanked by two circular towers. These entrance towers were much in the style of architecture peculiar to the castles of Edward I. of England. They were probably built after William le Fitz Warrene had been beleaguered in this castle by the insurgents of 1297. On that occasion the Bishop of Aberdeen, and Gratney Earl of Mar, were sent by Edward to the relief of this garrison, and directed to adopt such measures, in concert with Fitz Warrene, as they might think necessary to strengthen the fortifications. The result of their engineering skill was probably the erection of those massive circular towers which are so characteristic of the style of military architecture practised in the time of that monarch. It would seem that the fortifications and outworks thus added by Edward to the original stronghold now became the means

According to this view of the country of Moray, it extends from east to west by the side of the Firth, *i.e.*, from Speymouth to Beauly, 39 Scottish or about 60 English miles; and the River *Farar*, from Loch Monar to Beauly, runneth 30 Scottish miles from S.W. to N.E. Thus the utmost extent from N.E. to S.W. is 69 Scottish or 104 English miles. And if we take the breadth from the Firth at Inverness to the Braes of Glenfeshie in Badenoch it is about 38 Scottish, or 57 English miles.

of enabling the garrison to maintain a protracted defence against his troops. It held out for several weeks, but was at length stormed and taken in the spring of 1304. Its gallant commandant, de Bois, was apparently a scion of the family of Bosco or Wood of Redcastle, represented in the early part of the 13th century by Sir Andrew de Bosco, who married Elizabeth, Lady of Kilraveck, one of the three daughters of Sir John Bisset of Lovat. De Bois and the brave garrison he commanded were put to the sword; the only one of all the besieged who was not slain being the wife of de Bois, who contrived to make her escape in the disguise of a servant.

Sir Robert Lauderdale of Quarrelwood, in Morayshire, governor of the castle in 1334, maintained it against the Baliol faction. His daughter, marrying the Laird of Chisholm in Strathglass, their son, Sir Robert Chisholm of that ilk, became Laird of Quarrelwood, in right of his mother, and also constable of Urquhart Castle, in right of his grandfather. In 1359 the barony and Castle of Urquhart were disponed by David II. to William, Earl of Sutherland, and to his son John. In the Register of the Great Seal of Robert II., 1373, there is a grant of the Castle and Barony of Urquhart to his son, David Seneschalus, failing whom to Alexander Seneschalus. In 1509 they fell into the hands of the chief of the Clan Grant, in whose possession they abide.

Small remains of a small Religious house, which belonged to the Knights of St. John of Jerusalem, are adjacent to Castle Urquhart. (Ed.)

THE SITUATION OF THE COUNTRY OF MORAY.

This country lieth in the 57th degree of north latitude, and Speymouth is about 35 minutes east from Edinburgh. With respect to the neighbouring countries, the Moray Firth and the River of Farar separate it from Ross to the north, and from Speymouth towards the S.E. the south and S.W. It bordereth upon the Enzie, Strathdeveron, Strathdon, Braemar, Athole, Ranach, and Lochaber.

THE DIVISION OF THE COUNTRY.

The division of this country may be considered in a three-fold view.

I. The Natural Division, which is two-fold. First, into Lowlands and Highlands. The Lowlands are those plains that are not intermixed with mountains and hills, but are situated near the Firth, and are in some places four, in some six miles broad. The Highlands are the straths and valleys on the sides of rivers, separated from the Lowlands by mountains and hills. This points to the second natural division, which is made by the rivers that fall into the Firth. And here the strath or valley of Spey makes the first division; which, running from the Firth to the borders of Lochaber, is inclosed on both sides by a chain of hills, and is a barrier to the low country, covering it from one end to the other. In the

Lowlands, the other rivers divide the country from east to west into five unequal divisions. Thus, from Spey to Lossie, 6 miles; from Lossie to Ern or Findhorn, 9 miles; from Findhorn to Nairn, 7 miles; from Nairn to Ness, 12 miles; and from Ness to Farar, 5 miles. And all these rivers run almost parallel to one another, from S.W. to N.E.

II. The Civil or Political Division, into counties or shires, for the more easy distribution of justice to the people. A part of the county of Banff, the whole county of Elgin and Forres, the whole county of Nairn, and a part of the county of Inverness, lie within this province or country.

III. The Ecclesiastic Division, into Parishes, Presbyteries, Dioceses, and Commissariots. I here only mention the Political and Ecclesiastical divisions, of which I shall in the following parts treat at large.

PART II.

THE GEOGRAPHY OF MORAY.

IN viewing the geographical face of this country, I shall follow the Natural Division of it above mentioned, passing from one parish forward to another, and in every parish observing the situation of the church, the extent of the parish, the principal baronies, heritors, and seats or dwellings, and what else merits observation.

The valley of the River Spey makes the first branch of the Natural Division, and therefore I shall first describe this strath or valley, after I have given some account of

THE RIVER SPEY.

This river has its fountains on the borders of Lochaber. It floweth out of a small lake about half a mile in length, called Loch Spey, and running from S.W. to N.E. it watereth the countries of Badenoch, Strathspey, and Rothes, and then turning due north it discharges its stream into the Moray Firth at Germach [Garmouth] after a course of about 60 Scottish or 90 English miles. It seemeth to have its name from the Teutonic or Pictish word *Spe* (*Sputum*), because the rapidity of it raiseth much foam or froth. Many lesser rivers from the Grampian Mountains swell its stream so much that the manuscript *De Situ Albaniæ*, written in the 12th century, calleth it (in the Latin of these days) "Magnum et miserabile flumen, quod vocatur *Spe*."* The strath of this river is inclosed to the N. and W. by a ridge of hills, which, beginning in the parish of Urquhart near the sea, runs above Elgin, Forres, Inverness, and Loch Ness to Lochaber. And to the S. and E. a part of the Grampian Mountains runneth along Strathspey and Badenoch, and several glens jut into these mountains, which shall be described in their proper place.

[The Spey rises in the Braes of Lochaber, close on the water-shed with Lochaber, only ½ mile from Glenroy and 6 miles from Loch Laggan. Less than a mile below its source it expands into a tiny lake called Loch Spey. Measuring its run in a straight line, for 37 miles its course is in Inverness-shire, and over that distance it flows 15 miles eastward and 22 miles north-east. It receives on its left bank the Markie, the Calder, the Dulnain, and some half dozen burns. On its right there flow into it the Truim, the Tromie, the Feshie, and numerous minor streams. It traverses the parishes of Laggan, Kingussie, and Alvie, forming in its glen the seat of by far the greater part of their population. In the parish of Kingussie it averages from 80 to 100 feet in breadth, varies from 2 to 16 feet in depth, and moves at the mean rate of about 3 miles in the hour. In the parish of Alvie it expands into Loch Inch, is partly gentle and partly impetuous, and has a mean breadth of about 150 feet. Over the next 30 miles of its course, still measuring in a straight line, its direction continues to be N.E., and over the last 15, or from Craigellachie Bridge to the

* *Translation*—The large and dangerous river, which is called Spey.

Moray Firth at Garmouth, it is toward the north. Over 21 miles of these 45, it chiefly flows between Inverness-shire and Morayshire, yet runs across wings and intersecting parts of both counties; and over the remaining 24 chiefly divides Morayshire from Banffshire, yet cuts off considerable wings of the former, and at one place is touched by a tiny detached part of Nairnshire. It receives on its left bank the Dulnain, 2½ miles above Grantown; and on its right the Nethy at Abernethy, the Avon at Ballindalloch, and the Fiddich below Craigellachie. Its entire length, measuring in straight lines, is about 82 miles, but measured along the curvatures of its channel, it cannot be less than 120 miles. The valley or strath of the Spey is extensively covered with pine, birch, and alder, suggesting an image of Caledonia at the Roman invasion, or of a prairie in the wilds of America.]—(Ed.)

I proceed now to

THE PARISH OF BELLIE.

This parish in Irish is called *Bealidb*, i.e., *Broom*. It is situated on the east bank of the River Spey, at the mouth of it.

The Church standeth near the bank of the river, two miles above the firth.

The great ornament of this parish is the house of Gordon Castle, the seat of the Duke of Gordon, This house was founded by George, Earl of Huntly, who died A.D. 1507. It is a large and grand pile; but, consisting of several apartments built at different times, it cannot be very regular. The rooms of state are grand, well finished and furnished, with fine pictures; and the library containeth a valuable collection of books. The house is environed with parks and enclosures and much planting, old and young. The gardens are spacious, well laid out, and watered with a pond and *Jet d'eau*. But the house, by its low situation betwixt the river to the west and a high hill to the east, commandeth no view of the adjacent country. It was formerly called *the Bog of Gight*, in Irish, *Bog na gaoith*, i.e., the windy Bog.

[The original of this vast quadrangular Gothic pile was a gloomy tower in the centre of a morass called the *Bog of Gight Bogen-Gight*, accessible only by a narrow causeway and a drawbridge. The ferry, or ferry-boat across the Spey was for ages known as *Boat o' Bog*, now supplanted by the Bridge of Spey. The most ancient title of the Duke of Gordon was *the Gudeman o' the Bog*, but in those feudal times the said soubriqueted *Gudeman* was anything but good to those of his vassals *o' the Bog* who gainsaid him. Thomas Pennant, in his "Tour in Scotland," 1769, vol. i., p. 142, says:—"Castle Gordon, originally called the *Castle of the Bog of Gight*, inherits at present very little of its former [Moorish] splendour. By accident I met with an old print that shows it in all the magnificence described by a singular traveller of the middle of the last century. This gentleman, Richard Franks, made his journey in 1658, and went through Scotland as far as the Water of Brora, in Sutherland, to enjoy as he travelled the amusement of angling. In his "Northern Memoirs" (12mo., London, 1694) he says—"*Bogagieth*, the Marquis of Huntly's palace, all built of stone, facing the ocean, whose fair front (set prejudice aside) worthily deserves an Englishman's applause for her lofty and majestic towers and turrets that storm the air, and seemingly make dents in the very clouds. At first sight I must confess it struck me with admiration to gaze on so gaudy and regular a frontispiece, more especially to consider it in the nook of a nation." The principal pictures in Castle Gordon are (1) the first Marquis of Huntly, who, on his first arrival at Court, forgetting the usual obeisance, was asked why he did not bow; he begged His Majesty's pardon, and excused his want of respect by saying he was just come from a place where everybody bowed to him. (2) The second Marquis of Huntly, beheaded by the Covenanters. (3) His son, the gallant Lord Gordon, Montrose's friend, killed at the battle of Auldford. (4) Lord Lewis Gordon, a less generous warrior, the plague of the people of Murray, whence this proverb, "The guil, the Gordon, and the hooded-craw were the three worst things Murray ever saw." The guil is a weed that infests corn. Murray was then the seat of the Covenanters, hence the contrast of characters in these old lines—"If ye with Montrose gae, ye'l get sic and wae enough; if ye with Lord Lewis gae, ye'l get rob and rave enough." (5) The head of the second Countess of Huntly, daughter of James I. (6) Sir Peter Frazier, a full length, in armour. (7) A small fine portrait of the Abbe d'Aubigne sitting in his study. (8) A very fine head of St. John receiving the Revelation—a beautiful expression of attention and devotion.

The Duke of Gordon still keeps up the diversion of falconry, and had several fine hawks of the Peregrine and gentle falcon species, which breed in the rocks of Glenmore. I saw also here a true Highland greyhound, which is now become very scarce. It was of a very large size, strong, deep-chested, and covered with very long and rough hair. This kind was in great vogue in former days, and used in vast numbers at the magnificent stag-chases by the powerful chieftains. I also saw here a dog, the offspring of a wolf and Pomeranian bitch. It had much the appearance of the first, was very good-natured and sportive, but being slipped at a weak deer it instantly brought the animal down and tore out its throat. This dog was bred by Mr. Brook, animal merchant in London, who told me that the congress between the wolf and the bitch was immediate, and the produce at the litter was ten."

The old Cross of Fochabers stands in the Castle Park, to which is attached a portion of the original *Jougs.*]—(Ed.)

Close by the castle standeth the village of Fochaber, so called, in my opinion, from the Irish *Fo-hobir*, i.e., below the Well; for above it, in the face of the hill, is a well or fountain, the waters whereof serve the town. The town is a burgh of barony, hath a weekly market, and in the centre of it there is a court-house, with a steeple of modern architecture. It has a post-office, and at the west of it is a passage over Spey, called the Boat of Bog, upon the post-road.

[THE FAMILY OF GORDON, DUKE OF GORDON.

Of this family, which took their surname from the lands which they possessed in the shire of Berwick, there are, besides these in Britain, several in Muscovy, who make a great figure there.

THE FAMILY OF GORDON; DUKE OF GORDON. 53

In the time of King Malcolm IV., which is 750 years ago, this family was very numerous, and flourished in the county aforesaid, one of which was Bertram de Gordon, who, at the siege of Chalne in Aquitain, as it is said, wounded to death King Richard I. of England.

About 550 years since, upon the fall of Commins, the superiority of the county of Mar, or Aberdeen, was given to this family by King Robert de Bruce, and upon that occasion they removed thither from their original country; where the family and their branches possessed many considerable baronies, among which is the Lordship of Gordon; and now they enjoy as many in the north and west, there being of this family, besides his Grace the Duke, the Earls of Aboyn and Aberdeen, and the Viscount Kenmure.

This family had also many lands bestowed upon them for their fidelity to their princes; but suffered much by their adhering to Queen Mary, King Charles I., and King James VII., and are descended from Richard de Gordon, who, in 1267, gave lands to the Abbey of Kelso.

To Richard succeeded Thomas, his son, who was also a benefactor to the aforesaid Abbey; and Thomas, his son, according to the devotion of those times, taking upon him the sign of the cross, left his inheritance to his daughter Alicia, which daughter being married to Adam Gordon, her kinsman, by him had Sir Adam Gordon, Knight, their son and heir.

Sir Adam, who succeeded, lived in the year 1303, and confirmed all the donations made to Kelso by Richard, Thomas, and Adam Gordon, his progenitors; and being a zealous assertor of the independency and freedom of his native country, stood in such high favour with King Robert Bruce, that the said King, in consideration of his good services, gave him the Lordship of Strathbogy, in which he was succeeded by Sir Alexander, his son.

To Sir Alexander, who was next heir, and in 1346 lost his life at the battle of Durham in behalf of King David II., succeeded Sir John Gordon, his son, which Sir John, in the 28th of the said King, obtained a charter for erecting all his lands into an entire barony of Strathbogy.

To Sir John succeeded Sir David, his son, who was the 2nd Baron; and he being slain in 1401 at the battle of Homildon, in the service of his country, left issue by Elizabeth, his wife, daughter to the Lord Keith, an only daughter of her name, who was his heir; and she, in 1408, married Sir Alexander Seaton, second son to Sir William Seaton of that ilk, to whom Robert, Duke of Albany, in the third year of his government, gave a charter and confirmation of the lands and baronies of Gordon, Huntley, Strathbogy, and several others, by him had Alexander Seaton, who succeeded, and William Seaton of Meldrum.

Alexander, who was heir to the baronies aforesaid, and the 3rd Baron thereof, was also one of the hostages for the ransom of King James I., and in 1437 was joined in commission with John, Bishop of Glasgow, Sir Walter Ogilvy, and Sir John Forrester, Knights, to treat of a peace with England, which they happily concluded.

In the reign of King James II. he resumed the surname of Gordon, and placed the arms of that name in the first quarter, and for his noble services performed to that King in his minority was made Sheriff of Inverness and created Earl of Huntly, and had also divers manors and lordships (as Badzenoch, &c.) given him, which he long enjoyed.

This Earl, marrying to his first wife Honora, daughter and heir to Robert Keith, grandson to Sir William Keith, Marishal of Scotland, and Honora his wife, heiress to the Lord Frazer, by her had no issue, but with whom he got the lands of Touch, Fraser, Aboyne, Glentanner, Glenmuick, and Cluny. By his second wife, who was Giles, daughter and heir to John Hay, Baron of Tullibody, Touch, and Enzie, he had Sir Alexander Gordon, Knight, who was the first of the family of Touch. By his third wife, who was Margaret, daughter to William Lord Chrichton, Chancellor of Scotland, he had a son named George, and three daughters, whereof Jane was married to James Dunbar, Earl of Murray; Elizabeth to William, Earl of Marishal; and Christian to William, Lord Forbes.

To Alexander, Earl of Huntly, succeeded George, his son by the third wife (the honour being so limited), which George was one of the Privy Council to King James III., as he was to James IV., and by him made Lord Lieutenant of the north of Scotland and Lord High Chancellor of that kingdom, in which eminent station he continued till his death, being the space of eight years.

He married to his first wife, the Lady Jane Steuart, daughter to King James I., and after her decease, Agnes, daughter to William, Earl of Errol, and, dying in 1507, left issue (but by which of his wives is not said), three sons and four daughters; of the sons, Alexander, the eldest, succeeded his father; Adam, the second, was Earl of Sutherland; and Sir James was Admiral of Scotland. And of the daughters, which were Catherine, Janet, Agnes, and Mary, the eldest was married to Perkin Warbeck, the pretended Duke of York; the second, first to Alexander, son and heir to David, Earl of Crawford, and after, to Patrick, Lord Gray; the third, to Sir James Ogilvie of Finlater; and the youngest, to Sir William Sinclair of Westraw, in the county of Caithness.

Alexander, who succeeded his father, and was the 3rd Earl of Huntly, was one of the Privy Council to King James IV., which Prince he accompanied to the battle of Flodden, and commanded the van of the army with valour and conduct; and surviving that fatal day was, in the minority of James V., made Lord Lieutenant of the north, beyond the River of Forth, and one of his Majesty's Governors.

He married Jane, daughter to the Earl of Athole, and by her had a son named John, who died in his life time, leaving issue by Jane, his wife, natural daughter to King James IV., by Margaret, daughter to John, Lord Drummond, three sons and two daughters, whereof George succeeded his grandfather; Alexander was Bishop of Galloway; and William Bishop of Aberdeen: and of the daughters, which were Janet and Isabel, the eldest was married to Colin, Earl of Argyle, and the youngest to the Lord Innermeath.

George, who was heir to his grandfather, and the 4th Earl of Huntly, was a nobleman of great and eminent parts, and thereby, in 1536, became one of the Privy Council and Lord Lieutenant of Scotland during his Majesty's going to France to espouse Queen Magdalen; and, upon the death of his master, was one of the Peers who signed and sealed that association to oppose the intended match between Queen Mary and Edward VI. of England. In the 4th of Queen Mary, 1546, he was appointed Lord High Chancellor of Scotland; and afterwards, in consideration of his extraordinary services at the battle of Pinkie Cleugh, in defence of his country against the English (and other his services to the Crown), he had a grant of the Earldom of Murray and the Lordship of Abernethy, which he enjoyed for divers years, and died in 1563. He married Elizabeth, daughter to Robert, son and heir to William, Earl of Marishal, and by her had five sons and three daughters, of which George, the second son, was next heir; and of the daughters, who were Jane, Elizabeth, and Margaret, the eldest was married to Alexander, Earl of Sutherland, the second to John, Earl of Athole, and the youngest to Lord Forbes.

George, who succeeded, and was the 5th Earl of Huntly, was one of the Privy Council to Queen Mary, Lord High Chancellor of Scotland, and Lieutenant-General of all her Majesty's forces in the north, and dying 1576, left issue by Anne his wife, daughter to James, Duke of Chatelherault, George, his only son, and a daughter named Jane, who was married to George, Earl of Caithness.

George, who was the 6th Earl, and 1st Marquis, of Huntly, and heir to his father, was a nobleman of great spirit and courage, and was much in the favour of King James VI., by whom he was made Lord Lieutenant of the north, Knight of the Bath, and created Marquis of Huntly, which title he lived to enjoy 35 years. He died at Dundee in 1636, " was convoyit with sum freindis to the Kirk of Belly," where the corpse was kept a night while on its transit to Elgin Cathedral.

He married Henrietta, daughter to Esme, Duke of Lennox, and by her had two sons and four daughters; Anne married to James, Earl of Murray, Elizabeth to Alexander, Earl of Linlithgow, Mary to William, Marquis of Douglas, and Jane to Claud, Lord Strabane, of the kingdom of Ireland; and of the sons, which were George and John, the eldest succeeded his father.

George last mentioned, who was the 2nd Marquis of Huntly, was captain of the Scots Gens-d'Armes to Lewis XIII. of France, while he was only Lord Gordon; and upon the breaking out of the troubles in the reign of King Charles I. he, being very firm to that Prince's interests, had a commission to be Lieutenant of the north during the rage of the civil war, and at the end thereof, on the 30th of March, 1649, was beheaded at Edinburgh by the Covenanters.

He married Anne, daughter to Archibald, Earl of Argyle, by whom he had issue, three sons and three daughters; of the sons, George, the eldest, was killed at the battle of Aldford in his father's lifetime; Lewis, the second, was Marquis of Huntly, and Charles, the youngest, was created Earl of Aboyn; and of the three daughters, which were Anne, Henrietta, and Jane, the eldest was married to James, Earl of Perth; the second, first to George, Lord Seaton, and secondly to John, Earl of Traquhar; and the youngest to Thomas, Earl of Haddington.

Lewis, who was the 3rd Marquis of Huntly, married Isabel, daughter to Sir John Grant of that ilk, and by her had a son named George and three daughters; of which, Agnes was married to the Count de Crolly, Mary to James, Earl of Perth, and Jane to Charles, Earl of Dunfermline, and George, their brother, succeeded his father.

George, who was the 4th Marquis of Huntly, was, by King Charles II., created Duke of Gordon in 1684; and by James VII. made one of the Lords of the Treasury, one of the Privy Council, Governor of Edinburgh Castle, and Knight of the most noble Order of the Thistle; and at the Revolution held out the aforesaid Castle for some time for his Majesty's interest, but at last, seeing no hope of relief from his master, he surrendered it to King William's troops.

He married the Lady Elizabeth Howard, second daughter to Henry, Duke of Norfolk, in England, and dying at Leith in 1716, by her left issue, one son and one daughter; Jane, married to James, Lord Drummond, and Alexander, 2nd Duke, married Henrietta, daughter of Charles, Earl of Peterborough and Monmouth, and by her had four sons and seven daughters, viz.—Cosmo George, Marquis of Huntly, who succeeded his father; Charles, died 1780; Lewis, died 1754; Adam, a Major-General in the army, he married Sept. 2, 1767, Jane, daughter of John Drummond, Esq., and widow of James, late Duke of Athol, which lady died Feb. 22, 1795; Henrietta, who died Feb., 1789; Mary, who died July 26, 1782; Anne, married to William, Earl of Aberdeen, and died June 22, 1791; Betty, married to the Rev. Mr. Skelly; Jane, died unmarried in 1792; Catherine, married to Francis, Earl of Wemys; Charlotte.

Cosmo George, the 3rd Duke, named after the Duke of Tuscany, succeeded his father Alexander, who died in November, 1728. He, in 1741, married, at Dunkeld,

Catherine Gordon, daughter of William, Earl of Aberdeen, by whom, who died in 1779, he had three sons and three daughters; Alexander, the 4th Duke; William, married March 1, 1781, Frances Irvine, second daughter of the last Viscount Irvine, who was born July 12, 1761, by whom he had a son, born March 6, 1782, named Francis; George, died unmarried Nov. 1, 1793; Susan, married 1767 to John, late Earl of Westmoreland, to whom she was second wife, and after his death she married, secondly, Dec. 28, 1778, Colonel John Woodford, of the Foot Guards, by whom she had issue; Anne, married in 1782 to the Rev. Alexander Chalmers, and died Jan. 17, 1792; Catherine, married to Thomas Booker, Esq., an officer in the 53rd Regiment of Foot, and died Jan. 3, 1797. The Duchess, their mother, married, secondly, General Staates Long Morris, and died Dec. 10, 1779. Cosmo George, dying in France in Aug., 1752, was succeeded by his eldest son, Alexander, 4th Duke, who married, Oct. 25, 1767, Jane, daughter of Sir William Maxwell, Bart., by whom he had issue; George, Marquis of Huntly, married in July, 1794, to Miss Maxwell, his cousin; Charlotte, married Sep., 1789, to Charles, 4th Duke of Richmond and Lennox, by whom she had issue; Madeline married, Feb. 3, 1789, Sir Robert Sinclair and had issue; Susannah married, Oct. 7, 1793, to the Duke of Manchester; Louisa married on April 17, 1797, Lord Broome, son to the Marquis Cornwallis; Georgiana; Alexander, born Dec., 1776; a son born Nov. 12, 1785. The ladies were all born at Gordon Castle.

Long before the decease of the Lady Jane Maxwell, the 4th Duchess, the lecherous eyes of her husband, Duke Alexander, were set on Jean Christie, whose face and figure fascinated him. She was of humble descent, and resided in Fochabers, where he regularly visited her, and even aired her in his carriage. She bore his Grace nine children, to whom, "after proclamation on three several Sabbaths," she was married "on the 30th day of July, 1820, by the Rev. William Rennie, minister of the parish of Bellie." Excepting this escapade, Jean Christie's charities and multifarious good works to the people about the place were most praiseworthy. She was buried at Bellie Churchyard on the 2nd August, 1824, æt. 54, in a vault under a fine mausoleum supported by 12 pillars.

Her name is not recorded upon a marble slab to Adam, her son. [See page 61.]

Alexander died in 1827, and was succeeded by his son George, 5th and last Duke. He married Elizabeth, daughter of Alexander Brodie of Arnhall, and died without issue in 1836. His corpse was brought by sea in one of his Majesty's ships to the coast near Gordon Castle, where it lay in state before being taken to the vault in Elgin Cathedral. Charles, 5th Duke of Richmond, after the decease of the above, his maternal uncle, assumed the additional surname of Gordon. The title is now Richmond and Gordon.*

ARMS.—1st, Sapphire, three boars' heads erased topaz, for Gordon; 2nd, Topaz, three lions' heads erased ruby, for Badenoch; 3rd, topaz, three crescents within a double tressure ruby, for Seaton; 4th, Sapphire, three cinquefoils pearls, for Frazer, supported by two greyhounds pearl, each gorged with a plain collar ruby, charged with three buckles topaz. Crest in a Marquis' coronet of the last—a stag's head guardant proper. *Mottoes.*—On Crest, "Bydand"; on Arms, "Animo non astutia." [*By courage, not by craft.*]—(ED.)

St. Mary's Aisle, Elgin Cathedral, has for ages been allotted for the sepulture of the family of Gordon.

The following are yet traceable; albeit they are fast following the state of the Royal Vault in Holyrood, wherein a respectable sow would scarcely be put to litter by an Irishman, certainly by no Scotchman.

I. Alexander de Seton, Lord of Gordon, created Earl of Huntly by King James II. His coffin is under a sarcophagus, having a knight in armour on the top. The Inscription runs:—

* Shaw's history of the family, being so meagre, has been expunged, and the above substituted, mainly borrowed from the rare " British Compendium, or Rudiments of Honour," &c. vol. II. London, 1725; and Kearsley's " Complete Peerage," &c. London, 1798. Among the several Histories and Genealogical Trees, not two accord as to dates, intermarriages, and procreations. The numerous bastards are omitted. The chief work from which compilers draw is, " The History of the Ancient, Noble, and Illustrious Family of Gordon, from their first arrival in Scotland, in Malcolm the Third's time, to the year 1690," by William Gordon, of Old Aberdeen, published by Thomas Ruddiman in 1716. Gaps of amour and escalade can be inter-

𝕳𝖎𝖈 jacet nobilis et potens 𝔇ominus 𝔄lexander 𝔊ordon, primus comes de 𝕳untly, 𝔇ominus de 𝔊ordon et 𝔅adzenoth, qui obiit apud 𝕳untly, 15 𝔍ulii, anno domini, 1470.

Translation—Here lies a noble and powerful lord, Alexander Gordon, first Earl of Huntly, Lord of Gordon and Badenoch, who died the 15th July in the year of our Lord, 1470.

II. Adam Gordon, Dean of Caithness, died in 1523.

III. George, 5th Earl of Huntly, died at Strathbogy in May, 1576.

IV. George, 1st Marquis of Huntly, died 13th June, 1636.

V. Lady Anne Gordon, Countess of Moray, died at Elgin, 19th Jan., 1640.

VI. Alexander, Duke of Gordon, died 10th Aug., 1682.

VII. Alexander, 2nd Duke of Gordon, died 28th Nov., 1728.

VIII. "The most illustrious Princess Elizabeth Howard, senior Duchess of Gordon, died July 16th, 1732, aged seventy-five." [Died at Edinburgh.]

IX. "His Grace Cosmo George, Duke of Gordon, Marquis and Earl of Huntly, Earl of Enzie, Viscount of Inverness, Lord Gordon of Badenoch, died at Bretuil, August 5th, 1752, aged thirty-three."

X. "Sacred to the memory of Her Grace, Henrietta, Duchess of Gordon, who was the only daughter of Charles Mordaunt, Earl of Peterborough and Monmouth, who conquered Spain. She was born April 3, 1682, and married in 1706 to Alexander, Marquis of Huntly, afterwards Duke of Gordon, to whom she bore five sons and seven daughters. She died at Prestonhall the 11th day of October, 1760, aged seventy-eight years."

The device, medallion, and effigy are fast decaying.

XI. "Kathrin, Dowager Duchess of Gordon, died 16th December, 1777, aged sixty." [Wife of No. IX.]

lined by the adventurous reader. If the family did not originate from the lands, and in the parish of Gordon, in Berwickshire, Charlemagne, or even Julius Cæsar, the ancestral line may find the end of its clue in the loins of Adam and Eve, but not when they basked in the Garden of Eden. For certain, the Gordons had their residence in Elgin, on the north side of College Street, the site of which is now within the grounds of Grant Lodge. George, Earl of Huntly, was retoured to his father in a tenement within the Burgh of Elgin, 20th July, 1373.—(ED.)

XII. Lord Alexander Gordon, died 8th Jan., 1808, aged 22.

XIII. Alexander, 4th Duke of Gordon, died at London, 17th June, 1827, aged 84.

XIV. George, 5th and last Duke of Gordon, died at London, 28th May, 1836.

XV. Elizabeth Brodie, wife and widow of George, 5th Duke, died at Huntly Lodge, 31st Jan., 1864, aged 69.*

EPITAPHS IN BELLIE CHURCHYARD.

I. In this Vault are deposited the remains of ADAM GORDON of Newtongarrie, son of Alexander, fourth Duke of Gordon, who died at Burnside, 14th Aug., 1834, in the 37th year of his age. Deeply regretted by all his friends. This marble was placed here by his spouse, Jane Grant, as a testimony of her affection. [See page 58.]

Jane Grant (like her mother-in-law, Jean Christie) was of lowly parentage. She resided in Buckie or its vicinity, and subsequently married —— Reid, a bank agent in Fochabers.

Adam Gordon, after his forefathers' example, left procreations with and without wedlock.

Near the Churchyard gate is a marble slab within an enclosure with this Inscription:—

II. This tablet is placed by Jean, fifth Duchess of Gordon, to the memory of her dear infant daughter, CHARLOTTE, who died the 10th of Dec., 1810; and also to her beloved mother, Mrs. Susan Robertson, who died the 2nd of June, 1822, in her 91st year.

III. In the only remaining fragment of the Kirk at Bellie, a much defaced tablet, with Latin inscription, bears the name of

"GULIELMUS ANNAND,"

who appears to have died in 1770, aged 70.

IV. The gravestone of Mr. William Sanders, which (Shaw says) bore that "he lived 108 years, and was minister of Bellie 77 years," is now not visible. It was in Mr. Sanders' time, on the 15th Sept., 1632, that the Earl of Angus "was mareit at the Kirk of Bellie with Lady Mary Gordon [third] dochter to the Marquess [of Huntly], be Maister Robert Douglass, minister at Glen-

* See "Life and Letters of Elizabeth, last Duchess of Gordon, by Rev. A. Moody Stuart." London: Nisbet & Co., 1865.—(ED.)

bervie, whome the Erll of Angous brocht with him of purpoiss."

On the 28th Nov. following, the Master of Abercorn and Huntly's youngest daughter were married in the same place, " be ane Irish minister."

V. Near the middle of the churchyard :—

Svb hoc cippo tvmvlatvr corpvs exsangve ELIZABETHÆ MILNS, Angligenæ, Andreæ Hossack, ivnioris, qvondam sponsæ, principis Dvcissæ Gordon, qvondam ancillæ, qvæ obiit tertio Octobris, anno Dom. 1687.

Translation.—Beneath this stone is interred the body of ELIZABETH MILNS, a native of England, spouse of Andrew Hossack, junior, and formerly chief maid to the first Duchess of Gordon, who died 3rd October, 1687.

VI. From a flat slab :—

Heir lyes ELSPET GORDON, spous to Alex. Gordon of Upper Dalochie, alies Major, who departed May 12, 1690.

VII. Here lyes ISSOBELL KNIGHT, spous to Androu Hay, wywer in Fochabers. Shee departed the 13 of Feb., 1712. Manney hath donn werteusly, but shee heath excideth them all.

VIII. Here lie the remains of JAMES ROSS, Esq., who, with unblemished integrity, conducted for many years the important affairs of the great family of Gordon, and, whilst zealously anxious to promote their interest, raised no fortune to himself. He departed this life the 8th Sept., 1782, aged 50 years. And of KATHERINE GORDON, his wife, who discharged the duties of a daughter, a wife, and a mother, with a piety and affection, offering bright example to their descendants. She was born 1st Jan., 1743; died 17th Sep., 1795.

IX. Sacred to the memory of JOHN ROSS, Esq., some time Professor of Oriental Languages in King's College, Aberdeen, who, after passing a long life in the practice of virtues which rendered him an ornament and blessing to society, was removed to that better world, where he will meet their just reward, on 9th July, 1814, in the 84th year of his age. This humble tablet has been inscribed by parental affection.

X. Sacred to the memory of JOHN MENZIES, Esq., who died 15th March, 1831, aged 72. The best eulogium of his character is, that for the long period of nearly 50 years, during which time he acted as cashier to the Duke of Gordon, his employer never, sustained any loss by his incorrectness or neglect of duty ; and that the many thousands with whom he transacted business were equally satisfied with the integrity of his conduct, against which no complaint was ever heard, even from those who were not his friends.

The above panegyrics may be true, but they are specimens of that fulsome style of praise which is unfit to appear above a grave. *On whose soul may God have mercy*, is the most appropriate petition for all *Esquires*.

XI. Erected by Lieut.-Col. William Marshall, as a sincere but inadequate tribute to the memory of a revered parent, 1857.

This stone was originally placed by William Marshall over the graves of his son, Major ALEX. MARSHALL, who died at Keithmore, 31st Jan., 1807, in his 33rd year; and of JEAN GILES, who died at Newfield Cottage, Dandalieth, 13th Dec., 1824, in the 85th year of her age, whose remains lie both here interred.

Here also lie the remains of WILLIAM MARSHALL, Esq., husband of Jean Giles, a man of virtue and integrity. From a humble station in life he rose to distinction by the industrious cultivation of a natural talent; eventually he became factor on the estate of Alexander, Duke of Gordon, an office which he held for many years, performing its duties with fidelity and to the satisfaction of his employer and the tenantry. Although self-taught, he made considerable progress in mechanics and other branches of natural science, to which his leisure-hours were frequently devoted. But he was chiefly noted for his skill and fine taste in music, the Scottish airs and melodies composed by him being widely known and appreciated. He died, universally esteemed, at Newfield Cottage, Dandaleith, 29th May, 1833, in his 85th year.

Of a family of six children, besides the above-named Alexander, FRANCIS, a jeweller, died in London; JOHN, a Captain in the army, died in India; and GEORGE, a Lieutenant in the army, died in Spain. JANE, an only daughter, widow of John M'Innes, Esq., Dandaleith; and WILLIAM, a retired Lieut.-Col. in the army, being the sole present survivors.

[Another of that class of vainglorious epitaphs so disgusting to the good and inappropriate to the tomb. The worthy factor was, in the first place, a footman or lackey at Gordon Castle. Marshall's music to the song " O' a' the airts the wind can blaw" drew forth from Burns a complimentary letter. Not only did he excel as a firstrate 'fiddler, but as a composer of national airs and beautiful Strathspeys. He was also an ingenious clockmaker, a specimen of which is preserved in Gordon Castle. His son, Major Alexander Marshall, served in India, at the siege of Seringapatam. Captain John, of the 26th Regiment, was present in the Peninsular War, and died of cholera at Madras in 1829. Lieutenant George, of the 92nd Regiment, died from fatigue in 1812. Lieutenant-Colonel William (the 4th son, the erector of the monument) became a Lieutenant in the Gordon Fencibles in his 18th year, served in almost all the engagements during the French Revolution, including those of Aboukir and Corunna. He was so severely wounded at Waterloo that his right arm had to be amputated. After this he was employed in India during the rebellion of 1837, and afterwards in various responsible military offices at home. In 1838 he retired and came to reside at Newfield Cottage, near Craigellachie, where he died on the 29th Aug., 1870, æt. 91.]—(ED.)

XII. Here lyes the body of GEORGE GEDDES, late in Mains of Kempcairn, who dyed the twenty-first day of Octr., 1746.

In memory of CATHERINE MILNE, of the Mill of Towie, and relict of Thomas Geddes of Dallachy and Todholes; she survived her husband 33 years, and died the first September, 1821, aged 87.

XIII. In this burying-ground are interred the remains of THOMAS GEDDES, of Dallachy, who died in 1789, aged ——; and of his son, JOHN GEDDES, in Orbliston, who died 23rd Dec., 1817, aged 64, by whose disconsolate widow this simple record is placed over his grave as a small token of her remembrance of his affection and worth.

XIV. GEO. ANDERSON, farmer, Burnside, "a man distinguished for ardent piety and pure benevolence, whose manners were as simple as his morals were unblemished," died 1779, aged 69; his wife, HELEN SHAND, died 1792, aged 71.

Unknown to pomp, and bred to rural soil,
 To him the Christian's faith and hope were given;
Unskilled in art, nor trained in courtly guile,
 He lived to God and died—to wake in heaven.

XV. In same grave are deposited the remains of the Rev. JOHN ANDERSON, who was 27 years minister of the parish of Kingussie and 11 of Bellie, previous to his retirement from the church, and who died on the 22nd of April, 1830, in the 80th year of his age.

[The General Assembly objecting to Mr. Anderson holding the conjoint offices of a parish minister and commissioner upon the Gordon estates, he gave up the former in 1819 for the more lucrative latter.]—(ED.)

XVI. Erected at the expense of his fellow-servants to JOHN BARONDON, who died at Gordon Castle, Aug. 16, 1853, aged 39.

It was in the bloom of manhood's prime
When death to me was sent;
All you that have a longer time,
Be careful and repent.

O, the grave, whilst it covers each fault, each defect,
Leaves untarnished the worth of the just;
His memory we'll cherish with tender respect,
Whilst his body consumes in the dust.

Among the more interesting features within the policies of Gordon Castle are the Quarry Gardens—at one time presenting unseemly holes, filled with stagnant water and hillocks of quarry debris. This is now the most enchanting of places. Apart from nice walks and flower-beds, there are old carved stones, said to have been brought from Huntly Castle. Some of these have in monogram, the initials of the first Marquis and Marchioness of Huntly, and are oval-shaped; but the centre ornaments and inscriptions are defaced. The two texts which follow (Ps. xxxiv. 9; Phil. ii. 10), dated 1614, are the only parts decipherable:—

TIMETE. DOMINVM. OMNES. SANCTI. EIVS.
QVIA. NON. EST. INOPIA. TIMENTIB. EVM.

As there are traces of "a glory" or halo upon another slab, it had probably been adorned with a representation of our Lord :—

OMNE. GENV. FLECTATVR. .... NOMINE IESV.

Translation.—At the name of Jesus every knee shall bow.

BELLIE.

[*Situation, Soil, Climate.*—The name is Gaelic. Three etymological explanations have been suggested. One supposes it *Bealidh*, signifying *broom;* very unlikely to be right, considering that when the names of places were anciently imposed, the parish could not have been peculiarly distinguished by that shrub. Another, which supposes the name to be *Beulaith, the ford mouth*, is more unfortunate still. The hardy inhabitants of ancient times found the river almost everywhere fordable. The parish on the other bank must have had an equal claim to this significantly figurative epithet; and the channel of the river, shifted almost by every flood, has in every age made the shallow to-day the whirlpool to-morrow. But as ancient record concurs with present appearance to establish that the sea once flowed farther in upon the shore, it having retired almost half a mile on the coast of this parish: even within the memory of people still alive, it can be hardly doubted that the curvature in the bank where Gordon Castle stands was once a bay of the ocean. It must be presumed that the Camp near the Church of Bellie was formed by the Romans in connection with their fleet, when under Agricola they made the circuit of the isle. Whether a barbarian town existed upon their arrival, or whether their general practice of reconciling themselves, like the adventurers of present times, to the savages whom they visited, might have induced a settlement in this vicinity. Such an establishment, in that situation, would naturally be denominated by the natives *Ball-li,* or *Ball-lith,* the *town of the flood;* and the tradition, that Fochabers once stood near the churchyard of Bellie, and the Roman camp, corroborates this explanation of the name.

The parish is in the form of a triangle: the one side, from south to north along the Spey, is about 5 miles; the other along the coast easterly, from the influx of the river to the mouth of the brook of Tynete, is about 4; and the returning side, from the mouth of that brook back to Ordyfish on the bank of the Spey, is nearly equal to 6. From the angle at Ordyfish, the surface of the parish seems divided into three different flats, each rising about 20 feet above the other, and spreading like the quadrants of the concentric circles which the fall of a stone forms in a pond The lowest is along the bed of the river, and so little above the level of the stream, that much of it is laid under water by every flood. The second flat begins also near Ordyfish, and continues spreading like the first as it tends towards the coast; but the first encroaches upon it in the curvature where Gordon Castle stands. And the third, or highest flat, from near the same corner, is less regular than the others, encroaching also in some places on the second, where the mountain seems as if projected on the plain.

Upon the bank of the river the soil is thin, upon a sole

of gravel, the bottom either of the shifting river or of the retiring ocean. Near the coast, where the more still waters had deposited more sediment, it is a deep and fertile loam. Upon the higher flats the soil is of a kindly mould, save where it stretches back into the mountain, where it is moorish, wet, and spongy. In some places it is of a deep red colour, by a ferruginous or ocreous substance, superinduced by the streams from the mountain, which in this quarter, under the moorish surface, is composed of a vast deep bed of clay gravel, of that quality and colour; and each rill, during heavy rain, or a sudden thaw of snow, appears a wondrous torrent of thick deep red gore.

The air, though healthful, is rather cold and dry, yet temperate on the whole, and the winters generally mild.

State of Property.—Of all this parish, the valued rent of which is £3,082 8s. Scots, the Duke of Gordon is proprietor, excepting one farm in its outskirts belonging to the Earl of Findlater. Towards the southern end of the parish, on the second flat, is the town of Fochabers; a Gaelic name, which, like the parish, has received more than one explanation. The most probable refers it to the numerous fountains, where the village was lately placed. The other, which refers it to the field destined for the *weapon shew*, will be generally rejected, on the consideration that it must have obtained its name before either the practice or the statutes requiring meetings for the exhibition or the exercise of arms were introduced. The turbulent state of society in ancient times generally raised a village in the vicinity of every castle, for the mutual security which both the fortress and the people afforded to each other: but in the peaceful security which the wisdom and energy of the present constitution has so long maintained, it is more pleasant to have the palace environed by the ornamented grounds of an extensive park. In this regard, the Duke of Gordon, several years ago purchased the property of the town, then situated not far from his gate, and feued off the present village, at a handsome yet commodious distance. This new town is a clean neat burgh of barony; all its streets are straight, crossing each other at right angles; and the great road to London conducted through the centre of its grand square; three sides of which, pretty uniformly built, are the mansions of the inhabitants. The fourth is occupied by the public buildings, the church, detached in the middle between two large handsome houses of uniform exterior, one occupied as the manse, the other containing the parochial school and town hall.

Off the highway, between the west end of the town and the river, is the great gate to Gordon Castle, consisting of a lofty arch between two neat domes, elegantly finished, with neat square lodges upon the abutments. Its front bears some resemblance to the outline of the castle, and it is similarly embellished by a handsome battlement. Within the gate the road winds about a mile through a green parterre, skirted with flowering shrubbery and groups of tall spreading trees, till it is lost in an oval before the front of the castle. There is, besides this, another approach from the east, sweeping for several miles through the varied scenery of the park, enlivened by different pleasant views of the country around, the river, and the ocean, till it also terminates at the great door of this princely mansion.

The situation of the Castle is on the lowest of the flats that have been described. It commands a long extended view of the whole plain, with all its wood, and a variety of sheets of the river glittering onwards to the sea; comprehending also the town and shipping of Garmach, or Garmouth, and a large handsome edifice that terminates the plain on the shore, the hall and other buildings for the accommodation of the salmon fishery.

The Castle was originally built by George the 2nd Earl of Huntly; altered and enlarged in every succeeding age. It has of late been almost built of new by his Grace, in all the elegant magnificence of modern architecture. It extends in front to the goodly length of 568 feet, from east to west; being however of different depths, the breaks make a variety of light and shade, which takes off the appearance of excess in uniformity. The body of the building is of 4 storeys; and in its southern front stands the six-storeyed tower entire of the original castle, by much ingenuity making a part of the modern palace, and rising 84 feet high. The wings are magnificent pavilions of two lofty storeys, connected by galleries of two lower storeys; and beyond the pavilions, buildings are extended, equally to either hand, of one floor and an attic storey. The whole of this vast edifice, designed by Baxter, architect, Edinburgh, externally is of white hard Elgin freestone, smoothly cut in the most elegant manner in the quarries of Drainie, or Duffus, and finished all around, like the gate, by a rich cornice and a handsome battlement.

The hall of this magnificent structure is embellished by a copy of the Apollo Belvidere, and of the Venus de Medicis, beautifully executed of statuary marble, by Harwood. Here also, by the same ingenious statuary, are busts of Homer, Caracalla, M. Aurelius, Faustina, and a Vestal. At the bottom of the great stairs, are busts also of J. Cæsar, Cicero, and Seneca, all raised on elegant pedestals of Sienna marble. With these last, stands a bust of Cosmo III. Duke of Tuscany, a connexion of the family of Gordon, on an elevated pedestal of painted timber. The stairs and passages are kept warm by a stove placed in this sumptuous apartment.

Two spacious halls for the different ranks of servants, with two baths, cellars, and other requisite accommodations, occupy the rest of the ground floor.

The first floor contains the dining-room, drawing-room, breakfast-room, the bed-chamber of state, with its dressing-room, and several other elegant apartments. All the rooms are judiciously proportioned, sumptuously finished, and the distribution of light managed to the greatest advantage. The sideboard is within the recess of the dining-room, separated by lofty Corinthian columns of Scagliola, in imitation of verd antique marble.

In this room are copies, by Angelica Kauffman, of Venus and Adonis, and of Danaë, by Titian; of Abraham and Hagar, of Joseph and Potiphar's wife, by Guercino; of Dido and St. Cecilia, by Domenichino; besides several portraits.

In the drawing-room is a portrait of the Duke by Raeburn, and of the Duchess by Sir Joshua Reynolds, and some beautiful screens done by the young ladies.

In the breakfast-room is a copy, by Angelica Kauffman, of the celebrated St. Peter and St. Paul, the masterpiece of Guido Rheni, esteemed the most valuable in the Sampieri palace at Bologna, and one of the best paintings in the world: 10,000 sequins, it is said, had been offered for it. It represents St. Paul rebuking the Apostle for his base dissimulation with the Jews, respecting the obligation of the ceremonial law, and concealing his communications with the uncircumcised, related in the Epistle to the Galatians; and the Apostle is represented as much ashamed of his mean hypocrisy. By the same master, there is also a copy of Herodias and the Baptist's head in the charger: and a copy by Guercino of the Persian Sibyl. On each side of the chimney is an original painting by Kauffman, Ulysses and Calypso, Bacchus and Ariadne. Opposite to these is a highly finished full-length portrait of the Duke, leaning on a horse, a gun in his hand, and dead game lying near, by Pompeijo Battoni of Rome. A fine small original of the Abbe d'Aubignie in his study, and a strikingly expressive head of St. John receiving the Revelation in Patmos, contribute also their embellishment to this magnificent room.

The upper storeys are occupied by bed-chambers, except the library in the third, and the music-room in the fourth floor, both directly over the dining-room, and of its dimensions. In all these numerous apartments are valuable paintings, many of them family portraits, descriptive of the dresses of their respective times; some fine hunting and pastoral pieces by Rosa de Tivoli; beautiful ruins, and a curious caricature group of Scots and English travellers, acquainted with the Duke, who happened to meet at Florence.

The library contains several thousand volumes, and is well furnished with geographical and astronomical instruments. There is a folio MS. of the Vulgate Bible, and two MS. Missals, elegantly illuminated. There is also a very clean MS. of Bernard Gordon's Lillium Medicinae, mentioning at the end the names of the copiers, and the year 1319.

Gordon Castle being situated on that range of flat ground where the sea had formed a semicircular bay, or where the river had winded in a wide-bending sweep, is of course environed on one side by the second range of higher ground. This bank, where nature has done much, is also highly ornamented by the embellishments of art, being on the side of a great park, containing 10 or 12 square miles. The wood, without the appearance of design, is prettily disposed upon the plain, and on the mountain above: it spreads a boundless forest, affording cover for vast numbers of mountain deer, and containing in its skirts an ample inclosure flocked with fallow deer. These ornamented grounds, which spread so far on every side around the castle, occupy the upper part of the parish, the town of Fochabers included, with what may be called its borough lands, but which are held from the Duke only from year to year.

The lower part is parcelled out into small farms, partly occupied in detached acres, intermingled with each other's possessions, and several of the tenants along the river pay their rents by the wages of their employment in the fishery. In the higher ranges of the district, the farms are less hampered, but none so large as to admit of the most advantageous system of agriculture. The average rent from the acre, including the lands and meadows in the park of Gordon Castle, may be estimated at £1 3s. sterling.

At Gordon Castle there is a plank, cut from near the root of a tree in the celebrated forest of Glenmore, 6 feet broad. A brass plate upon it bears the following Inscription :—

"In the year 1783, William Osborne, Esq., merchant, of Hull, purchased of the Duke of Gordon the forest of Glenmore, the whole of which he cut down in the space of 22 years, and built during that time, at the mouth of the river Spey, where never vessel was built before, 47 sail of ships, of upwards of 19,000 tons burthen. The largest of them of 1000 tons, and three others but little inferior in size; one now in the service of His Majesty, and the Harbles East India Company. This undertaking was completed at the expense (for labour only) of above £70,000. To His Grace the Duke of Gordon this plank is offered as a specimen of the growth of one of the trees in the above forest, by His Grace's most obt. servt., W. Osborne, Hull, Sept. 26, 1806."

State Ecclesiastical.—The Church, until of late, was near the Roman Camp, about a mile northward from the Castle, and nearer to the sea. It is now placed in the town of Fochabers: a building that would be ornamental to any city of the empire. It was designed and executed by the celebrated architect, Mr. Baxter of Edinburgh: it is built of freestone from the Drainie quarries, neatly cut. In its front is an elegant portico, raised on Doric columns, and from behind the pediment springs a light and handsome steeple, about 100 feet in height. Within, it is provided with a stove, and fitted up and finished in the most complete and neatest manner for the accommodation of 1,200 people, and at the cost of £2,000 sterling.

The stipend, including the allowance for the Communion, is £72 6s. 4½d. and a glebe near the town of 13 acres. It is hardly necessary to mention, that the right of patronage appertains to his Grace, or that the burying-ground is continued where the old church stood.

To this parish appertains a portion of the Enzie mission. The chapel is situated about 5 miles from the town, on the confines of the parish of Rathven. For this establishment, two general contributions were made over all the Church of Scotland, before or about the year 1730; and though at present the amount would be accounted trifling, yet by the thrifty management of the Presbytery of Fordyce, under whose care it was originally placed, it accumulated to a capital sufficient to purchase a glebe of 8 acres, with a house, and a provision of £50 yearly, for the minister, besides a fund for keeping the buildings always in repair. The Duke of Gordon sold the ground for this accommodation, and gave security for the capital, for which pious concern the General Assembly voted to him the thanks of the Church. The management has been since preposterously placed under a committee of 7 clergymen, mostly of Edinburgh, and 7 laymen of the profession of the law, continued from one General Assembly to another—unconnected with this country, unacquainted also and unconcerned about its particular interests.

In the town of Fochabers there is a neat Roman Catholic chapel, and another about 4 miles distant, where the clergyman of this communion resides. His income is supposed to be paid in part from funds in the disposal of foreign universities.

[A handsome Roman Catholic Church was erected in 1828, an Episcopal in 1834, and a Free in 1844.

Milne's Institution.—A free school, built in 1846, was from a bequest of 100,000 dollars, or £20,000, left by a native, Alexander Milne, a servant at Gordon Castle, who died at Louisiana in 1839.]—(ED.)

Schools, a radical branch of the state of this realm, both civil and ecclesiastic, may be regarded as the workshops in which mankind are formed of the raw material. Much, therefore, among the middle and lower orders of society must ever depend upon the discretion and abilities of a schoolmaster. But how little ought to be expected in the man, whose most assiduous toil scarcely earns £20 in the year, and who, although the efficient parent of all that distinguishes civilization from barbarism, and government from anarchy, is nevertheless neglected, despised, starved. The salary of the parochial school is 14 bolls of meal, with the other statutory dues; the number of scholars generally 60.

In the vicinity of the Enzie Chapel, the Society for Christian Knowledge have established a School, with an appointment of £10 yearly to the master, and a temporary allowance of £5 yearly to his wife, for her attention to the female pupils. The scholars in all are accounted about 100. The Duke bestows the accommodations which the Society require.

The provision for the poor is considerable. Besides the money contributed by the families which attend the church, there is a sum bearing yearly interest: both are divided among the poor, without regard to their being Dissenters from the National Church: and in addition to these, there is a pension by the Duke to 10 decayed labourers, who had been employed in the service of his Grace.

The members of the Established Church are 1,100; those of the Church of Rome are 650; there are a few of the Scots Episcopalians, and some Antiburgher Seceders, amounting together to the number of 20.

Miscellaneous Information.—Upon the farm of Upper Dallachy, about a mile from the shore, there lately was a low conical mount. It was known by the name of "the Green Cairn." Tradition recognized it as the tomb of a chief of ancient renown; and it remained unviolated, through all the changes of many generations, until a few years ago. It consisted of about 12 feet deep of rich mould, incumbent on an accumulation of small fragments of stone, nearly of the same height, surrounded at the base by a double row of stone erect, similar to the circles of the Druid temples. Among this great accumulation of fragments, was a stone coffin of unpolished flags: a small quantity of black ashes was its whole contents. Near the circumference, about two feet under the surface, was also found an urn, the rude workmanship of the potter, about eight inches in diameter, and one foot in height; and on shaking out the mould with which it was filled, a piece of polished gold appeared, in form like the handle of a vase. It was 3-10ths of an inch thick, its ends about an inch asunder; on them the solder, or the appearance of silver, remained, which by the application of aquafortis was dissolved. To form a conjecture of its use is in vain: its value in bullion was about £12 sterling.

Besides the salmon fishery in the river, which by its valued rent must appertain to Speymouth, although the buildings for its accommodation are on the coast of this parish, there is also still a salmon fishery in the salt water of some consideration.

A small proportion of the parish, answering to £242 8s. Scots of the valued rent, on which also a part of Gordon Castle stands, is in the county of Moray: the greater part of the Castle and of the Parish are within the sheriffdom of Banff. In its ecclesiastical jurisdiction, it is in the Synod and Commissariot of Moray, and in the Presbytery of Strathbogie.]—(*Survey of Province of Moray.*)

[The patronage of the Kirk of Bellie belonged to the Priory of Urquhart, in consequence of a grant of territory by David I. about 1150-3, which included Finfans, on the west of the Spey, and Fochoper (Fochabers), on the east, with a common for pasturage and a fishing on the Spey.

As to the proprietary history of the district, it appears that, about 1238, King Alexander acquired the second teinds of the lands of Fochobyr and others from the Bishop of Moray in exchange for lands and teinds in another part of that province. At a later date other parts of Fochabers were exchanged for the lands of Wynn (? Whinnyhaugh) and Bynin (? Binns). From the Chartulary of Moray it appears that in 1362 John the Hay of Tulybothuyl (Tillibody) had a charter of the whole lands from the Spey to the Burn of Tynet, which are described as lying within the Forest of Awne or Enzie. About 12 years later the same Baron, with consent of his son, founded a Chapel at "the Geth" (Gycht) in honour of God and of the blessed Virgin Mary and of all Saints. This was endowed with an annuity of £20 and 4 acres of land at Ladardach, with a horse for the chaplain, and pasture for 12 cows and a bull, 60 sheep and lambs, 2 horses, "one of which, being the chaplain's palfrey, was to have pasture in the same field with the lord's own stud," while the jurisdiction of the foundation was given to the Bishop and Chapter of Moray. This chapel appears to have been situated somewhere about Gordon Castle. The old fairs or markets of SS. Catherine and Mungo, and the Holyrood, long held in the neighbourhood of Fochabers, seem to indicate that there were either altarages within the chapel, or that chapels in different parts of the parish were dedicated thereto.

George Chalmers, the author of "Caledonia," &c., was a native of Fochabers. Born, 1742. Died in London. 1825.

The Eldest Son of the Great Montrose.—It is scarcely known in the north that the dust of a son of the great Marquis of Montrose sleeps inside the old Parish Church of Bellie, near Fochabers. The fact is alluded to in the Report made by Mr. William Fraser on the papers belonging to the Duke of Montrose in the recently issued Report of the Royal Commission on Historical Manuscripts. Mr. Fraser, in quoting the Bond of Union subscribed on 30th January, 1645, at Killiwheen, now Fort-Augustus, says— "The first signature [to the Bond] is that of Montrose, and the second that of the Earl of Seaforth. The third signature is that of Lord Graham, eldest son of the Marquis, then a youth of 15 years of age, who accompanied his father in this winter campaign, during which he became suddenly indisposed at the Bog, near Gordon Castle, where he died after a few days' illness. He was buried in the Parish Church of Bellie." The above passage is quite corroborated by the great chronicler of the "Trubles," John Spalding of Aberdeen, who says— "Ye heir on the uther leaf how Montrose comes to the Bog. His eldest sone, the Lord Grahame, was in his company, a proper youth—about 16 yeiris old, and of singular expectatioun. He takis seiknes, deis in the Bog in a few dayis, and is bureit in the Kirk o' Bellie, to his fatheris gryt greif." It might have been thought the Marquis would have seen that some stone should have been placed to tell where reposed the remains of the hope of his house; but the pressure of public affairs had probably been too great, the struggle too intense, to permit him to attend to the gratification of his own feelings. At all events, if any memorial ever was erected, it now no longer exists. The Rev. Robert Cushny, minister of Bellie, having applied to the oldest and most intelligent of the inhabitants of Bellie, some of them persons who had in their youth worshipped in the old Parish Church, which stood in the churchyard, about two miles from Fochabers, found none who had any recollection of having ever seen any record or mark of the interment of the Marquis of Montrose's eldest son there. It seems that Dr. Bremner, Banff, made inquiries about the matter 20 years ago, at the instance of some of the members of the Spalding Club. William Sievewright, mason in Fochabers, the person to whom Dr. Bremner applied, questioned the gravedigger, who had held the office for 40 years, on the subject, and was informed by him that he had never come upon any stone, or fragment of a stone, which he could imagine to have marked the grave of such a person; although he had carefully examined any stone that had the appearance of having been placed as a gravestone, for the purpose of preserving such. The fact that he was interred, not in the Churchyard, but in the *Kirk* of Bellie, may account for the circumstance of there being now no visible record of the interment, supposing there had ever been such; as there is a quantity of what had no doubt been debris of the old church, in which interments had afterwards taken place. It seems clear from Spalding's narrative that Lord Graham's death had occurred between the 4th and 10th of March, 1645, probably on the 5th or 6th; for Montrose had reached Turriff about the 10th of March, after sundry plunderings at Cullen, the ravaging of the land around the Craig of Boyne, and making that visit to Banff, when, in terms of the old chronicler, the relentless Montrose " plundered the same pitifully, leaving neither merchandise, goods, nor geir; they saw no man on the streit, bot was stript naikit to the skin."]—(ED.)

THE PARISH OF DUNDURCOS

Is next to Bellie, up the river : so called from *Dun* a hill, *Dur* water, and *Cos* foot, for there the river runneth at the foot of the hill. It is situated on both sides of the river.

On the west side, the Church * standeth about half a mile from the south end of the parish, about 3½ miles south of Speymouth Church, and 1 mile north of Rothes.

North from the church lie the lands of Garbaty, the property of Sir Robert Gordon of Gordonston, and below these, on the river, are the lands of Orton, lately belonging to a branch of the family of Innes, and now to the Earl of Fife. Near to the church is a part of the Lordship of Rothes, and now the property of the Earl of Findlater.

On the east side of the river the parish stretches about 4 miles in length, and in some parts more than a mile in breadth. In the north end is Ordewhish, pertaining to the Duke of Gordon. South of which, on the river side, is Cairntie, lately purchased by Sir Ludovick Grant from Alexander Hay, whose ancestors had been for some generations heritors of it. And south and east of Cairntie is the barony of Mulben, the freehold of Sir James Grant. This, it is said, was the first land that the family of Grant had on the River Spey, and which they obtained by

---

* The roofless Church still stands. The workmen who were employed to take off the slates, &c., on its suppression, were stoned into the Spey by the ireful Abigails of the Kirkton; and one young man, while fording the river in trying to escape, was drowned. The old Manse is now a well-kept farm-house.—(ED.)

marriage with the daughter and heir of Wiseman of Mulben, about 350 years ago.

A brook that falleth into the river at the passage-boat, called the Boat of Bridge, was formerly called Orkil; and the lands on the banks of it were called Inverorkil, which lands Muriel de Polloc mortified, in the 13th century *ineunte*, for building an hospital there, of which hospital some vestiges still remain. And at the mouth of this brook there was a bridge of wood over the river, the pier of which, on the east side, is yet to be seen. It was called *Pons de Spe* (the Bridge of Spey), and was the only bridge I have found upon that river till of late.

[At the beginning of the 13th century, Muriel de Pollock, daughter of Peter de Pollock, heiress of Rothes, bequeathed her estate of Inverorkil, or Inverlochtie, where a bridge was first built by her, for an Hospital to God, the blessed Virgin Mary, and S. Nicholas (the patron Saint of all who travel by water) for the reception of poor travellers. The wooden bridge existed at the Reformation, but having fallen into neglect and disrepair it was swept away by the Spey, and its place was supplied by a ferryboat, whence the spot was termed "Boat o' Brig." This again was supplanted about 50 years ago by the present iron suspension-bridge, 235 feet in span, and now the railway viaduct runs parallel with it, conducting through the precipitous birchy ravines of Auchroisk on to Mulben. The ruins of S. Nicholas' Hospital and Chapel remained in considerable extent till cleared away for the approach of the first iron suspension bridge (built on a plan by Captain Brown for £3,500), when many human bones were disinterred, but no other article of curiosity. Shaw gives imperfect copies of the several Charters bearing on this little Hospital and Chapel. The sequel is a correct Inventory of the whole of the Charters thereanent, as carefully collected by Professor Cosmo Innes in the *Registrum Episcopatus Moraviensis*, and also in the *Antiquities of the Shires of Aberdeen and Banff*: Spalding Club:—

1. Charters of the Hospital of St. Nicholas beside the Spey, at Orchil, A.D. 1228, A.D. 1242.
2. Charter by King Alexander II. of the land of Robenfeld, for the maintenance of the Bridge of Spey. A.D. 1228.
3. Charter by Muriel of Pollock of the land of Inverorkil, for the endowment of an hospital for poor wayfarers, A.D. 1224, A.D. 1244. Witnesses—Andrew, Bishop of Moray; Nicholas, Vicar of Rothes; and Symon, Vicar of Dundurkus.
4. Charter by King Alexander II. to the Chapel of St. Nicholas beside the Spey, for the support of a chaplain, of four merks yearly from the rents of his mills of Nairn, A.D. 1232.
5. Agreement as to the Church of Rothes between the Prior of St. Andrews and the Bishop of Murray on the one part, and the Lady Muriel of Rothes and the Hospital of St. Nicholas beside the Bridge of Spey on the other side, A.D. 1235.
6. Charter by Muriel of Rothes, the daughter of Peter of Polloc, to the Hospital of St. Nicholas beside the Bridge of Spey of a piece of land beside the Hospital, and of liberty to have a mill on the Hospital's land of Inverorkil, with a mill-dam and mill-race, A.D. 1238.
7. Charter by Walter of Murray, the son of William of Murray, to the Hospital of St. Nicholas beside the Bridge of Spey of his land of Agynway (of the measure of one davach), A.D. 1224, A.D. 1242.
8. Charter by Eva Morthach daughter of Walter Murdoch and of Muriel of Polloc, Lady of Rothes, the daughter of Peter of Polloc, Lady of Rothes, to the Hospital of St. Nicholas beside the Bridge of Spey of all her right and claims in the Church of Rothes, A.D. 1235, A.D. 1242. This Eva Morthach or Murdoch married a knight of the surname of Watson, and their daughter married in 1286 Sir Norman Leslie of Garioch, whose name the family of Rothes still bears.
9. Charter by Andrew, Bishop of Murray, to the Hospital of St. Nicholas beside the Bridge of Spey of the Church of Rothes, A.D. 1235, A.D. 1242.] (ED.)

In the south corner of the parish, on the river's bank, are the lands of Aitkenwa, for several generations the property of a branch of the family of

Rothes, and now pertaining to the Earl of Findlater, as a part of the barony of Rothes.

The whole of this parish is in the county of Elgin.

Next to it is

THE PARISH OF ROTHES.

This parish in Irish is called *Rauis q. Raudbuis*, i.e., Red water, from the red banks of the river and brooks. It extendeth on the river side, in a beautiful plain, from N.N.E. to S.S.W. about 2 miles, and in the lower end a defile, called the Glen of Rothes, stretcheth among the hills towards Elgin, 3 miles to the N.N.W.

The Church standeth upon the side of a brook, a quarter of a mile from the river, and half a mile from the north end of the parish—1 mile south of Dundurcos Church, 3 miles north of Aberlour, and about 5 miles N.E. of Knockando.

In the year 1238, Eva de Mortach (daughter of Muriel de Polloc, who was daughter of Petrus de Polloc) was Domina de Rothes (*Chart. Mor.*) In the end of King Alexander III.'s reign, Norman Leslie of Leslie, in the Garioch, married the daughter and heiress, it is said, of Watson of Rothes, and from that time the barony continued to be the property of the family of Leslie until, in the beginning of this century, Captain John Grant of Easter Elchies made a purchase of it. And his grandson, John Grant, Baron of Exchequer, sold the Barony of Rothes and the Baronies of Easter Elchies and Edinvillie, anno 1758, to James, Earl of Findlater.

The east side of the Glen of Rothes pertaineth in feu-holding to Robert Innes of Blackhills, and the west side is the feu property of Robert Cumming of Logie.

Near the church stood the castle or fortalice of Rothes, which carries the marks of an ancient building. It stood on a green mount, surrounded by a dry ditch or fosse, and is now in ruins.

[Edward I. took up his quarters in the castle or manor-house of "Rosers," or "Roseise," as Rothes is designated in the different versions of the Journal or Diary of his expedition. Two etchings of the present ruin are given in *Rhind's Sketches of Moray*. The keep was several storeys in height. Several houses in Rothes have been built from the stones of this fort, which the villagers burned nearly 200 years ago, as it became a refuge for tramps and thieves. Grant of Elchies purchased it about 1700, and eight years afterwards it was bought by the Earl of Findlater, and it is now the inheritance of the Earl of Seafield.] (ED.)

The whole of this parish is in the county of Elgin or Moray.

[*Situation, Soil, Climate.*—The River Spey has been described as holding a course nearly from west to east, and almost parallel to the Firth, through the districts of Badenoch and Strathspey. Had this course been continued, it would have fallen into the sea near Portsoy, or have probably conjoined its stream with the waters of the Deveron. The mountain of Beneagen, lying across this course at a little distance from the lower Craigellachie, bends it into a direction nearly from south to north; in which, save sundry short inflexions, it hastens more directly, and almost at right angles, to the sea. The plains of Rothes lie in the same direction for 9 miles along its western bank; the estate of Oakenwall only occupying about the space of a mile, in the form of a peninsula, at the bottom of the mountain, on the other side. Besides the defile called the Glen of Rothes, opened through the hill towards Elgin, there are two other valleys stretching along the sides of their respective streams westward into the hills, where many improvements have within the space of 50 years been made, now yielding a rent, with others on the banks of smaller brooks, of more than £150. The hills, at certain distances bending near to the bank of the river, have shaped the country into four detached plains—Dunnalieth, or Dandaleith, Rothes, Dundurcos, and Orton. Besides the plains, the slopes along the bottom of the hills are closely cultivated: the banks of the river in many places are fringed with stripes of natural wood; and extensive well disposed plantations occupy the uncultivated sides of the hill. The northern frontier of the parish skirts along the confines of Dollas, Birnie, Elgin, St Andrews-Lhanbryd, and Speymouth.

The soil along the river may, in general, be described as a fertile loam; in some places, a purer clay; and in others, rather surcharged with sand, superinduced by the floods: along the bottom of the hills, it is a sharp gravelly mould, a little encumbered by the smaller loose stone: in the improvements within the limits of the mountain, it is moorish, in some places inclining to clay, in others to sand.

The climate below Craigellachie, though more rainy, is not colder than in the open plain of Moray; yet, being more distant from the sea, the snow lies deeper, and the harvests are, in general, more late.

The Gaelic name *rathuish* signifies the bending of the water, *rath*, or *roth*, signifying a wheel, nearly as in the Latin.

State of Property.—Six proprietors possess the parish. The only family seat is at Orton,* the property of the

* The estate of Orton belonged to a family named Dumbreck. The Earl of Fife purchased it about the middle of last century and left it to his youngest son, the Hon. Arthur Duff, who died in 1805. Richard Wharton, his nephew, succeeded him, and

honourable Arthur Duff of the family of Fife. A level plain of fertile corn-field spreads backward about a mile from the river; a green bank sweeps circular upon the other side, presenting near its margin above an elevated enchanting situation for the house, a modern large elegant building of four storeys, with a neat pavillion roof: besides the hall, a parlour and three bed-chambers occupy the ground floor: on the first floor is a magnificent suite of public-rooms; the paintings, though pretty numerous, are for the most part family and other portraits; there is a specimen or two of the polygraphic art, landscapes no way distinguishable from common paintings: on the third floor the library occupies a spacious room, fitted up in an elegant and commodious manner. Eastward on the same plain with the house, is a thriving orchard, within the skirts of a sheltering grove; under the bank is the garden, and a considerable extent of wall for the more delicate fruitage: the bank offers an inviting walk, with its ornamented shrubbery; groves judiciously disposed, and circling belts afford their shade and shelter to the circumjacent fields; and a great extent of flourishing plantation, fir, larix, and forest trees, clothes the side of the mountain behind. On one prominent intermediate height, a neat modern watch-tower commands the course of the river, Gordon Castle, and its decorated environs, and all the plain northward, and a great extent of the sea. The valued rent is £412 Scots.

Garbity on the south of Orton, and Inchberry on the north, the property of the Duke of Gordon, are valued at £324 3s. Inchberry is connected with his Grace's property of Speymouth, and parted from his lands in Bellie only by the river.

To the Earl of Findlater, connected with his property in St. Andrews-Lhanbryd, Elgin, Birnie, and Knockando, appertains the Lordship of Rothes, amounting to the valuation of £1,621 14s. 10d. Scots.

In the year 1766 a village was begun to be built on the

took the surname of Duff on marrying his cousin, Lady Anne Duff, 2nd daughter of Alexander, 3rd Earl of Fife, who bore a son and three daughters. He died in 1862 and was succeeded by his son, Captain Alexander Thomas Wharton Duff, late 93rd Regiment. (ED.)

plain of Rothes, upon leases of 38 years, and the life-rent thereafter of the possessor, after which the building becomes the property of the landlord: each tenement is the eighth part of an acre, at the rent of 10s. yearly; from an half to two acres of land, at the rate of a guinea the acre, save where the soil is greatly inferior, is occupied with each tenement, but without any lease. The village at present accommodates about 300 inhabitants. In the year 1796 there were set off 41 additional tenements, for its farther enlargement. The establishment of no manufacture has been yet proposed, though a considerable stream, working a corn and fulling mill, washes the whole length of its streets: a few artizans only supply the exigencies of the country. Pitcraiggy, and the glen, in which there is a snug commodious house and garden, on the margin of a little brook under the side of a hill, covered with a considerable extent of birch, called the Torwood, is the property of Robert Cuming of Logie, Esq. The valued rent is £74 15s. The estate of Auchnaroth, on which there is a great extent of various plantation, and many smaller rising groves, is the property of William Robertson, Esq., merchant of Elgin. The valued rent is £35 Scots. Oakenwall, in the county of Banff, the property of David M'Dowal Grant of Arndilly, Esq., adjoining to his other property, is valued at £130: extending the valuation of the parish to £2,597 4s. 10d. Scots.

There are several farms of very commodious extent, rising to the extent of £80 of rent: several are from £10 to about £40: the rents of the generality of the possessions in the newer lands in the hills are even under £10. The whole number of acres under culture are about 2,500, and the present real rent does not much exceed the sum of £1,200 sterling.

State Ecclesiastical.—Although a chapel in Roman Catholic times stood, no doubt, on the farm of Chapelhill, yet the parish remained unaltered in its extent, from the first establishment of parochial districts until the year 1782, when the suppressed parish of Dundurcos was divided between those of Boharm and Rothes. Experience hath shown that the general accommodation of the people hath not been thereby in any degree impaired.

The church, moved from its ancient station in the burying-ground, is commodiously placed in the village.

About the year 1630, Mr. John Wemyss, brother to the Earl of Wemyss, and minister of the parish, made a private agreement with the proprietors, fixing the stipend at £20 12s. and 45 bolls of oatmeal, and which was first changed by the annexation of part of Dundurcos. It is now established by a decreet in 1794 to be £54 4s. 4d., 63 bolls of meal, and 35 of barley, the communion allowance included. The whole glebe at Dundurcos was by excambion annexed to the glebe of Rothes, which now consists of about 16 acres. One third of the right of patronage, by the annexation from Dundurcos, appertains to the Crown, and the other two-thirds to the Earl of Findlater.

The salary of the school has been lately, with some opposition, augmented from £1 12s. and 6 bolls of meal, to an establishment of £11 2s. 2½d., with the customary fees from about 40 scholars, and the perquisites of the office of session clerk.

The number of poor is 30: the provision for their support, raised from the people in common form, aided by two endowments, amounting together to £1, is equal to an annual dividend of £15 sterling.

The members of the national Church are 1,450.

The dissenters, about 50, assume the profession of any preacher who pleases to officiate in the old church at Dundurcos, which, when first vacated on the suppression of the parish, was occupied by an insane preacher, and, since he wandered off, by persons generally unknown, professing to be Methodists.

Miscellaneous Information.—The people are in every case obliging, frugal, industrious, and discreet, and much attached to the national religion and government. In Roman Catholic times, the parish was under the peculiar protection of St. Lawrence. The rights of his fair were long ago, by purchase, translated to the town of Forres; but his well, a fountain distinguished by the purity and lightness of its water, is still recognised.

On the estate of Orton, there was a chapel dedicated to the Virgin Mary. There also was a sacred well, which, like the patent medicines of the passing times, was for many ages of the most distinguished celebrity, for the miraculous cure of all manner of disease. The passing generation have seen pilgrimages from the most remote parts of the Highlands, and from the Western Isles; but they are now wholly discontinued.* The tomb-stone of the first minister of the Presbyterian Establishment is still entire, in the tomb of a family of the same lineage: it simply relates, that "HERE LIES ANE NOBLEMAN, MR. JAMES LESLIE, PARSON OF ROTHES, BROTHER-GERMAN TO GEORGE, UMQUHILE EARL OF THE SAME, WHO DEPARTED IN THE LORD 13TH OCTOBER, 1576." The copy of the Solemn League and Covenant, which was subscribed, at Rothes in the year 1643, is still extant; by which it appears, that in this quarter the subscription of it was not rigorously enforced. It is printed at Edinburgh by Evan Tyler, printer to the King's Majestie, on two sheets of small coarse paper, in quarto. The first contains the approbations of the General Assembly and of the Convention of Estates, both dated on the 17th Aug., 1643, and the ordinance of the estates for swearing and subscribing the Covenant, dated 11th Oct. thereafter: and the blank pages are for the subscribers' names, which are, Mr. Rob. Tod, minister of the gospel at Rothes—Leslie—Patrick Leslie, elder—Walter Leslie—Robert Leslie—Wm. Innes —John Guthrie, elder—Wm. Farquhare, who subscribes also for nine others, elders, adding a docket, "Thir are in name of the elders that could not subscribe themselves, who professed their consent formalie, and that I, William Farquhare, clerk to the session, should subscribe for them."] (*Survey of the Province of Moray.*)

[The vale of Rothes is beautiful and fertile, but in the great flood of the 3rd and 4th Aug., 1829, the Spey, fed

* A mausoleum, erected in 1844, like a small Gothic chapel, now covers this once famous well. Inside are mural tablets with the names of the various members of the Duff family buried. In clearing out the foundations of St. Mary's Chapel, among other objects, T. Mackenzie, the architect, discovered a fragment of a stone of the Anglo-Norman style, which proved that the Chapel dated from 1066 to 1135. The mausoleum bears the following inscription:—" Quo primum loco Moraviensis Christiani Sacellum Mariæ Virginis in honorem Posuerunt hoc Mausolcum ut sub ejustecto Reliquiæ sui ipsius suorumque requiescant in pace. Sepulchri memor extruendum curavit Ricardus Wharton Duff de Orton Armiger Anno Salutis 1844."—(ED.)

with many streams and burns, devastated the village and haughs unprecedentedly; overtopping lofty trees and leaving marks of sad disaster and woe.

Benrinnes towers aloft, just beyond the south-east boundary, and invites a tourist to survey a large portion of the 9 surrounding counties. The village of late has been almost rebuilt, and instead of about "250 straw-thatched cottages arranged in 4 streets" (the characteristic 30 years ago), there are now several respectable residences of two storeys. The Glengrant Burn and the Burn of Rothes intersect the little town. The Glengrant Distillery (capable of running off 1,600 gallons of whisky a week) is the principal industry.] (ED.)

THE PARISH OF KNOCKANDO.

In Irish *Knoc-canach*, i.e., the Merkat hill, is bounded by the river [Spey] to the south and east, by the hills on the north and west, and extends by the side of the river about 6 miles in length, and generally 1 mile in breadth, and in some parts 2 miles.

The Church standeth a quarter of a mile from the river, about 2 miles below the south-west end of the parish, 2 miles north of Inveravon, 5 miles south-west of Rothes, and about 3 miles south-west of Aberlour.

In the lower end of the parish, on the borders of Rothes, is a rocky hill called Craig Eleachie,*

* CRAIGELLACHIE AND BRIDGE.

"Stand Fast Craigellachie" was the slogan or war-cry of the Clan Grant, shouted often and long along the beetling cliffs so graphically alluded to by the painter Ruskin in his "Two Paths":—" In one of the loveliest districts of Scotland, where the peat cottages are darkest, just at the western foot of the great mass of the Grampians, which encircles the sources of the Spey and the Dee, the main road, which traverses the chain, winds *i.e.*, the Echoing or Sounding Craig; and from it to another craig called Elachie, on the borders of Badenoch, stretcheth the country of Strathspey,

round the foot of a broken rock, called the Crag or Craig-ellachie. There is nothing remarkable in either its height or form; it is darkened with a few scattered pines and birch trees, and touched along the summit with a flush of heather; but it constitutes a sort of headland or leading promontory in the group of hills to which it belongs—a sort of initial letter of the mountains; and thus stands in the mind of the inhabitants of the district—the Clan Grant—for a type of the country upon themselves. Their sense of this is beautifully indicated by the war-cry of the Clan—'Stand Fast Craigellachie.' You may think long over these words without exhausting the deep wells of feeling and thought contained in them—the love of the native land, and the assurance of faithfulness to it. You could not but have felt, if you passed beneath it at the time when so many of England's dearest children were being defended by the strength of heart of men born at its foot, how often among the delicate Indian palaces, whose marble was pallid with horror, and whose vermilion was darkened with blood, the remembrance of its rough grey rocks and purple heaths must have risen before the sight of the Highland soldiers—how often the hailing of the shot and the shrieking of the battle would pass away from his hearing and leave only the whisper of the old pine branches—'Stand Fast Craigellachie.'"

Craigellachie is a lofty, romantic, quartz crag, of similar appearance to the rock of the same name at Aviemore, which Ruskin paints so well. This is the Lower Craigellachie. The reach of the Spey above and below it is finely picturesque. A single-arched metal bridge, 150 feet in span, with a round embattled tower at each corner, 50 feet high, resting in the parish of Knockando-side of the Spey, at the foot of a solid red rock (which gives its name to the bridge) and on a strong pillar of mason work on the Aberlour-side, erected in 1815 at an expense of £8,200 (one half raised by subscription and the other half given by Government), was the design of Thomas Telford, civil engineer, and the undertaking was carried out by Simpson of Shrewsbury. (Thomas Telford, born at Westerkirk, in Dumfries-shire, 9th August, 1757, celebrated *inter alia* for the Menai Bridge. Died unmarried at Abingdon Street, Westminster, 2nd Sept., 1834. Buried in Westminster Abbey beside Robert Stephenson.) This was a great undertaking at the time, and opened up most convenient commonly said to be between the two Craig Elachies, extending about 22 miles in length but unequal in breadth—a country inferior to few, if to any, in the North of Scotland for the conveniences of life. Besides abundance of grain for the inhabitants, it is beautified and enriched with much wood and timber, watered by many rivulets, and well stored with cattle, great and small. And as the most considerable inhabitants of it are gentlemen of the name of Grant, I shall, before I describe this parish, give a succinct account of

THE FAMILY OF GRANT.

From what country to fetch the Grants originally I know not. Some make the names *Suene*, *Allan*, &c., indications of a Norwegian extraction. Others make the surname, *Grande*, of French original. These two may be compounded by fetching them from Norway into Normandy in France, and thence into Britain with William the Norman Conqueror. But, if we allow them a Scottish origin, the name will bear us out. For, in the Irish, Grant signifies Gray or Hoary.

communication which for ages was obstructed. The easy access cut abruptly into the opposite towering wooded rock, the Spey rolling deeply underneath, the lightness yet stability of this graceful bridge, the most beautiful vista of mountains in their various altitudes and distances, with the lovely vales of birches and firs, the seats and dwellings under the eye, present so fascinating a landscape that no tourist can forget this enchanting spot of wonder, love, and praise. (ED.)

And one tribe of the Grants is called *Keran*, or *Kiaran*, much the same with Gray or Grant. But in this I determine nothing.

Not to carry up their antiquity (as an inexact and unchronological Tree of the family doth) to Woden the Heathen, their descendants can be traced back 500 years, with strong presumptions of a much higher antiquity—(1) In an Agreement betwixt the Bishop of Moray and Bisset of Lovat, anno 1258, "Robertus de Grant vicecomes de Inverness" is witness (*Chart. Mor.*) (2) Joannes de Grant was one of those Barons, with Radulphus his brother, whom King Edward I. sent prisoners from Berwick to London, anno 1296. They were not liberate till 30th July, 1297, when they were obliged to engage to serve King Edward abroad "contra quoscunque inimicos d. d. Regis" (*Rym.*, vol. ii., p. 776). (3) Robertus de Grant is one of the Barons in Ragman's Roll (*Prynne*, vol. iii., p. 657) about anno 1300, and the author of the Remarks on that Roll calleth him the ancestor of the family of Grant (*Nisb. Herald*, vol. ii., *Remarks on Ragman's Roll*, p. 35). (4) John de Grant was one of the commanders in the battle of Halidonhill, anno 1333; and, anno 1359, the same gentleman, with Sir Robert Erskine and Norman Lesly, were ambassadors to the Court of France to renew the ancient league (*Abercr. Hist. Folio*, vol. ii., p. 124); and (5) Robert Grant, Esq., was much in favour with King Robert II.;

and in 1385 was one of those Barons among whom were distributed 50,000 crowns of gold, remitted from France to animate the Scots to invade England (*Rym.*). Men of such distinction and eminence in those early ages are an undeniable historical presumption, that the Name and Clan were, even in these days, numerous, powerful, and much respected. I cannot, indeed, instruct that these five gentlemen were the successive representatives of the family, although I think it highly probable. But the following descents, from father to son, admit of no question, viz. :—(6) Maude or Matildis, heiress, married Andrew Steuart, son of Sir John Steuart, Sheriff of Bute, who was son of King Robert II. (*Geneal. Tree*); and their son was (7) Patrick, who married the daughter and heiress of Wiseman of Mulben, and by her was father of (8) John Roy. This gentleman married Bigla Cumming, heiress of Glenchernich [or Duthel]. He had two sons, viz., Duncan, his heir, and Duncan, progenitor of the Clan Donachie or family of Gartenbeg. (9) Duncan, whom in 1479 I find designed Duncan Grant of Freuchie (*Cart. pen. Kilr.*), married Muriel, daughter of Malcolm, Laird of M'Intosh, by whom he had John, his heir, and Patrick, ancestor of the family of Ballindalach. (10) John, the Bard-Roy, or Red Poet, married Elizabeth Ogilvie, daughter of Findlater, by whom he had John, his heir. He had likewise a natural son, called John More, ancestor of the family of Glenmoriston. (11) John, by his lady, a daughter, it is said, of Rothes, had three sons, viz., James, his heir; John, of whom Corimonie is descended; and Patrick, ancestor of Bonhard. (12) James, called *Shemuis nan Creach*, i.e., the Ravager, married a daughter of Lord Forbes, and dying anno 1553, was succeeded by his son (13) John Baold, *i.e.*, Simple, who, by his first wife, Margaret, daughter of Steuart, Earl of Athole, had Duncan, his heir, and Patrick, ancestor to Rothemurchus; and by his second wife, Isobel Barclay, daughter of Towie, he had Archibald of Bellentom. (14) Duncan died 1581, before his father, who died 1585, and his wife, Margaret, daughter of the Laird of M'Intosh, left John, his heir; Patrick, of whom is Easter Elchies; and Mr. James, of whom are Moyness and Lurg. (15) John of Freuchie, who died anno 1622, leaving by his wife, Lilias Moray, daughter of Tullibardin (16), Sir John, called Sir John Sell the Land, who, by Mary Ogilvie, daughter of Finlater, had eight sons, of whom James succeeded him. Colonels John and Patrick left no male issue, nor did Alexander nor George, governor of Dumbarton. Of the other three, Mungo of Kincherdie was ancestor to Knockando and to Kincherdie; the 7th was Robert of Muckerach; and the 8th Thomas of Belmacaan. Sir John died anno 1637. (17) James married Mary Steuart, daughter of the Earl of Moray, and dying anno 1663 left two sons, Ludovick and Patrick of Wester Elchies. I need not descend farther to mention (18) Ludovick, who died in 1718, father of (19) Brigadier Alexander, who, dying 1719, was succeeded by his brother (20) Sir James. He, dying 1747, was succeeded by his son (21), Sir Ludovick, to whom, anno 1773, succeeded his son (22), Sir James, now living.

I have dwelt thus much on the descents of the House of Grant, that the branches of it might appear, and to avoid repetitions. Besides the branches above-named, there are other three that claim a higher antiquity, viz.:—The Clan Alan, or family of Achernack; the Clan Chiaran, or family of Dillachaple; and the Clan Phadrick, or family of Tullochgorm. These contend that they sprung from the House of Grant before they came from Stratherick into Strathspey. That the ancient residence of the Grants was in Stratherick cannot reasonably be questioned. The names of their ancient or old seats in Stratherick (as Gartmore, Gartbeg, Dillachapel, &c.) are given to their new seats in Strathspey. But at what precise time they came into Strathspey (surely not all at one time) I pretend not to determine. The Laird of Grant was designed of Freuchie before 1479, and I think it probable that they began to come to Speyside about, or before the year 1400.

The armorial bearing of Grant is—Gules, three antique crowns Or. Crest, a burning hill proper. Motto above the Crest, CRAIGELLACHIE. Below the Shield, STAND FAST. Supporters, two savages proper.

GRANT OF GRANT.*

[The sirname of Grant is of great antiquity in Scotland: but historians do not exactly agree about their origin,—some alleging that they are of the ancient Scots, denominated Caledonians when the Picts inhabited the south ot Scotland; others that they came from Denmark; others from England; and others again from France.

Although we cannot with certainty fix the precise time of their settlement in Scotland, or whether they were of the aborigines of the country, yet we have incontestible proof from our histories and records that they were a powerful family, and made a considerable figure in that kingdom about 600 years ago.

We shall therefore pass over the traditional part of their history, and proceed to deduce their descent from

I. Gregorius, or Gregory de Grant, Sheriff Principal of Inverness in the reign of King Alexander II., who succeeded to the crown of Scotland in 1214, and died 1249. At that time, and till 1583, the shire of Inverness comprehended, besides, all Ross, Sutherland, and Caithness. He married Mary Bizzet, a daughter of the family of Lovat, with whom he got the lands of Stratherrick, &c., and by her he had several sons—(1) Sir Lawrence his heir; (2) Robert; (3) Lucas, of whom Dellachapple; (4) Allan, of whom Achernack. Whether Lucas or Allan was the eldest is disputed.

Gregorius de Grant died in the reign of King Alexander III., and was succeeded by his eldest son.

* Rev. James Chapman, son of Robert Chapman, merchant, Inverness, minister of Cromdale in 1702, gave great attention to the pedigree of the Grants. At his death in 1737, æt. 63, there was found in his repositories a History of the Clan, tracing it to the 6th or 7th century, or rather to Odin, god of the Saxons. Sir Archibald Grant of Monymusk has printed the MS., taken chiefly from a Norwegian genealogist. We have almost reprinted what is given by Grant in his Edition of *Shaw*, in preference to the details given by Robert Young in his "Annals of Elgin"; but these two writers diverge greatly. (ED.)

II. Sir Lawrence de Grant. In a competition in 1258 between Archibald, Bishop of Moray, and John Bizzet, father of Walter Bizzet, mentioned in "Rymer's Federa," this "Dominus Laurentius de Grant" is particularly mentioned as a friend and kinsman of the said Bizzet, and to which deed Robert de Grant, brother to the said Lawrence is a witness. These Grants resided in Stratherrick, a part at that period of the Province of Moray.

Sir Lawrence had two sons—(1) Sir John his heir; (2) Rudulphus de Grant, who being firmly attached to the Bruce interest against Baliol, was, with his eldest brother Sir John, and his uncle Robert de Grant, taken prisoners by King Edward I. of England in 1296. Robert, as possessing less influence and weight, obtained his freedom at Berwick; but Sir John and his brother were carried to London, whence they were liberated on bail in 1297. Sir Lawrence was succeeded by his heir,

III. Sir John Grant the first. He was a great hero and patriot, and joined Sir William Wallace in defence of the liberties of his country. He was succeeded by his eldest son,

IV. Sir John Grant the second. He is mentioned as a commander in the right wing of the army in the battle of Halidonhill, 19th July, 1333, in which he commanded a battalion of his own name and followers. He received the honour of knighthood from King David II. after the return of that monarch from England in spring 1359, and in the same year he, with Sir Robert Erskine, progenitor of the Earl of Mar, and Norman Leslie, ancestor of the Earls of Rothes, were appointed ambassadors extraordinary to the court of France, to renew the ancient league betwixt Scotland and that kingdom, and to negociate other affairs of State, which embassy they discharged honourably. The Earldom of Moray, after the death of Earl John Randolph, in the battle of Durham in 1346 fell to the gift of the Crown, as did many of the lands belonging to the Cummings; and considering the esteem in which Sir John Grant stood with the King, there is a strong probability that at this time he received a royal gift of part of their lands on Speyside, as soon after his family are denominated *of Freuchy,* now called *Castle Grant,* which is situated within a short distance of the river Spey. There is a Safe Conduct from King Edward

III., "Domino Johanni Grant militi et Elizabeth, his spouse," &c. to travel into that kingdom, with 10 servants to attend them, in 1363. He afterwards got another Safe Conduct to repair to the court of England upon affairs of state in 1366. He died in the end of the reign of King David II., and by Elizabeth, his wife, left a son, Sir Robert, his heir, and a daughter, Agnes, married to Sir Richard Cumming, progenitor of Altyre, &c.

V. Sir Robert.—As Sir John had been much in favour with King David II., so this Robert was respected by his successor King Robert II. In 1385, on a war breaking out betwixt France and England, the King of France remitted 40,000 francs to be divided amongst the nobility and principal gentry of Scotland, for the purpose of animating the Scots to make an irruption into England, and thereby a diversion in favour of France, of which sum Sir Robert had a proportion as chief of the family. He was a man much esteemed for his conduct and fortitude. He died in the reign of King Robert III., and was succeeded by his son,

VI. Malcolm de Grant, who began to make a figure as head of the Clan soon after Sir Robert's death, though then but a young man. He was one of those gentlemen of rank and distinction mentioned in a convention for settling certain differences between Thomas Dunbar, Earl of Moray, and "Alexander de Insulis Dominus de Lochaber." He died about the beginning of the reign of King James I., and was succeeded by his son,

VII. Sir Patrick Grant, who by a charter in the archives of Castle Grant, is designed "Patricius le Grant Dominus de Stratherrock," by which he gives in liferent to Elizabeth his daughter, and William Pilche, burgess of Inverness, her husband, the Davoch of Dreggie, and the half Davoch of Glenbeg in Inverallen of Strathspey. Sir Patrick was twice married. His first lady was daughter and heiress of Wiseman of Mulben; and his second a daughter of Maclean of Douart, who was killed in the battle of Harlaw in 1411. She was the mother of his son and successor Sir John. Sir Patrick was a man of activity and prudence, and, to increase the fortune of his family, projected and accomplished the marriage of his son with Matilda, the heiress of Gilbert Cumming of Glenchernick. He was succeeded by his said son,

VIII. Sir John, Sheriff Principal of Inverness. Among the arms at Castle Grant, there is a musket with this Inscription on the barrel, "Dominus Johannes Grant, Miles, Vicecomes de Inverness, anno 1434," accompanied by the three antique crowns of the family arms. By his lady Matilda Cumming, heiress of the estate of Glenchernick, he had three sons—Duncan, the oldest, succeeded him in the family honours and estates. The next was ancestor of the Clan-Phadric, or House of Tullochgorum, of whom are sprung the Guns and Groats, or Groots in Caithness, who boast of including in their Tribe the great Hugo Grotius, who in the Dutch language is called *Hugo Groot*. The other son was progenitor of the Clan Donachie, or House of Gartenbeg. In this Sir John's time, his mother being a daughter of Maclean of Douart, an ardent friendship commenced betwixt the two families of Grant and Maclean, which continued for several successive generations, and in memorial of which, agreeably to the romantic ideas of the times, on the decease of the Chief of either, the sword of the deceased was transmitted to the survivor as a pledge of reciprocal attachment. Sir John was succeeded by his son and heir,

IX. Sir Duncan Grant, who in a charter under the Great Seal, anno 1442, is designated "Dominus de eodem et de Freuchie." A precept of Sasine by the Earl of Moray for infefting Sir Duncan in some lands in Moray, begins thus, "Archibaldus Comes Moraviæ et Magister de Douglas," &c., dated at Elgin, 31st August, 1453. There is likewise a Retour of Sir Duncan Grant, Fruquhie, Knight as heir to his "guidsire" (grandsire or grandfather) Gilbert of Glenchernick, dated 6th February, 1468. And a precept of Sasine on said Retour by King James III., in favour of Sir Duncan Grant Knight, as heir to his guidesire Gilbert Cumming, of Glenchernick, on the lands of Congash, dated 3rd March, and 9th year of the King's reign (1469).

We find him one of the arbiters in settling a debate in 1479 between Duncan Macintosh, Captain of the Clan Chattan, and Hutcheon, or Hugh Rose, Baron of Kilravock (*Writs of Kilravock*). He married Muriel, daughter of Malcolm, Laird of Macintosh, by whom he had twin sons, John, his heir, and Patrick, and a daughter, named Catherine who was second wife of Duncan, Laird of

Macintosh. Sir Duncan Grant's second son Patrick, was the progenitor of the family of Ballindalloch, from whom are descended the Grants of Tomvullin, Tulloch, Dunlugas, Advie, Dalvey, and Rothmais, &c. Of this family Sir William Grant, Master of the Rolls, and representative in Parliament for the county of Banff, is a Cadet (1810).

X. John, the eldest son of Sir Duncan, had two sons. John, the eldest, and William, the progenitor of the Grants of Blairfindy in Glenlivet. By a precept of Sasine from George, Earl of Huntly, for infefting this John Grant, in Farmerstown, in the County of Aberdeen, and Kinrara, in the County of Inverness, dated at Bog of Gight, 8th September, 1478, he is called the son and heir of Sir Duncan Grant of Fruquhie. Dying, however, before his father, Sir Duncan was succeeded by his oldest grandson,

XI. John Grant of that Ilk and of Fruquhie, who in 1484 married Margaret Ogilvie, daughter of Sir James Ogilvie, of Deskford, Knight. In the contract of marriage, he is called "the Oye" (grandson), and apparent heir of Sir Duncan Grant of Fruquhie, Knight; and among others therein named as witnesses, is the foresaid William Grant, ancestor of the Blairfindy Grants.

In 1493 a Crown charter is granted in favour of this John Grant of Fruquhie, annexing and creating for him and his heirs, all and hail the lands of Fruquhie, the two Culquoichs, Dellifour, and Achnagaln, the two Congashes and Glenlochy in the County of Inverness, five parts of Linkwood, five parts of Barmuckity, and Garbaty, half the lands of Inchberry, with the half of Ordequish, the half of Mulben, and the lands of Sheriffstown, in the County of Elgin, into a Barony, to be called the Barony of Fruquhie, with full and ample powers, civil and criminal, dated 4th January, 1493. And another Crown charter is granted by King James IV. to the said John Grant, on Glenchernick and Ballindalloch, dated 4th February, 1498. He was succeeded in the estate by his son and heir,

XII. John, called "the Bard," because he was a poet, who married Elizabeth, a daughter of John 6th, the Earl of Rothes, by whom he had three sons and three daughters; first, James, who succeeded him; second, John, the progenitor of the families of Coromony and Sheuglie, in Urquhart, from the last mentioned of which, Charles Grant, Esq., M.P., for the County of Inverness, and chairman of the Court of Directors of the East India Company, is lineally descended; and third, Patrick, of whom are sprung the Grants of Bonhard, in Perthshire. The daughters were, first, Isobel, married to Sir Archibald Campbell, of Calder; second, Catherine, to John Haliburton, of Pictur, and after his death to Hugh Lord Lovat; and third, Agnes, married to Donald, son and apparent heir of Ewen Allanson, Captain of the Clan Cameron, by Contract dated 1520. In 1509 King James IV. grants him a Feu Charter upon the lands and Lordship of Urquhart, and at the same time another Feu Charter upon the lands and Barony of Corrimony, to his son John, now represented by his descendant James Grant, Esquire, of Corrimony, Advocate. John, died about the year 1527, and was succeeded by his eldest son,

XIII. James, commonly called *Shemish-nan-creach*, a term expressive of the bold and daring character, which, in conformity with the genius of the times, led him to resent any injury or insult offered to his Clan, by ravaging the territories of their enemies.

He was much in esteem and favour with his sovereign, as his predecessors had always been, and was much employed by the King and his Government in quelling insurrections and disturbances in the northern counties, upon several important occasions, as the writs in his family archives bear. James was married to Elizabeth, daughter of Lord Forbes, and of Catherine Stewart, daughter of John, Earl of Athol, by whom he had a son, John, who succeeded him, and two daughters, Marion, married to John Fraser, brother to Hugh Lord Lovat, and Janet, married the 26th January, 1552, to Alexander Sutherland, of Duffus.

In 1534, King James V. writes a letter to this James, Laird of Grant, " praying and charging him, with his kin, friends, and partakers, to pass with his Lieutenant-General upon Hector Macintosh, cawand himself Captain of the Clanchattan and others, his accomplices and partakers, and inward them to slachter hership and fire, &c., taking their goods to himself for his labour. Given under the Sign-Manuel at Stirling, the 13th May, and of his reign the twenty-first year (Signed) James R." Addressed thus,—" To our well beloved James the Grant of Fruchy."

And on the 28th of July, 1535, at Stirling, the same King grants under his Seal and Sign-Manuel to his loveit and Servitour, James Grant, of Fruchie, and all and sundry his kinsmen, friends, householdmen, tenants, servants, and inhabitants of his lands of Strathspey, Mulben, and Urquhart, and all other his lands within the realm, an exemption from appearance in any of his Majesty's Courts of Lieutenancy, Warrandry, Admiral Courts, Chamberlain Courts, Sheriff Courts, Bailie Courts, Burrow Courts, or any other temporal courts within the realm, for any action whatever, or at the instance of any person whatever, except before the Lords of Council and Session only.

In 1544, James grants a Commission of Bailery to his trusty and well beloved friend Alexander Cumming, of Altyre, upon the lands and Barony of Kinloss, for all the days of his life. He died in 1553, and was succeeded by his son,

XIV. John Grant, of Freuchy, in 1560 was a Member of Parliament when the Protestant religion was established. He was twice married. First in 1555, to Margaret Stewart, daughter of John 3rd, Earl of Athol, by Mary, daughter of Colin, Earl of Argyle. By this lady he had two sons and two daughters: the eldest son was Duncan, and the second Patrick, progenitor of the family of Rothiemurchus. To this Patrick, John gave a feu charter on the lands of Over Findlarg or Mukerach, 26th September, 1583, but redeemable, and on his afterwards acquiring the lands of Rothiemurchus, he gave them to Patrick and redeemed Mukerach. His eldest daughter Catherine, was married to Colin M'Kenzie, Laird of Kintail; and his second daughter Mary, to Abergeldy. After the death of his first wife, Lady Margaret Stewart, he married Isobel Barclay, who brought him one son, Archibald, the progenitor of the family of Ballintomb, now represented by Sir Archibald Grant, of Monymusk.

XV. Duncan, his eldest son, married Margaret, daughter of William, Laird of Macintosh, by whom he had four sons. John, who succeeded his grandfather; Patrick, of whom the family of Easter Elchies is descended; Robert, ancestor of the family of Lurg, and James, of Ardnellie. Duncan died in 1581, before his father, who lived till 1585. John was succeeded by his grandson the son of Duncan.

XVI. John Grant of Freuchy. The chiefs of the family of Grant for several generations took the addition of Freuchy; but this gentleman was peculiarly called, and to this day is known by the name of *John of Freuchy*. He was much employed in public affairs, and was offered a patent of dignity by King James in 1610, but he declined accepting it. He purchased the Lordship of Abernethy from the Earl of Moray, for 22,000 merks, and the Estate of Lethen from the Falconers (now Halkerton) who had long been the proprietors. Along the north side of the Spey, his property extended as far as Rothes, he had the estates of Mulben, Cairnty, Mulderies, the Kinminities, Couperhill, and others near Keith; the Baronies of Cromdale and Freuchy, the Lordships of Glenchernick and Urquhart, besides many others; and in short was accounted the most opulent and extensive land proprietor in the north. He exchanged with the Earl of Huntly, the lands then belonging to the family of Grant, in Glenlivet and Strathaven, for the lands of Gartenmore, Tulloch, and Rymore, in Abernethy, and of Curr, Clury, and Tullochgorum, in the Parish of Inverallan, which were a part of the sixteen Davochs of the Lordship of Badenoch, and to which the Lake and Castle of Lochindorb are a pertinent. In the Deed of excambion, Huntly reserved a servitude upon that part of the woods of Abernethy, which lie westward of *Star na Manach* (the Monk's Bridge), at the foot of the hill of Rymore, for repairing the House of Gordon Castle and Blairfindy, which servitude was abolished by a Decree arbitral settling the marches betwixt the families of Gordon and Grant, recorded in the Books of Session, 21st December, 1771. To his brother Patrick, he gave Easter Elchies, to his brother James, the ancestor of the Moynes family, he gave Ardnellie, in Rothes, and to Robert he wadsetted the Davoch of Lurg and Clachaig; being burdened with the portion of his aunt, the Lady Kintail, he paid it by adjudging the lands of Macdonald, of Glengary, who had joined Ewan Macallin, of Lochiel, in plundering and burning the lands of Urquhart, which adjudication he assigned to Kintail. He married Lillias Murray, daughter of John, Earl of Athol, by Catherine, daughter of Lord Drummond. King James VI. and his Queen honoured the marriage with their presence. This lady brought him one son, John, his heir, and four daughters, viz., Janet, married to Sutherland, of Duffus; Mary, to Sir Lachlan Macintosh, of that Ilk; Lillias, to Innes, of Balvenie; and Catherine, to Ogilvie, of Kempcairn. He had also a natural son named Duncan, progenitor of the family of Clury. He died in 1622, leaving an opulent and free estate to his son.

XVII. Sir John Grant, of Freuchy, who entered into possession of his fortune with every advantage, but by the profuse and expensive style in which he lived, his frequent attendance at Court, and residing chiefly at Edinburgh, he considerably impaired it, and sold the estate of Lethen, one of his father's acquisitions, to Alexander Brodie. He married Mary Ogilvie, daughter of Walter Lord Ogilvie, of Deskford, and of Marion, daughter of William, Earl of Morton, who brought him a family of eight sons and three daughters, viz. (1) James, his successor. (2) John, who entering the army was soon advanced to the rank of Colonel, and died a bachelor. (3) Patrick, afterwards tutor to his nephew Ludovick, Laird of Grant; he was likewise a Colonel in the time of the civil wars; he married a daughter of Sutherland, Earl of Duffus, by whom he had three daughters—Mary, married to Patrick Grant, of Rothiemurchus; ——, married to Fraser, of Belladrum; and Anne, married to William Grant, of Dellay. (4) Alexander, married to Isobel Nairn, daughter to Nairn, of Morenge, by whom he had two daughters. (5) George, a major in the army, and appointed by King Charles II. governor of Dumbarton Castle; he died a bachelor. (6) Robert, married a daughter of Dunbar, of Bennagefield, and by her had a son, the father of Robert Oge, of Milton of Mukerach. (7) Mungo, of whom are descended the Grants, of Tomdow, Knockando, Kinchirdy, and Tullochgriban. (8) Thomas, of Bellimacaan, in Urquhart, who married Mary, daughter of Colin Campbell, of Clunies, son of Sir John Campbell, of Calder, by whom he had Ludovick, of Achnastank, the father of Captain Thomas Grant; Patrick Grant, of Culvullin, the father of George Grant, of Bellifurth; and a

THE GRANTS OF FREUCHIE. 103

daughter, married to Mungo Grant, of Mullochard. Sir John's daughters were—(1) Mary, married in 1644 to Lord Lewis Gordon, who, after the death of his father and his elder brother, George Lord Gordon, who was killed at the battle of Alford in 1645, became Marquis of Huntly, and was father by this lady of George, the first Duke of Gordon; Lewis dying in 1653, she married the Earl of Airly and lived to a great age, having died about the year 1712. (2) Anne, married in 1640, to Kenneth Mackenzie, of Gairloch. (3) Lillias, married to Sir John Byres, of Cotts; Sir John died at Edinburgh in 1637, and was interred beside his father, John, of Freuchy, in the Abbey Church of Holyrood House; he was succeeded by his eldest son,

XVIII. James, who became representative of the family in times of the greatest confusion and convulsions, both in Church and State. In the summer after his father's death, when the troubles began on account of imposing a public Liturgy and Canons on the Church, it was not to be expected Grant would be (as indeed few were) allowed to stand neutral, accordingly he openly joined the Covenanters in 1638 and 1639, and afterwards subscribed the Solemn League and Covenant in 1643. He was at the same time a steady Royalist, and much respected by his Sovereign. In 1640, he married Mary Stewart, daughter of James, Earl of Moray, by Ann, daughter of the Marquis of Huntly. Of this marriage there were two sons and three daughters that arrived at the years of maturity. The eldest son, Ludovick, succeeded him in the estate. The second son, Patrick, founded the family of Easter Elchies. Of the daughters, Mary was married to Ogilvie, of Boyne; Margaret, to Sir Alexander Hamilton, of Haggs; and Anne, to Roderick Mackenzie, of Redcastle. Had the Laird of Grant lived in better times, he would have made a brighter figure, as a man of solid judgment, a firm friend, a true patriot, and a good economist; but having found the estate greatly burdened by his father's profusion, he could not possibly avoid adding to its incumbrances, owing to the troublesome times in which he happened to live. He lived to see the restoration of King Charles II., and was a Member of the Parliament that met in January 1661. In the year 1663, he went to Edinburgh to see justice done to his kinsman, Allan

Grant, of Tulloch, in a criminal prosecution for manslaughter; and although he was successful in preserving the life of his friend, he could not prolong his own. He died there that year, and was buried in the Abbey Church at Holyrood House.

XIX. Ludovick, his eldest son and successor, being a minor at the time of his father's death, came under the inspection of his uncle Colonel Patrick Grant, as tutor. He was a Member of Parliament in 1690, and one of the committee appointed by that Parliament to visit the universities, colleges, and schools, and to purge them of all insufficient, immoral, and disloyal teachers. He was likewise one of the Lords Commissioners for the plantation of Kirks and valuation of Teinds (Acts Parliament 1690), and so zealous was he to have legal ministers planted in his own estates, that he removed John Stewart at Cromdale, Suene Grant at Duthil, and James Grant at Abernethy, and shut up their churches in 1690 or 1691, till ministers properly qualified for discharging the sacred functions were found.

He was twice married; first, to Janet Brodie, by whom he had four sons and four daughters, who survived their parents. The two elder, Alexander and James, came successively to the estate, and represented the family. The third son, George, entered the army, soon attained the rank of major, and was appointed governor of Fort George. Retiring afterwards he purchased the estate of Culbin and Moy, and dying a bachelor, he left it to his nephew, Sir Ludovick Grant, of Grant. The fourth son, Lewis, a Colonel in the Army, was one of those brave men sent to the West Indies in 1740, under the command of Lieutenant-General Cathcart, where next year he unfortunately died of the disease of the climate. The Estate of Dunphail, which he purchased before he set out on that expedition, he also left to his nephew, Sir Ludovick Grant.

Elizabeth, the eldest daughter, was married to Hugh Rose, Baron of Kilravock. Ann, the second, to Colonel William Grant, of Ballindalloch. Janet, the third daughter, to Sir Roderick Mackenzie, of Scatwell; and Margaret, the fourth, was married in 1717 to Simon Lord Lovat. Their mother died in 1697, and some years after her death, Ludovick married Jean Houston, daughter of Sir

John Houston, by whom he had no children. Dying in 1718, he was interred in the Abbey Church of Holyrood House, and was succeeded by his eldest son,

XX. Alexander Grant, of Grant, who had the command of a regiment of foot, was governor of Sheerness, and rose to the rank of Brigadier General. During the course of the war in Queen Anne's reign, he served with the greatest applause. He was the inseparable companion of that great general and patriot, John, Duke of Argyle, and shared the same fate with him both in the dangers of the field and in the smiles and frowns of the Court. He was one of the commissioners for settling the Articles of Union of the two kingdoms, and a member of the first five British Parliaments. In 1704 he was appointed Lord Lieutenant and High Sheriff of the County of Inverness; and in 1715, by a new commission, he was appointed Lord Lieutenant and High Sheriff of Inverness and Banff. It may with justice be said that he was one of the first rate men of his day in the nation. He was equally qualified for the Camp and the Court, and alike uncorrupted and faithful in both. He married, first, Elizabeth Stewart, eldest daughter of James Lord Down, son and apparent heir of Alexander, 6th Earl of Moray; second Anne, daughter of the Right Honourable John Smith, Speaker of the House of Commons, and one of the maids of honour to Queen Anne, but had no surviving children by either. He died at Edinburgh in 1719, and was interred in the Abbey Church of Holyrood House. He was succeeded by his next brother,

XXI. James, the second son of Ludovick, Laird of Grant. He having, by the indulgent care of his grandfather, Alexander Brodie, of Lethen, been provided with an independent fortune upon his coming of age, his inclination led him to a country life, and in 1702 he married Ann Colquhoun, daughter and heiress of Sir Humphry Colquhoun, of Luss, the chief of an honourable family of considerable antiquity in the County of Lennox. In the marriage articles it was provided that this James Grant, of Pluscarden (the Estate of Pluscarden having been delivered to him when purchased), should, as is usual in such cases, assume the sirname of *Colquhoun*, and if he should happen to succeed to the estate of Grant, that his eldest son should bear the name of Grant, and his second son the name of Colquhoun. Sir Humphry Colquhoun resigned his patent of baronet and obtained a new one in his own favour, whom failing to the said James his son-in-law, whom failing to the heirs male of the body of the said Anne Colquhoun his daughter, whom failing to the heirs male whomsoever of the said Humphry himself, upon whose death James Grant, of Pluscarden, his son-in-law, entered upon the possession and assumed the title of *Luss*, together with the sirname and arms of that family, and in virtue of the new patent was called Sir James Colquhoun. His elder brother, brigadier Alexander Grant dying, Sir James succeeded him, and resumed his paternal sirname of Grant. He retained the baronetage, it being vested in his person, and the estate of Luss went to his second surviving son, according to the settlement in the entail. He was several times a member of Parliament, and was justly esteemed, respected, and honoured by all ranks. To his clan he was indulgent, if not to a fault, and to his tenants always just and kind.

By his wife, Anne Colquhoun, he had five sons and five daughters—(1) Humphry, who, at the age of 20, died a bachelor in his father's lifetime. (2) Ludovick, afterwards Sir Ludovick. (3) James, a major in the army, who, upon his brother Ludovick becoming heir of the estate of Grant, retired from the army, succeeded him in the estate of Luss, and married Helen, sister to the Earl of Sutherland. (4) Francis, a general in the army, married Miss Cox, and left a numerous family. (5) Charles, an officer in the Navy, was captain of a 74 gun ship, and was at the taking of Manilla.—Of the daughters, Jean, the eldest, was married in 1722, to William Lord Braco, was mother of the late James, Earl of Fife, also of his brother Alexander, who succeeded him, and grandmother of the present Earl of Fife. Anne, the second, married in 1727 Sir Harry Innes, of Innes, and was mother of the late, and grandmother of the present Duke of Roxburgh. Sophia, the third, died unmarried. Penuel, the fourth, married in 1739 Captain Alexander Grant, of Ballindalloch, the elder brother of the late General James Grant. And Clementina, the fifth, was married to Sir William Dunbar, of Durn, Bart. Sir James died at London in January 1747, and was succeeded by his son,

XXII. Sir Ludovick Grant, of Grant, Bart., who after

a course of liberal education, to qualify him for the Bar, was admitted Advocate in 1728. On the death, however, of his elder brother, Humphry, he became heir apparent of the family, and his father devolving upon him the whole care and burden of the estate, he laid down the practice of the law, and represented his father as chief of the Clan. During the Rebellion in 1745 and 1746, he, as all his ancestors had invariably done, stood firmly attached to Protestant succession and the Revolution interest, and accordingly raised a number of his clan and vassals, in defence of his King and the established Constitution. He was representative in Parliament for the County of Moray, from the year 1741 till 1761, when his son Sir James was elected in his stead. He married (1) Marion Dalrymple, daughter of Sir Robert Dalrymple, of North Berwick, by whom he had a daughter who died unmarried, aged about 19. He married secondly Lady Margaret Ogilvie, eldest daughter of James, Earl of Findlater and Seafield, by Elizabeth, daughter of Thomas, Earl of Kinnoul. By this lady (who died in January 1757), he had one son, James (born in May 1738), who succeeded him, and 11 daughters, of whom 6 survived their father; viz.—(1) Mariana, died at Coulnakyle, 28th March, 1807. (2) Anne Hope, married to Robert Dalry Waddilove, D.D., Dean of Ripon. (3) Penuel, married to Henry Mackenzie, Esq. of the Exchequer, author of "The Man of Feeling," &c., &c. (4) Mary. (5) Helen, married to Sir Alexander Penrose Cumming Gordon, of Altyre and Gordonstown, Baronet. And (6) Elizabeth, died unmarried 27th March, 1804.

Sir Ludovick died at Castle Grant, the 18th March, 1773, and was interred at Duthil, the family burying-place. He was succeeded by his son,

XXIII. Sir James Grant, of Grant, Baronet, who married at Bath, in January 1763, Jane Duff, only child of Alexander Duff, of Hatton, Esq., by Lady Anne Duff, eldest daughter of William, first Earl of Fife. By this lady he had 7 sons and 6 daughters, the survivors of whom were 2 sons and 3 daughters, viz.—(1) Lewis Alexander, afterwards Earl of Seafield. (2) Alexander, died at Castle Grant, 21st March, 1772. (3) James Thomas, of the Bengal Civil Service, died (Judge of Furrackabad) 18th July, 1804. (4) Francis William, Colonel of the Inverness Militia, M.P. for the Elgin District of Burghs in 1802, for the Inverness District of Burghs in 1806-7, and for many successive Parliaments for the County of Elgin; afterwards Earl of Seafield. (5) Robert Henry. (6) Alexander Hope, died at Castle Grant, 1793. (7) Dundas Charles, died at Castle Grant, 1788. First daughter, Anne Margaret, a dignified personage who resided for many years at Grant Lodge, Elgin. (2) Margaret, married at Edinburgh, 10th June, 1795, to Francis Stewart, of Lesmurdie and Newmills, afterwards Major-General. (3) Jane. (4) Penuel. (5) Christina Teresa, died at Elgin, 16th July, 1793. (6) Mary Sophia, died at Castle Grant, 26th Feb., 1788.

At different periods Sir James represented the counties of Moray and Banff in Parliament. In 1793 he levied the first Regiment of Fencible Infantry, and in the year following, the 97th Regiment of the Line. He was general Cashier of Excise for Scotland, and Lord-Lieutenant of the county of Inverness from the year 1794, the time when that office was revived in Scotland, till 1809, when the infirm state of his health obliged him to resign it to his Sovereign, who appointed his son to succeed him. This illustrious Chief died at Castle Grant, on the 18th of February, 1811, æt. 73. His remains were interred at Duthil. He was succeeded by his son,

XXIV. Sir Lewis Alexander Grant, who, on the death at Dresden, in Saxony, 5th Oct., 1811 (without issue), of James, 7th Earl of Findlater, and 4th Earl of Seafield, succeeded to the titles of Earl of Seafield, Viscount Redhaven, and Baron Ogilvie, of Deskford and Cullen. In 1822, George IV. was pleased to advance his Lordship's brothers and sisters to the same rank as they would have attained had their father lived to be the Earl of Seafield. Sir Lewis Alexander died unmarried in 1840, and was succeeded by his next surviving brother,

XXV. Francis William, 6th Earl of Seafield, born 6th March, 1778. Marr., 1st, 20th May, 1811, Mary Anne, only daughter of John Charles Dunn, of Higham House, and by her, who died 27th Feb., 1840, had issue—(1) Francis William, born 5th Oct., 1814, died unmarried, 11th March, 1840. (2) John Charles (present Earl). (3) James, born 27th Dec., 1817, three times married, and has issue, one son surviving by each of his two first marriages. (4) Lewis Alexander, born 18th Sep., 1820, married, and has issue. (5) George Henry Essex, born 13th Feb., 1825, married, and had two sons and two daughters. (6) Edward Alexander, born 17th June, 1833, died 1844. Daughter, Jane, married 20th July, 1843, to Major-General Edward Walker. Forester Walker, C.B., died 16th Sep., 1861. He married, 2ndly, 17th Aug., 1843, Louisa Emma, 2nd daughter of the late Robert George Maunsell, of Limerick, without issue. His Lordship died 30th July, 1853.

XXVI. Sir John Charles Grant Ogilvie succeeded his father, as 7th Earl of Seafield, 1853; created a Peer of the United Kingdom, by the title of Baron Strathspey, 14th Aug., 1858. Married 12th Aug., 1850, the Hon. Caroline Stuart, youngest daughter of Walter Robert, 11th Lord Blantyre, and has Ian Charles (Viscount Redhaven), an Officer in the 1st Life Guards, born at Edinburgh, 7th Oct., 1851.

The armorial bearings of Grant are quarterly quartered, first and fourth grand, quarters quarterly. First and fourth, Argent, a lion passant guardant Gules, crowned with an imperial crown Or; second and third Argent, a cross engrailed Sable, for Ogilvie; second and third grand quarters Gules, three antique crowns Or, for Grant. Above the shield is placed an Earl's coronet, over which is an helmet befitting his Lordship's degree, mantling Gules, doubled Ermine, next to which, above the achievement are two crests, that on the dexter side being on a torse, Argent and Gules, a lion rampant guar. of the second, holding in his paws a plummet, Or, and having above it on an escrol Tout Jour; and that on the sinister side being upon a torse, Gules, and Or, a burning hill, Proper, having upon an escrol above it, Craig-Elachie. The shield is encircled with an Orange Tawney ribbon, pendant, wherefrom is the badge of a Baronet of Nova Scotia; and on a compartment below the shield, whereon is the motto STAND FAST; are placed for supporters, on the dexter side a lion rampant guardant Or, armed Gules, and on the sinister, a savage or naked man, bearing upon his left shoulder a club, Proper, and wreathed about the head and middle with laurel Vert.] (*Grant's Ed.*)

I now return to describe the Parish of Knockando. In the north-east end, next to Rothes, is the barony of Easter Elchies, which has been the heritage of a branch of the House of Grant for above 150 years, and during six generations, but sold as above-mentioned. It is accommodated with a good house, spacious inclosures, and much barren wood near the river. Next up the river is the barony of Wester Elchies. About the year 1620 this was the heritage of Mr. Lachlan Grant; thereafter it came to Patrick, the first of this family, whose son, James, was father of Ludowick, who died 1757, father of James, then a minor.

Farther up the river is Bellintom, the patrimonial estate of (1) Archibald of Bellintom, whose sons were, Archibald, John of Aruntullie, and Alexander of Alachie. (2) Archibald was father of (3) Sir Francis of Cullen, late Lord of Session, created a Baronet anno 1705, and whose sons are (4) Sir Archibald of Monimusk, who in 1758 purchased from Sir Ludowick Grant the freehold of Bellintom and some superiorities, by which he' is a Baron in the county of Moray; William of Prestongrange, late Lord of Session and Justiciary, and Mr. Francis. Next to Bellintom, up the river, is the barony of Knockando, with a good house of modern architecture on the bank of the river. The first of this family was Mungo of Kincherdie, whose eldest son James purchased Knockando from Ludowick, Laird of Grant. James was father of Ludowick, who died 1751, and of Alexander Grant of Grantfield; and Ludowick was father of James, whose son Ludowick is now living. And in the south-west end of the parish is the barony of Kirdels, the freehold of James Grant of Ballendaloch. All these baronies within the shire of Moray are richly accommodated with salmon fishing in the river and woods on the banks of it.

[The mansion of Easter Elchies now belongs to the Earl of Seafield. It is beautifully situated, elevated on the left bank of the Spey, nearly opposite Aberlour, and is three storeys high, with a slated turret and dome. Part of the house is said to be contemporary with Lord Elchies. It 1857 it was quite altered and almost rebuilt. Patrick Grant, 2nd son of Duncan, the 15th Laird of Grant, was the *pater familias* of Easter Elchies. Patrick, Lord Elchies, Judge of the Court of Session, came from his loins, and took his title from this property. He died in 1754, and his son, Baron Grant, sold Easter Elchies to the Earl of Findlater; and, as stated, belongs now to the Earl of Seafield. Adjacent is the sequestered churchyard, with a fragment of the Church of Macallan, which was joined to Knockando about the date of the old mansion.

Wester Elchies is a castellated building, standing upon a picturesque elevation. Two chairs are in the hall brought from the old Castle of Rothes. The chief attraction is an observatory—a white stone edifice, erected by J. W. Grant after his return from 44 years' residence in Bengal. Herein was placed a giant telescope, the trophy of the great Exhibition of 1851. A sphinx is placed on either side of the entrance, and above the doorway is incised, " He made the stars also." Mr. Grant fetched home several curious slabs, supposed to be portions of a ruined Hindoo temple near Gour.

Robert Grant, son of Alexander Grant, died in the house of Wester Elchies in 1803. His son Charles succeeded, who died in the Isle of Wight in 1828. The above J. W. Grant heired the estate and died in 1865. His eldest son, William Grant of Carron, succeeded, who died in 1865.

The present proprietor is Henry Alexander Grant, youngest son of the above, by Margaret, daughter of the Rev. Thomas Wilson of Gamrie, county of Banff; born

1827, succeeded his brother in 1877, married 1873 Mary Jane, eldest daughter of William P. Jackson, resident Magistrate at Natal, and has, with others, issue, James William Hamilton, born 1876.

Knockando House is beautifully and loftily situated on the banks of the Spey, surrounded by woods, on the estate of Wester Elchies. It was built in 1732—a plain house of two storeys. The family arms, with the motto, "Honour and Virtue," underneath which is the name of the founder, "Lud. Grant," are cut on the pediment.

Remains of chapels and religious houses, and also of a Druidical temple, are pointed out in the parish.

Sir Thomas Dick Lauder thus graphically describes the Morayshire floods in this region in 1829 :—" The Knockando Burn, entering from the left, is extremely small; but it was swollen by the flood to a size equal to that of the Spey in its ordinary state. The high promontory, on the neck of which the manse of Knockando stands, shoots forwards towards the steep opposite banks of the burn, interrupting the continuity of its haughs by a narrow pass, leaving room only at the base of the precipice for two cottages, a small garden, and a road. Where the glen opens, a little way above, there stood a carding mill, a meal mill, and the houses of their occupants. Of the two cottages at the bottom of the promontory, one was inhabited by the old bellman, his wife, and daughter, and a blind beggar-woman, who had that night sought quarters with them; the other was tenanted by a poor lame woman, who kept a school for girls and young children. After the flood the prospect here was melancholy—the burn that formerly wound through the beautiful haugh above the promontory had cut a channel as broad as that of the Spey from one end of it to the other. The whole wood was gone, the carding mill had disappeared, the miller's house was in ruins, and the banks below were strewed with pales, gates, bridges, rafts, engines, wool, yarn, and half-woven webs, all utterly destroyed. A new road had recently been made, and all the burns were substantially bridged; but with the exception of one arch, all yielded to the pressure of the flood. Mr. Grant of Wester Elchies' damage is estimated at £820. The parish of Knockando returned 12 cases of families rendered destitute by this calamity."] (ED.)

KNOCKANDO.

[*Situation, Soil, Climate.*—The parish extends 15 miles along the north side of the Spey, from Cromdale at the west to the lower Craig Elachy, which terminates the district of Strathspey at the east, on the borders of the parish of Rothes. It is separated from Inveravon by the river, and extends northwards into the hills about 6 miles, to the limits of Dollas and Birnie.

The soil, along the banks of the river, and by the sides of the brooks winding through the hills from the west and north, is a sandy gravel. In other situations, it is a deep wet clay; a very great proportion is of moorish quality, and wet. There is naturally so little mixture of calcareous earth, that no part, without the application of lime, will produce bear, clover, or pease. In the higher part of the district, a boll of bear, in common, is but half the weight of that quantity raised upon the coast; and it requires two bolls of the oats to yield one of meal.

The climate is healthful: but, from its general elevation, and the swampy quality of so great a proportion of the surface, it is severe and cold; heavy rains falling in the spring and autumn, and much frost and snow prevailing in the winter months.

State of Property.—The valued rent of the parish amounts to £1,987 18s. 10d., of which Robert Grant, Esq., holds £1,247 7s. 4d. for Wester Elchies, Ballnatom, and Knockando. The family seat is at Wester Elchies; where improvements have been for some time begun, and are making a gradual advance. A village was built on the moor of Ballnatom, about the year 1760, by Sir Archibald Grant of Monymusk, and some improvement, to the extent of about 24 acres, at the first was made: but instead of continuing progressive, it has for several years been rather retrograde. The roads, only formed, not completed, have fallen into so much disrepair, that to a wheel carriage the village is only accessible from the east; by the south and west roads, the approach on horseback requires the most careful circumspection.

By an accidental fire, in 1783, many of the houses were consumed, and their naked roofless walls suggest the idea of Tadmor in the desert, or of some other eastern city, on which judgment denounced by some ancient prophet hath been in part accomplished, for it still retains the number of about fourscore worthy inhabitants.

General Grant of Ballnadallach has Kirkdales, Glenarder, Pitcroy, and Delnapot, at £426 10s., and the Earl of Findlater has Easter Elchies, at £314 1s. 6d. Knockando and Easter Elchies were once the mansions of their respective owners, and are still embellished by manor houses, gardens, and plantations. Some of the farms are of considerable extent; but, in general, they do not much exceed 30 arable acres. The real rent, including £10 arising from the salmon fishery, may be estimated about £2,000 sterling: cultivated by 150 ploughs: and the best arable acre is valued at 14s. The parish supports about 300 horses, 3,000 cattle, and 5,000 sheep.

State Ecclesiastical.—The parish of Macallan, that is, St. Colin, comprised in Easter and Wester Elchies, was united to Knockando during the regency of the Earl of Morton. They were again disjoined during the establishment of Prelacy, for 16 years prior to the Revolution: since which, they have made one parish under the name of Knockando, signifying in the Gaelic *the market hill.* The stipend is £93 5s. 6d. and 27 bolls of meal. The glebe is 16 acres, of which 11 are arable. The right of patronage appertains to Sir James Grant of Grant. The salary of the parochial school is 10 bolls of meal and £2 sterling, the value of the office of session clerk, and the customary fees of about 40 scholars. The Society for Christian Knowledge have established a school in Ballnatom, for the accommodation of the eastern quarter of the parish. The number of the poor on the session roll is 20: the fund for their support arises from the contributions made by the families in their assemblies for public worship, about £6 sterling in the year, and as much, the Interest of a bequeathment under the care of the session. The whole inhabitants are of the National Church, amounting to 1,500.

Miscellaneous Information.—The people are, in general, sober, discreet, and very economical, but deficient in the article of industry. The navigation of timber in rafts from Strathspey to Garmach is frequently undertaken by some of them. They make a journey to the forest, and conduct the raft by two men to Garmach, returning home generally within the week, at the medium hire of two guineas for each trip; of which 7s. and maintenance is allowed by the master-floater to his coadjutor, generally a young man learning the business.

At the rock of Tomdow, in this parish, the river dashes with such rapidity at right angles against the cliff, that by the violence of the collision the rafts were shattered. To avoid this charybdis, the York Building Company, when established at Coulnacoill, cut a new channel along the hypothenuse, and by this course the floating business is still carried on. Capt. Shank of the Navy resided at Knockando House in the year 1786. After having maturely considered the course of the Spey, he would have undertaken to render the river navigable, for flat-bottomed vessels of 40 tons, from its influx up to Grantown. There being no trade or manufacture adequate to the expense, the execution, if practicable, was deferred till some future age, when the superior improvement of the country may require such accommodation.] (*Survey of Province of Moray.*)

EPITAPHS IN ELCHIES CHURCHYARD.

The *Kirk of Elchies* became ruinous about 1760. The Easter Elchies burial-aisle is in the south-east corner, which is still roofed, but the place is ill-cared for. In the east wall is an elegant monument with a tablet, flanked by two Corinthian pillars, bearing the following:—

I. Sub hoc marmore in Christi adventum conduntur cineres JOANNIS GRANT de Elchies, viri æternum lugendi, qui, dum, inter vivos, nunquam, adeo sibi suisq quam aliis officia præ-stare solicitus fuit; amicum certissimum amicis, egenis levamen promptum, singulis hospitem liberalissimum ubiq se præstitit; de patria vero, propter operam ei in bello posteriore civili non minus fideliter quam feliciter navatam, optime meritus, et postquam tam in sacris quam negotiis secularibus omnium cujuscunq generis virtutum constanti exercitio veræ nobilitatis character-isticon adeptus esset, a virtutis Auctore vocatus, fatis cessit Martii IV^{to}, anno salutis humanæ MDCCXV, ætatis LVI^{to}, hoc unicum, ædificium in debitæ filialis observantiæ, justiq doloris tesseram, Patricio, filio unico, extruendum relinquens.

Translation.

Under this marble, until the advent of Christ, lie the ashes of John Grant of Elchies, an ever-to-be lamented man, who, while among the living, was never so anxious to promote the interests of himself and his family, as those of others; to his friends he ever showed himself a very sure friend, to the needy a ready benefactor, to all a very liberal host; by the not less loyal than successful services which he rendered to his native land during the late Civil War, he earned a just title to the deepest gratitude of his countrymen; and, after he had by the constant practice of every kind of excellence in sacred as well as in secular affairs, acquired the distinctive mark of true nobility, being summoned by the Author of virtue, he departed this life 4th March, 1715, in his 56th year, leaving this unique structure to be erected by his only son, Patrick, in token of due filial respect and just regret.

II. Here lyes ane honest woman called Mariorie Chalmers, spous to William M'Conachie, in Hillhall, who departed this lyfe the —— day of Dec., 1687.

III. Here lyes ane honest woman called Isabel Warden, spous to John Sharp, in Hillhall, who departed the 29 day of December 1704.

IV. Here lyes the body of Alexander Cumming, lawful son of Robert Cumming indweller in Colargreen, who dept. the 3 day of October 1707 years.

V. Under this stone is laid til the coming of Christ, the dust of an honest man called John Proctor, sometime indweller in Clayfurs at Easter Elkies. He died the . . . and Elspet Grant, his first spouse, who died the 29 of July 1709, and . . .

VI. Upon a stone bearing representation of a rake, hedge-shears, and a pruning knife, are the initials, G.M. C.C. Adjoining:—

Jean Gray, wf. of John Shakell, mercht., Elgin, died in "the flower of her age," 1732, a. 22:—

In one coffin, below this stone,
Lys both the mother and the son.

EPITAPHS IN KNOCKANDO CHURCHYARD.

The Kirk of Knockando, which is a long narrow building with outside stairs to the galleries, has a commanding position upon a rising ground, from which there is a fine view of mountain scenery. A slab over the kirk-door bears the following text and date: the date refers to the building of the present place of worship:—

Rom. x. 14. 15.

The three slabs figured at Plate CV. *Stuart's Sculptured Stones of Scotland,* Vol. II., are now placed in the graveyard of the parish, but are said to have been brought thither from an old burying-ground called Pulvrenan, on the bank of the river below Knockando House, about 50 years ago. The stones are much weathered and are undressed.

The Inscription on No. 3. is in runes. Professor George Stephens of Copenhagen read it as "SINNIK." This appears to be the name of a man, and it occurs on another Runic monument at Sanda Södermanland in Sweden. The Inscription at Knockando is in Scandinavian runes of the oldest and simplest class, and may date from the 9th or 10th century.

The Church has lately been much improved by the enlargement of the windows, &c.; and an inscribed slab of white marble, set in black, is in the Wester Elchies loft.

I. Sacred to the memory of Margaret, wife of James William Grant, Esq. of Elchies, who died in London, Jan. 28, 1855, born April 10, 1791. Her mortal remains were laid in Kensal Green Cemetery, in the sure and certain hope of the resurrection to eternal life. Isa. xxvi. 3.

II. A Templar's tomb (formed of composite) within an enclosure in the church-yard, covers the ashes of the husband of the above-named lady. It bears the words "CRAIG-O'-CROACHAN" (the Slogan, or war-cry of the Grants), also this Inscription :—

III.   THE VAULT OF ELCHIES.
In remembrance of James William Grant of Elchies, in this county, who died the 17th day of Dec., 1865, aged 77 years. His mortal remains are laid in this vault.
Jesu mercy.

Grants appear to have occupied *Wester Elchies* from at least 1565. In the Rental of the Bishopric of Moray of this date, it is stated that *Wester Elchies*, with the mill and fishings of the same, the "ferrie cobbill," also Kincardie, with fishings on the Spey, were held by James Grant, for the annual payment of £16 9d. Scots. This old branch of the Grants (who were cadets of Grant of Grant), held Wester Elchies, &c., for several generations.

IV. A fragment which bears a shield with the Dunbar

and Grant arms impaled, the initials I.D., and these
words:—

. . . . ODEY OF MARY D. . . . .
LAVFVL DAVGHTER TO. . . . . . .

The above Stone was found in the old offices of the
Manse a few years ago,—supposed to be a fatal stone of
malediction against all future ministers in the parish, by
reason of the minister refusing to give the workmen " *a
founding pint*" of drink at the building of the manse.
From April 1788 until Dec. 1866, seven ministers here all
died young, excepting Dr. Asher, who was translated to
Inveravon after having been seven years at Knockando.

V. In memory of the Rev. John Wink, minister of Knockando, who, after 11 years of faithful service, died 11th March
1851, aged 54.

VI. In memory of the Rev. Francis W. Grant, who, after
3 years of an earnest ministry, died 25th Jan. 1855, in the
32nd year of his age. By his sister, Margaret, teacher,
Kirknewton.

VII. Erected by the Parishioners of Knockando in affectionate remembrance of the Rev. John Clarke, minister of
Knockando, who, after an acceptable ministry of 11 years,
died 18th Dec. 1866, aged 47.

In addition to the above, other three parish ministers
are buried at Knockando, who have no tombstones—viz.,
Messrs. Francis Grant, who died in 1805; Lauchlan
M'Pherson, who died in 1826; and George Gordon, who
died in 1839.

VIII. . . . Lean, an honest and laborious man that
died 17th June, 1746, and of Margaret Wallace, his wife, a
woman of unaffected simplicity and cheerfulness in manners,
with unspotted integrity, and by her industry reared a young
family. She died 16th May, 1769. This monument is erected
by Alex. M'Lean, their dutiful son, gardener at London.

IX. William Watson, Excise Officer, d. 1834, a. 34; his dr.
Hannah d. 1840, aged 9 years.

To Death's despotic sceptre all must bend,
He spares not parent, child, nor weeping friend;
Not manhood's bloom, nor youth's fair tender flow'r,
Can move his pity, or resist his pow'r.
Meagre consumption here a Father laid,
And burning fever slew his lovely maid,

'Twas sin that gave tyrannic pow'r to Death,
And at his summons, these resigned their breath,
Until their Saviour calls them from the grave,
Destroys grim Death, and shews his pow'r to save.

X. Erected by Isabella M'Quine in memory of her son James Robertson upar Tamdo, who died the 5th My 1840, aged 21 years:—

Remember friends as you pas bay
What you are now so once was I.

XI. In memory of the Rev. Andrew Sprott, who was born at Stranraer, in July 1806, ordained at West Kilbride in 1837, inducted at Archiestown in April 1845, and died 4 May 1864. A laborious and faithful minister greatly beloved.

XII. In affectionate and hallowed remembrance of the Rev. John Munro, for 50 years the pastor of the Congregational Church of this parish. He was an eminently devout, able, and faithful minister of Christ, greatly beloved and respected in all the relations both of private and public life. He finished his long, laborious, and useful course, March 20, 1853, in the 79th year of his age.
"Well done," &c.

Upon a headstone :—

XIII. Erected by Helen, Jessie, and Isabella Tulloch, in memory of their beloved parents Margaret Gillan, who died on the 19th Feb. 1840, aged 55 years; and her husband Alexander Tulloch, farmer, Crofthead, who died on the 17th Oct. 1840, aged 55 years.

Alex. Tulloch was killed by his son-in-law, Peter Cameron, Ballintomb. Cameron, who was tried for the murder at Inverness, 14th April, 1841, pleaded that he had no intention to kill Tulloch, but only intended to maim or disable him, so as to prevent him from marrying a woman to whom he was attached. Cameron was found guilty of culpable homicide, and transported for life. It is added that, under the circumstances, much sympathy was felt for Cameron.] (*Jervise's Epitaphs.*)

THE PARISH OF BOHARM.

Anciently and truly written, *Bocharn;* for, over against the plains of Rothes, and on the east bank of the river [Spey], is a high hill called

Ben-eggin, i.e. The Hill with clefts, and round a great part of the hill this parish windeth: Hence called *Bocharn*, i.e. a bow or arch about the cairn or hill. It is in length about 4 miles, and in few places above half a mile in breadth, lying on the east side of a brook that runneth into the water of Fiddich.

The Church standeth on the south side of the hill, 2 miles west of Botrifnie, 2 miles north east of Aberlour, 2½ miles south east of Rothes, and about 3 miles north of Mortlich.

This parish (all in the county of Banff),* was, in the reign of King William the Lion, about anno 1210, the property of William Moray, son of William, and grandson of Freskyn Moray of Duffus. He is designed, Dominus de Petty, Brachlie, Bocharin, &c. (*Cart. Mor.*) and from his son Walter, descended Sir Andrew Moray Lord Bothwell. Willielmus filius Willielmi Freskin, had his castle and seat in Boharm, probably at Galival, where some vestiges do still remain.

At this time, the freeholds are, *Arntullie*, the seat of Alexander Grant, of which he purchased the freehold from Sir Ludovick Grant, anno 1757. His father, Thomas of Achoinany and Arntullie, died 1758, and was son of Walter, son of John of Arntullie, second son of Archibald

---

* With the exception of the lands of Cairntie, Auchroisk, Mulben, and Muldeary, part of the heritage of the Earl of Seafield, which are in the county of Moray. Originally this territory was in the parish of Dundurcos. (ED.)

the first of Bellintom. It is pleasantly situated at the foot of Ben-eggin, on the bank of Spey, and capable of great improvement, by inclosing and planting. This gentleman is likewise proprietor of Galival and of Newton, which lately pertained to a gentleman of the name of Anderson. To the east of the church are the lands of *Achmadies*, the property of Sir James Grant. And thence northward is the barony of *Auchluncart*,* which, for several generations, pertained to a branch of the House of Innes, and by an heiress came to a son of Stewart of Tanachie. This parish is well accommodated with moss ground for fuel, and generally is a rich and fertile soil, very early in ripening about Arntullie, but cold and late on the south-east side of the hill.

[The Church of the parish of Arndilly, in early times called Artendol, stood on the eminence which is now the site of the mansion-house of Arndilly, on the banks of the Spey, in the south-west corner of the present parish. Vestiges of such ecclesiastical occupation of this lovely spot remained till within the memory of man; the ruins of the church being cleared away to make room for part of the offices of the mansion-house, and an equivalent being then given for the glebe, which now forms part of the lawn. It is conjectured that the Church at Arndilly

* The present proprietor is Andrew Steuart, only son of Patrick Steuart, by Rachael, daughter of the late Lachlan Gordon, of Park; born 1822; married 1847 Elizabeth Georgiana Graham, 3rd daughter of the late Thomas Gordon, of Park, and has issue. Educated at Trinity College, Cambridge (B.A. 1844); entered at the Inner Temple 1851, but was not called to the Bar, although fond of law-pleas; was M.P. for Cambridge 1857-62. Auchluncart House, a large tame erection, with poor gateways, was built about 1750. (ED.)

having been allowed to go to ruin, perhaps even before the Reformation, the chapel of the castle of Bucharm, in a much more convenient situation, became the place of worship for the whole district, and gave name to the parish. In the year 1788, the parish of Dundurcos, lying due north from Boharm, on both sides of the Spey, was suppressed, and the part of it which lay to the east of the river was annexed to Boharm, except one small property, Aikenway, which, with the lands on the west side of the river, was annexed to Rothes. This annexation added to Boharm upwards of a third, both in extent of surface, and in the number of population. The old parish is in the county of Banff; the annexation, excepting a small fragment in Banffshire, is in the county of Elgin. A stone, which was in the wall of the old church at Arndilly, is now built into the wall of one of the wings of the mansion-house. It has rude figures carved on it. Another stone, having very nearly the same figures upon it, was taken out of the foundation of the old church of Inveravon; and a third is built into the wall of the Abbey of Deer. (The New Statistical Account of Scotland, number xxxviii., pp. 355, 356, 364. See also The Statistical Account of Scotland, vol. xvii., p. 364, Edin. 1796. See No. 2 Plate xv., vol. i., Stuart's Sculp. Stones of Scotland).

The ruin of the Castle of Gallvall is the only remain of antiquity in the parish. It was built fronting the east, on the north side of the valley, towards the western end, where the declivity hath fallen more gently into an inclined plain, and that a promontory into the deep defile formed by the course of the stream of Aldermy; snugly sheltered from the northern blast, with an enlivening extent of arable field rising behind; on either side a luxuriant landscape spread westward on the winding banks of the Fiddich. It appears to have been a simple structure of 119 feet by 24 feet within, divided by an internal wall, so as to form 2 halls on the ground floor; one 65 and the other 54 feet in length. The windows were only 20 inches wide, though the walls were 8 feet thick. The front and corners were neatly finished with free-stone. The front and gables are now entirely broken down; but within these fifty years they stood to the height of several storeys. This bulky fabric, on the eastern front, had lower external accommodations. A domestic chapel stood in its own consecrated burying ground (forsaken only in the course of the last sixty years), about 50 yards from the north end of the castle; and, though only 24 feet by 12 feet within, must have been the parent of the present parish church, which was erected in the year 1618. (The Statistical Account of Scotland, vol. xvii., pp. 363, 364).

The Castle of Bucharn, now Galval, is an interesting remain, situated on a fine eminence between the brook Aldernie and the Fiddich, having the vale of Balveny stretching out in front; the vale of Boharm to the east; the lower part of the valley of the Fiddich to the west; and a great extent of well cultivated fields and beautiful woodlands all around. Little of the building is now standing. Under a stone in the floor of the oratory of the castle, a silver ring was lately found, having a small shield fixed upon it which exhibited two martial figures; this is now at Arndilly. (The New Statistical Account of Scotland, number xxxviii, pp. 364, 365.)

The rivulet Aldernie above mentioned, conveys to the Fiddich the waters of the upper part of the parish; while those of the lower part, uniting where the eastern valley meets with the circular valley, form the Orchill, now called The Burn of Mulben, which thence descending very rapidly to the Spey, which it joins at the place called Boat of Bridge, has cut a very romantic channel for itself in the rocks through which it passes. (The New Statistical Account of Scotland, vol. xvii., p. 359.)

The old Church of Boharm is located on the summit of a beautifully wooded rocky ravine, in grand contrast with the site of its bald successor, which, when erected, was unprotected and unadorned by dyke, whin-bush, or tree. The belfry-gable remains with its bell, which is only *clinkit* at the funerals of the heritors or members of their families. "The aul' kirkyard" is shamefully kept—a few sheep being the conservative gardeners. An economical conjoint tomb divided by causeway-stones in the inside, is set aside in a corner for the mortal remains of Auchluncart and Arndilly. The public road from Mulben Station hereto is tedious and uninteresting: there is no danger of being led captive either by the lust of the eye or by the pride of life.] (ED.)

BOHARM.

[*Situation, Soil, Climate.*—Bocharn, the ancient name, in the Gaelic denotes, in one respect, the situation of the parish, *the bending about the hill,* lying around the eastern side of the hill of Beneagen, from the river Spey at the south, till it meets the river again on the northern end of the mountain; its breadth stretches back to Botriphnie and Keith, and its length extends to Bellie, from the confines of Mortlach and Aberlaur. The country behind the mountain may be conceived as an extensive valley, having all the arable land hanging on the acclivities of both sides of the rivulets which wind their courses from the middle of the dale to the river at either end of the mountain. The soil on the banks of the river may be accounted sandy, light, and warm; on the eastern side of the hill, it is a stiff, deep, wet clay, generally on a bed of lime-stone. The climate also, like the soil, is cold and wet: the clouds, borne aloft from the ocean, appear sometimes as if attracted by the mountain, and at other times as if dashed upon its summit by the winds from the north, or from the northwest. The seed-time can seldom be commenced till the spring be well advanced: and, in general, the season of harvest encroaches far upon the winter.

State of Property.—The parish is possessed by four proprietors. In its southern quarter, sheltered from the east and north, by a curvature of the mountain, is the family seat of Arndilly, the property of David Macdowal Grant, Esq., a magnificent modern house, making the front of a small court of lower buildings; it is pleasantly situated on an elevated ground, rising from a pretty extensive plain, which has the river winding around it: the plantations stretch behind upon the sides of the mountain, farther than the house on either quarter commands, presenting a pleasant riding of several miles, diversified by the different sweeps of the river, and the fertile plains of Rothes on the farther side; while the ornamented banks of a brook, gushing from the angle of the mountain, with the gardens and enclosed fields, add to the natural beauties of this elegant situation. The valued rent of the whole domain in the parish, Papeen, Newton, Galdwal, and Auchmadies, amount to £840 Scots. The barony of Auchluncart, with the family seat, recently improved into the elegance of modern fashion, with the convenience of a kitchen garden, and the shelter of a little grove, is the property of Andrew Steuart, Esq., writer to the signet, amounting to the valuation of £1000. The farm of Knockan, a part of the estate of John Duff of Drummuir, which has run over the hill from the parish of Botriphnie, is valued at £100. The rest of the parish appertains to the Earl of Findlater, of which the valuation only of the lands of Boat of Brigg, amounting to £100, is within the county of Banff; the lands of Cairnty, Auchrosk, Mulderies, and Mulben, amounting to £1437, 9s. 2d., belong to the county of Moray: extending the total valuation of the parish to the sum of £3577, 9s. 2d. Scots. The farms are, in general, of considerable, though of various extent. The average rent of the acre of arable land may be estimated at 18s.

State Ecclesiastical.—In Roman Catholic times there were three chapels in the parish of Boharm: St. Nicholas at the Boat of Brigg, the chapel at the Castle of Galival, and the third at Arndilly, then named Artendol. St. Nicholas, it may be presumed, was suppressed and added to Dundurcos about the Reformation; and there is reason to believe, that Arndilly and the district of Galival were formed into the parish of Boharm prior to the year 1618. In the year 1682, Dundurcos being suppressed, the territory of St. Nicholas was then conjoined: and of late a new church has been built, about 3 miles eastward from the old fabric, in a situation pretty centrical to the present parish; where the glebe, about 30 acres, has been also located, and the residence has also been fixed. The value of the living, as presently constituted, is £44, and 72 bolls in bear and meal. The right of patronage appertains to the Earl of Fife; but the Crown has obtained a share by the annexation from Dundurcos. The school has not been in a flourishing state for many years: a sorry cottage, is incommodiously situated behind the old church. The salary is only a wretched pittance of £5, 11s., about half the wages of an ordinary farm servant, as the fees of teaching, and the whole emoluments of the office of session clerk, about £3, 10s., do not defray the expense of daily bread alone.

The number of the poor is about 26: and the provision

for their support, contributed in the church in the usual manner, with 10s. an ancient yearly endowment in the parish of Dundurcos, amounts to nearly £7 in the whole. The number of the people is about 1300; and, except those who occasionally support the vagabonds that ply about the old church of Dundurcos, they are all of the national Establishment.]—(*Survey of Province of Moray.*)

South from Boharm, on the rivulets of Fiddich and Dulenan, lieth

THE PARISH OF MORTLICH OR MORTLACH.

This parish, in ancient writings is called *Morthlach*, probably from *Mor-lag*, i.e. a Great Hollow, for it is a deep hollow, surrounded with hills. Before I enter this parish, I shall a little describe the two rivulets that water it.

Fiddich, q. *Fiodhidh*, i.e. Woody, because its sides are covered with wood, hath its rise in the hills south of Mortlich towards Strathdon, and running N.-E. about 3 miles, turneth almost due west for a mile, and then, after a course of 3 miles due north, it falleth into Spey.

The other rivulet *Dulenan* (properly *Juilan*, from Tuil, a flood, because of its impetuous current), takes its rise in the hills of Glenlivat, and running N.-E. parallel to Fiddich (but separated from it by a ridge of hills) 3 miles, it mixes with it 3 miles above Spey.

The parish is in length from N. to S. 4 miles, and as much in breadth from E. to W. besides some skirts that lye near to *Botrishny, Glass,*

Cabrach. It is all environed with hills, except a small opening to the north.

The Church standeth on Dulenan, a little above the confluence with Fiddich, 2 miles S.-S.-E. of Aberlour, and about 3 miles south of Boharm. The parish (all in the shire of Banff) consists of the Barony of Kininvie, the Lordship of Belvenie, and the Barony of Auchindune.

The House of Kininvie stands upon the rivulet Fiddich on the east side, environed with natural wood. A branch of the family of Lesly of Balquhan has enjoyed this Barony about 250 years, and of this branch the Earl of Leven is descended. Next up to Fiddich-side and the west-side of Dullen, are the lands of Balvenie, which comprehend Bochram, Little Tullich, Park-beg, Clunie-More, Clunie-beg, Pitvaich, Littoch, &c. Of the Commissioners sent to London, 19 August, 1423, to relieve King James I., was James Douglas of Balvenie (*Rym. Fœd.* vol. x., p. 298), and 1446 John, son of James, Earl of Douglas, was created Lord Balvenie, who, being forfeited 1455, for joining in his brother's rebellion, King James II. granted Balvenie to his uterine brother, John Steuart, Earl of Athole. That family sold it to Aberneathie Lord Salton, who, about 1606, disponed it to Lord Ochiltree. From him it came to Sir Robert Innes of Invermarkie, and from Sir Robert's heirs to Sutherland of Kinminity. About anno 1666, Alexander Lord Salton reduced his father's disposition to Lord Ochiltree, and conveyed the lands in 1670 to Arthur Forbes, brother to Blackton, from whom Alexander Duff of Braco adjudged them, and got possession about 1687, and they are now the property of the Earl of Fife.

Upon an eminence on the west bank of Fiddich, stood the castle of Balvenie, the ancient seat of the Lordship, commanding a pleasant view of the valley; and half a mile below it, in a moist, low, and unwholesome soil, there is built a fine house of modern architecture, one of the seats of the Earl of Fife, adorned with gardens and planting.

In the south of the parish, betwixt the rivulets of Fiddich and Dulen, is the barony of Auchindune. This was formerly a part of the Lordship of Deskford, and Auchindune and forest of Fiddich were a part of the barony of Ogilvie, erected in 1527 (*Pen. Findl.*). Afterwards it was purchased by, and is now the property of the family of Gordon. The castle stood on a mount above the water of Fiddich; and from it Glenfiddich stretches S.-W. about 3 miles among the hills; where is fine pasture ground and a forest of red deer. Upon the head of Dulen lieth Glenriness, a fertile valley, 2 miles long.

The south side of it is a part of the barony of Auchindune, and the north side a part of the lordship of Balvenie. Along the north side runneth Benrinnes, a high hill, and a land mark for sailors in sailing into the Moray Frith.

[*The Castle of Auchindune* lies about 3 miles northeast of Dufftown. The ruin is a high square tower, on a bleak dreary knoll, 600 feet high. In the centre of the ruin is a remarkable Gothic arch. Tradition says that it was built by Cochrane, the favourite of James III. Until 1535 it was the property of the Ogilvies of Deskford, and then passed to the Gordons. The like old tale exists of it as of the burning of the Castle of Frendraught and the bonnie House of Airlie. Auchindoun was the domicile of Adam o' Gordon, the Marquis of Huntly. In 1592, William, Laird of MacIntosh and Chief of the Clan Chattan, had given offence to Gordon, of whom the MacIntoshes held certain lands, and who came to Auchindoun to seek redress. Unfortunately Adam o' Gordon was not at home, but his young wife was, who, listening to his errand, said that her husband desired the head of the Captain of the Chattans to be stuck on the portcullis of the castle. This fired the blood of the MacIntosh to siege, whereupon the vassals of Adam o' Gordon within Auchindoun turned out in defence. Lady Gordon, with a claymore, struck off the head of the MacIntosh then and there. Soon this defeat got wind, and the Clan Chattan, in dead of night, surrounded and set on fire the stronghold of Auchindoun. A ballad, "Helen of Auchindoun," is given in my "Book of the Chronicles of Keith," pp. 305-318. "The glacks o' Balloch," mentioned in the song "Roy's Wife of Aldivalloch," are a pass near the Castle of Auchindune. Mrs. Grant of Carron is the authoress, born at Aberlour in 1745; died at Bath about 1814. "Tibbie Fowler o' the Glen" is said to have lived in the Braes of Auchindune. This is very dubious; the style of the lyric, and the illusion to "Tintock tap," in the Upper Ward of Lanarkshire, discard the fancy.

Not one solitary tree is near this weird fastness; albeit, Queen Victoria (when on a brief stay with the Duke of Richmond at Glenfiddich) sketched dismal-looking Auchindune from several points of view. Its elevated solitude inspires the visitor with strange feelings.

Some few years ago a curious massive solid gold ring, having three links, was found among rubbish dug up at the castle. It seemed to have been intended for a puzzle or pass-sign, as the motto inscribed upon it could only be read when the links were placed in a certain way.

Balvenie Castle.—S. Waloch is said to have had a mission at Balvenie (Bp. Forbes' *Kalendar of Scottish Saints*) long before the time of S. Moloch. A well at Balvenie was noted in old times for its virtues in curing various diseases.

It is further averred that Bp. Beyn lived at Balvenie, and conferred the name *Bal-Beyn*, i.e., Beynstown, upon the locality. More probably its origin is to be found in the Gaelic compound *Bal-bhana*, the town of green fields, which aptly describes the verdant aspect of the place and its pretty surroundings.

The Cumins are said to have been early proprietors of the lordship of Balvenie, which, being afterwards held by the great family of Douglas, was forfeited by Sir John Douglas, Lord of Balvenie, in 1455. About 1460, Sir John Stewart, Earl of Athole, uterine brother of James II., had a gift of Balvenie from the Crown on the occasion of his marriage with Lady Margaret Douglas, "the fair maid of Galloway." She left two daughters; and the Earl having married as his second wife a daughter of the Earl of Orkney, she bore him a son, from whom descended the Stewarts, afterwards designed of Belvenie. The Stewarts sold Balvenie about 1606, from which date until 1687, when the property was acquired by Alexander Duff of Braco, ancestor of the Earl of Fife, it had several owners, including the Inneses.

The Castle, which is guarded on the north by a great ditch, with built sides, is popularly said to have been first erected by the Danes, and has a large parlour in it, yet called the Danes' Hall. The western portion appears to be the oldest, and the south-east part bears unmistakable evidence of the Stewarts. The national arms occupy a niche over the entrance door, upon which hangs a strong gate or *yett* of curiously wrought iron, and the Atholl legend is boldly carved upon the front wall:—

FVRTH. FORTVIN. AND. FIL. THI. FATRIS.

A shield within the castle court is charged with the Atholl and Gordon arms impaled. These possibly refer to the 4th Earl of Atholl, who died in 1579, and to his lady, a daughter of the house of Huntly. Upon another slab is a much defaced coat, over which is the motto, "SPES. MEA. XVS."—*Christ, my hope.*

In its palmy days the House of Balvenie had consisted of a large square, occupying a Scotch acre in extent, with a strong lofty tower at the gateway and turrets at each of the four angles of the building. The castle was unroofed about 160 years ago, since which time it has gradually become so much dilapidated that restoration would be almost impracticable. Had this been gone about at the time when the first Earl of Fife built a costly, but now neglected mansion, a little farther down the valley, Balvenie might have been at this day one of the noblest seats, as it is one of the most interesting ruins in the north. Billings * gives two capital engravings of it in his *Baronial and Ecclesiastical Antiquities of Scotland*, and there is a good view (1787) in Cordiner's *Remark. Ruins.*

Edinglassie Castle was far inferior either to Auchindoun or Balveny. In 1690, the year of the engagement on the Haughs of Cromdale, some of the Highland clans, on their march from Strathspey through Mortlach to Strathbogy, pillaged and burnt the house. Whereupon Gordon, the laird, with his tribe, seized 18 of the katerans at random on their return, a few weeks after, and hanged them *seriatim* on the trees in his garden. So many kindred *scare-crows* never perched there before nor since. They were afterwards burnt, and the spot is still known as "*the Hielanmen's mossie.*"] (ED.)

MORTLACH.

[*Situation, Soil, Climate.*—The principal part of this parish is a valley nearly parallel to the course of the Spey, extending eastward from the eastern quarter of Inveravon along the southern side of Aberlour, from which it i. separated by a ridge of mountain, raised into three high rounded summits, named the Conval Hills. Through this valley, the stream of Dullan holds a straight, and, as its name imports, a rapid course, until near its termination in the Spey; where, bent almost into a right angle, it turns across the end of the Conval Hills from south to north. But having run about two-thirds of its course, it resigns its name to another stream, the Fiddich; which,

* *N.B.*—Billings makes a gross blunder in stating that Balveny Castle is in "the parish of Marnoch." Even if this was an error of the press, it is not corrected in any page of *errata*, but passes on as a verity, to be copied by others. (ED.)

rising near the eastern borders of the parish of Inveravon, occupies the bottom of a woody vale, as it name imports, nearly parallel to that of Dullan. At the distance of 3 miles on the south, across this space, turning direct, it hastens to join its neighbour with both its water and its wood, forming the country together into the figure of the letter [h] inverted, as thus [y]. But to the parish another vale appertains, stretched towards the south-east, from the other side of the hill which bends the course of the Fiddich. Through this vale, the brook of Marky winds down to the river Deveron; which there, for almost a quarter of a mile, forms the limit of the parish, and bounds the county of Banff with that of Aberdeen, enlarging the form of the parish to something resembling the capital letter [K]. Its greatest length, along the course of the Dullan, is about 12 miles; and the breadth, over Glenfiddich and Glenriness, is not less than 6. No alteration either in the natural appearance of the country, or in its name, has taken place for more than 800 years. In the charter granted by Malcolm II. about 1010, to the first bishop of this ancient see, its name is written MURTHLAC, nearly the same as at present; but its etymology is not ascertained. MORTIS LACUS, *the death lake*, is entitled to equal respect only with the burlesque derivations of the Dean of St. Patrick. The more probable Gaelic source, which makes the name imply *the great hollow*, is neither satisfactory in sound construction, nor in comparative signification, as the hollow in all of the six surrounding parishes is of as great or greater extent than here. The arable fields may be from 4 to 5000 acres. They lie, in general, pretty high along the Dullan and the Fiddich, and the banks of the brook of Marky, disjoined from the rest of the parish. The sloping sides of the rills which fall into these streams, and the more gentle declivities of the mountains, are also partly under cultivation. There are some little plains along the windings of the streams, but they are not considerable. The extent of meadow grass and coarser pasturage, with the moor and heath-covered hills, may amount to twenty times as much as the cultivated field. The soil, for the most part, is a deep fertile loamy clay; the exceptions of its inclining in some places to a sandy or a moorish soil, scarcely merits notice. The air is pure and wholesome, though rather moist than dry. Fair weather is sometimes enjoyed on the farms below, when fogs, or showers of rain, or of snow, are gloomily chilling on the surrounding heights above. Its political situation places it in the county of Banff. In the ecclesiastical view, it is under the jurisdiction of the Presbytery of Strathbogie, the Commissariot of Aberdeen, and the Synod of Moray.

State of Property.—The parish is the property of five proprietors. The Earl of Fife has the lordship of Balvenie, on which there is an ample handsome regular modern Seat, situated in a wide opening of the vale, upon the banks of the Fiddich, after its union with the Dullan, in a plain at the bottom of the eminence which is occupied by the old castle. To his Lordship also pertains Glenmarkie, Edinglassy, and Dullanside, valued altogether in the cess roll of the county of Banff at £1920 Scots. The Duke of Gordon has the lordship of Auchnadun, Glenfiddich, with a commodious hunting Seat, and Glenrinness, amounting altogether to the valuation of £1620 Scots. James Leslie, Esq., holds the barony of Kininvie and the lands of Tullich, a valuation of £450 Scots, and resides in the manor house of Kininvie, the commodious habitation of his very remote ancestors. The small property of Buchrome is a part of the estate of Andrew Steuart of Auchlunkart, Esq., valued at £90 Scots; and the farm of Lochend, on the confines of the parish of Botriphnie, a part of the estate of Duff of Drumuir, is valued at £20 Scots; making the whole valued rent of the parish amount to the sum of £4100 Scots. The farms are unequal in extent, from a rent of £5 to £80 sterling. The mean rent of the acre is about 15s.

State Ecclesiastical.—The church is situated on the bank of the Dullan, a little above its confluence with Fiddich. It is venerable merely on account of its age. It is the cathedral of the second bishopric of Scotland. Its walls are supposed to have stood since the beginning of the 11th century, and they are still deemed to be more durable than any building of the present day. They have none of that magnificence or elegant decoration of the cathedrals of succeeding ages. The simplicity of the doors and windows, and of the whole edifice, bears witness to its age. The windows are narrow slits, 6 feet in height, and only 10 inches wide on the outside, but sloped so much as to measure 12 feet wide within. It is 90 feet in length, and 28 in breadth, having 27 feet in the east end, where no doubt the choir and altar were, a few feet higher than the rest of the building. The bodies of Bean, the first bishop, Donortius, the second, and Cormac, the third, are supposed to be here interred. Nectan, the fourth, in the 14th year of his incumbency, was translated by David I. to Aberdeen; which, then becoming the seat of the diocese, assumed also the name, having remained at Mortlach for the space of 129 years after its erection in the year 1010. Its revenue here was but small, comprehending only the churches of Mortlach, Cloveth, and Dalmeth, with all their lands. The glebe on which the manse is placed is close by the church, extending to 6 acres, and comprehending a small orchard and kitchen garden. The patronage belongs to the Crown, and the stipend is £63 2s. sterling, and 16 bolls bear and 32 of meal, in which the allowance for the communion is included. The whole emoluments of the schoolmaster (the salary, an annual donation bequeathed by Duff of Dipple, the fees, and the perquisites of the office of session clerk), do not exceed 20 guineas a-year, for which 40 scholars have a respectable mediocrity of education. Dr. Alex. Moir of St. Croix, a native, and for some time the schoolmaster of the parish, bequeathed £600 sterling to the care of the Professors of King's College, Aberdeen, for completing the education in that University of 4 boys taught in this school, which must be certified by the minister, the donation being so adjusted as to have one of the 4 boys beginning with it each year; and if 2 or more apply together, the best scholar is preferred. This endowment has continued almost 40 years, and though inadequate now to defray the whole expense at Aberdeen, has been of important service to many of the youth of this parish.

The fund for the support of the poor consists partly of the sum of £4, 3s. 4d., being the yearly interest of a capital bequeathed also by Dipple, who, by his endowments for the support of the schools, and provisions of this kind in the parishes in which his property lay, showed the kindest and most liberal attention both to the minds and to the bodies of the poor. To this sum, which was of great consideration in the age in which it was bequeathed, the tenants and their families who attend the church make, by their weekly contributions, the addition of about £16 more. From which, not what can be supposed a subsistence, but a scanty aid, is derived for the support of 60 of their indigent neighbours, the number of poor on the roll of the books of the church session. The members of the Established Church are 1837; and there are 43 Seceders, 37 Roman Catholics, and 1 Episcopalian.

Miscellaneous Information.—The people, with a few exceptions, are and long have been honest, industrious, sober, and humane, attached to the British constitution, and decent in their attendance on the ordinances of religion. In general, they are disposed to cheerfulness and contentment, but keenly alive to the sense of injustice or oppression. They are not fond of a military life, and the business of a soldier is in low estimation among them, being regarded as dissipated, slavish, and poor. It is frequently observed, that there was greater plenty of all kinds of game before the legal prohibitions had effect, as every one had then an interest in destroying those animals that prey upon them so much more successfully than man, and in taking care also of the eggs and of the young, about which they are now careless, at least, and indifferent. In the vicinity of the Duke of Gordon's seat in Glenfiddich, there is a great extent of fine natural birch wood, the residence of more than 1000 deer and roe, the natural and ancient inhabitants of the forest.

Balvenie Castle, in the lower end of the country, is embellished also by much natural wood on the banks of the Fiddich, chiefly aller, among which the elm, plane, and oak, prosper. The ash also shoots luxuriantly, and seems natural to the soil. And a great variety of flowering shrubs appear among the trees, the natives of the place. There are, besides, several extensive plantations of Scots fir upon the property of Buchrome, and on that of the Earl of Fife, on the whole nearly 400 acres. An arable and very fertile field, a sloping bank in the park around the castle, planted with fir, when it was built about 70 years ago, is now become fine timber full grown. In that age, it was the opinion that rich soil was requisite for such plantations; but the other groves, which at present decorate so much of the inarable waste around, seem now to require that this field, denominated from its fertility the "granary of the farm" to which it appertains, should be again restored to the more indispensable productions of the plough.

There are several chalybeate springs: one, near the old castle of Auchindune, has been found by a chemical examination to resemble the Peterhead water, and to be as light as it: they are of use in gravelish complaints, and in disorders of the stomach. In the wood also about Kininvie house, there is a spring of a petrifying quality. On this estate also, in the banks of a brook at Tullich, there is the appearance of alum, vitriol, and lead. There is everywhere plenty of stone for building, and some quarries also of pretty good slate, of a grey colour, and over all the country exhaustless treasures of limestone, locked up almost from the farmer, merely by the expense of fuel. There is marble also in the banks of both the streams, and in one place a laminated rock is fit for whetstone and hones.

It was in this parish that Malcolm II. in the year 1010, gained that victory over the Danes which terminated their depredations in the kingdom. This event, so important then, makes the place to be respected as classic ground. In the preceding year, Malcolm had been wounded, defeated, and obliged to leave the Danes in possession of the coast of Moray. Returning with a more powerful army, the intruders, informed of his approach, solicitous to prevent his arrival in the open country, moved forward to oppose him in the hills. The Battle was begun near the Church of Mortlach. In the beginning of the attack, when pushing on with over-ardent impetuosity, three thanes, Kenneth of the Isles, Dunbar of Lothian, and Græme of Strathern were slain; and the Scots, thereby struck with panic, were hurried into flight. The King, reluctantly borne along by the frighted crowd, passed by the Church dedicated to St. Molocus, and gained the height of a steep and narrow pass near its western end. Here, by the situation of the ground, he was enabled to stop, and to collect his broken host. Reanimated on the occasion by the King's vow of enlarging the Chapel by three lengths of his spear, and having now also the advantage of the ground, they turned with enthusiasm on the foe disarrayed by their pursuit. Euecus, their leader, was slain by the prowess alone of the King, and the Danes in their turn fled; but their rout was final and complete, although they also attempted to rally on the eminence opposite on the east, near to the old Castle of Balvenie. Many monuments of this victory remain. An entrenchment, yet distinct on the lowest summit of the Conval hills, is still known as "the Danish camp." A bulky cylindrical Stone, placed over the grave of Euecus, was only of late rolled a few yards off its station at the corpse, for building the fence of a corn-field. At a very little distance from the chieftain's grave, on the south, near to the north-west corner of the plantation of Tomnamuid, a small squared spot of ground has been ever recognised as the common grave of the slaughtered Danes. The addition to the west end of the Church, 24 feet in length, the triple measure of Malcolm's spear, in the performance of his vow, is still obviously distinct; and three holes in this votive addition still record the barbarous triumph with which the heads of three Danes of distinction had been there originally placed. It is hardly thirty years ago since the last mouldered away. An Obelisk, raised on the glebe on the bank of the Dullan, about 6 feet in height, the sculpture on its two opposite sides now nearly by time effaced, hath almost ceased to tell the purpose of its own erection. Human bones, broken sabres, and pieces of other ancient armour, have from time to time been accidentally discovered. About 40 years ago, a chain of gold, supposed to have been the ornament of some chieftain's neck, was by the plough turned up on the glebe. If the stratagem of damming up the Dullan, where its channel through a rock is contracted to the span of the stream, for discharging an artificial torrent on the unsuspecting Danes below, and thereby dividing their strength, had been at any time practised, it must have been on some other occasion than that of this engagement. If an enemy could be by these means surprised, the facility with which it might be accomplished might naturally suggest such a simple expedient.

In the history of this parish, another occurrence may be mentioned. Although the interest of King James in Scotland became evidently desperate, on the death of Viscount Dundee in the Battle of Killicranky in 1689, yet, in a council of the Jacobite chiefs in the beginning of the year thereafter, it was determined to attempt another campaign. But until the seed season should be completed, when greater numbers might be raised, a party of 1500 men was sent down to employ and fatigue the revolutionary troops. They plundered the country through which they marched, and burnt the House of Ediuglassie, at that time the property of Mr. Gordon, who lying in wait for their return, a few weeks afterwards, seized at random 18 of the stragglers, whom he immediately hanged on the trees of his garden. They were buried together in a corner of the nearest waste, still distinguished by the name of the *Highlandmen's mossie.—(Survey of Moray.)*].

RUNIC OBELISK.

[The Stone of Mortlach is erected on a haugh on the banks of the Dullan, immediately below the height on which the old Church of Mortlach is built. It has been supposed, although without any probability, that the stone was erected to commemorate a victory which Malcolm II. is said to have achieved over the Northmen at this place in 1010. An engraving of it appeared in the *Archæologia*, vol. xxii., plate 3, and an etching of it is given in Rhind's *Sketches of Moray*, p. 129. In both cases, however, the bird which surmounts the serpent has been omitted. It indeed required the practised eye and touch of the artist to detect its traces on the rough weather-beaten surface of the stone; but a close examination reveals the figure exactly as it appears on Plate VII., vol. I., of Stuart's *Sculptured Stones of Scotland*.] (ED.)

THE BATTLE OF MORTLACH.

(Ex. "The Scottish Chronicle; or, a Complete History and Description of Scotland," &c., by the reverend and learned Mr. Raphael Hollinshead.* Arbroath, 1805. Vol. i., p. 327.)

In the first brunt three valiant Captaines, that is to wit, Kenneth of Isla, Gryme of Stratherne, and Patrike of Dunbar,

* Hollinshead was born in London, but the date is unknown. He died between 1578 and '82. He never travelled 40 miles distance from London. The above Work was first written in Latin by Hector Boethius, translated into the Scottish tongue by John Ballenden, Archdeacon of Moray, and then (assisted by Wm. Harrison) into English by Hollinshead. It was published originally in two folios in 1570, in 1587, and latterly in 1805. (ED.)

THE BATTLE OF MORTLACH.

rushing ouer fiercely on their enimies, were slain, and gaue occasion to many of the Scottishe men to flee, but the place was such, that they could not well make theyr course any way forth, by reason of ye narrownesse thereof, fenced on either side with deepe trenches full of water and mudde, also a trauerse were laid sundrie trees, as it had bene of purpose to impeach the passage, deuised in that sort (as was thought) in time of some ciuill warres.

Here though Malcome, liake a valiant champion, did his best to stay them that fled, yet was he borne backe with the preasse, til he came to ye mids of this place, where stood a Chappell dedicate in the honour of Saint Molok, the which Malcome beholding, cast up his handes towardes heauen, making his prayer on this wise:

"Great God of vertue, rewarder of pietie, and punisher o sinne, we thy people seeking to defende our natiue countrey graunted to vs of thy beneuolence, as now destitute of al mortal help, and thus oppressed with the injurious inuasion of Danes, do flee vnto thee in this our extreeme necessitie, beseeching thee to haue compassion upon our miserable estate: Remoue (oh merciful Lorde) this dreadful terror from the people. And oh thou mother of God, the sicker refuge of mortall people in their distresse and miseries: and thou, S. Molok to whom this chappell was dedicate, help vs at this present, and in the honour of you, I here make a vow to build a cathedral Church for a Bishops sea, to remain as a monument to testifie vnto our posteritie, that by your support our realme hath been defended."

Scarcely had Malcolme made an ende of this prayer when diuerse of the Nobles with a loude voyce, as though they had bin assured yt his praier was herd, cried to their companies: stand good fellowes, for surely it is the pleasure of Almightie God, that we returne and renew the battayle against our enimies.

Hereupon rose a wonderfull noyse amongst the souldiers, ech one encouraging other to withstand the enimies, and to fight in most manfull wise in defence of theyr countrey and aunctent liberties, and foorthwith as it had bene by miracle they returned vpon their enimies, making great slaughter on eche side, without regarde to theyr liues or bloudy woundes, which they boldly and without feare receyued.

Herewith Malcolme also with a bushment of stoute warriors came vpon Euetus, who was praunsing up and downe the fielde without any helmet on his head, as though the Scottes had bene already without recouery clearely discomfitted, and so there was he beaten downe, beside his horse, and amongst the footemen slayne out of hande. The residue of the Danes beholding the slaughter of their Captaine, stayed from further pursute on the Scottes. Hereof ensued great boldnesse to the Scottes and discouragement to the Danes. Albeit the batayle continued still a long space, the souldiers doying theyr best on eyther side, till at length the Danes were put to flight, many of them being slaine, and but fewe taken. Olanus beholding the discomfiture of his people, and how his companion in authoritie was slain, fled into Murrayland with a small companie about him.

As this Battle is among the most important, so it is, perhaps, one of the best authenticated of all the contests of that early period. In addition to the above and similar narratives, we have the unanimous testimony of tradition, national and local, as to the actual occurrence, and as to the site, of the struggle. In the neighbourhood of the old castle there is still pointed out a spot said to mark the pit in which a great number of the Danes who fell in the battle were interred; and also, in the same locality, built into a rustic dyke, there is shown the stone which was said to have been placed over the remains of Euetus, the Danish leader, who was killed in the engagement. In addition to all these, we have the erection of the church and founding of the see, both well-authenticated historical events. Mr. W. F. Skene opines otherwise.

HOUSE OF BALVENIE.

Less than a mile below the Castle, and close to the river, and quite in view from the Station, is situated the new House of Balvenie, a noble mansion erected by the first Earl of Fife, who for some time resided in it. His Lordship did much to beautify the grounds around the mansion. Receiving with his second lady, the daughter of Sir James Grant of Grant, a large number of young natural firs from the Forest of Abernethy, these were planted on the hill-sides around, and formed extensive plantations, some of the fine old trees yet remaining. The trees were carried with a portion of the native earth attached to the root of each, and were thus planted.

HOUSE OF KININVIE.

Of the western portion, which is the most ancient, all that now remains is a spiral staircase, with a sort of tower

HOUSE OF KININVIE; TOWER OF TULLICH.

of four flats, surmounted by a curious place of the description called a *keep*, but popularly known in the locality by the name of "Belmydearie," the tradition being that here one of the old lairds had maintained a mistress, whose name, it is presumed, must have been "Bell." So much for the ingenuity exercised in tracing the derivation of names. The roof of the old part of the building is very steep, and the original slates are still on it. With much taste, the present proprietor studiously preserves the older portion of the building in nearly its ancient state, having merely modernized it so far as to have a couple of good old-fashioned bed-rooms within it.

A considerable portion of the remainder of the mansion was erected by James Leslie of Kininvie. This, indeed, is explicitly set forth in the following inscription, which was placed over the old entry door of that part of the house which he erected:—

JACOBUS LESLIE DE TULLICH, JOANNIS LESLIE DE KININ-VIE TERTIUS NATUS, PATERNÆ HÆREDITATIS EMPTOR ANTE-RIOREM HUJUS ÆDIFICII PARTIM ÆDIFICANDUM ADVERSAM Q. REPARANDUM CURAVIT, IN CUJUS TESTIMONIUM PALADA-MENTUM HOC EXTRUXIT ANNO PARTUS.
CIƆ IƆ CC XX V.

On the entry door being shut up in 1842, the stone got a place a little higher up, in its present position. Above it is another stone, containing the following :—

QUÆ JUNCTA FIRMA.
JACOBUS LESLIE DE KININVIE HAC POSSESSIONE DE TULLICH AB ILLO EMPTA PULUDAMENTUN HOC EXTRUENDUM CURAVIT ANNO 1726.

This latter stone originally occupied a very prominent place in the old Tower of Tullich, a separate estate adjoining Kininvie, belonging to the family, and which was accustomed to be give over to the eldest son. This tower shared the fate of many such buildings, having been demolished by the Goths of the day. On the decay of the tower, the stone in question was built into the wall of the farm-house of Kininvie; but, in 1842, it was removed to its present more fitting and more honourable position. In the same old mansion or Tower of Tullich were found several other ancient tablets in pretty fair preservation; and, of these, two have been placed over upper windows in the House of Kininvie. On one is the Tullich coat of arms, without, however, any lettering save the words, "1610 ZEIRIS." The other also contains the arms, and the letters " M O " and " L M." We should also mention that there is a third stone with the family arms, and the motto " Hold Fast."

Several additions and improvements on the House were commenced in 1840 by the late Archibald Young Leslie, and much was done during the short period of his lairdship; and his intentions, both as regards the building and the alterations on the garden, lands, &c., having been fully carried out by his son, the present proprietor, the house is now one of the most pleasing in appearance, the most interesting in association, and picturesque in situation, of any in the county.

The Leslies are cadets of the ancient line of the Rothes family. The property of Kininvie has been in their possession since an early period of the 16th century. A charter of the lands granted by John, 3rd Earl of Atholl, to Alexander Lesly is dated in 1521. The present proprietor derives his title through a daughter of that James de Tullich who built the portion of the House of Kininvie described in one of the foregoing inscriptions as the "anteriorem." This laird had a numerous family; and at his decease the property came in succession into the hand of two of his sons, James and Alexander Leslie, both of whom died without issue. The property then reverted to the family of his eldest daughter, Jane, who had married Robert Young of Monymusk—their eldest son, Archibald, assuming the surname of Leslie, and succeeding to the Kininvie and Tullich estates in 1840. This gentleman dying in the following year, he was succeeded by his son, Mr. George A. Young Leslie, the present proprietor.

Nearly opposite to the House of Kininvie is the House of Buchromb. The view stretches down to the sudden detour the river makes to the west, on its way to the Spey at Craigellachie, and the scenery in some parts is strikingly wild and beautiful.

RESTORATION OF MORTLACH PARISH KIRK.

From June till December, 1876, a much needed transformation went on. In the course of the operations there were raised from the floor of the church several slab-stones, upon one of which was sculptured a cross and sword. The cross is encircled with *fleur de lis* at each of the points. An inscription had been on the outer rim of the stone, but the apparently Saxon letters are quite illegible. It is to be regretted that this relic should be again trampled under foot, being now along with other lettered stones used in the flooring of the east end.

The Church is in the form of the letter T. The top of the letter represents the main section or nave of the building standing east and west; the leg of the letter representing the north aisle. The date of its foundation is lost; and no accuracy accompanies statements of the times at which it was successively enlarged. It was erected at a time when the surface of the ground floor was about 6 feet under its present level; the modern elevation of surface being due to accumulation. The examination of the main section of the church shows that part of the walls, above 4 feet thick, are composed of small round stones, such as may be found on the margin of the Dullan, embedded in mortar, on the same principle as a modern concrete wall. At a point 18 feet from the west end of the main section, the walls were found to have been extended westward, the extension being in a different and evidently later style of masonry. At the point where the addition had been begun there was on the outer surface of the wall a mark of the junction of the two styles of work. Popular belief was that this mark indicated *the three spears' length added to the church* by King Malcolm in virtue of a vow on the eve of battle, before defeating the Danes. The masonry of the oldest part of the church is believed to belong to about the 11th century, and the addition at the west end is of later date. In the old Statistical Account, Mr. Gordon, then minister of the parish, describes the church as an oblong square of about 90 feet by 28 feet, and this measurement corresponds to the main section of the building as at present. The church had been roofed 80 years before Mr. Gordon wrote. He urged the renewal of the roof, and the sacrifice of veneration for the antiquity of the church by remodelling it in a more convenient form. In 1826 the church was modernized by an addition made to it. That addition was at the north aisle. Probably, at the same time, the galleries were added; and the churchyard was certainly then extended on the north and west. No later alteration was made upon the building till 1876; and the only change in the outward form now is an addition of 10 feet to the north wing, and an improvement in the outside stair leading to the east gallery.

The addition to the north aisle has improved the aspect of the building. Formerly, a door was in the centre of the north gable; and two doors were in the south wall. The latter have been permanently closed; and the only entrances to the lower part of the church are now by doors on either side of the north gable. The two arched windows formerly in the north gable have been removed to the side walls of the extension of the north aisle; and in the centre of the north gable has been placed a handsome triple window, 15 feet high, with freestone mullions. The north wing is thus lighted from the gable, and by two large windows in each of the side walls, the former especially being of service to those seated in the enlarged gallery. The old belfry surmounting the north gable has been removed, and a new and more ornate steeple added, with chamber for the bell. It may be noted that it is a modern instrument; but in a receptacle in the wall of the church there yet lies the ancient hand-bell. Persons still recollect the old "Ronach Bell" having been used to summon the people to church; and also at funerals the bellman went before the coffin and rung the bell while the body was being carried to the churchyard and during interment.

In excavating at the west end of the main section of the church, near the junction of the old wall with the north aisle, a very interesting discovery was made. A circular-headed doorway was found in the old wall, the head of the door being only about 18 inches above the present level of the floor. In the side of the doorway was found an opening about 6 inches square, penetrating the wall a distance of 6 feet. The aperture had been made for the bar by which the door was secured in the inside. This had been one of the old entrances to the church. The doorway is 3 feet wide, and its existence shows that the level of the first floor of the building must have been about 6 feet under the present surface. Excavation was not made to any depth at this point, but the old archway is now exposed to view within the vestry. The new

STONE EFFIGY OF THE KNIGHT OF KININVIE.

vestry is at the north-west angle of the nave and aisle, and in forming it about 4 feet of the space was provided by removing a portion of the ancient wall.

The west end of the church has been greatly improved. The old curve in the gallery towards the north has been removed, and the gallery squared by the front being placed straight across the aisle. An old window with four panes in the west gable wall has been enlarged into an arched window, which lights both the lower floor and the gallery.

The greatest change has been effected in the east end of the nave. The old gallery has been removed, and the features of the wall, against which the Altar stood in pre-Reformation times, have been brought into prominence. In renovating this part of the church, several new features were disclosed. Two lancet windows were underneath the gallery in the east gable wall; and a small square window above the gallery. On removing the plaster from the wall, it was found that the square window had been formed by closing up the bottom and top of an old lancet window. The architect has restored the window to its ancient form, and the gable wall has now the 3 lancet lights, about 6 feet high and a foot wide at the outside, the aperture widening to several feet inside. The members of the family of Findlater of Balvenie have the lancets filled with memorial windows. The old gallery-stair in the east nave almost hid from view the statue of the Knight of Kininvie standing against the wall. The recumbent statue had evidently been placed in an upright position to be out of the way; but an arched niche has been made in the wall at the north-east corner, and the knight laid on his back. The figure is in armour, the head resting on a pillow, arms folded across the breast, and feet touching the side of a dog couchant. The stone-effigy is believed to be that of Alexander Leslie, who bought the estate of Kininvie from the Earl of Athol in 1521, built the House of Kininvie, and was buried within the Church of Mortlach about 1549.

The mural monument on the south wall of the aisle to the Laird and Lady of Keithmore has long been an object of interest within the church; but there has now been opened to view the two busts in stone which were known to exist in niches in the wall below the tablet. The figures are in freestone and very much worn, but they mark the spot near which, within the church, the great-grandfather and great-grandmother of the present Earl of Fife were buried. The inscription is—

I. Hoc conduntur tumulo reliquiæ ALEXANDRI DUFF de Keithmore et HELENÆ GRANT, uxoris suæ charissimæ, qui quadraginta annos et ultra felici et fæcundo connubio juncti, vixerunt. Uterq quidem ingenue natus, ille ex nobilissimis Fifæ Thanis per Vetustam familiam de Craighead, paulo abhinc superstitem proxime et legitime oriundus; illa ex splendida et potenti Grantœrum familia eodem quoq modo originem trahens. Ortu non obscuri, suis tamen virtutibus illustriores, opibus affluxerunt, et liberis ingenue educatis floruere; pie, juste, et sobrie vixerunt, et sic in Domino mortem obiere, illa Anno Domini 1694, ætatis suæ sexagesimo.

Translation.—In this tomb are laid the remains of Alexander Duff of Keithmore, and Helen Grant, his dearly beloved wife, who lived in a happy and fruitful union for more than 40 years. Both were well born, he being very nearly and lawfully descended from the most noble Thanes of Fife, through the old family of Craighead, not long extinct, and she deriving her origin, in like manner, from the renowned and powerful family of the Grants. Of distinguished birth, yet more illustrious for their virtues, they abounded in wealth, were happy in a flourishing family of liberally educated children, lived piously, justly, and soberly, and so died in the Lord, the A.D. 1694, in the 60th year of her age.

"JOANNIS FAID ME FECIT" is cut on the monument.

The property of Keithmore was a wadset which Duff received from the Marquis of Huntly about 1640–6. It is in Auchindoun, and the house commands a good view of the ruin and of the vale of the Fiddich, &c. It belongs to the Duke of Richmond and Gordon. Two slabs on the farm are pointed out; one dated 1680, with the Alexander Duff initials, arms, and family motto—VIRTUTE ET OPERA —as well as the "strype of water," by the side of which Keithmore's wife, fearing the approach of King William's dragoons, had a bag of gold and silver coins secreted by "her grandchild, old Lesmurdy, a boy then 17 or 18 years of age."

II. Another marble tablet near the Keithmore monument bears:—

M.O.V.S. : M![r] Hugonis Innes, filij honorabilis viri Joannis Innes de Leichnet, qui, cum annos triginta quatuor sacra in hoc templo peregisset obijt anno Christi MDCCCXXXII, natus annos LXVIII. Posuit hoc monumentum pia ac dilectissimæ conjux Eliz. Abernethie, filia domini de Mayen.

Translation.—Sacred to the memory of Mr. Hugh Innes, son of an honourable man, John Innes of Leichnet, who was minister of this church for 34 years, and died in 1732, aged 68 years. His pious and dearly beloved wife, Elizabeth Abernethy, daughter of the Laird of Mayen, erected this monument.

Anecdotes are narrated of the superior bodily strength of the above shepherd, often exhibited in herding his flock. Mrs. Innes, of Mayen in Rothiemay, is buried at Banff. Her husband's successor, Rev. Walter Sime, who died in 1763 of putrid fever, was one of 13 victims to an uncommon mortality then in the parish of that malady, whose bodies lay unburied at the same time. The frost was so intense that fires had to be kindled in the churchyard to soften the ground for digging the graves.

A most desirable operation would have been to have dug to the foundation of the walls of the oldest part of the church. Excavations were made to a depth of 9 feet below the present surface, but without reaching the foundation, or revealing anything new. Bones were exhumed, but there was nothing to indicate who the persons were.

At the north-east angle of the nave, an iron "joug" attached to a chain, which had been fixed in the wall, was dug up. It is hung on the east wall of the nave. The excavations would have been made in a more thorough manner but for the cost, antiquarian research not being among the objects contemplated by the heritors and congregation, who provided the funds.

During the operations, the whole series of inscribed stones catalogued in the Minute-book of the Kirk-Session of the parish in 1811 by the Rev. Wm. Cowie, then schoolmaster at Mortlach, afterwards minister at Cairnie, were looked for. They were all found with one exception. The whole of those found have been laid in the floor of the east nave. Mr. Cowie did good service in copying the inscriptions, which, if not now, will soon be beyond legibility.

III. Among them is a slab upon which is cut a cross, of the wheel-pattern, and a sword, with the following:—

Hic. jacet. honorabilis. bir. Johannes. Gordon. de. Brobland. qui. obiit. apud. Bochrom. anno. Dni. mdxxxiij.

Translation.—Here lies an honourable man, John Gordon of Broadland, who died at Buchrome in the year of our Lord 1533.

IV. Another slab, which lay under the stair, had only the name of Gordon legible, but was supposed to be of the same century.

From the passage was taken the stone which, in 1811, bore these words round the margin, having the Innes coat of arms:—

Hic. iacet. . . . . . [? cons]tabularius. de. balbenie. qbi. obiit. die. mensis. . . . . . anno. dni. mcccxx. . . . n. sponsa. . . . . . . nna. innes. eius. que. obiit. . . . . die. mensis. decembris. anno. dni. mccccxxix.

Translation.—Here lies . . . . . constable of Balvenie, who died on the . . . . day of . . . in the year of our Lord 1420. Here also lies spouse . . . NNA INNES, who died Dec. 1429.

V. From under the Pittyvaich seat a slab was found:—

. . . . . u. resurrectionis. hic. in. pace. requiescunt. cineres. u.

Translation.—Here rest in peace the ashes of . . . . till the resurrection. . . .

VI. Four marble tablets within the church are respectfully inscribed:—

Sacred to the memory of Major Ludovick Stewart, Pittyvaich, and formerly of H.M. 24th Regt. of Foot, who died on the 25th of Dec., 1848, aged 66 years. Also, of his wife, MARGARET FRASER, who died on the 17th of Oct., 1859, aged 62 years. Their children, GORDON ELLIOT, Lieut. 22nd Regt., Bombay, died 12th Jan., 1849, aged 24 years.

[Two daughters named.]

VII. Sacred to the memory of Mrs. Ann Stewart, late of Pittyvaich, whose remains are deposited in this churchyard. She died 5th Feb., 1823, aged 81 years.

The title "of" is vainglorious. The Stewarts were proprietors of Nothing, being merely tenants of Pittyvaich, of which the Earl of Fife is the proprietor. Even to the grave, some people carry empty vanity and poor pride, the cause of the fall.

VIII. Sacred to the memory of the Rev. Morris Forsyth, minister of the Gospel at Mortlach, who departed this life 19th Feb., 1838, in the 68th year of his age, and 33rd of his ministry.

IX. A tablet built into the east wall:—
To the memory of Major John Cameron, C.B., E.I.C. Native Infantry, on the establishment of St. George, who, after serving his country in India for 32 years, both in a civil and military capacity, and particularly in most of the principal events during that period, died on the 15th of June, 1838, while officiating as President at the court of Hyderabad, aged 42 years.

This tablet has been erected to his memory, and placed in the church of his native parish, by a few of his friends in India, as a mark of esteem and affection for his public and private character.

X. Probably the oldest slab in the churchyard is one with a bold carving of the Farquharson arms near the centre. An inscription, closely run on, and oddly arranged toward the close, is cut in relief round the margin. The sequel is not far from the original, difficult to make out—

hic jacet honorabilis vir robertus farquharson de lauchtitvany qui obiit mar de qunto meri anno dni m⁰ qu⁰ sexto cum sua propiquiet.

Translation.—Here rests with his kindred an honourable man, ROBERT FARQUHARSON of Lauchtitvany, who died at noon on the [5th or 15th] of March [1417 or 1517].

Before the 15th century the Cumings owned Lochterlandich and other property on the north side of Glenrinnes, as well as in Glenlivat, which prove that the above tombstone relates to some of the Cumings who took the name of Farquharson, after Cuming of Kellas was refused burial in the ancestral tomb at Altyre,

XI. A flat slab, which lay in the passage towards the west end of the church in 1811, now in the churchyard near to the south wall, presents a shield in the centre with the Moir and Reid arms impaled. The following inscription is round the sides of the stone:—

HEIR. LYES. ANE. HONEST. MAN. CALLED. IOHNE. MOIR. HVSBAND. TO. ELSPET. REID. WHO. WAS. KILLED. . . . . . EFENCE. OF. HIS. OVIN. HOVS. AT. THE. VALK. MILN. OF. BALVENIE. THE. 13. DAY. OF. OCTOBER. 1660. MEMENTO. MORI.

According to tradition, Moir, who was reputed rich, was attacked by "the cateran band" and killed by a gun-shot while barricading the door of his house. Whether "Iohne" had been an ancestor of Dr. Alexander Moir, a native, and once schoolmaster of Mortlach, who so generously left the interest of £600 for educational purposes to the parish, is uncertain, though not improbable.

XII. Upon a slab, with mortuary emblems:—

Hir lys the corps of the decessed IANAT CATTACH, vho departed this life Iuly 3, 1751, spovs to Iohn Mackendie in Belmern, hir age is 72.

XIII. Upon a broken table-shaped stone is:—

Here lies the body of ALEXANDER CANTLIE, late in Newton of Clunymore, who died 16th June, 1807, aged — years. Done by the care of his brother, Francis Cantlie, masson.

XIV. John Spence, Balandy, d. 1777, a. 82.
My God who gave me strength to walk
The world to and fro,
And by his mighty handy work,
I'm here interred below.
So in the silent grave I ly
Along with many more,
Until the day that I appear
My Saviour Christ before.

XV. Rudely cut upon a flat, undressed granite boulder—

Heir lies the dust of Alex. Farquhar, who lived at Priests-well, and died May 22, 1733, aged 76 years. And of Barbara Gordon, his spouse, who died Nov. 1736, aged 70. . . . .

XVI. This stone is erected by Alex. Anderson, Officer of Excise, in memory of his spouse, HELEN GORDON, who died 3rd March, 1810, aged 23, daughter of John Gordon in Tomnavollan, who left 3 children, John, Alex., and Margaret.

In memory of John Gordon, in Tomnavollan, who died 6th June, 1831, aged 92 years. I.H.S.

✠ His spouse, MARGARET GORDON, died 13th July, 1844, in the 78th year of her age, and left no family alive but an only son William.

[This William died on Saturday, the 30th Jan., 1875, æt. 84. He was my 2nd cousin. He had no sympathy with modern ideas of advance. For half a century the whole steading was of the most primitive make-shift caste. *Tamoul*, as he was called from the farm, in his garb was equally unadorned, the same tattered rags having done duty for years gone by. However, on high occasions, as rejoicings connected with the Duke of Richmond on the marriage of the Earl of March, he appeared *bon-ton* at the dinner given in honour of the event at Tomintoul. While most penurious, when "an auld acquaintance" paid him a visit at the roadside farm-house (if such it could be designated) *Tamoul* was kind and hospitable, setting down bread and cheese and a bottle of "real Glenlivat." He held the appointment of collector of seat-rents for the Roman Catholic Chapel at Tombae, and was proud of the original mode in which he kept the roll, somewhat puzzling to all but the patentee. The contributors were classified in three separate divisions—*Good*, *Bad*, and *Indifferent*. He was a rigid dunner, and after Mass pursued delinquents with foot and tongue. He lived in celibacy, nevertheless he left the fruits of his loins. The popular mind of the district magnified his ample means into an immense horde, which, at his death, amounted to about £7,000.] (ED.)

XVII. Here lies the body of William Kelman, farmer in Lessmurdie, who died April 26, 1793, aged 80; and Helen M'Barnat, his spouse, who died 1st Dec., 1785, aged 75.

XVIII. In memory of Mr. Alexander Thomson, who taught the school of Mortlach 23 years, and died March the 21st, 1804, in the 57th year of his age. This stone is placed here by his friends and pupils, as a mark of respect for his character as a worthy member of society, and an unwearied teacher of youth.

XIX. Within an enclosure :—

The Rev. Alexander Grant, late minister of Glenrinnes, was interred here, Aug. 1, 1806, and his mother in 1777. This stone was repaired in 1807 by George Grant in Drumfurrich. Here lie also the remains of the said George Grant, brother of the Rev. Alexander Grant, who departed this life at Elgin, 23 April, 1816, aged 85, in memory whereof this inscription has been added by desire of his son, Alex. Grant, late of the Island of Jamaica, on visiting his native county from London in Aug., 1829. Janet Donaldson, relict of Geo. Grant, Drumfurrich, died 1834, aged 78. By her son, Alex. Grant, Aberlour, 1844.

The above-named Alex. Grant, of the Island of Jamaica,

bought the estate of Aberlour from James Gordon, Esq. A sister of Mr. Grant's married Dr. M'Pherson, farmer, Garbity, and their daughter, Miss M'Pherson-Grant, succeeded by her uncle's will. (See under ABERLOUR.)

XX. From a table-stone:—

In memory of Robert Lorimer, senior, who departed this life at Glenbeg in a good old age, about the year 1702. His sons, William, James, and Thomas, all died unmarried. His fourth son, Robert, junior, lived in Myreside, and died there. This monument was erected by his grandson, Dr. John Lorimer of London, in the year 1795.

Dr. Lorimer left £200 for the maintenance of a bursar at the school of Mortlach, and a like sum to enable him, if so inclined, to prosecute his studies at Marischal College, Aberdeen.

XXI. Upon a table-shaped stone, enclosed by a railing:—

This stone was placed here by John M'Innes, Dandalieth, in memory of his parents, John M'Innes, Braehead, who died 21st Nov., 1816, aged 84; Margaret Luke, his spouse, who died 4th Feb., 1813, aged 74. . . . . John M'Innes, died at Dandalieth, 19th May, 1850, aged 74, and is here interred.

XXII. A monument of Peterhead granite bears:—

This stone is erected by James Sturm of London in memory of his parents, Alexander Sturm, merchant, Dufftown, who died 7th April, 1848, aged 65; and Margaret Murray, his wife, who died 6th May, 1847, aged 75.

The erector of this monument, who died at Hampstead, May 7, 1869, aged 57, was sometime a clothier in Aberdeen. He afterwards became a furniture dealer in London, and left upwards of £25,000. Besides handsome legacies to relatives and friends, he left £500 to each of eight charitable institutions in London. He also left a legacy of £500 to the National Life-Boat Institution, directing that a boat, named James Sturm, should be employed on the coast of his native county. He bequeathed £2,000 to found two scholarships for five years each in the University of Aberdeen, for natives of Mortlach, of the age of fifteen years, who have been taught in the school of that parish; also £500 for the education of females of Mortlach in the principles of the Established Church of Scotland; and a farther sum of £500, a portion of which, and interest, to be expended for the relief of infirm poor persons of the village of Dufftown.

XXIII. Here lys in hope of a blessed resurrection Barbara Barren, spouse to John Barren, dyster in Menelock, who departed this life the 12th of January, 1779, her age forty-one. Also there son George, who departed the 13th of Oct., 1769, in the fifth month of his age.

The above John Barren gifted a pewter-basin to the kirk, which is thus inscribed:—"Given by John Barren, elder, to the Kirk of Mortlach. Mr. John Tough, minister, 1768." Some profane wag has scratched a verse of doggerel rhyme upon the basin, the first couplet of which runs thus:—

"This basen was presented by me, John Barren,
Who ever took the Scripture for my warran'."

XXIV. Helen Clark, mentioned in the next inscription, was a sister of the late Sir James Clark, M.D.:—

✠ In pious memory of John Gordon, who succeeded to the farm of Tullochalum, 1771, and died there 1820, aged 82. Mary Dawson, his spouse, died 1824, aged 72. And of their children, William, who died in Jamaica, 1802; Anne, died at Tullochalum, 1811; Thomas, Capt. 92nd Regt., "Gordon Highlanders," died in Jamaica, 1819; James, died at Aberdeen, 1824; Rev. John, died at Edinburgh, 1832; George, S.S.C., Edinburgh, died at Paisley, 1868. Also of Helen Clark, the beloved wife of Alex. Gordon, who died at Tullochalum, 1822, aged 28 years. R.I.P.

XXV. From a stone in the east wall of the churchyard:—

Erected in memory of William M'Connochie, late farmer in Boghead of Auchendown, who died 13 Dec., 1824, aged 81. Done by his son John—

Omnes eôdem cogimur: omnium
Versatur urnâ, seriùs, ociùs,
Sors exitura, et nos in æternum
Exilium impositura cymbæ.

The above, from Horace's Ode to Dellius, is thus translated by Dr. Francis:—

" We all must tread the paths of Fate;
And ever shakes the mortal urn,
Whose lot embarks us, soon or late,
On Charon's boat, ah! never to return."

XXVI. A table-shaped stone (enclosed) bears :—

This stone was placed here by the Parishioners of Mortlach as a mark of respect to the memory of the Rev. George Grant, who discharged with fidelity the duties of a minister of this parish for the space of eleven years, and died 10th Oct., 1804, in the 44th year of his age. Also interred here the remains of Harriet Ann Stuart or Grant, thereafter Irvine, widow of the said Rev. George Grant, who died at Aberdeen, 5th Sept., 1847, in the 69th year of her age.

Erected by a few friends in memory of John Utley Wignall, Inland Revenue Officer, who died at Dufftown, 17th Jan., 1866, aged 27 years.

XXVII. Within the church is a stone effigy in armour. It is built into the north wall, in an upright posture. This had at first formed part of a recess-tomb, like those at Fordyce; and being placed near to the old Kininvie sepulture, the figure in all probability represents Alexander Leslie (a descendant of the fourth Baron of Balquhain), who acquired Kininvie from the Earl of Athol in 1521. Four years later, Leslie built the House of Kininvie, part of which building still stands, and dying about 1549, he was interred within the Kirk of Mortlach, where the family long continued to bury. Their tomb is now outside the church. The first Baron of Kininvie left several sons. Walter, the eldest, who succeeded to Kininvie, died in 1562, and the third son, George, received the lands of Drummuir from his father. It was a grandson of George of Drummuir who became Earl of Leven; and the eldest daughter of the fifth Leslie of Kininvie was mother of Archbishop Sharp.

XXVIII. The following, from a tablet at Mortlach, erected by the Archbishop's uncle, is in memory of his (the sixth laird's) wife :—

Here lyeth the pious, verteous gentlewoman, Helen Grant, goodwife of Kininvie, daughter to Belentom, who lived with her husband, John Leslie of Kininvie, 60 years, and departed the 11 of May, 1712, the 82 year of her age.

XXIX. The seventh laird, who was Provost of Banff, sold Kininvie and Tulloch, in 1703, to his third brother, James, who built the middle part of the House of Kininvie in 1725, and died in 1732. He was twice married, and the following inscription relates to his first wife :—

Here lyeth Helen Carmichaell, daughter to —— Carmichaell of Clapertounehall, in the countie of Midle Lothian, and spous to James Leslie of Tullich, who departed this life the 15 day of May, 1717. I.L: H C. Memor lethi fugit hora.

XXX. Another slab bears the name of a brother-in-law of the eighth laird :—

Here lyeth the pious and vorthie gentleman, John Grant of Navie, who was married to Helen Leslie, daughter to John Leslie of Kininvie, who departed the last of August, —-7—. J.G : H L.

The eighth laird of Kininvie and Tullich entailed the estates in 1730, and dying two years afterwards he was succeeded by his only child, James, as ninth laird. The ninth laird married a daughter of Stewart of Lesmurdie, by whom he had three sons and three daughters. The first and third sons both succeeded. The first, who sold Buchromb in 1795, had an only daughter, and the second died unmarried in 1839, in which year the estates came to the son of their eldest sister, Jean, by Robert Young, factor and commissioner to Sir A. Grant of Monymusk. This son, who was a solicitor in Banff, and took a leading part in the affairs of the county, married a daughter of James Donaldson of Kinairdy in Marnoch, and a marble tablet at Mortlach bears this record of their deaths :—

XXXI. Sacred to the memory of Archd. Young-Leslie of Kininvie, who departed this life 31 Oct., 1841, aged 74. And of his spouse, Jane Donaldson, who died on 30 Nov. of the same year, aged 63. This tablet is erected by their children.

The above were the parents of the present laird, of whose lady and a daughter there is the following record :—

XXXII. Sacred to the memory of Barbara King Stewart, the beloved wife of George A. Y. Leslie of Kininvie, and daughter of Gen. William Stewart of Elgin, C.B., who died 12th Aug., 1853, in her 36th year ; and Mary Jane, their infant daughter.

Mr. Geo. A. Y. Leslie had three sons and three daughters. The eldest son, Archibald, an officer in the 23rd R. Welsh Fusiliers, lately constructed a family tree, from which, and notes kindly furnished by my friend, Robert Young, writer, Elgin (author of excellent histories of Burghead, the Parish of New Spynie, &c.), this notice of the Kininvie family is mainly compiled.] (*Jervise's Epitaphs.*—ED.)

156 BRANCHES OF THE DUFF FAMILY.

Before I proceed to the next parish, I shall give some account of

THE FAMILY OF DUFF.

The family of M'Duff, Earl of Fife (descended, in my opinion, of King Duffus, who was murdered in Forres about anno 965), was ancient and eminent, and flourished until the year 1385. The sirnames of *Weem, M'Intosh, Tosheach, Shaw, Spens, Fife, Duff,* &c., are branches of that great family. I have before me a genealogical manuscript account lately written, deducing the Lord Braco from the family of Fife. It consists of three successive branches.

I. The Earls of *Athole* of the name *de Strathbolgie,* descended of the Earls of Fife, thus: (1) David, son of Duncan, the 6th Earl. In a donation to the See of Moray, by Malcolm the 7th Earl, "David filius quondam Duncani Comitis de Fife, frater meus, anno 1226," is witness. "Collatio Malcomi Com. de Fyfe, Episc. Morav. Test. Duncano et Davide fratribus meis. Conventio inter Andream Episc. Morav. et nobilem virum Davidem de Strathbolgie filium quondam Duncani Comitis de Fyfe, anno 1232." (*Cart. Moray*).

Translation.—David my brother, the son of the late Duncan, Earl of Fife, in the year 1226.—The Contribution of Malcolm, Earl of Fife, to the Bishop of Moray, witnessed by Duncan and David my brothers. The Covenant between Andrew, Bishop of Moray, and the Nobleman, David of Strathbolgie, the son of the late Earl of Fife, in the year 1232.

He was father of (2) John de Strathbolgie, who became Earl of Athole in right of his wife Ada, co-heiress of Henry, Earl of Athole, and was father of (3) David, who married Isabel, co-heiress of Lord Chilam, and died 1284. His son (4) John, executed at London, 1308. His son (5) David, killed at Kilblain anno 1335, by his wife Joan, daughter of John the Red Cuming Lord Badenoch, had several sons, whereof the eldest (6) David, was forfeited for abetting the English interest, and died in England anno 1375, without male issue. This deduction of the Earls of Athole is instructed from the Chartulary of Moray and Sir Wm. Dugdale.

II. Branch, deduces the *Duffs* of *Muldavid* and *Craighead* thus: (1) John, second son of David, the 5th Earl of Athole, quitted the name of de Strathbolgie and assumed that of Duff, and had the lands of Muldavid and Craighead, &c. His son was (2) David, &c. The line was carried down by eleven generations, to John Duff, writer in Aberdeen, who died in Holland anno 1717, without issue; and in him the direct line of Craighead became extinct. I confess all the descents are well instructed, except the first. But one will desiderate, how doth it appear, that John, called the first of Craighead, was the 2nd son of David, 5th Earl of Athole? Or was at all his son? That ever he bore the name of Strathbolgie? That he assumed the name Duff? And for what reasons he did so? For all, or any of those, there is no voucher. Be it as it may, I pass on to

III. Branch, The family of *Clunybeg* and *Braco*. The direct line of Craighead becoming extinct in John Duff anno 1717, his grandfather John (who died about 1660), was twice married. By his first wife Isabel Allan, he had John, father of the foresaid John the writer. And by his second wife, daughter of John Gordon of Carnborraw, he had (1) Adam Duff of Clunybeg, who, by his wife, daughter of Gordon of Birkenburn, had Alexander of Keithmore, William, ancestor of Drummuir and Crombie, John, ancestor of Cornfindie, Peter and Adam. Clunybeg died anno 1677. (2) Alexander of Keithmore, married Helen, daughter of Alexander Grant of Allachie, and had Alexander of Braco, William of Dipple, and Patrick of Craigston. (3) Alexander of Braco married Margaret, daughter of Sir William Gordon of Lessmore, Bart., and had (4) William, who, leaving no male issue, was succeeded by his uncle (5) William of Dipple, heir male and of entail, who, by his wife, daughter of Sir George Gordon of Edinglassie, has left a son (6) William. This gentleman married Jean, eldest daughter of Sir James Grant of Grant, and hath a numerous issue. In 1735, he was created Baron Braco of Kilbryde in the county of Cavan in Ireland; and, by patent to him and his heirs male, dated 10th

April, 1759, he was created Viscount MacDuff and Earl Fife of that kingdom.

William, second son of Clunybeg, was father of Alexander, who married Katherine Duff eldest daughter and heiress of Adam Duff of Drummuir, and by her had Robert of Drummuir, John of Couldbin, and William of Muirton. Robert was father of Archibald, now of Drummuir. William had a second son, James, father of William Duff of Crombie advocate. Of Clunybeg's 3rd son, John, is descended Duff of Corsindae. And of Keithmore's son, Patrick of Craigston, are descended Hatton, Kemnay, Craigston, &c.

The armorial bearing of Duff, Earl Fife, of the Kingdom of Ireland, is quarterly, 1 and 4, Or, a lion rampant Gules, armed and langued azure, for Fife; 2 and 3, Vert, a fess danzette Ermine, betwixt a hart's head cabossed in chief, and two escallops in base, Or, for Duff of Braco. Crest, a demy lion Gules, holding in his dexter paw a broad sword erected in pale proper, hilted and pomelled. Or, motto above the crest, DEUS JUVAUIT. And below the shield, VIRTUTE ET OPERA. Supporters, two savages wreathed about the heads and middles with laurel, holding branches of trees in their hands, all proper.

Translation.—Crest, GOD WILL HELP. Below the shield, BY COURAGE AND LABOUR.

FAMILY OF DUFF, EARL OF FIFE.

[This family has a clear Charter-descent for about 500 years. The Duffs were settled as landed proprietors in Banffshire in the reign of David II. The first recorded was

1. John Duff, who was proprietor of the lands of Muldavit, near Cullen.

In the Church of Cullen, upon the arch of a recess tomb, there was a recumbent effigy, and before it lay a flat slab adorned with the incised figures of a Knight in armour. Both these were removed, in 1792, at the request of the Earl of Fife, to the mausoleum near Duff House. The effigy and slab both relate to the above.

𝔥𝔦𝔠. 𝔍𝔞𝔠𝔢𝔱. 𝔍𝔬𝔥𝔞𝔫𝔢𝔰. 𝔇𝔟𝔣. 𝔇𝔢. 𝔐𝔲𝔩𝔟𝔞𝔟𝔦𝔱. 𝔢𝔱. 𝔅𝔞𝔩𝔟𝔞𝔟𝔦. 𝔬𝔟𝔦𝔦𝔱. 𝔈. 𝔍𝔘𝔏𝔍𝔍. 1404.

Around the margin of the slab is:—

𝔥𝔦𝔠. 𝔍𝔞𝔠𝔢𝔱. 𝔍𝔬𝔥𝔞𝔫𝔢𝔰. 𝔇𝔟𝔣. 𝔡𝔢. 𝔐𝔲𝔩𝔟𝔞𝔟𝔦𝔱. 𝔅𝔞𝔩𝔟𝔞𝔟𝔦. 𝔮𝔲𝔦. 𝔬𝔭𝔢. 𝔢𝔱 𝔬𝔭𝔢𝔯𝔞. 𝔟𝔦𝔯𝔱𝔲𝔱𝔢. 𝔞𝔠. 𝔣𝔯𝔲𝔤𝔞𝔩𝔦𝔱𝔞𝔱𝔢. 𝔞𝔩𝔱𝔬. 𝔠𝔬𝔫𝔰𝔦𝔩𝔦𝔬. 𝔢𝔱. 𝔦𝔫𝔱𝔯𝔢𝔭𝔦𝔡𝔬. 𝔠𝔬𝔯𝔡𝔢. 𝔭𝔞𝔱𝔢𝔯𝔫𝔬𝔰. 𝔩𝔦𝔪𝔦𝔱𝔢𝔰. 𝔞𝔪𝔭𝔩𝔦𝔞𝔟𝔦𝔱. 𝔬𝔟. 𝔦𝔫𝔢𝔠𝔬𝔯^m. 𝔪𝔢𝔫𝔱𝔢𝔪. 𝔦𝔫𝔢𝔠𝔬𝔯^m. 𝔪𝔢𝔫𝔱𝔢𝔪. 𝔦𝔲𝔟𝔦^m. 𝔣𝔦𝔟^m. 𝔭𝔯𝔢𝔠𝔩^m. 𝔬𝔟^t. 1404.

An engraving of this monument is given in *Cordiner's Remarkable Ruins*.

The mausoleum near Duff House is of Gothic architecture, surrounded with shrubbery, and forms a striking ornament to the park. The windows are of stained glass, and in front are two fine statues of Faith and Hope. In the middle of last century were visible considerable ruins of St. Mary's Chapel, built by King Robert Bruce in 1324, upon the site of which the Duff mausoleum is erected. The adjacent grounds were also devoted by his Royal Charter for the building and support of a Carmelite monastery. (ED.)

2. David Duff of Muldavit was probably a son of the preceding John Duff. He obtained a Crown Charter in the year 1404, in favour of himself and Mary Chalmers, his wife, of the lands of Muldavit. He had also the lands of Craighead, Baldavie, Auchingall, and others.

3. John Duff, his son, succeeded, and lived in the reign of King James I.

4. John Duff of Muldavit and Craighead succeeded, and had a Crown Charter from King James II., "Johanni Duff, filio et heredi Johannis Duff," of various lands, dated 12th February, 1442. He wadset his lands of Muldavit to James Innes of that ilk, under redemption.

5. John Duff, designed Burgess of Cullen, son of the preceding, confirmed his father's wadset of the lands of Muldavit to the Laird of Innes, who obtained a Crown Charter thereon in 1481. He left a son,

6. Andrew Duff of Muldavit, who redeemed the property from the Laird of Innes, and got a Crown Charter thereon, dated June, 1504, to "Andreæ Duff, de omnibus et singulis terris de Maldavit, in vice comitatu de Banff, quæ fuerunt Johannis Duff, avi dicti Andreæ." He married Helen Hay, grandchild of John Hay, Lord of Forest

of Boyne, Enzie, &c. After the death of her husband, this lady built an aisle on the south side of the Church of Cullen, which was long called the Duff's Aisle. Andrew Duff left two sons—1st, John, his heir; and 2nd, George, who was a Churchman. He himself died in the year 1519.

7. John Duff succeeded, and was infeft on Chancery precept as heir to his father, Andrew, 16th May, 1520. He had two sons—1st, George ; 2nd, John.

8. George Duff, who never married. He resigned his lands to his brother John.

9. John Duff of Muldavit and Craighead * got a charter under the Great Seal, 26th November, 1550—"Johanni Duff, fratri germano Georgii Duff de Maldavit, terrarum de Maldavit, cum molendino, &c. He died about the year 1580.

10. John Duff, son of the preceding, succeeded. Got a charter under the Great Seal, previous to his father's death, as heir-apparent, 10th July, 1575, which was renewed 24th February, 1610. He married Agnes Gordon, by whom he had a son, John, with whose consent, and that of his wife, he sold the Estate of Muldavit, to James Hay of Rannes, in the year 1626. He died in the year 1627.

11. John Duff succeeded his father, and married, first, Isabel Allan, by whom he had a son, John; second, Margaret, daughter of John Gordon of Cairnburrow, by whom he had a son, Adam Duff of Clunybeg, and a daughter, Margaret, married to John Meldrum of Laithers.

12. John Duff, eldest son of the last John Duff, was a merchant in Aberdeen, and had a charter—"Johanni Duff, mercatori burgen burgi de Aberdeen, dimidiato terrarum de Boghall." He died in the reign of King Charles II.

13. John Duff, son of the preceding, was an Advocate in Aberdeen, and much respected as a man of business, and also privately. He died, without issue, in the year 1718, and in him ended the succession of John Duff of Muldavit (No. 11), by his first wife, Isabel Allan.

14. Adam Duff of Clunybeg, son of John Duff, (No. 11),

* Craighead was the place of residence of the family. According to Gordon of Straloch's map it stood on the high bank above the burn, nearly opposite Cullen House.

by his second wife, Margaret Gordon, was born in 1598. He settled at Clunybeg, in the parish of Mortlach, and became a great farmer, merchant, and trader, dealing in all country produce. He was a man of great sense, shrewdness, and sagacity, and began the foundation of the wealth of the family. He was fined by the Covenanting party, in the year 1646, in 500 merks, as a supporter of the Royalist side, to which he was attached. He married Beatrix Gordon, daughter of John Gordon of Birkenburn, by whom he had six sons and two daughters, viz:—Alexander, his heir; John, ancestor of the Duffs of Corsindae, died 1696, aged 73; William,* a merchant in Inverness, ancestor of the Duffs of Drummuir and Crombie, died October, 1715, aged 83; George, married, and had issue. Two other sons died unmarried. Two daughters, Jean and Helen, were married. Adam Duff of Clunybeg died in April, 1674, aged 76.

Alexander and John, the two eldest sons of Clunybeg, in their early days supported the Royalist cause, and fought under Montrose in his wars. They were both bold, daring men, particularly John, who was taken prisoner by the Covenanters, and would certainly have perished on the scaffold, if he had not contrived to make his escape from an escort of soldiers, who were conveying him to Edinburgh for trial.

15. Alexander Duff, eldest son of Adam Duff, of Clunybeg, obtained from the Marquis of Huntly a wadset of the lands of Keithmore, in Mortlach, which long continued to be the residence of the family, having only been redeemed in the following century. He was a very prudent, careful man; had abundance of money, and an extensive wadsetter and purchaser of land. He acquired the extensive Estate and Lordship of Balvenie, either in wadset or by purchase, and also the considerable property in Glenrinnes, belonging to the Cumings of Lochtervandich, with many other estates. He was a great farmer and moneylender. He married Helen, daughter of Alexander Grant

* William Duff's son, Alexander, was Provost of Inverness, and married Katherine, daughter and heiress of Adam Duff of Drummuir. The Duffs of Drummuir are an old family. I have not seen their pedigree; but the estate was small, and was enlarged to its present dimensions by the money made by the Duffs at Inverness. (R. Y.)

of Allachie, brother of Archibald Grant of Ballintomb, ancestor of the family of Monymusk. By this lady it has been stated that he got 100,000 merks of tocher, more than £5000 sterling, a very large sum for those days. She was a most prudent, industrious, and very hospitable person, and much of the future prosperity of the family proceeded from her. By this lady Keithmore had three sons and four daughters, viz.:—
1. Alexander of Braco. 2. William Duff, merchant in Inverness and Elgin, afterwards of Dipple and Braco. 3. Patrick Duff of Craigston, ancestor of Hatton. 1st. daughter, Margaret, married to James Stewart of Lesmurdie. 2nd, Jean, married to George Meldrum of Crombie. 3rd, Mary, married to Andrew Fraser, physician in Inverness; secondly to Thomas Tulloch of Tannochy, County of Elgin. 4th, Elizabeth, married to a brother of Sir James Calder of Muirton. Keithmore died in the year 1700, aged 76. His wife, Helen Grant, died 1694, aged 60. They were interred within the Parish Church of Mortlach, where a monument with a Latin inscription is placed to their memory.

The arms of the Duffs at this period were—Vert a fess daunzette ermine, between a buck's head cabossed in chief, and two escalops Or.

16. Alexander Duff of Braco succeeded his father, Keithmore, but did not long survive him. He purchased many estates in the County of Banff, particularly in Mortlach, Aberlour, Keith, and Grange Parishes. He married Margaret, daughter of Sir William Gordon of Lesmore, Bart., by whom he had one son, William Duff of Braco, and three daughters, viz.:—1. Margaret, married to Gordon of Glengerrack. 2. Helen, married William Gordon of Farskine. 3. Mary, married to Alexander Abercrombie of Tullibodie, Advocate. He was a member for the County of Banff to the Scots Parliament, and supported strongly the party opposed to the union with England, of which the Duke of Hamilton was the leader. He died in the year 1705, two years before the union, not much above fifty years of age, and was buried in the aisle of the Parish Church of Grange, where a monument was erected to his memory.

17. William Duff of Braco, only son of the preceding, was an amiable and accomplished gentleman, of very

different tastes from his father; liberal and generous in his nature, and very kind to his numerous tenantry. He had travelled much abroad, and had seen a great deal of the world. He married Helen Taylor, a female in humble life, but a very excellent person, by whom he had one daughter, Margaret, married to Patrick Duff of Premnay. His marriage, perhaps, and other incidents contingent upon it, brought on a continued melancholy, and he died at Balvenie Castle, in January, 1718, a young man, much regretted by his tenantry and friends. The succession fell to the heir-male, in virtue of the settlements of the estates, and the uncle of this proprietor, and the nearest heir-male was

18. William Duff of Dipple. This gentleman was second son of Keithmore, and had a very limited patrimony from his father—a sum of 10,000 merks Scots, or something more than £500 stg., and with this small allowance, and a promise of succession to his father's wadset of Keithmore, he began the world. He was born about the year 1654, and, when arrived at a suitable age, was bound apprentice to his uncle, William Duff, merchant in Inverness, then largely engaged in trade, with whom he eventually became a partner. He was a prudent, sagacious, careful man; very honourable in his dealings, and greatly esteemed over all the North of Scotland for integrity and justice in all his transactions. He acquired a very considerable fortune, and, like the rest of his family, lent largely on wadsets. His only purchases of land were in Morayshire, to which he was much attached. He acquired there the estates of Dipple, Pluscarden, Oldmills, Coxton, Quarrelwood, Aldroughty, Mosstowie, and Sheriffmill, Inverlochty, and others. He married, first, Helen Gordon, daughter of Sir George Gordon, of Edinglassie, by whom he had one son, William, afterwards Lord Braco and Earl of Fife, and four daughters, viz.:—1st. Helen, married to the Honourable William Sutherland of Rosscommon, third son of James Lord Duffus, by whom she had no issue. This lady long survived her husband, lived in the Castle of Quarrelwood, and was known by the name of Lady Rosscommon. 2nd. Catherine, married to Alexander Duff of Hatton. 3rd. Elizabeth, married to Thomas Donaldson of Kinnairdie. 4th. Isabella, married to Alexander Macintosh of Blervie, to whom she had

twenty-two children. Numerous descendants of this marriage still exist over the North of Scotland. William Duff of Dipple married, second, Jane, daughter of Sir William Dunbar of Durn, Baronet, by whom he had one son, Alexander, who died in 1721, aged five years, and four daughters, viz.:—1st. Anne, married to William Baird of Auchmedden. 2nd. Janet, married to Sir James Kinloch of Kinloch, Baronet. 3rd. Mary, married to General James Abercrombie of Glassaugh. 4th. Henrietta, a very excellent, charitable person, who died unmarried. During the last nineteen years of his life, Mr. Duff lived in Elgin, where he carried on his business, principally as a private banker, lending on mortgage and wadsets. He is said to have had his place of business in the old house on the north side of the High Street of Elgin, near the Little Cross, still in good repair, and there is no doubt he lived himself in the house, also on the north side of the High Street, which he purchased along with the Estate of Coxton, from Sir George Innes, and which still exists, although in a very dilapidated state, bearing on the eastmost window a star, for Innes, and the date, 1677. It was sold by Lord Braco, in 1747, to Robert Anderson, Sheriff-Substitute of Morayshire, who had married his Lordship's niece, Elizabeth Mackintosh. Mr. Duff died in the year 1722, but the place of his burial I have failed to discover. He had previously, in 1718, by the death of his nephew, William Duff of Braco, succeeded to the whole estates of the principal branch of the Duff family, which he is said to have left all clear to his son, besides £30,000 sterling in ready-money, a very large sum for that period. He was about 68 years of age at the time of his death at Elgin, in 1722.

19. William Duff, only son of the preceding, succeeded his father in his large estates. He was a Member of Parliament for the County of Banff in 1727; created a Peer of Ireland, by the title of Lord Braco of Kilbride, on 28th July, 1735, and Earl of Fife and Viscount Macduff, 26th April, 1759—the patent being limited in both cases to him and the heirs-male of his body. He was a careful manager of his affairs, and purchased considerable estates in the Counties of Aberdeen, Banff, and Moray. In the last county he acquired Milton, Blervie, and other estates, so that with what his father left him he had a very fine

estate in Morayshire. He married, first, Lady Janet Ogilvie, second daughter of James 4th Earl of Findlater, and 1st Earl of Seafield, Chancellor of Scotland, and widow of Hugh Forbes, Younger of Craigievar, by whom he had no issue. He married, second, Jane Grant, daughter of Sir James Grant of Grant, Baronet, by whom, who died 16th January, 1788, in the 83rd year of her age, he had 7 sons and 7 daughters, viz.:—1. William, who died unmarried in London, 26th March, 1753, in his 27th year. 2. James 2nd Earl of Fife. 3. Alexander 3rd Earl of Fife. 4. Patrick, who died young. 5. George, long Convener of the County of Elgin—a most worthy, estimable gentleman. He died at Elgin, at his residence, South College, 23rd November, 1818. 6. Ludovick, who died at Blervie, without issue, 19th November, 1796. 7. Arthur, Advocate, Member of Parliament for the County of Elgin, 1774; died unmarried at Orton, 26th April, 1805. He was long Comptroller of Excise for Scotland. The Earl of Fife left his third son, Alexander, the Estate of Echt, in Aberdeenshire; to George, his fifth son, the Estates of Milton, Inverlochty, and Barmuckity, in Morayshire; to Ludovick, his sixth son, the estate of Blervie; and, to Arthur, his seventh son, the estate of Orton. There are now no descendants of all these 7 sons, except of Alexander, the third son only. 1st daughter, Lady Anne, married to Alexander Duff of Hatton, and died in Edinburgh, 5th June, 1805. She had an only child, Jane; married 4th January, 1763, to Sir James Grant of Grant, Baronet. 2. Janet, married, first in 1745, to Sir William Gordon of Park, who engaged in the Rebellion that year, was attainted, and died at Douay, 3rd June, 1751. By him she had two sons, born abroad. She married, second, George Hay of Mountblairy, and died at Carnousie, 3rd March, 1758, aged 30. 3. Lady Jane, married, 25th October, 1753, to Keith Urquhart of Meldrum, by whom she had issue—James Urquhart of Meldrum, long Sheriff-Depute of Banffshire; a son, Lewis; and two daughters, Anne and Mary. 4. Lady Helen, married, in 1764, to Robert Duff of Logie and Fetteresso, Vice-Admiral in the Royal Navy, by whom she had three sons and one daughter, viz.:— Robert William Duff of Fetteresso and Culter; Adam Duff, Sheriff of Forfarshire; James Alexander Duff, an Officer in the Army; and Jane, married to James Clerk

JAMES DUFF, THE SECOND EARL OF FIFE. 167

of Chesterhall. 5. Lady Sophia Henrietta, married to Thomas Wharton, Commissioner of Excise, by whom she had the late Richard Wharton Duff of Orton, and two daughters, Jane and Mary. 6. Lady Catherine, died, unmarried, 25th April, 1765. 7. Lady Margaret, married at Edinburgh, 6th March, 1768, to James Brodie of Brodie, and died, burnt to death, at Brodie House, 24th April, 1786; leaving two sons, James and William, and three daughters, Jane Anne Catherine, Margaret, and Charlotte. William Earl of Fife, while a great economist, had a taste for magnificence and fine buildings. Shortly after his succession, in the year 1724, he built the new Castle or House of Balvenie. The family having taken a dislike to the fine old Castle, allowed it to go to decay, and between the years 1740 and 1745, he erected the grand building of Duff House, at a cost of £70,000, an immense sum for those days. His Lordship died at Rothiemay, on the 8th September, 1763. A monument is erected to his memory, and that of Jane Countess of Fife, his wife, in the mausoleum at Duff House.

20. James 2nd Earl of Fife succeeded his father. He was born 29th September, 1729. He was elected Member of Parliament for the County of Banff in 1754, 1761, 1768, 1774, and 1780; and for the County of Elgin in 1784. He was a man of great talents, and nearly doubled the property of the family by judicious purchases of estates. He planted about 14,000 acres of barren ground, and was a great agriculturist, and a most extensive improver of land. His Lordship has had the name of being rather a hard man; but this perhaps arises from the fact that he was very exact and precise in all his accounts and transactions. For, to do him all justice, it must be recorded that in the year 1783, which was a season of famine, he gave his tenants in the Highlands a reduction of 20 per cent. from their rents, and sold his own grain, and imported cargos from England, which he disposed of to the poor, at a personal loss of £3000. He was kind and hospitable to his tenants, and entertained the more respectable of them very frequently at his own table, when he visited his different estates. He was a man of immense political power in the North, and is said, in the year 1784, to have returned the Members for the Counties of Aberdeen, Banff, and Moray. His purchases of land in

Morayshire were great. In 1767 he purchased from the family of Innes of that ilk the extensive and beautiful Estate of Innès, and from cadets of the same family he shortly afterwards acquired the Estates of Inchbroom, Dunkinty, and Leuchars. In 1777 he acquired, by excambion, from the Duke of Gordon, the Lordship of Urquhart, and the lands of Ardgay, Leggat, and part of Kintrae, in the Parishes of Alves and Spynie. Shortly thereafter he bought from the family of Brodie the Estates of Spynie, Monaughty, and Aslisk. He also purchased the Estate of Rosehaugh, in Spynie Parish. In his own and his father's time the large Estates in the Parish of Glass, and Glenbucket, Delgaty, and Braemar, were acquired, and by the death of his brother, Lewis, he succeeded to the Estate of Blervie. His Lordship was Lord-Lieutenant of the County of Banff, and was created a British Peer by the title of Baron Fife, with limitation to the heirs-male of his own body. He married, 5th June, 1769, Lady Dorothea Sinclair, only child of Alexander 9th Earl of Caithness, by whom he had no issue. He died at his house in Whitehall, London, on 28th January, 1809, in the 80th year of his age, and was interred in the mausoleum at Duff House. His British Peerage became extinct. His estates, held in fee simple, he left in trust for certain purposes, and the entailed estates and Irish titles descended to his immediate younger brother, Alexander Duff of Echt.

21. Alexander 3rd Earl of Fife, born 1731, succeeded in 1809, was a member of the Faculty of Advocates, being admitted in 1754. He married, at Careston, 17th August, 1775, Mary, eldest daughter of George Skene of Skene and Careston, by whom he had—James 4th Earl of Fife, Alexander, a General in the army, father of the fifth Earl. Lady Jane, married, on 2nd December, 1802, Major Alexander Francis Tayler, of the 26th Regiment of Foot, by whom there was issue. Lady Anne, married, at Duff House, 16th October, 1809, Richard Wharton Duff, Esq. of Orton, by whom there was also issue. His Lordship died 7th April, 1811, and was succeeded by his eldest son,

22. James 4th Earl, born 6th October, 1776. His Lordship married, at London, 9th September, 1799, Maria Caroline Manners, second daughter of John Manners of

JAMES, THE FIFTH EARL OF FIFE.   169

Grantham Grange, and sister of Louisa Duchess of St. Albans, who died 20th December, 1805, without issue. He entered the Spanish Army, and was wounded at the battle of Talavera, in 1809, and again severely at the storming of Fort Matagorda, near Cadiz, in 1810. He was a great friend and companion of George IV., who created him a Peer of the United Kingdom, by the title of Baron Fife, 27th April, 1827. He was a Knight of the Order of St. Ferdinand of Spain, and of the Sword. Like the rest of his family, his Lordship was a great politician. He succeeded his uncle, Mr. Skene of Skene and Careston, to these fine estates in 1827, a great addition to the fortune of the family. After mixing much in the world, and seeing society in all its ranks and grades, he, in his latter years, lived at Duff House, in a very retired way; died there the 9th March, 1857, and was buried at the mausoleum.

23. James 5th Earl of Fife, nephew to the preceding Earl, and eldest son of General Sir Alexander Duff of Delgaty, succeeded. His Lordship was born 6th July, 1814; is Lord-Lieutenant of the County of Banff, and long represented the same county in Parliament. He was created a Peer of the United Kingdom, by the title of Baron Skene, in 1857. He married, 16th March, 1846, Lady Agnes Georgiana Elizabeth Hay, daughter of William George 17th Earl of Errol, by Lady Elizabeth Fitzclarence, natural daughter of King William IV., and of course cousin to Queen Victoria, and has issue—Alexander William George Viscount Macduff, born 10th November, 1849. 1st daughter, Anne Elizabeth Clementina, born 1847, married, 17th October, 1865, to John Villiers Stuart, fifth and present Marquis Townshend, and has issue. 2nd, Ida Louisa Alice, born 1848, married, 3rd June, 1867, to Adrian Elias Hope, Esq., and has issue. Obtained divorce 1873; married, 2nd, 1880, William Wilson. 3rd, Alexina, born 1851, married 2nd July, 1870, Henry Aubrey Coventry, Lieutenant 10th Hussars. 4th, Agnes Cecil Emmeline, born 20th February, married, 1st, 4th October, 1871, to Viscount Dupplin, and was divorced 1876. She married, 2nd, 5th August, 1876, Herbert Flowers. The Countess of Fife died on the 18th December, 1869, and was buried in the mausoleum of Duff House. His Lordship's brother, the Honourable George Skene Duff of Milton, for

some time represented in Parliament the Elgin District of Burghs, and is now Lord-Lieutenant of the County of Elgin.] (*Young's History of the Parish of Spynie.*)

THE PARISH OF ABERLAURE OR ABERLOUR,

All in the County of Banff, is called also *Skirdrustan*. It extendeth on the bank of Spey, from the mouth of Fiddich, 3 miles to the south-west; and, on all other sides, is environed with hills, and no where above a mile in breadth, except a small skirt in Glenrinnes.

The Church standeth on the bank of the river, where a brook, flowing from the hills towards Mortlach, falleth into it 2 miles north-west of Mortlach, 2 miles near to the west of Boharm, and $3\frac{1}{2}$ miles north-east of Inveravon. At the confluence of Fiddich and Spey, there is a passage-boat, and another at the church. The parish is now the property of five heritors.

In the lower end is Mudhouse, a feu pertaining to Mr. Anderson. Next up the river is the heritage of Gordon of Aberlaure. Further up the river, and on the south-east of the brook, is Alachie. This was the heritage of Alexander Grant, third son of Bellentom, by whose daughter it came in mortgage to Duff of Keithmore, and was lately redeemed by Sir Ludowick Grant, who in 1758 disponed it to James Grant of Carron. In the face of the hill south-west from Alachie, is Edinville. This was the property of Gordon of Faskine, from whom it came to Grant of Easter Elchies, and is now the property of the Earl of Findlater. The lands of Mudhouse, Aberlour, Alachie, and Edinvillie, were a part of the Lordship of Balvenie; and the lands of Carron were Church lands, and now hold of the family of Gordon.

Below Edinvillie towards the side of the river, is the Barony of Kinermonie. This was a part of the Lordship of Balvenie, and given by Innes of Balvenie to his second son, whose heirs exchanged it for Orton, and now it is the property of the Earl of Fife.

In the west end of the parish is Carron, at the foot of the hill of that name. It continued above 200 years the property of a branch of the family of Grant of Glenmoriston, and Colonel John Grant, the last of Carron, being killed before Carthagena anno 1741, without male issue, Charles Grant of Ringorum became the male heir. From him Captain Lewis Grant of Achterblair, a branch of the Clan Allan (and who married Colonel Grant's eldest daughter), purchased his right, and now Captain James Grant, his son, enjoyeth it, and in 1767 was Baron of Mulderie, in the County of Moray.

ABERLOUR.

[*Situation, Soil, Climate.*—Aberlour extends 9 miles from the borders of Inveravon on the west, along the southern bank of the Spey, to the influx of the Fiddich at the east, on the borders of Boharm. There spreading backward about a mile of arable ground, it rises to the summit of the Conval hills, by which it is separated from Mortlach. It gradually increases its breadth to the western frontier, where it is nearly equal to its length.

The narrow vale of Glenrinnes may be regarded as a continuation of the parish of Mortlach. It is detached from the body of this parish by the mountain of Benrinness, between which and the Convals a narrow pass (called Glackharnis) opens a level communication. The brook Dulnan winds in its bottom, and its northern side only appertains to the parish of Aberlour.

The soil upon the river is a light mould upon a bed of sand; and as the country extends back toward the hills, it becomes a deep clay. The climate, on the whole, is temperate; along the river it is warm, and the harvests are more early than in Glenrinness, where there is never occasion to complain for want of rain.

State of Property.—The parish appertains to five proprietors. The only family-seat is Aberlour, the estate of Patrick Gordon, Esq., and the mansion of his ancestors. It is embellished by a garden, enclosed fields, with some natural and some planted wood. The valued rent is £250 Scots.

Edinvillie is the property of David Macdowal Grant of Arndilly. It is also improved by a commodious house, well cultivated fields, and some natural wood. The valued rent is £350.

The estate of Carron is the property of Robert Grant of Elchies, Esq., from which it is separated only by the river. Having been once a family-seat, it still displays a handsome mansion house, gardens, enclosed fields, and plantation. The valued rent is £400.

Except the Earl of Findlater's property of Mudhouse, valued at £50, the rest of the parish appertains to the Earl of Fife, at the valuation of £1167; extending the total valuation of the parish to £2217 Scots.

There are several farms of considerable extent, from £40 to about £70 sterling of rent: but the parish is generally occupied in small possessions, from about £5 to about £16 sterling of rent; and the mean rent of the acre may be estimated at 14s.

State Ecclesiastical.—The ancient name of the parish was *Skirdurstan*, literally St. Durstan's shire or division, from the original Gaelic, signifying to cut, there being no word in that language answering more nearly to that of parish.

The church, a mean ancient fabric, is situated near the influx of a considerable and rumbling stream, as its present appellation imports.

The stipend is £58 6s. 8d. and 18 bolls of meal. The glebe is about 6 acres, of which nearly 5 are under the plough. The Earl of Fife is the patron.

In the valley of Glenrinness there is a missionary establishment for the accommodation of the remote extremities of Aberlour and Mortlach, with an appointment by the Royal Bounty of £30 yearly. The school is in the vicinity of the church, a commodious building, floored and finished within. The landholders of the parish have been in the use of paying to Mr. Hall, the present incumbent, about £11 sterling of salary, which, with £1 as the fee of the session-clerk, and the perquisites of that office, and the customary rates of payment, makes the appointment equal to about £20 yearly, as the school retains about 30 scholars.

The Society for Christian Knowledge once established a school in Glenrinness, adding thereby a great accommodation to that sequestered district; but the landholders refusing to countenance the establishment, by the petty conveniences which the rules of the Society require, it has been for some time wholly withdrawn.

The number of the poor enrolled is 21 : the provision for their support arises from the money contributed by the people who attend the church, about £5 yearly ; and sundry bequeathments, with savings by the session in times of plenty, have created a fund at interest producing yearly £4 8s. and 3½ bolls of meal, and a small sum retained for answering urgent exigencies. The members of the national Church are 910, and the Dissenters 11 (of the Church of Rome).

Miscellaneous Information.— On the stream (the Burn of Aberlour), which passes by the church, a little farther up, there is a pretty water-fall (the Linn of Ruthrie), of consideration in this quarter of the country. The stream precipitates itself from a height of 30 feet, and, broken in its fall, dashes into a gloomy circular pool of unknown depth [?], environed by a rocky mound more than twice the height of the fall. The bason below is easily accessible; and the surrounding rock, by reverberating, increases greatly the din.

The people, with anticipated satisfaction, contemplate two great promised accommodations—a post office at Aberlour, and a bridge over the Spey, a little farther up than the church. By these, it is certain, the state of the country all around will, in a short time, be improved in a variety of circumstances, beyond what could be at present believed.

The sentiments and manners of the people are in no respect different from those of their neighbours in the adjoining parishes.]—(*Survey of the Province of Moray.*)

THE ABERLOUR SUCCESSION CASE.

The action at the instance of Mrs. and Mr. Yeatman against the trustees of the late Miss Macpherson Grant of Aberlour came on for trial upon the 28th Dec., 1877, in the Second Division of the Court of Session before the Lord Justice-Clerk (Moncrieff) and a jury.

The pursuers in the case were Mrs. Charlotte Temple or Yeatman, residing at West Lodge, Iwerne Minster, Blandford, spouse of Harry Farr Yeatman of West Lodge aforesaid, retired commander Royal Navy, and the said Harry Farr Yeatman as administrator in law for his said spouse and for his own interest. The defenders were James Proctor, residing in Tarland; Margaret Proctor, residing in Banchory; and Alex Proctor, Bachelor of Medicine, Rhynie, all in the county of Aberdeen; and John Falconer, S.S.C., Edinburgh, sole accepting trustee under the trust disposition and settlement of the now deceased Miss Margaret Gordon Macpherson Grant of Aberlour, dated 8th March, 1873.

The purpose of the action was to reduce a deed of revocation executed by Miss Macpherson Grant on 2nd November, 1876, whereby she revoked all her previous settlements, and in particular the settlement dated 8th March, 1873. The effect of the deed of revocation, if allowed to stand, was to throw Miss Macpherson Grant's large fortune, amounting to upwards of a quarter of a million, into intestacy, and to allow the defenders, Mr. James Proctor and Miss Margaret Proctor, to succeed to the moveable estate, which was the most valuable; and also to allow the defender, Mr. Alex. F. Proctor, to succeed to the heritable estate, as Miss Macpherson Grant's heir-at-law. If the deed of revocation was reduced, and the settlement of 8th March, 1873, allowed to stand, the result would have been that the female pursuer practically succeeded to the whole of Miss Macpherson Grant's means, with the exception of £9500 of legacies.

For the pursuers there appeared the Lord Advocate, Mr. Fraser, and Mr. Pearson, instructed by Messrs. Boyd, Macdonald, & Co., S.S.C. For the heirs *in mobilibus* there appeared Mr. Balfour and Mr. Macintosh, instructed by Mr. T. J. Gordon, W.S. For the heir-at-law there appeared Mr. Asher and Mr. C. J. Guthrie, instructed by Messrs. Gibson-Craig, Dalziel, and Brodies, W.S.

The issues laid before the jury were:—

(1) Whether said deed of revocation is not the deed of the deceased Miss Macpherson Grant.

(2) Whether, at the date of said deed, Miss Macpherson Grant was weak and facile in mind, and easily imposed upon, and whether Simon Keir, tenant of Burnside, Duffus, by Elgin, taking advantage of her weakness and facility, did, by fraud or circumvention, impetrate and obtain the said deed of revocation from the said Miss Macpherson Grant, to her lesion?

A third issue had been proposed by the pursuers but disallowed by the Court—viz., Whether in granting said deed of revocation Miss Macpherson Grant was under essential error as to the import and effect?

Mr. Fraser opened the case for the pursuers. He said that Miss Macpherson Grant was the daughter of Dr. Macpherson, and succeeded as heiress to her uncle, Alexander Grant, who died in 1854. Miss Grant bought the estate of Lauriston, near Edinburgh. She sometimes made journeys to London, and in 1864 she was introduced there to Miss Temple, the female pursuer, the daughter of the High Sheriff of the county of Wilts. Miss Grant died on 14th April, 1877, between the age of 40 and 50. In 1864 Miss Temple came to Aberlour on a visit. She turned ill and remained there from the autumn till spring of 1865. The intimacy ripened into the warmest friendship. Miss Temple having determined to terminate her visit to Aberlour, came back to her father's residence, where she remained for some weeks, when she received a telegram from Miss Grant, asking her to come up to London. She went, and the friendship was resumed. Miss Grant went to see Miss Temple's friends at that time. Her father and mother are now dead, but you will hear from herself what was then proposed. It was that Miss Grant beseeched Miss Temple's parents to let her take their daughter to live with her and adopt her, and make her her heiress, she loved her so much. The parents paused a little, but were at length overcome by Miss Grant's entreaties, and Miss Temple agreed to go. I don't say there was a contract whereby Miss Grant, on the footing of Miss Temple going to live with her was to make her her heiress, but there was plainly an honourable understanding, which was immediately carried out. She went to her London solicitors, and directed them to prepare a will, which was done. By that will, executed in 1865, Miss Grant conveyed to trustees the whole of her means and estates for the purpose of paying certain legacies. But there was a previous will by which the whole of her property would have gone to the Episcopal Church. By the will of 1865 the trustees are directed to convey her estates to her own issue, and failing them to Miss Temple and her heirs. She first directs that the whole estate shall be entailed, and all her money was to be spent in purchasing other lands to be entailed on the same series of heirs. She thus contemplated having issue herself. After her own issue the estate was to go to an old aunt, Margaret Gordon, and failing her and her issue to Miss Temple. That was the carrying out of the expressed intention of Miss Grant. That deed was executed in London. She goes to the office and brings out the pen to Miss Temple, who was waiting in the carriage, saying to her, "Do you know what I have been doing? I have been making you my heir, and here is the pen I did it with; keep it!" Down to 1866 Miss Temple lived with Miss Grant, aiding her in all her schemes, comforting her in her sorrows, and nursing her in sicknesses, which were many. Miss Temple's will remained untouched. By it she gave the estate of Lauriston to her father. Her aunt died in 1866, and her father in 1871. It then became necessary for Miss Grant to rearrange her will so as to make a distribution of her estate consistent with the altered state of things, for if riches confer great privileges, they also entail great responsibilities and cares.

In 1872 a new will is made by her on 31st May, also prepared by her London solicitors, in which the legacies are still continued. As to the residue of her estate, she directed her trustees to convey the same to her own issue, whom failing Miss Temple and her heirs, whom failing Miss Temple's nephew. Miss Grant's Scotch lawyers, on seeing the deed, thought it not suitable to convey the estate according to Scotch law. Miss Grant then got very restless about the matter. She writes to her Elgin agent requesting him to communicate with her London solicitor and also her Edinburgh solicitor, as she wished the matter put beyond all question. Messrs. Gibson-Craig & Co. were employed to make the new will, and it was executed on 8th March, 1873. By the will Miss Grant directs her trustees, to whom her whole property was conveyed in trust, to pay a legacy of £20,000 to Miss Temple, so as to provide against the contingency of her not succeeding to the estate by the resistance of any heirs of Miss Grant's own body. Then she provides that the heirs of entail shall assume the name and arms of Grant of Aberlour. This deed of 1873 was found with her representatives after her death. Miss Temple under it would now have been entitled to a conveyance of the whole of the properties. Miss Grant lived till 1877, and it is in reference to what she did three years after this deed that this inquiry has taken place. On 2nd November, 1876, a few weeks before she died, she executed a deed of revocation, revoking her settlements, and in particular the deed of 1873. The whole arrangements of this lady for the distribution of her estate were revoked. All the legacies she left were cancelled, and all her charitable bequests, which were made by separate deeds, go to the door. The whole of the lady's fortune is to be distributed, according to the rules of common law, amongst the next of kin and the heir. The defenders are persons excavated from obscurity, so far as Miss Grant was concerned. They happen by the accidence of existence to be nearest of kin by the father's side, but these were just about the last persons in the world upon whom she would have wished to bestow her fortune. Miss Grant's father was in a somewhat lower social position than her mother was, and it was the mother's brother who made the fortune, and he never liked the father or his connections, and that feeling seemed to have been handed down to the daughter. After getting her fortune, Miss Grant seemed to have given reins to herself. She got into a habit of tippling to a large extent, drinking not merely wine, but beer and brandy—a bottle and a half of brandy a-day sometimes. Miss Temple used arguments to wean her from that, and appealed to her self-respect, but without avail. She hid her failings when she could, and when she could not did her best to do so. On 11th December, 1875, there occurred an incident which had a most important effect upon any intellect Miss Grant then had. That was a fire which occurred in Aberlour House. She got so terrified and frightened she seemed to think there was a hole in her head, and asked people to look for it. She got her hair clipped sometimes twice a-day. She beseeched her attendants to look for the hole. She also thought that she had saved her servant from the fire and had carried her out. Another thing came to add to the misfortune. Miss Temple got married in February, 1876, and this was a great blow to Miss Grant. The deed of November, 1876, was written by Simon Keir, a London merchant. He calls himself tenant of Burnside. He was factor for Miss Grant's Jamaica estates. The produce of these estates was sent home, and sold by Milne and Co., who were appointed her agents in February, 1870. Mr. Keir, who was a partner of Milne & Co., had to account for the produce, and he had been doing so by sending accounts direct to Miss Grant. She was not a business woman, and this was troublesome. Miss Temple, a month before her marriage, wrote to Mr. Keir stating that she was going to be married, and that Miss Grant desired him in future to correspond with Mr. Falconer, W.S., Edinburgh, regarding the Jamaica estates, instead of with Milne & Co., and to send his accounts to Mr. Falconer. That was not agreeable to Mr. Keir. Miss Grant never wrote herself. If anything was to be written it was done by a maid, after Miss Temple left. In November, 1876, Mr. Keir comes down to Aberlour, and gets her to put her name to a deed of revocation. What arguments he used to operate upon that diseased and decayed mind we cannot know. This gentleman gets the document drawn out, and gets her to sign it. There is nothing more difficult than to dive into human motives for the reason of a man's conduct. We are driven to judge by the fair or the tortuous means adopted. What are the facts here? This lady was a person perfectly capable of paying for legal advice, who had got her three wills prepared by solicitors, and had a country agent at Elgin. Miss Grant goes on from bad to worse, from November 1876 to April 1877, till the whole scene closes. It is for you to determine the preparation of this new deed.

At the close of his address Mr. Fraser asked to be allowed to retire for a few minutes. Leave having been granted, counsel for the parties retired. After upwards of an hour they returned into Court, when

The Lord Advocate stated that parties had agreed upon terms of settlement, and in respect of that agreement, he asked his lordship to discharge the jury.

The Lord Justice-Clerk thereupon relieved the jury from further attendance.

The minute of settlement is in the following terms:—

The parties agree to compromise the case on the following terms:—

1. That a minute be lodged in process withdrawing on behalf of the pursuers and their children their grounds of action and all charges or imputations against Mr. Simon Keir, and consent to absolvitor, neither party being found entitled to expenses—the terms of the minute to be adjusted by the Lord Advocate and Mr. Asher.

2. The defenders shall pay to the pursuers the sum of £10,000, and the pursuers may elect to take the gold watch presented by Mrs. Yeatman to the late Miss Macpherson Grant, and a diamond star belonging to the latter, at a valuation— the value to be deducted from said £10,000.

3. All other legal proceedings in which the pursuers impeach the validity of the deed of revocation by Miss Grant of 2nd November, 1876, to be withdrawn—neither party being entitled to costs of suit.

Judgment was then pronounced in terms of this minute.

The Aberlour Succession Case thus came to a sudden end or collapse. Neither party to the litigation, which at one time threatened to be a long, a troublesome, and a costly one, deemed it necessary to prolong the conflict as to the intentions of Miss Macpherson Grant, and a compromise was entered into. In the language of Mr. Patrick Fraser (said newspapers of the time), three individuals of the name of Proctor have been "excavated from obscurity" and inherit, by the law of intestate succession, money and lands exceeding in value a quarter of a million. A certain Mrs. Yeatman, formerly Miss Temple, who, but for the friendship and regard and rather curious love of the deceased proprietrix of Aberlour, of several West India estates, and of large investments in the Three Per Cents., would undoubtedly never have arisen from that "obscurity" her counsel so kindly assigns to Miss Grant's next of kin—this Mrs. Yeatman receives £10,000; a poor sum in comparison with her expectations and her demands—not too large a sum by which to buy off a suitor to £300,000. The Episcopal Church of Scotland which had at one time—through the agency of its Primus, Bishop Eden, and the Rev. Charles Jupp, Incumbent of Aberlour—no small "hopes" of benefiting largely by the lady's death, was not even cut off with the proverbial shilling. Even the public were denied the full revelation of a curious, an interesting, and instructive romance, and were forbidden to inquire into a history that does not altogether reflect credit on several of the principal actors. They were foreclosed from a narrative, and particularly from certain correspondences, that, had the suit been closely pressed, must have come under the eye of the public, and told tales better fitted to humiliate than to edify. Mrs. Yeatman may in a sense be regarded as coming off with flying colours. Being *pursuer* in the lawsuit, her counsel had the advantage of making an opening statement of her case to the jury, only after which was the compromise negotiated. It was speedily concluded and immediately acted upon, but the other side had, of course, no opportunity of presenting their case. The "move" was an adroit one, and in its artistic effect might have been regarded as remarkably successful, had it not been that the allegations of the next of kin had already become pretty well known. By Mr. Fraser's eloquence, Mrs. Yeatman was depicted as Injured Innocence; according to the pleadings in the case, she has been held up by the next of kin as the Incarnation of Mischief. According to her own story, she only left her parents' home to dwell with Miss Macpherson Grant at that lady's request, and with the promise that she was to be made her heir. The contrary theory is that Miss Temple's continued and prolonged stay with Miss Grant was due to "mutual consent," and that something like a marriage had taken place between them. Each pledged herself to celibacy; Miss Grant "married" Miss Temple, placing on the latter's marriage-finger a suitable ring, and thenceforth designating her "Charley;" Miss Temple not only reciprocated the extraordinary affection, but likewise manifested similar extraordinary proofs of it—she termed herself "Wifie" in her letters to Miss Grant, she addressed the latter as "Jamie," and in short, a lot of remarkable tomfoolery went on between the two. It is this that constitutes the romance, the history of which—at least the investigation of which—is denied the public.

But what promised to be a *cause celebre* had been suddenly stopped, and the public have been denied the gratification of their "sensational" instincts, and certain exposures that would point many a moral and adorn many a tale have been withheld. One of the leading ecclesiastic characters had been dubbed by a probable witness—"a d——d Jesuit;" certain personages would, in all likelihood, have had to pass a *mauvais quart d'heure* in the witness-box; and a general picture would have been presented, containing a good deal of light and shade. From entering into these matters we are, however, practically foreclosed; and it will be sufficient, in a few words, to indicate the end of the "romance" as already made known. The "pact of celibacy"—if it did exist—was only kept on one side. Miss Temple, while charged with screening her "partner" from all possible suitors—even with cutting off her intercourse with friends and relations—herself succumbed to the charms of Captain Yeatman, and in due time became his wedded wife. An estrangement ensued between her and Miss Grant, and the latter substituted as her "companion" a young girl who fulfilled the capacity of maid. The latter days of the muscular, active, "strong-minded" lady of Aberlour form a sorrowful picture, on either alternative of the theories and allegations as to her habits. On the one side, it is said that she was rendered irritable by reflection on Miss Temple's breach of faith—her confidence in her quondam friend having been such that she refused a good offer of marriage, and the ultimate revulsion of feeling leading her to make a declaration that thenceforth she should cease to believe in religious people. On the other side, it was freely asserted that Miss Macpherson Grant became a victim to drink—that her abstention for years from tea and coffee, and her habitual practice of taking liquor six times a day had ultimately broken down her constitution, and produced her death before she had attained her 50th year. There were not wanting indications that Miss Macpherson Grant was opposed to the estate of Aberlour passing to Miss Temple and to her "brats of children"—as the "strong-minded" but none the less highly respected proprietrix of that fine Speyside property designated them; and on this ground alone, if on no other, the settlement was for the better and not for the worse, in behalf of "distant poor relations."—(*Local Newspapers.*)

Near the influx of the Burn of Aberlour, on the daugh of Allachie, stand the roofless walls of the old Church, bought by Grant of Elchies from the other heritors; and about 300 yards farther to the east, on the same plain, is the new Church, erected in 1812, accidentally burnt down by the overheating of the flue in the beginning of 1861, excepting the belfry and tower, which were built in 1840 by Grant of Aberlour. A still more elegant Church has since been erected. An old font, formed from a rude block of mica-schist, lies in the churchyard. It is large enough to immerse infants. The basin is 2 ft. wide by 1½ ft. deep. An imbecile person, who was rescued from suicide in the Spey, was kept one night within the Church for safety, and was found drowned in the font.

When the churchyard was recently enlarged and walled in at the expense of Miss Macpherson-Grant, the old manse and offices were removed, and a door-lintel was found having the initials M. R. S., and date of 1672. These correspond with the time of Mr. Robert Stephen, who was minister of Aberlour from 1669 until his death in 1705. His son, who was appointed his assistant and successor, was translated to Craig, in Forfarshire, in 1714.

EPITAPHS IN ABERLOUR CHURCHYARD.

I. The following tombstone relates to Mr. Stephen's immediate predecessor :—

Sub. spe. Beatæ. Resurrectionis. Hic. Requiescit. GEORGIUS.
SPEED. Pius. Doctus. Fidus. Pastor. Parochiæ. Aberlourensis.
Quam. Voto. Voce. Et. Vita. Diligenter. Instruxit. Annos. 28.
Et. Grandi. Piam. Expiravit. Animam. A. Æ. C. 1688. Sobrie.
Juste. Pie. Vixit. Haec. Tria. Perpetuo. Meditare. Adverbia.
Pauli. Hæc. Tria. Sint. Vitæ. Regula. Sancta. Tuæ. GEORGIUS.
Et MARGARITA. SPEEDII. Inhumantur. Hac. Tendimus. Omnes.
—M. G. S.

Translation.—Here resteth, in the hope of a blessed resurrection, GEORGE SPEED, a pious, learned, and faithful minister of the parish of Aberlour, which he diligently instructed for 28 years, by vow, voice, and life. He breathed out his pious spirit in 1688, at an advanced age. He lived soberly, justly, and piously. On these adverbs of Paul ever meditate. Be these three of thy life the sacred rule. GEORGE and MARGARET SPEED are interred here. Here we all tend.—MARGARET and GEORGE SPEED.

George Speed was schoolmaster at Keith in 1631, and afterwards at Fordyce. He became minister of Aberlour about 1640, and died in 1668. He provided that he should be buried in the churchyard, and not below the pulpit, as had long been the practice; quaintly remarking that, if laid there, "The rest o' the Aberlour folk at the last day would be o'er the hill o' Taminruie (an eminence between Aberlour and Craigellachie) afore he got oot o' the kirk."

II. A burial aisle, in the Perpendicular style of architecture, erected over the bodies of her father and mother by the late Miss Macpherson-Grant of Aberlour, adds considerably to the beauty of the churchyard. Here is also laid herself, who died 14th April, 1877, æt. 43.

III. A freestone monument in the north dyke, upon which the Innes and Barclay arms are carved, has :—
W. I : E. B : 1664.
WILLIAM INNES OF KINNERMONI CAWSED BVILD THIS TOMB IN THIS REMOTE PLACE FOR HIMSELF AND ELIZABETH BARCLAY HIS SPOVS, THAT NON MIGHT HAVE OCCASION TO RAIS THEIR BONES, AND WE REST HEIR IN HOPE OF THE RESURRECTION OF OVR BODIES [2 COR. v. 10.]
ANNA INNES, DAVGHTER TO THE SAID WILLIAM INNES, LYES HEIR, WHO DIED VNMARRIED THE 22 OF NOVEMBER, 1663.

No mention of the above laird of Kinermonie or his

wife is in the "Account of the Family of Innes," but, according to Douglas' *Baronage*, he was the second son of Sir Robert Innes of Balveny; and when the third baronet died, the succession devolved upon Walter, son of William Innes of Kinermonie. He became fourth baronet, and through him the line of the family was carried on. William Innes of Kinermonie mortified £350 Scots for the behoof of the poor of the parish.

The property of Kinermonie (anciently Kyneremonet) "was a part of the lordship of Balvenie, and was given by Innes of Balvenie to his second son, whose heir exchanged it for Ortown, and now (1775) it is the property of the Earl of Fife." The Knights Templars held the superiority of Kinermonie, where, continues Shaw, "are the walls of an old Gothic house; and the tradition of the country is that it was a religious house, and that all the religious in it were massacred in one night."

IV. From a slab, also in the kirkyard dyke:—

HIC ET INTUS EX OPPOSITO JACENT CINERES PROGENITOR .... ALEXANDRI GRANT DE RUDRIE. .... TEMPLUM SUB DUOBUS HIS .... CONDUNTUR EXUVIÆ JANETÆ GRANT, QUI CONJUGIS FILIÆ HELENÆ GRANT, DI .... JOANNIS LIBERORUM .... QUO .... HOC MONUMENTUM EXTRUENDUM CURAVIT SUPRA DESIGNAT ... ALEXANDRI.

Translation.—Here and within opposite lie the ashes of the ancestors of Alexander Grant of Rudrie. Inside the church, under these two stones, are interred the remains of Janet Grant, spouse of John Grant, and of her daughter Helen Grant, to whose memory the above-mentioned Alexander caused this monument to be erected.

Alexander Grant of Rudrie was probably one of the Grants of Allachie, and may have been related to the wife of Duff of Keithmore. The property of Ruthrie, now Lord Fife's, lies to the south of the church. The Burn of Aberlour runs past Ruthrie, and when in flood "the Linn of Ruthrie" becomes a romantic and picturesque waterfall.

V. From a flat stone:—

Opposite to this .... interred Isabel ..... ton, spous to Alexr. Martin in Aberlour, and their children, William and Margaret. She died Nov. 8, 1758, aged 63, and they in infancy.

VI. The next inscription probably refers to a descendant of the above :—

Pat. Martin, mason, Aberlour, d. 24th, and his wf., Elspet Stewart, on 29th Ap., 1780, a. 66.65. "They lived in, and was the first that inhabited, Gownie of Aberlour":—

    Twice 19 years they lived man and wife,
    Betwixt them there was heard no strife;
    In love they liv'd, both in one week did die,
    And in one grave both here they lie.

By their son, William Martin, china merchant in London.

Alexander Moir and son John (1775-6) :—

    No wonder tho' men do turn to clay
    When rocks, and stones, and monuments do decay.

And Robert Moir, late farmer in Sockach of Glenrinnes, son of the aforesaid Alexander Moir, who died January, 1800, aged 40, and his wife, Helen Stuart, who died February, 1820, aged 55.

VII. From an adjoining stone :—

Erected by Robert Gordon of Polduie in memory of Helen Green, his beloved spouse, who died May 14, 1791, in the 38 year of her age. A Patern of Virtue; remarkable for hospitality and charity; respected and lamented by all her acquaintances.

VIII. Abridged from a table-shaped stone :—

John Green and Elizabeth Stewart at Edinvillie had 8 sons and 3 daughters. John Green died at Shindow in 1798, aged 79, and his widow at Rinnachat in 1808, aged 82. Their son William, farmer, Ruthrie, and his wife, Helen Stewart, died in 1833, aged 73 and 63 respectively, having had 7 sons and four daughters.

Members of this family (an ancestor of whom bequeathed £66 13s. 4d. to the poor) still occupy the farm of Ruthrie, and are also bank agents in Aberlour.

IX. The next inscription possibly refers to John Proctor, who (Shaw says) left £66 13s. 4d. Scots to the poor of Aberlour :—

JOHN PROCTOR, LATE POSSESSOR IN SAUCHENBURN, HATH PUT ON THESE TWO GRAVESTONES UPON THIS BURIAL PLACE, WHERE HIS DECEAST PARENTS, WIFE AND CHILDREN LYETH.

These were probably ancestors of Mr. Proctor, Sheriff-

Substitute of Moray, who married a daughter of Gordon of Leitcheston. Their only son, Patrick Proctor of Halkerton, near Forfar, referred to in Sir Walter Scott's "Demonology" as the seneschal of Glamis Castle, was widely known. He and his son William were for about 90 years factors for the Earl of Strathmore, and the eldest son, John, was some time farmer of East Calcots, near Elgin. One of Sheriff Proctor's daughters, Isobel, married John Nicoll, corn merchant, Lossiemouth. Their son was Principal Nicoll of St. Andrews, who was the leader of the Church of Scotland, along with Dr. John Inglis, father of the present Lord Justice Clerk, for the ten years following the death of Principal Hill, in 1820.

X. Margt. Dick sp. to Jas. Grant, d. 1779 :—
She was the virtuous woman described in Prov. 31. The loving wife and affectionate mother. The pains she took in showing her children the beauties of a pious and virtuous life, and her charity to the poor and those in distress, leave no cause to doubt of her soul being in glory. This stone is deservedly erected to her memory by her husband.

XI. A tombstone to the memory of John Findlay Gownie of Aberlour, who died in 1813, aged 73, bears to have been erected or "done by his Natural Daughter, Margaret Findlay."

XII. Abridged from a stone within an enclosure :—
Rev. Wm. Grant, minister of Duthil, died 22d Aug., 1862, aged 76. Called to the ministry at the age of 24, he discharged his duties for 52 years. Mary Garioch, his wife, daughter of Dr. James Garioch, Old Meldrum, died 1866, aged 76.

Mr. Grant was previously at Kirkmichael. He was an able scholar and minister, and liberal in endowing from his own resources educational institutions in his own parish, &c. His brother-in-law, Mr. Garioch, of Old Meldrum, who seceded at the Disruption, was a liberal benefactor to the Free Church. (*Jerrise's Epitaphs.*)

As in many other parts of Scotland, the parish of Aberlour was divided into *Daughs* or Davachs, which were certain districts which were either under cultivation or capable of being so. As such they were assessable for public burdens, and, according to their extent, were also bound to furnish soldiers in time of war. The names of these seven Davachs are still preserved, viz., Aberlour (including Charlestown), Allachie, Carron, Drumfurrich, Edinvillie, Kinnermony, and Ruthrie.

The Village of Charlestown of Aberlour was founded about 1812 by Charles Grant of Elchies. He claimed descent from Patrick, 2nd son of James Grant of that ilk, who, in the time of Charles II., sided with the Parliament, while his clan joined the King. One of the family, who is said to have fought under Dundee at Killiecrankie (1689), was presented by the Viscount with a *snuff-mull*, silver-mounted, now at Elchies, having this inscription: "*Presented to John Grant Roy, laird of Ballindalloch, by Viscount Dundee.*" Charlestown was created a Burgh of Barony in 1814, and has a population of 501. The heritors of the parish are the Earl of Fife, Dr. Proctor of Aberlour House, and Henry Alexander Grant of Wester Elchies.

Sir Thomas Dick Lauder, in his "Moray Floods," gives affecting details of the sad catastrophe which befel Charles Cruickshanks in the memorable August of 1829.

The Manse of Aberlour, beautiful for site, was then inundated, and, in the consternation, the cellar was drained in more ways than one by some obliging hands. Part of the glebe was swept away.

Aberlour House is an elegant modern mansion of three storeys, with wings, built in the Grecian Doric. It stands on an eminence above the public highway and railway. A great portion was accidentally burnt down on the 11th Dec., 1875. A column with a stone globe on its summit, erected by Mr. Grant in 1839, in front of the mansion ominously fell prior to the event. The old house, formerly the seat of Gordons, who were Roman Catholics, stands to the eastward. The former proprietor, James Gordon, who had two thumbs on one hand, got involved in bankruptcy, chiefly by trafficking in a distillery. Latterly he resided in Fochabers until his death. An upright headstone, having a cross indented, marks his grave in the churchyard of Aberlour.

Carron House is situated about 3 miles from the village of Aberlour, on a choice haugh between the railway and the Spey. Graceful birches adorn the surrounding slopes, and the modern unpretending mansion is so embowered as to render it invisible till quite nigh. William Grant of

Wester Elchies resided here. Spalding details the gallant deeds of James Grant of Carron, known as James-au-Tuam, *i.e.*, James of the hill, who was a free-booter and an outlaw. In 1630 there dwelt at Carron a branch of the Grants of Glenmorriston, and at Ballindalloch there was a rival stock. Frequent raids were made upon the possessions of Ballindalloch. Roused by these and other assaults, Grant of Ballindalloch, hearing that John Grant of Carron and some of his vassals were in the Forest of Abernethy cutting timber, assassinated him, on the presumption that this John Grant was a partizan of his clansman, James-au-Tuam. The Earl of Moray, as Lord Lieutenant, tried to vindicate the rights of Ballindalloch, and "made a paction with three broken men to gar one devil ding another." James-au-Tuam was captured after another daring assail, and lay a prisoner in Edinburgh Castle for nearly two years, from which he escaped by means of ropes which his wife secreted in a cask of butter. Other desperate conflicts ensued between the two clans. Near the head of the Drum of Carron is shown the cave where this scion of Carron concealed himself from his pursuers, and this hiding-place was subsequently the resort of another renowned free-booter, James Macpherson, a famous fiddler, who was executed at the Cross of Banff, on the 16th Nov., 1700.

"Roy's wife of Aldivalloch" (sung to a Gaelic air, "An Caimbeallach dudh"), has the accepted authorship of Mrs. Grant of Carron, to mark her from another of the same, viz., Mrs. Grant of Laggan. The maiden name of the former authoress was Grant. She was born about the '45 near Aberlour, and was twice married, first to her cousin, Grant of Carron, about 1763; secondly to Dr. Murray, a physician in Bath, a famous flute-player and an Irishman. She died there in 1814, and the inspiriting ballad is her sole production known. Like most unique rhymes, the original has been contorted by modern reformers, by way of improvement.

Benrinnes, having a twin-shaped summit called "the Skurrins," is chiefly in the parish of Aberlour, although it extends to that of Inveravon. It rises steeply above the level of the sea 2,747 feet, and 1,876 feet above its very broad base. It is the highest mountain in the district, and, in a clear day, can be descried from the top

BENRINNES; ST. DROSTAN'S MONASTERY. 189

the Grampians on the south, and the mountains of Ross, Sutherland, and Caithness on the north and east, portions of nine counties far separated, from Caithness to Dumbarton. It also commands a view of the sea for many miles along the coasts of Moray and Banff, being a landmark to mariners. On the east shoulder there are a spring, which sometimes developes into a small pond, and a sort of cave wherein James-au-Tuam made his covert, hence his cognomen *James of the Hill.*

The *Lynn of Ruthrie*, a short way up the Burn of Aberlour, is a pretty cascade, and has a fall of about 30 feet, broken in its descent by a projecting rock, and received into a gloomy pool below. The wood-covered rocks rising above the waterfall, and reverberating its sound, contribute to the interest of the scene. The House of Ruthrie is in the immediate vicinity.

The prebendary of Aberlour was bound to provide a deacon to serve as his substitute in the Cathedral Church at Elgin. In 1238, "Andrew, canon of Abyrlouer," is one of the prebendaries who adhibit their signatures to the constitutions for the service of the Cathedral. On the 2nd Aug., 1473, Thomas of Saint Clair or Sinclair, is prebendary of Abirlour. On the 23rd Oct., 1487, and on the 8th May, 1489, Master Alexander Sutherland is prebendary of Abirlour. (*Regist. Episc. Moravien.*)

From *Brockie's M.S.*, p. 3,754, in the Library of Blairs College, near Aberdeen, it is stated that the monastery of S. Drostan, commonly Kil Drostan, now Aberlour, was situated on the right bank of the River Spey, where at the present day is S. Drostan's Church, in which formerly the relics of the Saint were garnished and kept with great veneration. S. Drostan was descended from the Kings of Scotland, was a scholar of S. Columba at Iona, and was sent to evangelize the people on the Spey, in the north of Scotland, where he fixed his monastery about A.D. 618. In the archives of the Scotch College of S. James, at Ratisbon, there is an old catalogue of monasteries in which occurs this ancient Monastery of Drostan, and in which it is stated that S. Drostan was sent to the north from Iona by Abbot Fergnus in A.D. 618. Camerarius places "S. Drostan, Abbot and Confessor," opposite the 11th July. Fordun says that the mother of this saint was S. Tynewenna, or, as she is also named, Monenna, or Modenna, and that Conrad; the son of the King of Demecia, married her, and that S. Drostan was their offspring. S. Tynewenna (according to Usserius) built seven churches in Scotland for holy women—1. Kilcase in Galloway; 2. Dundevenel, on the top of the hill; 3. Dumbarton; 4. Stirling, in the Castle; 5. Edinburgh; 6. Dunpelder, or Dunpeller, or Dunpenderlan, in East Lothian, where S. Kentigern was born; 7. Langfortin, near Alyth, in Angus.

S. Margaret's (Episcopal) Church was built in 1876 at a cost of £10,000. A small part of the nave was defrayed by Grant of Carron and the late Miss Macpherson-Grant, whose sudden death was a great loss. Had she lived the gain to the Episcopal Communion would have been great indeed. The nave was completed, and the chancel and transepts added by the Rev. Charles Jupp, the present and first incumbent. *The Orphanage, Convalescent Home, and Servants' Training Institution*, stand under the shade of S. Margaret's, in about 10 acres of land. The approach is very fine, and the grounds are tastefully laid out. There are also elegant schools and parsonage.

At Bateshaugh, in this parish, Mrs. Glass or Sellar died in March, 1876, aged 102 years.] (ED.)

I now proceed up the river to

THE PARISH OF INVERAVON.

Here I must trace the rivers of Avon and Livat that water this parish. The river Avon riseth out of a lake of that name, about 2 miles in length, situated in a deep valley between two of the highest hills in the kingdom, viz., Cairngorm and Cairngormloi; and running through Glenavon, and the parishes of Kirkmichael and Inveravon, it emptieth into Spey at Ballendallach, after a course of about 20 miles.

About 3 miles above the mouth of Avon, Livat

falleth into it, which rising in the hills towards Strathdon, watereth Glenlivat for 7 or 8 miles, and mixeth with Avon at Drumin. Both these waters are very impetuous; and Avon is so clear and deceiving, that, where to the eye it appeareth but a foot deep, it is commonly more than 3 feet.*

* The river Avon issues in a large stream from its loch in the very bosom of the Cairngorm mountains with so great pellucidity through its deep and narrow glen, that many accidents have occurred to strangers by its appearing fordable in places which proved to be of fatal depth. Hence the doggerel: "The water of Aven runs so clear, It would beguile a man of a hundred year." Loch Avon is surrounded by frightful precipices, rising on all sides, sheer up, almost to the very ridges of those towering heaps which are now admitted to be higher than any land in Great Britain. Nothing in our island can approach so near to the wilder and more savage parts of Swiss scenery. Cairngorm and Beinbainac rise almost perpendicularly from its northern and western edges; and the vast foundations of Benmacdui and Bein-main overhang its southern extremity, in frightful masses, that seem as if poised for immediate projection into the valley; so that, for several of the winter months, the sun never shines on the surface of the lake. These are the sources of the pure and transparent Avon, the glaciers which hang in their ample bosoms furnishing exhaustless supplies to its stream, by means of the cataracts they continually pour down into it. All traces of man are lost amid the grandeur of these regions. No tree or shrub is to be seen; and no living creature, save when the eagle soars from the verge of the cliff athwart the vacant ether, awakening the echoes with his scream; or when the ptarmigan flutters its low flight across the mountain brow; or perhaps when some straggling deer from the Forest of Mar, "That from the hunter's aim hath ta'en a hurt, may come to languish." How terribly grand would have been the feelings excited in the bosom of him who could have sat on the 4th of August, 1829, by the side of that solitary lake, to have beheld each furrow in the faces of the frowning cliffs converted into a separate cataract! How sublime their mingled sound, as they blended with the howling of the storm, the hoarse murmur of the agitated lake, and the chilling splash of the sheeted rain, heightened as these effects would have been by

ST. PETER'S CHURCH, INVERAVON.

This parish is very extensive, running on the bank of Spey from N.E. to S.W. above 3½ miles, and then S.S.E. above 8 miles.

The Church* standeth on the bank of Spey, a furlong east from the mouth of Avon, 3½ miles S.W. of Aberlaure, 2 miles S. of Knockando, 6 miles N.E. of Cromdale, and as many N. of Kirkmichael. Malcolm, Earl of Fife, gave this Church, and a Davach of land in Inveravon, to the Bishop of Moray, which sheweth that this was once a part of the estate of the Earls of Fife, and probably came to the Grants by the favour of Robert Steuart, Duke of Albany (uncle to Andrew Steuart, who married the heiress of Grant), to whom Isabel M'Duff, the heiress, disponed that great estate.

the conviction that there was probably no other mortal within a circuit of many miles.—(*The Moray Floods*, by Sir Thomas Dick Lauder. See also Professor Wilson's beautiful portraiture of the Avon in *Remarks on the Scenery of the Highlands*, pp. 43, 45, copied in Fullarton's *Gazetteer*.) (ED.)

* In 1829 the Church was so environed by a burn on one side and the Spey on the other, that it threatened to yield to the fate predicted that "the kirk of Inveravon would gang doon Spey fu' o' folk."

The Church of St. Peter of Strathouen was erected into a Prebend of the Cathedral Church of the Holy Trinity at Spyny, by Bricius Bishop of Murray, between 1208 and 1214, which was confirmed by Pope Innocent III., on the 22 Dec. 1214 (*Reg. Epis. Morar.*). There was preserved, until the end of the last century, in the library of the Scots College at Paris, a MS. Missal which, says Father Thomas Innes, "had belonged to Mr. James Gordon, the last chancellor of the church of Murray, and in that quality the last Catholic pastor of St. Peter of Inerawin, which was the parish where I served in Scotland 3 years." (ED.)

The whole lower end of the parish (except Coulchoich, pertaining to the Duke of Gordon) is the barony of Ballindalach. This, for above 200 years, was a part of the estate of the old family of Ballindalach, of whom Advie, Dellay, Dalvey, Tommavulin, &c., have descended. But being evicted and brought to a sale, was purchased by the Laird of Grant in the beginning of this century, and given by the Brigadier with his sister to Colonel William Grant, second son to Rothimurchus, whose son James (since the death of his nephew William, son of his elder brother Alexander, without issue) now possesseth it, and has a beautiful seat at the confluence of Spey and Avon.

Three miles above Ballindalach, upon the same side of Avon, beginneth Glenlivat [utterly destitute of wood], which runneth up S.E. on both sides of Livat 5 miles, and holdeth of the Duke of Gordon, either in property or in superiority.

In the face of Benrinnes, on the north side of Livat, is Morinsh, for several generations the property of Nairn of Morinsh, but now a part of the estate of Ballindalach.

On the west side of Avon, for 3 miles from the mouth of it, lieth the barony of Kilmachlie. This was a part of the estate of Alexander Steuart, 4th son of King Robert II. Earl of Buchan, and Lord Badenoch and Strathavon, who, having no legitimate children, gave the lands of Strathavon to his bastard son Sir Andrew, whose son Sir Walter sold Strathavon to the family of Gordon; or rather, it came to Thomas, bastard son of Alexander Steuart, Earl of Mar, who was bastard son of the Earl of Buchan, and Thomas sold it to Alexander Earl of Huntley. But Kilmachlie continued with a son of Sir Andrew and his descendants, until Ludovick Laird of Grant purchased it, and now it is a part of the estate of Ballindalach.

On the point where Avon and Livat join, stands the Castle of Drumin, which was the seat of the Barons of Strathavon, and is now the residence of Charles Steuart, of Drumin, a branch of Kilmachlie. Here there is an arch of a stone-bridge over Livat.

This parish is accommodated with much wood, rich pasture-ground, and plentiful salmon-fishing.

The barony of Ballindalach is in the county of Moray. The rest is in Banffshire.

[*Ballindalloch Castle*, or the *House of Ballindalloch*, the residence of Sir George Macpherson Grant, Bart., is a massive looking mansion, situated on the banks of the clear-flowing Avon, upon a low flat haugh richly wooded, at a short distance from its conflux with the Spey. Like many of the residences of our Highland gentry, it comprises, amid additions from time to time made by succeeding possessors, an imposing centre square tower, with which have been blended some beautiful copies of tall chimney spires and turrets, taken from some of the best of the olden Aberdeenshire castles. This contains the ancient door and turnpike stair, surmounted by a watch-tower termed *the Cape House*, with a window to each of the four sides, and an aperture in the wall immediately above the entrance; so as to admit of boiling lead, or missiles, being thrown down in the event of an enemy making good his approach. Over the chimney in one of the rooms is carved the date 1546. The *Cape House* seems to have been added by Patrick Grant in 1602; and about the beginning of last century a further addition was made of two large and commodious wings. Over the door-way is the family arms of Macpherson-Grant, with the inscriptions in Saxon letters:—𝔐𝔢 𝔏𝔬𝔯𝔡 𝔰𝔥𝔞𝔩𝔩 𝔭𝔯𝔢𝔰𝔢𝔯𝔳𝔢 𝔱𝔥𝔶 𝔤𝔬𝔦𝔫𝔤 𝔬𝔲𝔱 𝔞𝔫𝔡 𝔱𝔥𝔶 𝔠𝔬𝔪𝔦𝔫𝔤 𝔦𝔫. On one side, 𝔈𝔯𝔢𝔠𝔱𝔢𝔡 1546; on the other, 𝔑𝔢𝔰𝔱𝔬𝔯𝔢𝔡 1850. The chief gateway or entrance is at the Bridge of Avon; the style of architecture corresponds to that of the Castle. Over the arch is the family arms, with the motto—𝔗𝔬𝔲𝔠𝔥 𝔫𝔬𝔱 𝔱𝔥𝔢 𝔒𝔞𝔱 𝔟𝔬𝔱 𝔱𝔥𝔢 𝔊𝔩𝔬𝔳𝔢. The flood of 1829 poured violently for 24 hours through the vaulted passages of the old mansion. The dining-room had above 3 feet of water in it. The situation of the family, taken unawares, shut in by a raging deluge, was dreadful. The horses were standing 3 and 4 feet deep in the stables. This flood exceeded that of 1768 at Ballindalloch by 6 feet, and cost the proprietor upwards of £8000.

A little farther up the river, upon the edge of the high ground, and near a small stream called *the Castle Strype*, are to be seen the traces of a large building said to have been the former mansion of Ballindalloch. Tradition says that it would still have stood had not the building been prevented by unseen agency, the part built in the day-time having been always thrown down during the night. At length a voice was heard saying, "Build in the cow-haugh, and you shall meet with no interruption." The recommendation was followed, and the House of Ballindalloch was built where it now stands.

The Macphersons *of Invereshie* are the chiefs of a large tribe, which for ages has been distinguished under the designation of "Slioch Gillies," and which is composed of many considerable families, not only of the name of Macpherson, but of others, such as the Gillieses, Gillespies, &c. The founder of this tribe was *Gillies*, or *Elias Macpherson*, the first of Invereshie, who lived in the reign of Alexander III. He was a younger son of Ewan or Eugene *Baan* (the fair-complexioned), and brother of Kenneth Macpherson, ancestors of the Macphersons of *Cluny Macpherson*, in Inverness-shire. Ewan Baan was son of Murlach or Murdoch, and grandson of *Gillichattan*, chief of the powerful clan Chattan during the reign of David I., who, having devoted himself to the service of the Church, became Abbot of Kingussie, which he enjoyed till 1153, when, upon the demise, issueless, of his elder brother, *Diarmid*, the chieftainship devolved upon him. A few years subsequently, he procured from the Pope a dispensation to marry a daughter of the Thane of Calder. His son, *Ewan Baan*, was sometimes called Macpherson, which signifies "the son of a parson" (derived from his father's clerical profession); and surnames about that time becoming hereditary, it was perpetuated in his descendants.

Several of the lairds of Ballindalloch have followed the military profession, and others have devoted themselves to the improvement of their estate. General James Grant defeated Count d'Estainz, conquered St. Lucia, and was for many years Governor of Florida. At the time of his death, which took place at Ballindalloch in 1806, he was Governor of Stirling Castle. According to his own directions, his remains were buried in a favourite spot on the farm of the Mains, which commands a view of the Spey and of the Barony of Ballindalloch, and there a handsome Pillar has been erected, bearing a marble slab recording his appointments and the dates of his birth and death. General Grant was succeeded by George Macpherson Grant, who was created a baronet in 1838, and was an eminent agriculturist. He died in 1846, and was succeeded by his son, Sir John Macpherson Grant, who enjoyed the title but a few years, having died in 1851. The title and estates then devolved on his son, Sir George Macpherson Grant, the present baronet, when only 12 years of age. Sir George's mother, Marion-Helen, was the eldest daughter of Mungo Nutter Campbell of Ballimore, Argyllshire (she died in 1855). Born at Invereshie, Inverness-shire, 1839; mar., 1861, Frances Elizabeth, the youngest daughter of the Rev. Roger Pocklington, Vicar of Walesby, Notts; educated at Christ Church, Oxford, grad. B.A., 1861.

About a mile from the confluence of Avon and Livet, the rivulet *Tervy*, up Livet about half a mile, lies *Achbrake*; and at the distance of half a mile eastward from Achbrake, the burn of Altachoynachan falls into Tervy;

and about 1½ mile almost up this burn, and south-east from its mouth, the Battle of Altachoynachan, in Oct., 1594, was fought between Huntly and Argyle, in which the latter was defeated. (*The Stat. Acc. of Scotland*, vol. xiii., p. 35: Edinb., 1794).

The Battle of Altachoynachan, Altachoylachan, Glenlivat, Balrinnes, or Benrinnes, was fought upon an inclined plain near the Glenrinnes border of the parish, terminating in a flat ridge which descends rapidly to the burn of Altachoylachan, and flanked on the south by a somewhat precipitous shoulder of the contiguous mountain. About ¾ of a mile from the scene of action, a small knoll on the east bank of the stream Conlalt, commonly called *Lord Auchindown's Cairn*, ⅔ of it swept away by the flood of 1829, marks the place where Sir Patrick Gordon of Auchindown is supposed to have died. (*The New Stat. Acc. of Scotland*, number xi., p. 130. *Tytler's Hist. of Scotland*, vol. iv., pp. 223, 224: Nimmo, 1864. *The Battle of Balrinnes*, pp. 538-547, *in the Ballad Minstrelsy of Scotland*: Maurice Ogle & Co., Glasgow, 1871.)

On the 5th Feb., 1493, "the lordis of consale assignis to Alexander Tulloche the xv day of Aprile nixt to cum with continiatioune of dais to preif sufficiently that Walter Stewart of Straithovn knycht is awand to the said Alexander as are to vmquhile his faider the soume of ij^e merkis. And alse to preif sufficiently that Margrete laidy Dvn and Jonat Ogilby laidy Leis is awand him a croce of gold with a preciouse stane callit a ruby and vij orient perle with a pece of bane of Sanct Magnis hede and the price tharof. And ordinis him to haf letrez to summonde his witnes and the party to heer thaim sworne." (*Acta Dominorum Concilii*, p. 273.)

Kilmaichly. This old House, on the left bank of the Avon, occupies the flat summit of a green knoll, embosomed in a grove of ancient trees, and overlooking a rich assemblage of wooded banks and long withdrawing terraces and haughs. But its beauties have been already painted by the tender and glowing pencil of the "*Man of Feeling*," who has drawn a rural picture from it that would throw a charm over an infinitely less interesting reality. (See the 87th No. of *The Lounger*.) The old fir trees are still prominently observable, and the House

198 DRUIDICAL CIRCLES AND STONE AT INVERAVON.

and its accompaniments, though somewhat in decay, yet remain in a state sufficiently fresh to recall the author's fascinations. The old lady and her ancient butler are, indeed, no longer here in corporeal existence; but blunt must be the fancy of that individual who could visit this classic spot without finding it haunted by their venerable forms. The flood of 1768 cut a channel through the lower ground of Kilmaichly, isolating a part of it from the rest of the farm; and that of the 3rd and 4th of Aug., 1829, restored the river to its old bed.

A remarkable hill, long, flat-topped, and steep-sided in form, stretches down through the haughs, from the junction of the Livet with the Avon. It is evidently the remnant of a plain in which the rivers met at a much higher level. On this there is a Druidical Circle, and, on the top of the wooded Hill of Craggan, near the lower termination of the Duke's property, there are large remains of Cairns, and rude walls of fortification. *(The Moray Floods, by Sir Thomas Dick Lauder.)*

"The Stone," at Inveravon, lies in the churchyard of the parish, and is said to have been found under the foundation of the old church. Numerous traces of Stone-Circles are to be found in the parish, and rude Stone-Coffins have occasionally been discovered. (See No. 1 Plate XV., Vol. I. *Stuart's Sculptured Stones of Scotland*.)

There were upon an eminence on the east side of Avon, and a short way up from the House of Ballindalloch, a few long stones enclosing a small piece of ground, which was said to be a Druidical Temple. The most of the stones have been taken away, except one very broad, thick, and long stone, which stands still there. Opposite to this on the west side of Avon, upon a rising ground amidst the corn land of Bellaviller, is such another place, where several long broad stones encompass about 72 square yards of ground. Some of the long stones are broken, but several of them still stand whole. Such another Temple there is in the lower end of Glenlivet, on the east side of Avon, upon a hillock, or small rising ground, a little below the mouth of Livet, called *The Doun of Dilmore*. (*The Stat. Acc. of Scotland*, vol. xiii., pp. 42, 43.)

Rude Stone Coffins have occasionally been discovered

in the parish, under cairns to be removed to make way for the plough; and, in trenching a wood on the farm of Kilmaichlie, the labourers found some old urns and coins. Numerous traces of Druidical Temples are to be found. (*The New Stat. Acc. of Scotland*, number xi., pp. 132, 133.)

At Blairfindy are to be seen the ruins of a hunting-seat of the Earls of Huntly; and at Drummin, on a high promontory near the confluence of the Livet with the Avon, stands part of the old *Castle of Drummin*, now affording shelter only to jackdaws and pigeons. The wall, which is of great height and thickness, is pretty entire on the east and north and half of the west side, but the other half of the west and the whole south wall are gone, and the stability of a considerable part of what remains of the structure seems to rest on a single stone of a few inches in diameter. (*The New Stat. Acc. of Scotland*, number xi., p. 133.)

Besides the Churchyard of the parish, there are two other burying-places; one upon the east side of Livet, near 4 miles from the Parish Church, near the walls of the old Chapel of Dorman; and another, almost 5 miles higher up the glen, on the west side of Crombie, and opposite to the Bochle. It is called *the Buitterlach*, and was consecrated more than 40 years ago by two R. C. Bishops, to be a burying-ground for the Catholics, but few are yet buried in it. There was in old time also a chapel and burying-place on the east side of the Livet, about half-a-mile above the Protestant Meeting House, called *Chapel Christ*, but very little remains of the chapel are to be seen, and the burying-ground has been washed away by a small rivulet which runs between it and Nevie, and by the water of Livet. There was also once a chapel and burying-ground on the west side of Avon, on the estate of Kilmaichlie, almost opposite to the mouth of Livet, on a farm which is from it called *Chapeltown*. There are evident marks of graves, with stones set up at the heads of some of them; and hard by is an excellent spring, which emits a large stream of water. (*Stat. Acc. of Scotland*, vol. xiii., pp. 36, 37: Edinb., 1794.)

There were chapels at Phona, Nevie, Deskie, and Chapelton of Kilmaichlie; but no traces now remain of any of them except the latter, the outlines of which are still visible, with some appearances of graves close by. The burial-ground of Downan is still used, and occasionally that of Buitterlach, in the near neighbourhood of which there is a very large cairn, supposed to be raised over the grave of a person of note. A small spot in a field on the farm of Haughs of Kilmaichlie appears clearly to have been also a place of sepulture. In the immediate neighbourhood of the old chapel at Chapelton of Kilmaichlie is a very copious spring of water, cased with stones, indicating perhaps that it was in repute in times of old. (*The New Stat. Acc. of Scotland*, number xi., pp. 133, 125.)

ARCHÆOLOGY OF GLENLIVET.

[Glenlivet is by no means so prolific in remnants of the Bronze as in that of the Stone Period. This is, perhaps, owing to the perishable nature of the metal. Another reason is that ploughmen are so well accustomed to see pieces of metal corroded with rust in the earth, that they seldom, if ever, lift them. It is only when something of unusual shape or size attracts their attention that they pause to lift and examine it. It is to the mosses that we chiefly owe the preservation of anything that has been found. A few little things have, however, been found in the soil, and these tell us that Glenlivet was in the Bronze Period, as in the Stone, the scene of busy, active life.

A number of years ago, while workmen were trenching a piece of land on the farm of Thane, three stones were discovered in the form of a cromlech. The stones were removed, and the workmen went on digging. One of the workmen suddenly turned out some pieces of pottery, rudely ornamented. It could not be guessed at the time what the vessel had contained or how it had come to be there. We have no doubt, however, that the vessel was a cinerary urn formed of baked clay, and that it contained the ashes of perhaps some mighty chief in the far past. Near the urn was found a piece of bronze resembling, as our informant stated, a round buckle. From the description given, we have little hesitation in believing that the round buckle was a Celtic brooch, one of those beautiful ornaments that are so extremely rare.

At Cairnvreit, on the farm of Auchdregnie, some articles belonging to the Bronze Period have also been found, but very little has been preserved. Many years ago, in the piece of ground above-mentioned, was found a quantity of bronze rings, in addition to an implement resembling a saddler's needle. The rings, unfortunately, have disappeared long ago. Their size or shape cannot even be given with anything like accuracy. It is useless, therefore, to speculate whether they were ornaments or ring-money. If proper search were made in this piece of ground, so rich with riches of by-gone days, and under the eye of a competent archæologist, the search would be amply rewarded. These little things comprise everything, as far as we can learn, that have been found in the land. In the mosses the tale is not much brighter. Were it not that what has been found were in different parts of the locality, separated a considerable distance from each other, we would be inclined to think that, ere the dawn of the Bronze Period, the natives had all decamped, leaving a solitary family or two the sole occupiers of the desolate scene. This could scarcely be the case, however, or they must have migrated occasionally to procure their implements of bronze.

Three or four years ago, in the peat-moss of Vantauch, there was discovered a bronze vessel, or, as our informant said, a copper vessel, resembling a modern frying-pan. It looked like copper, and might have been three parts so; but there can be little doubt but that it belonged to the Bronze Period. It was found fully $4\frac{1}{2}$ feet in the solid moss, measured from the present surface. Six feet of solid moss had been taken from above that, however, within the memory of living men; and there might have been several feet cut before, which is very probable. The vessel was found under nearly 11 feet of solid moss, assuming that none had been cut before the present age. That in itself is sufficient to prove that it was of ancient date, but the vessel itself proves it more satisfactorily. The handle was of that peculiar twisted pattern so common in the Bronze Period, and which may be said to be peculiar to it. The vessel was also carefully mended in three or four parts, and well mended, as the finder stated. This proves the great value that must have been attached to it; but like many other objects of antiquity, it also has left the locality, it having been sold to a travelling stoneware merchant for a "bowl."

We have in our possession a perforated brazen ball, found in the moss of Blackward, with diagonal lines traced round it. It was found many feet under the surface of the moss; but we are by no means certain that it belongs to the Bronze Period. On the contrary, we are inclined to think that it belongs to a later date. It resembles very particularly the round ball that is attached to the hilt of a modern sword: yet it could scarcely have been attached to the hilt of an ancient sword, or probably the hilt would have been found with it, and perhaps part of the blade. It is, without doubt, however, of ancient date, whatever may have been its use. We have also in our possession an article which we take to have been an ornament. It is manufactured of a metal which, as far as we can judge, is neither brass nor bronze. It is round, about $2\frac{1}{2}$ inches in diameter, and resembles very much the ornaments that are used on horses' modern bridles. It has a very fair likeness of a fox head engraven on it. There are also two rough projections on the under side, by which it has been attached to something. We cannot conjecture what it has been used for. We have never seen anything of the kind described in any work on archæology; yet we are certainly of opinion that it is ancient. It was found in a piece of ground called the Carrachs. After the moss had all been removed, it was resting in the bed of clay, which proves that it is not a thing of yesterday.

The most important article, however, connected with the Bronze Period found in Glenlivet has yet to be mentioned. It is a chalice or cup. It was found underneath what must have been a very large monumental cairn, in a height near the farm-steading of Auchdregnie. The cairn having been driven away for the purpose of building a bridge and other purposes, this magnificent article of the Bronze Period was discovered. It was beautifully ornamented with flowers and other devices. Its great peculiarity was that it had neither handle nor stalk. It is probable, however, that the stalk might have been broken away. It was long kept at Auchdregnie, and only very lately went amissing. Not very far from the same spot was found part of a bronze spear, which was last seen keeping together a rent in a post of a sheep-flake. Such is the fate of many objects of antiquity; a melancholy fate indeed, when we consider that by these objects alone the degree of advancement of our early forefathers can be traced.

About 50 years ago, a man was busy trenching in a piece of ground called Betavochel. His spade came suddenly into contact with something hard, which, on examination, turned out to be a slab. The man (Farquharson) went immediately and told his brother, Dominie Farquharson, a man who acted as schoolmaster in the Braes. The dominie heard his brother's tale, and advised him to say nothing about the discovery until night, when they would go in company and lift the slab, when he doubted not but that as much gold would be found as would be a fortune to each. The shadows of night slowly fell, by far too slow for the impatience of the gold-seekers. Quietly they left their dwelling and proceeded to the spot. The ponderous slab was slowly lifted, disclosing four small apartments, in one of which was an earthen jar. Eagerly the dominie grasped it, and dashed aside the small flat stone that covered it. The surprise and disgust of the learned man may be better imagined than described, when he found that it only contained dust, human dust, the dust of centuries; but that did not move the dominie. He dashed the cinerary urn to the ground, smashing it in pieces, and fled from the spot, followed more slowly by his brother, doubtless equally disappointed. Next day other three slabs were taken out. This had no doubt been the burial-place of a family, at least the divisions inside would lead us to suppose so; but the family must have found another resting place, and this one alone was left to tell a tale of the past; and the dust was rudely scattered to the four winds of heaven, and the casket that had held it for ages was broken because it did not contain gold.

So far as we are aware, none of the tumuli in Glenlivet have been opened for scientific purposes. Those that have been opened have been opened accidentally. These tend to show that the burials have been made after the order of cremation. The long barrow, so far as we have yet seen, is altogether unknown in the district. Round barrows are pretty numerous.]   (J. G. PHILLIP.)

INVERAVON.

[*Situation, Soil, Climate.*—The river Avon, having escaped through a narrow pass from the parish of Kirkmichael, holds on its course in the same northerly direction, through the midst of this parish, for almost 14 miles, dashing into the Spey about a mile higher up on that river than the church: the name of the parish importing in the Gaelic this particular of the termination of the Avon. From the eastern limits of Cromdale to the western borders of Aberlour, the length of the parish along the Spey is 9 miles. The Avon having taken possession of the southerly quarter of this parish for about the course of 2 miles, receiving the stream of the Livet from its own valley of Glenlivet, extending easterly into the mountains with its lateral branches, the Tervie, Crombie, and Aultchoilnachan, for the space of 12 miles, forming a detached district of the parish. In the lower part of the country, the soil is light and dry, naturally producing broom. About the influx of the Livet, it is a fertile loam, and higher up in this district there is a marle pit. In some places the soil is moorish, in others it is clay on a bed of limestone, and everywhere over the whole parish, there is abundance of peat earth, furnishing in a dry season a sufficient compliment of fuel. Except one opening towards the north, where the country is washed by the Spey, it is everywhere environed by hills. The mountain of Benrinnes, rising on the eastern borders to the height of 2800 feet above the level of the sea, gives more cause, in general, to complain of the excess than of the deficiency of rain. On the banks of the Spey and on the plains of Ballnadallach, the climate is early and moderate. It is colder in the higher district of Glenlivet, the snow lying oftentimes pretty deep in the spring, when the sowing is diligently prosecuted below.

State of Property.—The family seat of Ballnadallach [Ballindalloch] (*the town of the level vale*) is pleasantly situated on the banks of the Avon, not farther from its confluence with the Spey than to maintain the connection with both rivers. The exterior of the building, and the artificial embellishment of the natural beauties, bespeak it the residence of opulence united with the most correct taste. The present great proprietor, General Grant, has expended almost £7000 sterling on decoration, united with permanent improvement. Similar to many of the seats of ancient families, the House was originally placed in the vicinity of very swampy ground, which has been completely laid dry by a number of costly but perennial drains. He has enlarged the park over a great extent of waste ground, rising on the eastern side of the valley, named BADNAGLASHAN, *the tufted boggy pasturage*, originally of no value, but now reduced to a state of such complete cultivation as might be easily let for a corn-farm of more than £200 sterling of rent. A long reach of an unsightly, precipitous, and craggy bank, which commanded the principal front of the House, hath been clothed with the delicate and rich variety of verdure which a luxuriantly shooting grove of different species of trees can produce. The park extends up the Avon for a considerable space, where it is terminated by a handsome bridge of three arches, connecting it with the other side. The highway bends behind the eastern limits of the park, across the bridge, and down along the margin of the western bank, exhibiting the delightful landscape below like a fair and animated painting, till it regains the less decorated country along the course of the Spey. In the Cess Book of the county of Banff, the valued rent of the domain in this parish, including that of Moreinch, Kilmaichly, and Pitchashe, is £1383 6s. 8d. Scots: but the House itself, with the park, and two or three of the adjoining farms, are placed, by their political connection, in the county of Moray, valued at £292 8d. Scots.

The rest of the parish is the property of the Duke of Gordon, and in the county of Banff, valued at £2290 Scots: extending the total valuation to £3965 7s. 4d. Scots. Though there are a number of the possessions but small, there are also many farms of very respectable extent. In the year 1768, the real rent of the whole was proved in the Court of Tithes to be £1148 sterling: since that time it may have increased nearly to the double of that amount.

State Ecclesiastical.—Inveravon falls into the Presbytery of Aberlour, which was erected into a separate independent jurisdiction from the Presbytery of Abernethy in 1709. Under the Prelatic dispensation, Inveravon was the seat of the Chancellor of the Diocese. The stipend, by decreet 1769, is £71 9s. and 48 bolls of meal, including the Communion-allowance. The glebe consists of little more than 4 acres, of which a little less than 3 are arable. Sir James Grant of Grant, Bart., is the patron of the parish. There is a commodious slated school-house in the vicinity of the church: the salary is 12 bolls of oatmeal, with the fees of nearly 40 scholars, and the emoluments of the office of session clerk. The Society for Christian Knowledge have established a school in Glenlivet, migratory about 8 miles from Deskie to Badnavochle: the appointment is £15 sterling. The number of scholars vibrates from 20 to 90: but from the versatile state of the establishment, it is not possible that any useful knowledge can be attained. The Royal Bounty supports a Missionary clergyman in the district of Glenlivet, with the pittance of £25: he conducts the ordinances of Divine worship for five successive Sundays at Auchbraek, about 2 miles above the influx of the Livet. On the sixth, at the distance of 7 miles farther up among the hills, where the country is thinly peopled, where there is no accommodation of a chapel, where one party is not pleased, and where the other is dissatisfied.

In Glenlivet, also, there has been a Roman Catholic establishment for almost 100 years, on the banks of the Crombie, in a very sequestered situation among the mountains which separate this district from the parishes of Cabrach, Glenbucket, and Strathdon. It was chosen on the account of its being so much removed from public view, in those times when the Christians of the Church of Rome were, by the civil law of Britain, and both its reformed churches, exposed to persecution. Its Gaelic appellation SCALAN, implies *an obscure* or *shadowy place*. It may be translated, *the dark* or *gloomy land;* and it denotes also the place where, in the days of other years, the hunter stalked in ambuscade for the bounding roe of the hill.

The school is properly the Bishop's seminary for educating a few of the Catholic youth in the principles of grammar and morality, and training them to a regularity of discipline, in preparation for the colleges on the continent; where they are, in general, entered into holy orders: although, on some occasions, the sacrament of ordination has been administered in the Scalan. The school at present contains from 8 to 12 students, under the care of a clergyman, who conducts their education, and superintends the management of the farm and the house. It is now proposed to remove this seminary to the vicinity of Aberdeen, where it is to be established on a more respectable foundation, and conducted on a more enlarged and comprehensive scale.

Upon the farm of Tombea, on the banks of the Livet, at the influx of the Crombie, the pastor of the people of the Catholic communion resides. Near his residence, the chapel, a neat, clean, slated fabric, is placed.

The contributions for the poor from the parochial and missionary churches amount to nearly £7 sterling in the year, distributed among 38 indigent individuals of the national Church. The Roman Catholics support their own poor, by funds of their own formation. Their number is nearly equal to that of the poor of the Establishment, the whole members of which amount to 1394, and those of the Church of Rome, the only dissenters in the parish are 850.

Miscellaneous Information.—The proprietors, inattentive to their concern in the provision established by the statutory law for the poor, disregarded an application in the year 1780 by the Session, to take a loan at legal interest of £100 sterling, accumulated by the most parsimonious and frugal management, unremitted for the space of many years. The Session therefore disposed of this capital, with the utmost caution, between two gentlemen of landed property, in other parishes; but though justly elated, no doubt, by their own provident address, they were taught the mortifying lesson that "riches are not always to men even of understanding." In a few years the affairs of both debtors fell into disorder, and their capital was in a great measure lost.

This parish in 1594 was distinguished by one of those events, the Battle of Glenlivet, which in the present times would be accounted peculiarly outrageous. The extremely imbecile administration of James VI. had at that time involved the nation into complicated misfortunes of the most inveterate anarchy. The Church, with the presumption not uncommon among upstarts, weakly interposed in the affairs of State, which were at the same embroiled by the contending interests of discordant nobles, and the imperious but selfish politics of the English Queen. Three noblemen, the Earls of Huntly, Errol, and Angus, from causes unnecessary to be stated here, had still persisted in the religion of their ancestors. By the incredible calumny of a conspiracy with the Spanish Monarch, the King, obliged to submit to the necessity of the times, reluctantly decreed their banishment and forfeiture; and excommunication, for the good of their souls, was added by the sentence of the Church. From a previous enmity to Huntly, the Earl of Argyle was appointed his Majesty's lieutenant to execute this mild correction, and his preparations for this holy war were aided and spurred on by the pious endeavours of Bruce of Kinnaird, a clergyman of Edinburgh. By their united influence and the hope of the plunder of the north, almost 10,000 rapacious warriors from the Western Isles, and all the coast from Kintyre to Lochaber, took the field. Elated with their own numbers, and gaping for the spoil, they hastened on through Badenoch towards the richer region of Strathbogie. In the vale of Glenlivet, their march was intercepted by a little band of scarce 1200 cavalry, which Huntly and Errol were only able, on the spur of the occasion, to muster. It is rather common than surprising, that an army presumptuous from their number should, by the resolution and caution of their condemned foe, have been foiled. The field of battle was the southern declivity of the valley, through which the brook of Aultchoilnachan winds its course, at the bottom of a heathy precipice almost perpendicular, upon the margin of which the forces of Argyle were marshalled, having the advantage of their enemy on the sloping ground below, which was however compensated by the effect of two small field-pieces, almost equally unknown among the forces of Argyle as among the powers of Montezuma, or the armies of Peru. The disorder which these occasioned was completed by the van, of 400 of the most gallant horsemen, led round the end of the precipice by Errol, charging the footmen furiously with the spear. The left wing had been without consideration entrusted to the command of a chief among the Grants, yet the vassal and friend of Huntly, who, by a previous concert, turned, at this crisis of the engagement, against the centre, which was led on by Argyle himself. Notwithstanding, the battle for more than two hours was maintained; but the centre at last gave way, under the vigour of Huntly's attack. Their rout left the van or right wing, which had commenced the fight, unsupported, which retreated unbroken and in order, though their leader, the chieftain of the Macleans of Mull, was slain. The attempt of Argyle to rally was in vain; and the whole of their baggage, the greater part of their arms, and more than 700 slain, were left upon the field, while 12 only of the opposing party fell. The carnage of the pursuit was prevented by the roughness of the ground. The whole country around was by this victory delivered from rapine and destruction. The ancestor of the Abyssinian traveller was grieved, and the King secretly rejoiced.] (*Survey of the Province of Moray.*)

CHURCHYARD EPITAPHS OF INVERAVON.

The Church, erected in 1809, stands on the south bank of the Spey; and S. Peter's Well, which was once considered an effectual cure for most diseases, is about 400 yards south-east of the Church. At no distant date, votive offerings were found in the Well; and Peter Fair, now held at Dalnashaugh, stood near the consecrated fountain.

A sculptured Stone, with a raven and other carvings, lies within the site of the old church. The burial-aisle of Grant of Ballandalloch, a recent building, stands apart from the church. It contains three tablets. The first, which is of Peterhead granite, bears:—

I. A tribute of filial affection and grateful esteem to the memory of Sir George Macpherson-Grant of Ballandalloch and Invereshie, Baronet. Born 25 Feb., 1781; died 24 Nov., 1846.

Sir George, who was long M.P. for Sutherlandshire, was created a baronet in 1838. He married Mary, eldest daughter of Carnegy of Craigo, in Angus. Their third son, Thomas, W.S., Edinburgh, succeeded to the valuable estate of Craigo, &c., on the death of his cousin Thomas, the last of the male line of that branch of the Carnegys. Sir George's eldest son, John, to whom the next inscription refers, only survived his father four years:—

II. This tablet is placed here by Dame Marion Helen Campbell in memory of her beloved husband, Sir John

Macpherson-Grant of Ballandalloch and Invereshie, Bart. Born 3 Augt., 1804; died 2d Dec., 1850.

The following, from a marble slab, records the death of Sir John's wife, who was a daughter of Campbell of Ballimore, Argyllshire:—

III. This tablet is placed by Sir George Macpherson-Grant of Ballandalloch and Invereshie, Baronet, in memory of his beloved mother, Dame Marion Helen Campbell. Born 12 Oct., 1810; died 5 June, 1855.

The Invereshie branch of the Macphersons claim descent from Gillies, third son of Ewan Baan (the fair Ewan), who lived in the time of Alex. II. He was of the Clan Chattan; and the succession of the clan having devolved upon the sons of Muriach, a parson or priest, the family is said to have assumed the name of Macparson, or *son of the parson*. George Macpherson of Invereshie and Dalraddie married Grace, daughter of Colonel Wm. Grant of Ballandalloch. On the death of his descendant, General James Grant, the Ballandalloch Estates came to George Macpherson, nephew, and subsequently heir of William of Invereshie, when he assumed the surname of *Macpherson-Grant*, and, as above noticed, was created a baronet. This family claim to be descended on the Grant side from John (son of Patrick of Grant), who lived during the first half of the 16th century. (See page 195.)

Besides the burial-aisle in the churchyard, a mausoleum, now surrounded by wood, erected in 1807, occupies an elevated position in the west corner of the Bowmoon Park, overlooking Ballandalloch Castle and a great part of Strathspey. Here, by special request, were deposited the ashes of the above-named General James Grant. The mausoleum is a square building of native granite, with a column rising from the centre, overtopped by a vase.

IV. A marble tablet upon the base of the column is thus inscribed:—

Memoriæ sacrum JACOBI GRANT de Ballandalloch, in exercitu Brittannico Ducis, undecimæ peditum legionis Præfecti, atque Castelli de Stirling Custodis, nati—die Novembris 1720, qui decessit 13 die Aprilis, 1806. Hoc monumentum posuit Georgius Macpherson-Grant de Ballandalloch.

The body of the General rests in the vault below. The

outer casing consists of a coffin-shaped tomb of light grey marble, set upon a large granite slab. Upon the top of the coffin are the Grant arms and motto, surrounded by nicely sculptured banners and other trophies of war. The following inscription (of the same import as that in Latin) is upon the top of the tomb below the family arms :—

V. James Grant of Ballandalloch, General in His Majesty's Army, Colonel of the 11th regiment of foot, and Governor of Stirling Castle, born Nov., 1720, died 13 April, 1806.

Gen. Grant, who succeeded to Ballandalloch on the death of his nephew, Col. W. Grant, about 1770, greatly distinguished himself during the American War, and was some years Governor of Florida.

VI. Heir lyes ane honest man caled William M'Willie, who livid in the Cories, who departed the 10 of Jvne, 1685; and Ketren Gordene, his spovsc.

VII. Here lyes the . . . . . James Stuart, late farmer in Cottertown of Balindalloch, who departed this life the 3 of . . . 1749, aged . . .

An enclosure on the south side of the kirk contains a number of tombstones to Grants who have tenanted farms in Inveravon. From these the next two inscriptions are copied :—

VIII. From motives of filial esteem and respect for the memories of John Grant, formerly in Glenarder, who died 12 Nov., 1797, aged 84 years; and William Grant, who was some time farmer at Dalnapot, who died 16 Jan., 1815, aged 39 this stone was placed over them by Peter Grant in Craigroy, grandson of the former and brother of the latter.

IX. Here lies the body of Charles Grant, farmer at Boat of Aven, who died Feb. 4, 1758, aged 76, and of his spouse, Anna Cumming, who died April 20, 1736, aged 63. In memory of them, John and Alex. Grants, their sons, erected this stone.

Those recorded in the last quoted Inscription were the direct ancestors of James Grant, writer, Elgin, who was fifteen years Provost of that city, and projector of the railways from Elgin to Craigellachie, and to Lossiemouth, &c.

X. William Grant, Esq., many years tacksman of Tombreckachie, terminated his earthly course with high and well merited esteem on Saturday, 3 June, 1815, at the advanced age of 85 years.

XI. Two separate and adjoining stones bear :—

James Grant, farmer, Pitgavenie, near Elgin, died 1771 : He was a pious and honest man, a tender husband, a most dutiful parent, and a good neighbour. His remains ly interred under this stone, which was placed over them by his son, Mr. James Grant, minister of Inveraven, who died 3 Feb., 1795, in the 77th year of his age, and 43d of his ministry.

XII. Mrs. Margaret Macgregor, died 7 Dec., 1841, daughter of Jas. Macgregor, Esq. of Pittyvaich. The Rev. Wm. Grant, minister of Inveravon, died 12 April, 1833, in the 75th year of his age, and 41st of his ministry.

XIII. Within an enclosure :—

Sacred to the memory of Thomas Stewart, Esq., late of Pittyvaich, who departed this life 5 Feb., 1815, aged 74.

XIV. In area of the old Kirk :—

The Rev. Wm. Spence, minister of the Gospel at Inveravon, died 30 July, 1807, in the 46th year of his age, and 12th of his ministry.

XV. This stone was erected here by John Hendrie, who died the 24th Dec., 1815, in the 63rd year of his age, with the concurrence of Penual Cameron, his spouse, who died 7 May, 1818, in the 57th year of her age, &c.

XVI. Peter Hay, merchant and farmer in Dalchwrich, placed this stone here on his burying place, and his remains are interred under it. He died Dec. 30, aged 73 years. He was a fair trader, an honest man, and peaceable neighbour. Death is certain, sin is the cause of it, but Christ is the cure.

XVII. Upon a granite headstone :—

Captain Grantt, tacksman of Advie and Molderie, interred here May, 1828, aged 90 years. He was the 7th in descent from Duncan, the 9th laird of Grant, and 6th from Patrick Grant of Ballandalloch, who held the lands of Advie, first in wadset and afterwards in tack. His youngest son, Capt. Lewis Grant of the 71st Regt., died May, 1812, of wounds received at the assault of Fort Napoleon and in the Tagus, when cheering and leading the Highlanders to victory. Erected by Col. W. Grant of Cloghill in memory of an honourable father, and a gallant brother; also to his grandson, Charles Grant Campbell, Esq., Assistant Surgeon R.N., who died at Rio de Janeiro, S. America, 6 Feb., 1851, in the prime of life, and faithful discharge of his duty.

XVIII. This stone is placed here in memory of William Falcener, late farmer in Pitchaish, who died at Mains of Kinermony, 4 May, 1793, in the 74th year of his age; and of seven of his children, who died infants.

XIX. An adjoining stone records the death of his wife, Anna Rose, in 1821, aged 78, also that of a number of their descendants. Three sons were merchants in New York, and another died farmer of Kinermony, 1849, aged 81.

Alex. M'Donald, farmer, Parkhead of Pitchash, d. 1809, a. 84—

Heav'nward directed all his days,
His life one act of prayer and praise;
With every modest grace inspired,
To make him lov'd, esteemed, admired.
Crown'd with a cheerfulness that show'd
How pure the source from whence it flow'd.
Such was the man whose thread, when run,
Finding the appointed time was come,
To rest he sunk, without one sigh,
The saint may sleep, but cannot die.

XX. Upon a headstone :—
Erected to the memory of James M'Donald, Esq., late of Morant Bay, Jamaeca, who died at Charleston of Aberlour, 6 April, 1836, aged 42; Francis M'Donald, Esq. of Morant Bay, died 19 June, 1833, aged 38, natives of this parish.

XXI. A costly tomb, composed of blue granite, with three marble slabs inserted, bears that—
Charles Stewart, Esq., Deskie, who died 30 Sep. 1826, aged 74, was upright in principle, disinterested in character, and the poor man's friend.
His widow, Mary, daughter of the late Jas. Gordon, Esq., Croughly, died 27 March, 1838, aged 66.
Ann Margaret, daughter of the above, spouse of Harry Lumsden, died 18 Nov., 1835, aged 27. Chas. Geo. Lumsden, Asst. Surg. K.R. Hussars, died at Meerut, Bengal, 1862, aged 30. [Two other sons and a daughter are recorded.]

XXII. Upon a table-shaped stone within same enclosure:—

This stone is erected here by Robert Stewart, tenant in Wester Deskie, in memory of his spouse, Elspat Gordon, who died Jan. 31, 1781, aged 50 years, who bore to him eleven children.

The parish being very large, burial-places were numerous. Apart from that at Inveravon, there were others at Chapelton, Haugh of Kilmaichlie, Lagmore, Bhuternich, Downan, &c. That of

DOWNAN,

Which is picturesquely situated near the junction of the Livet and the Avon, is still used for interments, and contains a number of tombstones. From one of these the following inscription is copied:—

XXIII. M'Lac Achbreack D. 1818 A.G 90 ✠ Also his spouse Grace Grant D 1814 AG 81.

From a better cut version of the above, upon the reverse of the same stone (where the last age is given as 80), it appears that the first-named was George M'Lachlan, farmer, Auchbreck.

The foundations of the old Place of worship, which appears to have been a small building, may be traced near the middle of the enclosure at Downan. A stone-slab bears a cross incised on both sides. It appears to be an object of some antiquity; and, according to tradition, near it lie some of those who fell at the battle of Glenlivet, which was fought not far from it, between the armies of James VI. and those of the Earls of Errol and Huntly, in 1594.

There was long a Roman Catholic seminary at Scalan, but on the institution of the College at Blairs, in Mary Culter, the students were transferred to that place.

Handsome Roman Catholic Chapels stand at Tombac and at the Braes of Glenlivet (S. Mary.) Over the principal entrance to the first ("The Church of the Incarnation") are the words—

CHRISTO ET PURÆ VIRGINI.

XXIV. A monument, built of granite, contains three separate tablets thus inscribed:—

✠ Sacred to the memory of William Gordon, Esq., Minmore who died 5 Nov., 1829, aged 74 years. R.I.P.

✠ O Death, I will be thy death. Osee, ch. 13.
Expecting a blessed resurrection, the mortal remains of Anne, the beloved wife of James Petrie, Esq., here repose,
In the fear of the Lord, which, &c.
In faith, without which, &c., please God.
In hope, the anchor, &c., sure and firm.
In charity, which never faileth.
She placidly resigned her spirit to its Creator, 7th Sep., 1858, aged 47 years :—
Her children rose up, &c.
Her husband, and he praised her.
Favour is deceitful, and beauty is vain.
The woman that feareth the Lord, she shall be praised, Prov., ch. 31.
Requiescat in pace.

XXV. ✠ IHS. Sacred to the memory of Mary Stewart, spouse of Capt. William Gordon, Minmore, who died 1 Oct., 1842, aged 63 years; of their son, Capt. John Gordon, H.E.I.S., who died at Singapore 4th July, 1833, aged 27 years; of their daughter, Elizabeth Stewart Forbes, who died at the Convent of Mercy, Glasgow, 10 April, 1834, aged 32; of their 3 sons and daughters, who died in infancy. Of Lewis Gordon, Esq., for many years Secretary to the Highland Agricultural Society of Scotland, who died at Aberdeen 23 January, 1839, aged 72. And of Sir Charles Gordon, who died at Edinburgh 25th Sep., 1845, aged 52. Requiescant in pace.

Gordons have been long resident at Minmore, and it is from one of them that the present Gordons of Abergeldie are descended in the male line. The above Sir Charles, who married a sister of Angus Fletcher of Dunans, Esq., was trained by his uncle, and ultimately succeeded him in the office of Secretary to the Highland Agricultural Society.

Further up the river Avon is

THE PARISH OF KIRKMICHAEL,

In the shire of Banff. This Glen and Strath was a part of the estate of M'Duff, Earl of Fife, in the 13th century, and was, anno 1389, June 22, resigned by Isabel M'Duff, heiress, in the hands of King Robert III., *in perpetuam remanentiam (Skene de Verborum Significatione titulo Arage.)* It came afterwards to Alexander, Lord Badenoch and Earl of Buchan, who left issue only three bastard sons, viz., Alexander (Earl of Mar in right of his wife), Sir Andrew of Sandhaugh, and Walter of Kinchardin. Sir Walter of Strathavon (son of Sir Andrew) sold Strathavon, except Kilmachlie and Drummin, to Alexander Earl of Huntley, who disponed it to his son Alexander, and he excambed it for the Barony of Clunie. Again, George Earl of Huntley, who died anno 1576, gave Strathavon to his son Alexander, whose son, Alexander Gordon of Dunkintie sold Strathavon to his cousin George Earl of Huntley. Since that time, all this parish (except the Davach of Delnaboe) holds of Huntley in property or superiority.

It is all environed with hills, except a small opening towards Inveravon, and extends in length, on both sides of the river, from north-east to south-west 7 miles: and about the middle of the parish, the rivulet Conglas (which riseth in the hills towards the River Don), after a course of 7 or 8 miles, falleth into Avon, and here the breadth of the parish is 3 miles.

The Church standeth on the east bank of Avon, 2 miles above the lower end of the parish, 6 miles south-west of Inveravon, 4 miles east of Cromdale, and 5 miles east-north-east of Abernethie.

On the west side of the river, at the foot of Cromdale hill, are from north to south the lands of Inveraurie, Inverlochie, and Forletter, the property of the Duke of Gordon.

Above these, on the banks of the river, is Delnaboe, for some generations the heritage of a branch of the Clan Allan, but now the property of Sir James Grant of Grant.

Above Delnaboe, on both sides of the river, are Achnahyle, once a mortgage of James Grant, brother to Easter Elchies; Dellavorar, for three generations the Wadset of a branch of the M'Gregors; and Gavelack. These, and some other possessions, are now wadsetted by William Gordon, grandson to Glenbucket.

Above Gavelack, Glenavon runneth into the Grampian hills about 12 miles, and is a rich pasture for cattle, and a forest for red deer.

On the east side of the river, below the church, is Dell; above the church is Ruthven-Camdale, where, in 1754, a bridge of three arches was built over the river on the military-road.

Next is Camdale Bhrid, or Brigida's Camdale. And on Conglas rivulet are several possessions, particularly Achriachan, which, for about 200 years, was the inheritance of a branch of the Farquharsons, but is now the property of the Duke of Gordon.

[There are four parishes of this name in Scotland, derived from the patron Saint Michael; one in Carrick, Ayrshire, another in Annandale, Dumfries-shire, another in Perthshire, and the fourth (the present) in Banffshire. It has been likened to the wings of a bat spread out, with curious symmetry, to the north and south, in a westward flight. Near the kirk there was a fountain, once highly celebrated, and anciently dedicated to St. Michael. It now lies neglected, choked with weeds, unhonoured and unfrequented. In better days, the winged guardian, under the semblance of a fly, was never absent from his duty. If the matron wished to know the issue of her husband's ailment, or the maiden that of her lover, they visited the well of St. Michael. Every movement of the sympathetic fly was regarded in silent awe; and, as he appeared cheerful or dejected, the votaries drew their presages.

On the summit of a hill called the Mealaghaneimh is a stone called Clachbhan (from *clach*, a stone, and *bean*, a woman). On one side it measures 20 feet, on the other it is lower and of a sloping form. In face of it two seats have been excavated, resembling that of an arm-chair. Till of late this stone used to be visited by pregnant women, not only of this, but from distant countries, impressed with the belief that by sitting in these seats the pains of travail would become easy to them. (*The Stat. Acc. of Scotland*, vol. xii., pp. 425, 429, 464, 465.)

Queen Victoria writes, in " Leaves from the Journal of our Life in the Highlands from 1848 to 1861," that "TOMINTOUL, which is in this parish, is the most tumble-down poor-looking place I ever saw—one long street with three inns, miserable, dirty-looking houses and people, and a sad look of wretchedness about it. *Grant* told me that it was the dirtiest, poorest village in the whole of the Highlands."]—(ED.)

KIRKMICHAEL.

[*Situation, Soil, Climate.*—The northern limits of Kirkmichael lie on the southern borders of Cromdale, and on the west it meets with Abernethy, in the mountains of Cairngorum, and it occupies the western extremity of the county of Banff. The length between the habitable extremes is 15 miles, and its greatest breadth about 5. The Avon, in the Gaelic denoting simply *the river*, takes its rise from a lake, to which itself has given its name, at the southern bottom of Cairngorum, and holding a course southerly, almost at right angles from the Spey, for nearly 10 miles, through a deep valley, the forest of Glenavon, and dashing down a cataract of 18 feet in height, meeting with the rivulet Builg, stealing from its parent lake through its own green solitary vale, parallel to the Spey, a wing of the forest, they proceed easterly in the same course, till they turn with the stream of Conlass into a northerly direction, right onwards to the Spey; forming a considerable river, on a bed chiefly of limestone, and thereby so extremely pellucid, as to represent a depth of three feet scarcely equal to one, whereby many have been to the loss of their lives deceived.

Along the Avon and its tributary brooks, the soil is a black sandy earth: on the more elevated plains, it is a pretty fertile mould; on the declivities, it is a red earthy gravel, or in some places a deep clay; and as it rises higher on the hills, it is a more sterile moorish gravel. There is little to recommend the climate, always cold in winter, and in summer seldom warm, subjecting the inhabitants to coughs, consumptions, and disorders of the lungs, by which many at an advanced period, and several in early life, are cut off; and nervous fevers, frequently fatal, prevail during the summer and autumn.

State of Property.—The parish is divided into ten little districts called davochs, from the Gaelic *daimh*, oxen, and *auch*, field, denoting as much land as can be ploughed in one season by 4 yoke of oxen. One of these, named Delnaboe, is the property of Sir James Grant, Bart., valued in the Cess Books of Banff at £233 6s. 8d. Scots; the other 9 appertain to the Duke of Gordon, amounting to the valuation of £1925 6s. 8d. Scots. Excluding the forest of Glenavon, and the mountain pasturage pertaining to Delnaboe, the whole parish contains 29,500 acres, of which about 1550 are arable; the whole real rent about £1100 sterling. The whole number of black cattle amounts to 1400, the sheep to 7050, goats to 310, and horses to 303. The mean quantity of meal produced yearly amounts to 2560 bolls, which being only about 2 bolls to each individual, excluding the potatoe and garden stuffs, would be equal to no more than two-thirds of the provisions annually required.

The village of Tomantoul, near the middle of the parish, contains 37 families. There is no manufacture; only some necessary articles of merchandise retailed; and the men occasionally hire as labourers by the day.

State Ecclesiastical.—The stipend is £68 6s. 8d. sterling, and £10 sterling allowed by the proprietors for keeping the parsonage buildings in repair. The glebe is nearly 10 acres, and might be let for £6 sterling. The right of patronage is the property of Sir James Grant. The salary of the parochial school is £8 6s. 8d., with the usual fees of education, and the perquisites of the office of session-clerk. The Society for Propagating Christian Knowledge have established a school in the village of Tomantoul, with an appointment of £13 10s., where nearly 50 scholars attend. The number of poor on the parish roll amounts to 32, and the yearly contributions in the parochial church amount to little more than £2 sterling. The members of the Established Church are 892, and 384 are of the Church of Rome, who have their own clergyman, and a handsome chapel in the village of Tomantoul.

Miscellaneous Information.—Although the usual proportion of persons conspicuous for honour and integrity, benevolence and uprightness in their transactions, may be found in this parish, yet among the generality, cunning has supplanted sincerity, and dissimulation, candour; profession supplies the place of sincerity, and flattery is used as a lure to betray the unwary. Obligations are rewarded by ingratitude; and when a favour is past, the benefit is no longer remembered. Opposed to interest, promises cease to be binding; and the most successful in the arts of deception acquire the esteem of uncommon abilities and merit. Suspended between barbarism and civilization, the mind is never so strongly influenced by virtue, as it is attracted by the magnetism of vice.

Mr. George Gordon of Foddaletter is justly entitled to be ranked among the number of eminent men. As a chemist and a botanist, his knowledge was considerable, and it was applied to the extension of useful arts. He discovered, that by a simple preparation of a species of moss produced by the rocks and stones of the mountains, an elegant purple dye might be made. He established a manufacture of this substance at Leith; but its extension was cut off by his premature death in the year 1765.

There is a fountain of mineral water in the parish, of the same kind with the wells of Pannanich; it is frequented by people subject to gravellish disorders, and complaints in the stomach.

At the end of Lochavon is a large natural cave, in a detached mass of stone, nearly 7 feet high and 12 in breadth. The cavity can contain 18 armed men. It is named *clachdhian*, the stone of shelter. People often lodge in it for a night, some from necessity, others in hunting and fishing.] (*Survey of the Province of Moray.*)

EPITAPHS IN KIRKMICHAEL CHURCHYARD.

The Church, a plain building, erected in 1807, stands upon the haugh, on the south side of the Aven. It contains five monuments: one is of freestone, and thus inscribed:—

I. Here lies the body of Ann Lindsay, spouse of John Gordon of Glenbucket, and daughter of the Right Hon. Sir Alexander Lindsay of Evelack, who departed this life on the 9th day of June, 1750, aged 50 years. Also Helen Reid, spouse of William Gordon, Esq. of Glenbucket, and daughter of the Right Hon. Sir John Reid of Barra, who died on the 5th of May, 1766, aged 52 years; and Lilias M'Hardy, spouse of John Gordon, Esq. of Glenbucket, and daughter of William M'Hardy, late in Delnilat, who died May 30, 1829, aged 78 years. And of Elspet Stewart, spouse of Charles Gordon, Esq., St. Bridget, and daughter of William Stewart, Esq., Ballentrewan, who died 2nd February, 1856, aged 63 years.

II. A slab in the churchyard, which has disappeared within the last year or two, bore the following epitaph to the lady first named in the above inscription:—

Here l . . . the body of M . . . Lindsey, lady Glenbucket, d . . . to the Hon. Sir Alexander Lindsay . . . Evlack, who in the 59th year of her . . . departed this life on the 9th of June, 1 . . .:—

    Her stately person, beauty, great,
    Her charity and lowly heart;
    Her meekness and obedience
    Her chastity and her good sense,
    Do all combine to eternise,
    Her fame and praise above the skies.

The Gordons of Glenbucket were descended of those of Rothiemay, whose grandfather was of the family of Lesmore (Nisbet). The Lindsays of Evelick (Perthshire), were descended of a younger brother of Sir Walter of Edzell. In 1666, a baronetcy was created in the Evelick branch of the Lindsays. The Reids, who bought Barra about 170 years ago, were created baronets in 1707.

III. Another tablet within the kirk, commemorates the death of John Steuart (of the Auchnakyle and Lynchork family), Captain in H.M. 39th regt., who died at Bangalore, E.I., in 1835, aged 46; also two of his brothers, Robert, who died at Jamaica in 1824, aged 25, and Charles, M.D., 86th regt., who died at Kurachee, E.I., in 1844, aged 40, &c.

IV. Upon a similar marble slab, built into the south wall, embellished with the Grant arms, is this inscription:—

To the memory of Patrick Grant, Esq. of Glenlochy, lately of Stocktoun, who died 15th April, 1783, aged 74; and of Beatrix, his wife (daughter of Donald Grant, Esq. of Inverlochy), who died 24th January, 1780, aged 69. This monument is erected in testimony of filial affection and gratitude to the best of parents, by John Grant, Chief-justice of Jamaica.

V. A table-shaped stone, outside the church, is inscribed as above, except that it bears to be erected "to the best of parents by Francis Grant of Kilgraston."

This branch of the Grants is descended from John of Freuchy, 4th son of Grant of Grant. The abovenamed John, long Chief-justice of Jamaica, bought the estate of Kilgraston, in Perthshire. He died issueless, and was succeeded by his younger brother, the above Francis Grant, who married a daughter of Oliphant of Rossie, and died in 1819. Francis was succeeded by his eldest son John, who married a sister of Lord Gray. Lord Gray and his elder sister having both died without issue, Mr. Grant's daughter (widow of the Hon. Mr. Murray), is now Baroness Gray. Sir Francis Grant, P.R.A., a well known portrait-painter, is the 4th son of the above Francis Grant; and the 5th son is the brave Lieut.-Gen. Sir James Hope Grant, late Commander-in-Chief at Madras.

VI. A beautifully executed monument of Aberdeen granite (upon which are carvings of the insignia of the Bath), a sword and shield cross ways, from which medals are suspended, and inscribed, Nive, Victoria, and To The British Army, 1793-4 bears,

Underneath lie the mortal remains of William Alexander Gordon, Lieut.-Gen. in H.M.S., Colonel of the 54th regt. of foot, C.B. Born at Croughly 21 March, 1769, died at Nairn, 10 Augt., 1856, aged 87.

Two monuments relating to the same family are within the church. One to James Gordon, Esq., Croughly, who died in 1812, aged 86, and his wife Anne Forbes, who died in 1818, aged 82 (the parents of Lieut.-Gen. Gordon). The second monument is to Robert Gordon, Esq., who died in 1828, aged 47, and to several of his children.

VII. Upon the top of a table-shaped tombstone in the churchyard :—

To preserve this burying ground, and in pious regard to the memory of Finlay Farquharson of Auchriachan, who possessed this place since 1569, son to Findlay Farquharson, Esq. of Invercauld; likewise William Farquharson who died anno 1719, aged 80 years, who was the 9th man of that family who possessed Auchriachan, and Janet Grant his spouse, who died anno 1720, aged 78. Also William Farquharson, son of Inver . . . who died anno 1723, aged 30, and Elizabeth Farquharson his spouse, who died anno 1772, aged 78; also Sophia M'Gregor, who died anno 1729, aged 59, spouse to Robert Farquharson in Auchriachan, who erected this monument, 1789.

The said Robert Farquharson died in 179 , William, his son died in April 1811, and Alexander, the last in the male line, died 11th Nov., 1835, aged 78. Janet Farquharson, Robert's eldest daughter, married James Cameron, Ballenlish, and this tablet is renewed by their son, Angus Cameron of Firhall, 1851 :—

These bodies low lie here consign'd to rest,
With hopes with all to rise among the blest:
Sweet be their sleep, and blessed their wakening,
Reader! pray for those that pray for thee.

Achriachan, which, for about 200 years, was the inheritance of a branch of the Farquharsons, is now (1775) the property of the Duke of Gordon.

VIII. Within a railed enclosure, upon a handsome granite cross:—

In memory of Capt. James Gordon, who died at Ivybank, Nairn, 9th April, 1867, aged 90. He served in the Peninsula with the 92nd Highlanders, and received the war medal with seven clasps. He was also present at Waterloo, and received the medal. He never made an enemy, or lost a friend.

IX. Near the above is the following record of another race of gallant Highlanders:—

Capt. Robert M'Gregor, of the Clan Alpine Fencibles, and 14th Battalion of Reserve, died at Delavorar, 5 Oct., 1816, in the 80th year of his age. His sons, Peter, Lieut. 17th regt. of foot, was killed at the head of the Grenadiers at the regt., at the storming of Fort Chumera, in the East Indies, in the 26th year of his age ; John, Lieut. in the 88th regt., was killed at the attack on Buenos Ayres, in the 17th year of his age ; James, Lieut. H.P. 84th regt., died at Delavorar, in his 32nd year.

[The deaths of other members of this family are also recorded.]

X. Here lies JAMES GRANT of Ruthven, Bailiff of Strathaven and Glenlivet, who, in the 73rd year of his age, departed this life, Dec. 9, an. 1743.

> This was a man remarkable
> At home, abroad, still hospitable ;
> A good companion, trusty friend,
> And still obliging to mankind.

Pallida mors, &c. *Translation.*—Pale death knocks with impartial foot at the cottages of the poor and the palaces of kings.

XI. Here lys the body of ISOBEL M'LACHLAN, spovs to James Grant, who departed this life . . . year of his age, Oct. 29, 1722.

A rudely-shaped Cross, formed out of a slab of gneiss, about 5 feet high, with a hole pierced through the shaft, between the arms of the cross, stands beside the monument of Captain James Gordon. It is said to have been used by the natives for resting their spears or lances upon, when they come to Divine service ; and a story is told of some of the more sacrilegious of the Highlanders having killed a priest by the side of the stone, for his being too strict in demanding attendance at church.

This, however, had very possibly been the Cross of S. Michael, round which, in byegone times, the people of these parts (as was customary elsewhere), had assembled for the purpose of buying and selling commodities—markets having been originally held in churchyards, and upon Sundays. As such, it is a relic of much local interest, and possibly of high antiquity.

A chapel dedicated to S. Bridget stood near Tomintoul in old times; and a spring in the limestone rock of Craigchalkie is known by the name of S. Jessie.

A *quoad sacra* church and manse were erected at the village about 1826. The Roman Catholics, being a numerous body in the district, have a chapel, school, and priest's house here. This inscription is over the front of the chapel:—

BENE FUNDATA EST DOMUS DOM. SUPRA FIRMAM PETRAM. DEO SUB TUTELA B. MARIAE VIRGINIS ET B. MICHAELIS ARCHANGELI DEDICATA 1837.

Translation.—The House of the Lord is well founded on a firm rock. Dedicated in 1837 to God, under the protection of the Blessed Virgin Mary, and the Blessed Archangel Michael.

The adjoining Cemetery contains several neat tombstones. One of these, erected in 1843, presents some orthographical peculiarities:

> Trouble sore, I shurely bore,
> Physicians was in vain,
> Till God above, by his great love,
> Relieved me of my pain.

> Adieu, dear friends, who laid me here,
> Where I must lie till Christ appear,
> And on that day I hope it'll be
> A joyful rising into me.

I now return to the banks of Spey to describe

THE PARISH OF CROMDALE,

That is, the crooked plain, about which the Spey windeth. There are three parishes united into one, viz., Advie, Cromdale, and Inverallen, stretching on the east side of the river above 6 miles, and on the west side near to 12 miles in length, and in the centre about 4 miles in breadth, flanked to the east by Cromdale Hill, and to the west by the hills of Brae-Moray.

The Church of Cromdale standeth on the south-east bank of the river, 6 miles south-west of Inveravon, 4 miles north-east of Abernethie, and 6 miles E.N.E. of Duthel.

The three parishes (except a few mortgages) are the property of the Laird of Grant.

In the lower end is the parish of Advie, consisting of the baronies of Advie on the east, and of Tulchen on the west side of the river. These, anciently a part of the estate of the Earl of Fife, came to the family of Ballendalach in the 15th century, and continued their property till they were sold to Brigadier Alexander Grant. Grant of Advie was a branch of the family of Ballendalach, and Grant of Dallay of Advie.

Next up the river on the east side is Dalvey, which for several generations pertained to a branch of the family of Ballendalach, and about anno 1680 Robert of Dalvey purchased Dunlugas, in the county of Banff, and sold Dalvey to James Grant of Gartenbeg, who in 1688 was created a baronet; and dying soon after the Revolution, and his brother Lewis dying about 1698, both without legitimate issue, the lands of Dalvey (by an agreement with the heir male) came to Patrick Grant of Inverladenan, the chief of the Clan Donachie, and now they are the property of the Laird of Grant.

Farther up on that side of the river is the barony of Cromdale. This (and I doubt not with it Advie and Dalvey) was a part of the estate of M'Duff, Earl of Fife, which, 22 June, 1389, Isabel M'Duff, daughter and heir of Duncan, Earl of Fife, resigned "ad perpetuam remanentiam, in the hands of King Robert III. the baronies of Strathurd, Strathbraan, Deasir, Toyer, with the isle of Tay and Logyahrie, all in Perthshire; the barony of Coul and O'neil in Aberdeenshire; the baronies of Cromdale and Affyne (probably Advie) in Inverness-shire; the lands of Strathavie and Abrondolie in Banffshire; the barony of Calder in Linlithgowshire; and Kilsyth in Stirlingshire (*Skene de Verb. signif. Tit. Arage*)." This was afterwards the property of Nairn, Baron of Cromdale, from whom Ludovick Grant of Grant purchased it.

In Cromdale is Dellachaple, the seat of the head of the Clan Chiaran; Lethindie, the seat of the ancient barons; Burnside, the residence of William Grant of the Clan Allan; &c.

Near the Church is the passage-boat.

Over against Cromdale, and on the west side of the river, is Achinarraw, where the Clan Chiaran first seated.

Next is Dunan, the first seat of the Clan Allan; and next thereto is the barony of Freuchie (*i.e.*, heathery, so called from a hillock covered with heath, near the House of Grant) or of Castle-Grant. This (as also Achinarraw, Dunan, and all the lands of Inveralan) was anciently a part of the estate of Cumming, Lord Badenoch. Here is the principal seat of the family of Grant. The house is a grand building, environed with gardens, inclosures, and much planting. The apartments in the house are well finished, and there is a valuable private library.

Two miles south the Church of Inveralan standeth on the west bank of the river. In the 13th century, about 1230, this Church, and probably lands about it, pertained to Walter Moray, Baron of Petty and son of William, son of Freskyn of Duffus. And anno 1236 King Alexander II. excambed with Andrew, Bishop of Moray, the three Davachs of Fynlarg (near the Church of Inveralan) for the forest of Cawood and Logynsythenach in Brae-Moray.

In the upper end of the parish is Tullochgorum, the seat of the chief of the Clan Phadrick for near to 400 years.

North-west from Tullochgorum is Clourie, a mortgage belonging to a branch of the House of Grant.

And north from Clourie is Muckerach, the first possession of the Grants of Rothemurchus, where they built a good house anno 1598, but now in ruins.

CROMDALE.

[*Situation, Soil, Climate.*—Although a wing of the county of Inverness might without design be stretched farther down upon the south than upon the north bank of the Spey, yet the disposition of the two counties in the parish of Cromdale appears to be the result of contrivance, merely arbitrary and political.

Cromdale originally was three unconnected parishes. Inverallan, on the eastern border of Duthil, and on the north bank of the Spey, was parted but unequally between both counties. Cromdale itself, within the jurisdiction of Inverness, extends farther down on both banks of the Spey; below which, Advie, the third of the original parishes, is continued to Knockando on the north, and to Inveravon on the south bank of the river; extending the present parish of Cromdale to 9 miles in length on the southern side of the river, and 18 upon the other. Its greatest breadth is 10 miles, from Kirkmichael in the county of Banff to the Castle and Lake of Lochnadorb, on the bank of which the counties of Nairn, Inverness, and Moray meet.

The soil is in general thin and dry, with the exception of the plains on the banks of the river, which in natural fertility are deemed equal to the fields along the shore of the firth. The climate is allowed to be extremely wholesome. While epidemical distempers are very rare, instances of longevity as far as 90 years are many, and not a few get beyond that extreme term of human existence.

State of Property.—The whole parish is the property of Sir James Grant of Grant, Bart. The valued rent of the district of Inverallan in the county of Inverness is £474 6s. 8d.; that of Cromdale in the same county £949 14s. 6d. In Moray the valuation of Inverallan is £182 10s. 10d.; and of Advie is £862 13s.; extending the valuation of the whole parish to the sum of £2,469 5s. Scots. The real rent at present may be estimated about £2,000 sterling.

The family seat of Castle-Grant rises on an eminence near the middle of the parish, on the north side of the river. The body of the House is four storeys in height; its northern front makes 3 sides of a quadrangle, having lower wings added to the length of the opposite sides. The original front towards the south is also elegant, though the workmanship of the 15th century. The accommodation consists of 20 handsome bed-chambers, exclusive of the public-rooms, the ground floor, the wings, and garrets. The paintings in the dining-room, which is a magnificent hall, 47 by 27 feet, and of a proportionable height, are—a portrait of Charles I. and Queen Henrietta, by Vandyke; the Virgin presenting her infant Son in the Temple, and offering her sacrifice; the aged Simeon, elated with the sight of his infant Lord, by Caracci; a full length of Magdalene, by Guido; a half length also, copied by Clark from Guercino; the marriage of Joseph and Mary; the adoration of the Wise Men of the East; Henry IV. of France taking leave of his Queen, by Rubens; Pygmalion and the Statue, by Poussin; Ruins at Rome, by Sanini; Head of Achilles, by Hamilton; two large landscapes; the landing of Æneas in Africa; Dido flying with Æneas from the storm, by Plymor; family portraits by Kneller, West, Ramsay, Allan, and Miss Reid; copies of the portraits of Guercino, Caracci, Angelo, and Fordano, by Clark at Rome; Still Life, Basketmaker, and Milkwoman.

The paintings in the drawing-room:—A half-length of Magdalene, by Guido; Venus mourning for Adonis, by Guercino; the celebrated painting by Hamilton of Achilles mourning over Patroclus, attended by Brisëis, Chrisëis, and chiefs of Greece—the prints of this painting, which are not uncommon, display much of its expression; copy by Clark of the Baptism of Constantine, by Volteria; eight small paintings in a frame, by Vandyke; a pencil drawing of Charles I. and his Queen, from Vandyke's original; a copy of Guercino's Persian Sibyl; Andromache offering sacrifice to Hector's Shade, by Morison of Rosybank; the Saviour on the Cross; Monks in a Cave; family portraits.

The paintings in the different bed-chambers:—Copy by Clarke of Guercino's Apostle Peter; three sea-pieces by Vandermere; the Holy Family, by Paragino; two paintings of the Civil Wars, by Burguiong; several portraits by Sir Peter Lely; two landscapes by Ponfract; Mars and Vulcan, an Italian drawing; the Resurrection of Lazarus; Adam and Eve; St. Veronica; the Judgment of Paris; Niobe and her Children.

In the hall are 30 portraits, by Watt, of gentlemen of the name of Grant, most of them exhibiting a true likeness of the original.

In the stair-case are:—A lady dressing, by Titian; Danaë receiving the Flower of Gold, by Corregio: Venus and Adonis, by Clark, from Lucas Fardano; An Encampment, by Bassau: a Highlander, a Piper, and an Old Woman, by Watt.

The House commands a pretty extensive and pleasing landscape. Southward the deep forest of Abernethy, its broad dark-green plain encroaching on the dusky side of the lofty Cairngorm, the pale rolling cloud seizing at times its summit, equalling its peerless elevation with the humbler hills, and the mountain anon discharging the hovering vapour, in lingering detachments, resumes its proud preeminence, and looks down upon its neighbours. Spread eastward, lies the wide-bending cultivated plain of Cromdale, its green level border illuminated by the blue-rolling river; and on the north and west, an irregularly curved range of hill displays upon its side the verdant mantle of flourishing plantation. The park itself is of great extent, diversified with the agreeable variety of thicket, grove, and forest, corn field and meadow; a double line of tall trees extends a cool shade over a long lane, by the lofty canopy of their intermingled foliage, impervious to the summer sun and the slighter shower; the trim garden, the ornamented shrubbery, and several pleasant ridings, may suggest a general idea of the environs of this respectable Mansion, the extent of which may be conceived by the compass occupied by the wood, nearly 4,000 acres.

About half the number of farms are rented at £7, £20, or £25 sterling, exclusive of some late improvements, and a few small lots for the accommodation of the labourers about the castle. The other half rent at or above £50 sterling, managed in the most approved system: the horses and cattle of a fine brood and figure, the implements of the best construction, and the buildings of the most substantial masonry and commodious form.

At the distance of nearly two miles westward of the

Castle is the village of Grantown. The first house was built in 1766, at that time in the midst of a pretty extensive uncultivated moor. It is built upon leases of 190, or ten nineteens of years, on an extent of 21 by 460 yards; rent free for the first 5 years, and 5s. yearly for the succeeding 14; for the second period of 19 years, 10s. yearly; growing to 11s. 8d. during the third; and to 15s. during the fourth; and £1 thereafter for the duration of the lease. The village, containing about 400 souls, is regularly constructed—the street 56 feet broad, and the great square 180 by 700 feet in length, decorated by a handsome town-house, for the accommodation of the Justice of Peace and Baron Courts. A brewery was from the first established, and a clause of the leases prohibits the vending of spirituous liquors without the written permission of the proprietor. A dozen of retail shops increase the movement of business; and weavers of wool, flax, and stocking manufactures, tailors, shoemakers, carpenters, masons, and blacksmiths, and two bakers, with a regularly bred and skilful surgeon, complete the accommodation of a very populous country around. The land improved about the village lets at 12s. the acre; to which the proprietor himself has added an extent of 60 acres in its vicinity improved by one year's fallowing the moor, and the manure of 60 bolls, or 240 firlots, of lime to each acre. In the environs of the village there is a pretty extensive bleachery, both of cloth and yarn, also a well constructed flax-mill, the operations of both conducted at present by a gentleman, a native of Ireland. The village possesses every inland advantage in the midst of a great and populous country; store of peat-fuel, wood, lime, slate, and stone, with the command of a stream of excellent water.

State Ecclesiastical.—The situation of the Church is centrical, on the south bank of the Spey, in the wide semicircular plain of Cromdale, which, in the original, expresses this situation; it is a modern, neat, well-finished building. The stipend, including the allowance for the communion, equal to that of Duthel and Abernethy, is £105. Part of the glebe, which still remains in what was the parish of Advie, together with the part at the present residence, might be let for nearly £9 of rent. The patronage is the right of the family of Grant. The salary

of the parochial school, which is near the Church, is
£11 2s. 3d. sterling, and the emoluments of the office of
session-clerk, about £4 sterling, besides the fees of education. There is also a school established in Grantown,
which, exclusive of the fees from nearly 70 scholars, for
education in French, Latin, Writing, Arithmetic, and
reading English, is an appointment of £25 yearly, of
which £10 arises from a bequeathed endowment under
the care of the Presbytery, £10 by the Society for Christian Knowledge, and £5 the gratuity of Sir James Grant.
There is also in the village a private schoolmistress, where
girls and children receive the rudiments of their education. Of late, also, an orphan Hospital has been established
in Grantown by a share of the fund bequeathed by the
late Lady Grant of Monymusk for the purposes of charity.
This fund was considerably diminished by a suit in
Chancery with the executors. One third part of this
bequeathment was, by her Ladyship's will, allocated for
Scotland: the object and the place to be appointed by
Dr. Gregory Grant of Edinburgh, without direction or
restraint. The capital for this Hospital amounts at
present to £5,000 stock in the 3 per cents. to which Sir
James Grant has added the sum of £150 sterling, and the
accommodation of a house equal to £12 of rent. The
plan of the Grantown Hospital is the same with that of
the orphan Hospital of Edinburgh; none are admitted
under 7 nor continued after 14 years of age, and at
present the number is limited to 30. Besides reading,
writing, and arithmetic, the girls are taught sewing,
weaving, and knitting with wires; and such trades as
can be conveniently carried on within doors are taught to
those of the boys who choose such employment. The
present establishment is a governess, with £10 sterling,
and 2 female servants; and the youth attend the schools
in the village, till the fund can admit of a teacher in the
hospital.

The contributions made in the Church for the poor
amount to £10 or £15 sterling; generally distributed to
30 individuals, though more are occasionally admitted to
a share of this provision. The whole inhabitants are of
the National Church, amounting to 3,000 souls.

Miscellaneous Information.—The people are industrious and of an obliging disposition. On public occasions

they are distinguished by the neatness of their attire; the women are also noted among their neighbours for cleanliness in their houses, and for the domestic manufacture of webs of woollen cloth.

The only antiquity in the parish is the Fortalix at Lochindorb, where a thick wall of mason work (20 feet even at this period, and supposed to have been much higher) surrounded an acre of land within the loch, with watch-towers at every corner, all entire. The entrance to the place is at a gate built of freestone, which has a grandeur in it that is easier felt than expressed. Several vestiges of houses are found within the walls, besides those of a church, which, without difficulty, can still be traced in the ruins. Great rafts or planks of oak, by the beating of the waters against the old walls, occasionally make their appearance, which confirms an opinion entertained of this place that it had been a national business, originally built upon an artificial island. Tradition says, and some credit is due to the report, that the particular account of this building was lost in the days of King Edward I. of England. The herb peculiar to that island, distinguished by the name of *Lochnadorb kail*, appears to be a mixture of red cabbage plants and common turnip, sown probably by the last possessor and never reaped, and since then degenerated through want of cultivation. They spring up annually in a thick bed without culture; in some favoured situation the root of the turnip is found almost of a pound weight, but, in general, the root is similar to that of cabbage plants; both are used as greens at the tables of the country people, and transplanted also into their gardens with the same view: when they run to seed on the island, young cattle are ferried in to feed on them.

The last battle in the revolutionary civil war, in 1690, was fought on the plain of Cromdale.* Colonel Living-

* *The Battle on the Haughs of Cromdale.*—By the death of Claverhouse (Viscount Dundee) at Killiecrankie on July, 1689, the cause of James II. became desperate. All his adherents were scattered or capitulated, except a few headed by Sir Ewen Cameron of Lochiel, who trusted to the approach of winter and the inaccessible nature of the mountains on the west coast, to which they retired. When the spring of 1690 began to open up, General Buchan was despatched with some 1500 men of the

ston, King William's general, defeated the forces of the Viscount Dundee with considerable slaughter, and many prisoners. It was, however, of little importance to the State, and needs not a particular relation here; it is celebrated in a well known Scots ballad ["The Haughs of Cromdale,"] happily descriptive of the humours and sentiments of the age.

The ancient name of Cromdale, *skir-na luac*, St. Luac's division or parish, to whom also a well was dedicated; and Inverallan is derived from the influx of the stream of Toperallan into the Spey, a well emitting a quantity of water at once sufficient to turn the machinery of a corn mill.

The names of many of the places in Strathspey are the same with those in Stratheric, it being ascertained that

Clans Maclean, Macdonald, Macpherson, Cameron, and Grant of Glenmorriston to lay waste the low country, and to divert and annoy King William's troops. On their march they plundered the inhabitants of Strathspey, and in Strathbogie they burnt the House of Edinglassie. Sir Thomas Livingston, who had been stationed at Inverness with a large force of cavalry and infantry, resolved to intercept them before they regained the interior of the country; but Buchan with his clans, hearing of the approach, betook themselves to the mountains. On the 1st of May, 1690, by dawn of day, Livingston arrived with his troops at Derraid, near Castle Grant, and ordered them to march into and through the woods and come down the Valley of Auchinarron, and cross the Spey at the ford below Dellachaple. On the 30th April, General Buchan and his troops had arrived at Cromdale and encamped at the farm of Lethendry, at the foot of the Hill of Cromdale, near the old Kirk of Cromdale, about 3 miles eastward, whereon Grantown now stands. Some of the outposts observing Livingston's troops fording the Spey at once gave the alarm, but the dragoons were on them before those in the camp had time even to put on their clothes. They hastened in confusion to the Hill of Cromdale, where they contended valiantly but were at last routed, leaving 400 slain and prisoners.

As regards the famous song in his *Jacobite Relics* Hogg says that it is the worst specimen of the truth of Scottish song that is to be met with, the Battle of Auldearn in 1645 and this one in 1690 being jumbled together. However, "The Bonny Haughs o' Cromdale" in rhythm and tune are imperishable. (ED.)

the ancestors of the family of Grant were once the possessors of that country on the banks of Loch Ness.] (*Survey of the Province of Moray.*)

EPITAPHS IN CROMDALE CHURCHYARD.

The burial-ground is surrounded by a substantial stone dyke. The monuments are modern. One within an enclosure, and in front of the kirk, exhibits a carving of the Grant arms, with this inscription:—

I. Sacred to the memory of Mrs. Grant of Burnside, daughter of George Macpherson, Esq., of Invereshie, who was a sincere Christian, an affectionate wife, and a dutiful kind parent, and was ever charitable and most amiable. She departed this life in 1835, in the 93rd year of her age.

The above refers to Jane, youngest daughter of Mr. Macpherson, by Grace, daughter of Col. Grant, and maternal aunt to the first Baronet of Ballindalloch. The father of Mrs. Grant's husband took part with Prince Charles, and was present at the battle of Prestonpans. He afterwards became a W.S., and died at Edinburgh in 1790.

The next inscription (abridged) refers to one of "The Men," or those who believed that their knowledge of the Scriptures was superior to that of their neighbours. (See Epitaphs in Duthil Churchyard, p. 259).

II. LACHLAN CAMERON, son of James Cameron, in Shenval of Delvey, "a man of good understanding and given to hospitality," died 1783, aged 43.

The next four inscriptions are from monuments within an enclosure:—

III. Sacred to the memory of ROBERT GRANT, Esq., of Kincorth, son of Mr. David Grant and of Margaret Grant, his wife, residenters in Lethendry in this parish, both of whom are here interred, descended from the Clan Chiarn branch of the family of Grant; an original member of the North West Company in Canada. In business he gained respect and confidence by honour and integrity. In all relations of private life exemplary. Born 3rd March, 1752; died at Kincorth, 10th August, 1801. Also in affectionate remembrance of Mrs. ANN GRANT, relict of the above Robert Grant, who died at Forres House, on the 19th of May, 1864, aged 95.

IV. In memory of Lewis Grant, Esq., sometime merchant in Bombay, second son of the late Robert Grant, Esq., of Kincorth; born at Kincorth, 12th Sept., 1801; died at the same place, 17th February, 1854. An affectionate and dutiful son, a most attached brother, an upright and amiable man. This monument is erected to record his virtues, by his afflicted and affectionate brothers.

V. In memory of MRS. ROBINA ANN GRANT, eldest daughter of the late Robert Grant, Esq., of Kincorth, and wife of John Peter Grant, Esq., residing at Invererne House, near Forres, by whom this stone is erected to record his affection and esteem. He died upon 11th Sept., 1850, aged 52 years. Her only sister, MRS. DAVINA GRANT, wife of Frederic Grant, Esq., of Mount Cyrus, Kincardineshire, where her mortal remains are deposited in the burying-ground of St. Cyrus parish. She died on 8th March, 1828, aged 27 years.

Robert and Lewis Grant were twins, and their mother was a daughter of the minister of Cromdale. The husband of their sister Robina was a son of Mrs. Grant of Laggan, the poetess.

VI. Sacred to the memory of ROBERT GRANT, of Kincorth, who died on the 10th August, 1801, in the 49th year of his age. Also in memory of LEWIS, infant son of Robert Grant and Edith Eaton, his wife, who died at Forres House, on the 17th November, 1861, aged 13 months.

From a table-shaped stone, enclosed :—

VII. Erected to the memory of ALEXANDER CARMICHAEL, of Congash, who died the 14th November, 1803, in the 64th year of his age. He was justly esteemed and sincerely regretted for his uniform integrity and general benevolence.

Lieut.-Col. LEWIS CARMICHAEL, born at Kinrara, June 26, 1792, died at Forres, August 8, 1844. Entering the army in 1809, as an Ensign in the 59th Regt. of Foot, he served his country 34 years with distinguished honours. At Vittoria, San Sabastian, Nivelle, Nive, and Waterloo, he earned the reputation of a zealous and intrepid officer; and at the assault of Bhurtpore, for a feat of extraordinary valour, he was officially thanked by the General in command, Sir Jasper Nicolls. His efforts in contributing to restore order in Canada during the commotions of 1838, &c., were duly appreciated and acknowledged by the Local Government, and by all the well affected in that Colony. As a man he was kind and generous, devoted to the interests of his country, beloved by his companions in arms, and esteemed by all who knew him. After a short but painful illness, which he bore with Christian submission to Divine Will, he died in the hope of a blessed resurrection. This monument his sorrowing sisters have erected to an affectionate and lamented brother, 1845.

VIII. There are five Tablets on the south side of the Church to a family of HOUSTON, the earliest recorded of whom, ALEX. HOUSTON, and his wife JANE CRUICKSHANK, lived in Grantown, and died respectively in 1808 and 1796. The deaths of two sons and two daughters are recorded. The eldest son, JAMES, and his wife HELEN MACDONALD, died in 1842 and 1863 respectively, and the following refers to one of their family:—

IX. In memory of ALEX. CRUICKSHANK HOUSTON, Lieut. 62nd Regiment, Bengal, N.I., "an officer of proved gallantry and great promise," born 25th March, 1829, at Kirkton of Inverallan, died 29th May, 1855, at Fort Abouzdie, in the Punjaub, where the officers of his regiment have erected a monument over his grave.

ADVIE.

The ruins of the Church of Advie occupy a hillock about 3 miles below the kirk and boat of Cromdale. A considerable portion of the walls of the church still remain, the east gable being the most entire. The walls are about 3 feet thick, and the inside measurement of the fabric is about 20 by 52 feet. The ruins of a roofless "watch-house" are near the south-west corner.

The kirkyard-dykes are in keeping with the crazy state of the kirk walls; but, being surrounded by a few ash and fir trees, the site is not destitute of picturesque beauty. Fine views of the shooting lodge of Tulchan, and a large part of the wilds of Spey, are obtained from it.

There are about a dozen grave-stones within the area of the ruins, and in the churchyard. From these the two inscriptions below are selected.

The former is upon a granite obelisk; the latter upon a plain headstone :—

I. In memory of the late ADAM STEWART, Esq., Mains of Dalvey, and of MARJORY GRANT, his spouse. Also of their sons, WILLIAM, surgeon in the 58th Regt., who died the . . . and GREGOR, surgeon in the 18th Regt., who died at Hong-Kong, on the 18th August, 1846.

James, younger son of Adam Stewart, became minister of the adjoining parish of Abernethy, where he died in 1862, aged 57. Being of an unostentatious, kindly disposition, he was much respected in his parish, while his attainments in literature and science gained him many friends at a distance. He was one of the best violinists in the north, and excelled in Strathspeys. "A thorough Highlander in feeling (Scott's *Fasti*), he had a treasure of Highland legends, and being gifted with a poetic genius, had several specimens of his verses printed in the *Banffshire Journal.*"

II. Erected by Peter Grant, Ballifurth, in memory of his son JOHN GRANT, who died May 15, 1843, aged 19 years. Remember man, &c.

6th May, 1874, ELSIE GRANT LIVINGSTON died in the faith, Prov. xiv. 13, aged 26.

By grace I say,
I hope alway,
I'll see my resurrection day.

Also, in memory of the foresaid PETER GRANT, late tenant, Ballifurth, who died on the 12th day of August, 1855, aged 78 years.

There is still a Mission Church, and regular service is held at Advie; but in addition to this parish, that of INVERALLAN is also united to Cromdale. The district of Inverallan was erected as a *quoad sacra* in 1869, and is known as the Church of GRANTOWN.

A good many traces of pre-historic remains have been found in the united parishes, such as stone-cists and urns, funeral cairns, and Druidical circles, the most of which have been described either in the Statistical Accounts, local Guide-books, or the Proceedings of the Society of Antiquaries of Scotland.

One point is curious.

It forms—1, boundary between the counties of Moray and Banff; 2, boundary between the parishes of Cromdale and Inveravon; 3, boundary between Seafield and Ballindalloch estates; 4, boundary between the Buchan and Moray "Nations" at the Aberdeen University; 5, boundary between Lower and Upper Strathspey; 6, boundary between the Gaelic and English speaking population (Gaelic being still regularly preached in Cromdale Church).

I now go up the river to

THE PARISH OF ABERNETHY,

That is, the mouth of *Nethie*, or the impetuous washy river. To this the parish of Kinchardine is united, and both lie on the south east side of the river. It extendeth from the borders of Cromdale to Rothiemurchus, 7 miles in length, and from Spey to Glenlochy, 5 miles in breadth, environed, except on the river, with a chain of hills. The barony of Kincardine is the property of the Duke of Gordon, and all the rest, except a few wadsets, the property of the Laird of Grant. Abernethy is in the county of Moray, and Kinchardine in the county of Inverness.

The Church standeth two furlongs from Spey, and as far from Nethie, 4 miles south west of Cromdale; 4 miles east of Duthel, and 6 miles north-east of Rothiemurchus.

The water of Nethie riseth in the hills near to Loch Avon, and watering the parish from south to north, after a course of near 7 miles, dischargeth into Spey.

The barony of Abernethy was a part of the estate of Cumming, Lord Badenoch, where he had a house or fort near the church. (See "Military History.") Upon the forfeiture of Cumming, it became a part of the Earldom of Moray, and as yet giveth the title of Lord Abernethy to that Earl. On the death of Earl

John Randulf anno 1346, the Earldom reverted to the Crown: and Abernethy, as a part of it, was given to " Delecto filio nostro Joanni de Dunbar, et Mariotæ sponsæ ejus, filiæ nostræ charissimæ, 9° Mart. anno regni 2° 1373."* (*Rotul. Rob.* II.) At what time the Lairds of Grant first obtained any part of Abernethy, I cannot determine; but they were in possession of the lower parts early in the 16th century, and thereafter they purchased the upper part in the 17th century, from the Earl of Moray.

Let it be observed that the Davachs of Gartenmore, Rymore, and Tulloch, in Abernethie, and the Davachs of Tullochgorum, Clourie, and Cour, in Inverallan, were a part of the Lordship of Badenoch; and about anno 1660, the family of Huntly excambed these lands with John of Freuchie, for lands in Strathavon and Glenlivat, reserving to Huntly a servitude upon the fir wood of Rymore, for repairing Gordon castle, and the castle of Blairfindie in Glenlivat, which servitude is still in force.

In the east end of the parish is Conegess, a mortgage pertaining to Mr. William Grant late minister of Abernethie; and a half mile above Conegess, is a bridge of four arches over Spey built on the military road in 1754.

---

* *Translation.*—Our well-beloved son John Dunbar, and Mariot his spouse, our dearest daughter, 9th of March, in the 2nd year of our reign, 1373.

A mile further up is Achernack, for about 300 years the residence of the Head of the Clan Allan. About the year 1560, James Grant of Achernack had a family of eight sons, whereof Duncan was heir: a 2nd, Gregor, founded the family of Gartmore; a 3rd, James, was ancestor of Auchterblair, now Carron; a 4th, John, was the first of the Grants of Easter Lethendie and Burnside; a 5th, Allan, was ancestor of Mulachard; a 6th, Mungo of Conegess; a 7th, Robert of Nevie; and the 8th, Andrew.

Near to Auchernack is a passage boat.

At the mouth of Nethie is Coulnakyle, a pleasant seat, where Sir James Grant has built a neat new house.

A mile up on Nethie, is *Letoch*, the mortgage of a gentleman of the Clan Allan; and a mile further up is *Lurg*, the seat of Robert Grant of Lurg, the 5th descent from Duncan heir of Grant, who died anno 1581.

Beyond Nethie, on the river Spey, is *Gartinmore* a mortgage of John Grant.

South from which is *Rymore*, and south-west thence is *Tulloch*, which had been for six generations the property of a branch of the family of Ballendalach, lately extinct.

A skirt of the parish of Abernethy lieth in a narrow valley called *Glenbruin* and *Glenlochie*, near the river Avon.

The barony of Kinchardine lieth on the river

Spey, betwixt Gartinmore and Rothiemurchus. The Church* is in the middle of it, a furlong from the river.

I observed above, that Walter Stewart of Kincardine was the 3rd son of the Earl of Buchan. His descendants for ten descents continued in good repute, till about the year 1683, John Roy, the last Baron (a silly ignorant man), was in a manner cheated out of his estate, by his brother-in-law Alexander M'Intosh, called the "sheriff Baine," who made him sell it to the Marquis of Huntly for a very trifle; and the family is extinct.

[Near the Parish Kirk there is a large oblong building called *The Red Castle* or *Castle Roy*, which appears never to have been roofed, has no loop-holes, and has only one entrance to the interior. Even "old wives' fables" fail to make up what is wanting. One side measures 30, the other 20 yards; the height is about 10.

Before 1745, *reiving*, or stealing cattle, was carried on to a great extent in this parish; and the county of Moray seems always to have been considered a fair field for plunder. It used to be a subject of regret that the cornstacks would not be driven like cattle. So great was the propensity to *reiving*, which was not considered a crime, that the Laird of Grant was obliged to build a stable within his court to prevent his own brother from making him *minus* of his best horses. The people of the district were in those times obliged to maintain a watch during the summer months for protecting their cattle; and those sentinels were regularly relieved at certain hours in military style.

* The Kirk of Kincardine is 8 miles distant from the village of Abernethy. The parish minister officiates two successive Sabbaths in the Kirk of Abernethy, and every third Sabbath in that of Kincardine. The latter has sittings for 600; the former for 1000. (ED.)

In the beginning of the 18th century, the only judges recognised in this district were the Bailies of the Regality appointed by the chiefs. Those functionaries were a set of the most ferocious despots, who set all law at defiance. One of them named Robert Grant, commonly called "Bailie More," lived in this parish. He was accustomed to hang people merely for disobliging him, and he seldom called juries. Another named James Grant, alias "Bailie Roy," or "the Red Bailie," on one occasion hanged a man; and after the unfortunate wight was dead, a jury was summoned who found him guilty as a matter of course, the said jury being all the creatures of "the Red Bailie." This personage coolly observed, when they gave their verdict of guilty, that it did not signify to the man whether he was hanged before or after the trial, as he would have been hanged at any rate. It appears that the Bailie had his own reasons for being in a hurry, as his victim possessed horses, cattle, sheep, and goats, all of which were driven to "the Bailie's" house. The children of the unfortunate man were reduced to beggary, and his wife became deranged, and drowned herself. On another occasion, this same "Bailie Roy" hanged two thieves, parboiled their heads, and set them up on spikes. He drowned two men in sacks at the Bridge of Bellimon, within a few hundred yards of the manse of Abernethy. When a man from Glenmore, in the barony of Kincardine, refused to assist him and his followers in the business, "the Bailie" said:— "I tell you what it is, my lad, if I had you within my regality, I would teach you better manners than to disobey my commands." Another of these wretches was "the Sheriff Baine" (probably the individual alluded to above by *Shaw*), who became so odious that the country people drowned him in Spey, near the kirk of Inverallan, about 2 miles from Abernethy.

Lords Cullen and Prestongrange, judges of the Court of Session, were connected with this parish. The Hon. John Grant, Chief Justice of Jamaica, and John Roy Stuart, the Gaelic poet, were natives. The latter was born in 1700 at Knock of Kincardine.

Tullochgorum farm-house, the pristine seat of the Clan Phatrick, on the left side of the Spey, nearly opposite the Kirk of Abernethy, has famous associations with the ancient poetry and music of Strathspey, and figures in the sarcastic lines of Sir Alexander Boswell, beginning, "Come the Grants of Tullochgorum," at which every Highland heart will beat.

In the Kincardine portion of the united parish, there are several lakes. The most considerable is Loch Morlach in Glenmore, of an oval shape, nearly 2 miles in diameter, and surrounded with old fir trees which rise gradually towards the mountains. There is also another small loch in Glenmore, which covers about an acre, which abounds in green trout. Loch Garten and Loch Maulachie, communicating with each other, lie northwest of Kincardine Kirk. Loch Pittenlish is south-west, at the Spey-side of the mountain range of Glenmore. At the foot of Cairngorum is Loch Avon; at the end of which, surrounded by mountains, is a large natural *Cave*, called by a name in Gaelic, signifying *the Sheltering Stone*, i.e., *the Blue Mountain*.

Cairngorum is one of the highest of the Grampians. It is 4050 feet above the level of the sea, and 1780 feet above Loch Avon, which is a mile from its base. It is of a conical shape; the sides and base are clothed with extensive fir woods, while its top is covered almost all the year round with snow. It has been long celebrated for beautiful rock crystals, called "*Cairngorum Stones*"— a species of *Topaz* much admired by Lapidaries. They were formerly found in great quantities, but are now more carefully sought for among the debris of the mountains brought down after a storm. They are hexagonal or six-sided prisms, extending from 1 inch to 6 or 8 inches in length, and of which specimens have been found weighing 10 lbs. of solid crystal. Generally the one end is rough, and often a part of the rock to which the gem was attached adheres to it. Topaz, beryl, amethyst, and garnet, also occur in this range of mountains. The following is a list of some of the rarer and more characteristic plants of this mountain district:—Aira alpina, Aira vivipera, Aiopecurus alpinus, Apargia Taraxaci, Arabis hispida, Arabis petrœa, Azalla procumbens, Betula namœ, Cetrariœ.] (ED.)

ABERNETHY.

[*Situation, Soil, Climate.*—The river Spey, expanded

to its greatest apparent magnitude, glides onward in a smooth unruffled course from Rothiemurchus along the northern border of the district of Kinchardine in the sheriffdom of Inverness, which is continued on the southern side of the river till it meets that of Moray near the middle of Abernethy, the lower end of which falls again within the county of Inverness, which stretches across from the parish of Cromdale, till it borders on the county of Banff in the parish of Kirkmichael, where there is a point at which the three counties meet.

Kinie-chairdin, in the Gaelic, signifies *the tribe of friends:* and Abernethy, where the church of that district is placed, denotes *the influx of the Nethy into the Spey.* The two districts extend the parish 15 miles along the banks of the Spey. It is nearly 12 miles to its southern border, in the extremities of the valleys of Glenlochy and Glenbruin, and the sources of the Nethy, which intersects the parish for the whole length of its course, which is only a brook in dry weather, but it is swelled by rain to such consideration, as to float down the timber to the saw-mills or to the Spey. There are several lakes in the parish: that of Glenmore is nearly circular, about 2 miles in diameter. It occupies the middle of an aged forest of firs, the largest and best timber in Scotland, and discharges a stream into Spey through a course of 6 miles, which, having been deepened and straighted, and a sluice and dam constructed, forming at pleasure an artificial flood, by which masts for the vessels even of the Navy, and the heaviest logs, are navigated into the Spey, which conveys them onwards to the Garmach dockyard. In this quarter is a deep hollow in a mountain; the bottom, of inconsiderable extent, forms a lake, neither taking in nor emitting any stream; but the rocky banks rise around to a great height, and are closely clothed with the ever-verdant pine, by the reflection of which the water is always seen of the deepest green colour, in every possible situation. It is stored with abundance of fat trout, which glitter in the same hue while viewed within the mound of this singular cavity.

The mountains of *Cairngorum*, the blue mountains, rise to a very conspicuous elevation on the southern boundary of the parish: they are never wholly free from snow; the forests cannot extend themselves to a great height on their sides, nor a tree rear its head within the region of the cold; even pasturage itself fails, and their rocky summits are covered with a downy coat of yellow sapless moss: from them the prospect is stretched over half the kingdom, from the mountains of Perthshire to the Caithness plains, and from the shores of Buchan to the sources of the Spey. The eye, accustomed to flowery pastures, and waving harvests, is astonished at the appearance and properties of mountainous regions: but these constitute a great part of the earth; and he that has never seen them must live unacquainted with much of the face of nature, and with one of the great scenes of human existence. The majestic features of the uncultivated wilderness, and extensive prospects of nature, gained from the lofty brows of rocky mountains, yield an expansion of fancy and a native elevation of thought, accompanied with impressions interesting and solemn, leaving on the memory traces of an entertainment serious and sublime.

The arable ground in the parish bears but a small proportion to the uncultivated: a great part of the surface is covered with wood; much more is rock, hill, and mountain: part of the arable soil is thin and dry, part wet and cold, and part kindly and deep: a stretch of 3 miles, containing many hundred acres of this fertile quality, along the bank of the Spey, is often overflowed. The air and climate become less genial as the ground rises towards the mountains, which occasion much frost and cold: but in healthfulness it is not exceeded by any part of the kingdom.

State of Property.—The district of Kinchardine, with all its wood, is the property of the Duke of Gordon. The particulars of the contract between his Grace and Messrs. Osbourn of Hull, and Dodsworth of York, for the marketable timber in the forest of Glenmore, are given under the parish of Speymouth. It only remains to be added here, that his Grace has also let to this company a considerable farm in the skirts of the forest, for their accommodation in the management of the timber; in their agricultural operations they have adopted the modern practice of the country. In the Cess-Books of the county of Inverness, Kinchardine stands valued at £400 Scots.

The district of Abernethy appertains to Sir James

Grant of Grant, Bart. The valuation of the Inverness-division is £903, 6s. 8d., and the Morayshire valuation amounts to £750, 9s. 4d. extending the valued rent of the whole parish to the sum of £1563 16s. Scots. The real rent of the Abernethy district, exclusive of the revenue for the sale of the wood, is about £1400 sterling. There are some farms in this part of the parish in a high degree of improvement, having substantial and commodious buildings, sufficient enclosures, and fields properly cultivated by able cattle, and implements of the best form, and brought to the highest state of productiveness by lime manure and green crops. The higher parts of the parish might be also much improved, particularly by the application of lime, which the vicinity both of the quarry and of the fuel solicit to provide: but the lands are let in run ridge, and without any certain lease, and every imagination of improvement must be thereby instantaneously and completely quashed. The only mode of melioration within the reach of these poor tenants is, not to overlook the summer pasturage, nor the winter forage, with greater numbers of sheep and cattle than can be kept in good condition. The productions of the cultivated land are chiefly black oats, and barley, rye, and potatoes. The crop is always precarious, and frequently misgives to a very distressing degree. Deducting the seed, and corn for the horses, the whole produce amounts to 2640 bolls, at an average of years; about 1½ bolls to each inhabitant, or provision only for six months of the year.

The revenue arising from the forest in the district of Abernethy, extending over 10,000 acres, is of great consideration. An uninterrupted manufacture of this timber hath been carried on for more than 60 years: though the wood, therefore, be in a very thriving state, it does not acquire the bulk, or hardness, or quantity of rosin, which is found in timber of more mature age. It is yet remembered in the country, since the only mode that was known of making deals, was, by splitting the timber with wedges, and trimming the boards with the adze or the ax; and an upper-room in Castle-Grant is floored with deals of this kind, never smoothed by the plane. In those days, the landlord got only a merk (1s. 1⅓d. sterling) in the year, for as much timber as a man could in this mode manufacture. By small gradations of 1s. 8d. and 3s. 4d. it had risen to 5s. 6d. about the year 1730, when the York Building Company purchased the timber of the woods of Abernethy, to the amount of nearly £7000 sterling. Great indeed was their beginning: every kind of implement of the best form, 120 work-horses, waggons, elegant wooden houses, saw-mills, and an iron foundry, all surprising novelties in the country. They had a commissary for provisions and forage, with a handsome appointment. They imparted much knowledge to the people, and taught them dexterity in many operations. Besides the saw-mills which they constructed, and the roads which they formed through the woods, Mr. Aaron Hill, the poet, the clerk to this establishment, first shewed the mode of binding 3 or 4 score of spars into a platform, by passing a rope through a hook of iron at both ends of each, thereby forming a raft of 2 or 4 lengths of the timber, on which also a quantity of deals or other wood is laid, to the value in whole of £10 or £20 sterling, and navigated down the river by a man seated at each end with an oar. Before this, they could only carry down a very small quantity of timber, bound together by a cord, conducted in a very hazardous manner, by a man seated in a vessel made of a hide, in a cylindrical or rather conical form, its inside extended by hoops of wood. It was managed by a paddle, and the timber tied to the conductor's leg by the noose of a rope, to be slipped as occasion required, that he might return behind the raft, to set it free from any shallow. This vessel the man carried home upon his shoulders by land, as the tackle of the rafts are yet brought back. Tradition relates, that this establishment was the most extravagant set ever known in the country, that their wasteful prodigality ruined themselves, and in part corrupted others. Their profusion was frequently displayed in bonfires of whole barrels of tar; and entire hogsheads of brandy were broached among the people, by which five men in one night died. It is likely, however, that a plan, wisely concerted for conciliating the favourable regard of the natives, might appear as astonishing wastefulness, among poor and simple Highlandmen, and, like other marvellous relations, might be exaggerated in the succeeding repetitions of it.

State Ecclesiastical.—The stipend, lately augmented, is

£105. The right of patronage belongs to the family of Grant. At Abernethy, the church is a neat well-finished building; that of Kinchardine, at the distance of 8 miles, is also in good condition. There is a burying ground at each, enclosed by a triple fence, a wall, a hedge, and a belt of wood. The establishment of the parochial school, exclusive of the fees, is £11 2s. 2d., and the perquisites of the office of session clerk. The Society for Christian Knowledge have established a school in Kinchardine, with an appointment of £9; and he has the best schoolhouse in the Highlands. The parish is likewise accommodated with a catechist, by the royal bounty. The contributions made in the assemblies for social worship, in behalf of the poor, amount to about £6 sterling, not sufficient to furnish them in shoes half the year. They are supported by the tenants, in begging from house to house; and in this mode 100 bolls of meal are distributed, supposed at a peck weekly, or 3 bolls in the year, from each tenant. The whole of the inhabitants, amounting to 1769, are of the national Church.

Miscellaneous Information.—The people are sagacious, well informed, frugal, very sober, and loyal to a degree that cannot be surpassed. Political or religious fanaticism have got no footing among them; neither misled by the doctrines of those vagabond fanatics that infest the coast, nor misled by the tenets of political pamphlets: they are only dissatisfied with the mode in which they are by the landlords obliged to hire their farms. Crystals of some value, similar to the kind at Bristol, are sometimes found about the bottom of the mountains of Cairngorum. They are for the most part found by chance, though some pretend to know the vein where they may be found by digging; yet it is an employment by no means worth following.] (*Survey of the Province of Moray.*)

I cross the River Spey to

DUTHIL PARISH,

Which lieth on the west side of the river, but the parish of Rothiemurchus that is united to it is on the east side. Duthil is divided into two parts by a ridge of hills running from south to north. The south-east side of these hills is called *Deasoil*, i.e., southward; and the north-west side is called *Tuathail*, i.e., northward; and hence is the name *Duthel*.

The rapid rivulet Tuilenan watereth this north side of the parish. It riseth in the hills betwixt Badenock and Strathern, and running north-east through Duthil, it turneth due east, and after a course of 16 miles falleth into Spey. There are upon it two stone bridges, one a furlong above the mouth of it and the other a mile above the Church.

The Church* standeth on the west side of Tuilenan, 6 miles W.-S.-W. of Cromdale, 4 miles west of Abernethy, and about 7 miles north of Alvie.

On Tuilenan, from north to south, lies Tulloch-griban, Mullachard, Achterblair, Inverladenan, &c., the seats of gentlemen of the name of Grant.

The Deasoil, or south side of the hills, stretcheth on the bank of Spey from Tullochgorum to the borders of Badenoch, 5 miles in length, and not 1 mile in breadth.

In the east end is Gartenbeg, the ancient seat of the Clan Donachie, of whom Sir Ludovick

---

* The bands of the Kirk door are very rare, made after the manner of a tree casting out its branches and covering the whole door after the manner of needle work. (*Account of the Country of Strathspey*, c. 1680.) (ED.)

Grant of Dalvey is now the representer. Lauchlan Grant, now of Gártenbeg, is of that family.

Upon the west bank of the river, where now the passage boat of Gartenmore crosseth, stood the house of Cumming of Glenchernich, as yet called Bigla's House, because Bigla, heiress of Glenchernich, married to the Laird of Grant, was the last of the Cummines that enjoyed that land. The house stood on a green moat, fenced by a dry ditch, the vestiges of which are yet to be seen. A current tradition beareth that at night a salmon net was cast out into the pool below the wall of the house, and a small rope, tied to the net and brought in at the window, had a bell hung at it, which rung when a salmon came into and shook the net.

Next is Kincherdie, the seat of a branch of the house of Grant.

Farther up is Aviemore, which (with Linechuirn) was the residence of a branch of the family of Glenmoriston, now extinct.

And on the borders of Badenoch is the Western Craigelachie, which word is a motto of the Grant's arms, and is the *Crie de guerre*, or war-cry of the clan.

This parish is in the shire of Moray for the most part, and the whole of it is a part of the estate of Grant.

[Three miles to the east of Duthil Manse the road passes close to the old tower of Muckerach, the high walls of which are visible at a great distance. It stands on the brink of a little dell, on the brow of a hill, which commands an outlook to the west as far as Upper Craigellachie and Aviemore, and eastward a great way over the valley of the Spey. It was the primeval seat of the family of Rothiemurchus, and was erected in 1598 by Patrick, second son of John, laird of Grant, and Margaret Stewart, daughter of the Earl of Athole, who was his first spouse. The founder's father was called John Baold, *the Simple*, and was the son of Shemis-nan-Creach, *the Ravager*, who died in 1550.

The lintel stone over the doorway has been carried off, but still exists in one of the farm houses at Rothiemurchus. It contains the year 1598, in which the Castle was finished, with the owner's arms (three antique crowns and three wolves' heads), and on the scroll, "IN GOD IS AL MY TREST." The building forms a most picturesque ruin and is beautifully situated, but it is a mere shell, its roof and all the interior partitions having fallen away. It was only a castellated mansion, and hence had not the solidity or thickness of wall sufficient to keep it as entire as many structures more ancient than itself.] (*Anderson's Guide to the Highlands.*)

DUTHIL.

[*Situation, Soil, Climate.*—The River Spey, on getting clear of the parish of Alvie, forms the boundary of the counties of Moray and Inverness. A part of the last county, still stretching down for 7 miles along the south side of the river, and for the breadth of 4 miles back to the bottom of the mountains, is distinguished by the name of the parish of Rothiemurchus, although it has been a part of Duthel since 1625, upwards of 170 years. From the borders of Alvie on the north side of the river, where the county of Moray meets with Inverness, Duthel extends down the river for 14 miles. From the influx of the Dulnan it extends backward along both banks of this rapid stream for almost 16 miles, near its sources to the north-west, in the mountainous desert which is interposed between the Spey and Findern, separating this parish from that of Moy and Dalarossie on the north. It was once distinguished by a Gaelic appellation, which signified ·the *valley of heroes;* its modern name, applying to the course of the Dulnan, which winds through a valley of almost 1,000 acres, imports *the excellent dale*. The soil towards the lower end of this district, which is widened into a plain of several miles, is rich and deep, but frequently overflowed by the Dulnan, which in the original signifies *floody*. Towards the upper end, and distant from the river, although shallow it is fertile throughout. The skirts of the hills are clothed with fir, birch, and aller, beyond which is the naked waste and the brown heath. In the Gaelic, *Rothemurchus* signifies the great plain of fir. Although some parts near the Spey be of a deep and fertile soil yet it is in general shallow. Its mountains beyond the forest extend backwards to Athol and Braemar on the south. The climate of the whole parish is extremely healthful; the common distempers are probably occasioned by imprudent changes of warmer clothing for the Highland garb.

State of Property.—The district of Duthil appertains to Sir James Grant of Grant, Bart. It is valued in the Cess-Books of Moray at £861 17s. 8d. Scots. The number of its arable acres is 2,183, all under corn and potatoes, excepting a few under turnip, cabbage, and sown grass; they are managed by 105 ploughs. There are besides, in natural pasturage and wood, 2,467 acres, and in moor and peat earth 4,650, exclusive of the mountainous waste. Its real rent may be nearly £1,100 sterling. The only articles of export are black cattle, of which the district supports 1,022; and sheep, which amount to 3,424; and besides these there are also 315 horses.

The whole district of Rothiemurchus is the property of John Peter Grant, Esq., valued in the Cess-Books of the county of Inverness at £425 Scots. Its real rent amounts to about £300 sterling, and as much may be drawn yearly by the sale of timber. From the number of people employed in its manufacture an importation of grain is required for this district, but that of Duthel supplies its own inhabitants with provisions. The black cattle in Rothiemurchus amount to the number of 180, and sheep to 2,300, and the horses to 95.

State Ecclesiastical.—The value of the living, both glebes excluded, is £105 sterling. The residence is at the Church of Duthel only. Public worship is performed but each third Sunday at Rothiemurchus. The right of patronage appertains to Sir James Grant. The salary and perquisites of office in the parochial school amount nearly to £12 in the year, the number of scholars about 30. There are two schools established by the Society for Christian Knowledge. In the district of Rothiemurchus the appointment is £10 sterling, and the perquisites drawn in the country are valued at £5 more; the number of scholars about 30. In the Duthel district the appointment is £9, with a few conveniences furnished by the tenants. The number of poor in the whole parish is 23, and the contributions made by their neighbours in both churches are about £8 yearly. The whole inhabitants are of the Established Church, amounting to 1,110.

Miscellaneous Information.—There are several chalybeate fountains; that at Auchterblair has been found of use in gravelish complaints. The people are extremely industrious in the cultivation of their possessions.

The country distinguished by the appellation of Strathspey begins where Duthel borders with Alvie, at a lofty rocky precipice called *Craigelachy*, the rock of alarm, the war-cry of the Clan Grant, and a motto in their armorial coat, distant almost 40 miles from a similar precipice of the same name, where the parish of Knockando borders with Rothes. Near the centre of the district of Rothiemurchus there is a mountain of limestone, and plenty of fuel in the country. In this quarter are also two small lakes, and by the romantic situation of the surrounding hills are formed 5 very remarkable echoes. In one of them, named Lochnellan, the island lake, are the walls entire of a very ancient castle.] (*Survey of the Province of Moray.*)

EPITAPHS IN THE CHURCHYARD OF DUTHIL.

A rude baptismal font of granite stands at the Church of Duthil. According to the *Old Stat. Account*, vol. iv., p. 311, the Kirk was built in 1400, which is possibly a misprint for 1600 or some later date. It stood until about 1826, when the present house was erected.

A mausoleum of granite, belonging to the Earls of Seafield, adjoins the Church, and there, it is said, the Grants of Castle Grant have had their place of burial since the year 1585. The first of the Grants is said to have been

Gregory (Sheriff of Inverness in the time of Alexander II.), who married a daughter of Bisset, Lord of Lovat. From that time the surname frequently occurs in charters and other authentic documents. It was in consequence of Sir Ludovick Grant having married Margaret, daughter of the 5th Earl of Seafield, that Grant of Grant succeeded to the estates and titles of the earldom of Seafield, &c.

The mausoleum was built in 1837 from a design by Mr. Playfair, Edinburgh. It is a square structure of dressed granite, situated at the east end of the Church. The walls are embattled all round, and in each of the three sides of the structure are arched doorways with iron doors. Above the front doorway is engraved in a slab the armorial bearings of the family, with the motto STAND FAST. Within the mausoleum are two memorial records. One of these is a large marble slab, encased in black marble frame, on the west wall, which is inscribed as follows:—

Sacred to the memory of Sir James Grant of Grant, Bart., Lord Lieutenant of the County of Inverness, &c., &c., who died at Castle Grant on the 18th day of February, 1811, aged 73 years. And to his spouse, Jane, only daughter of Alexander Duff of Hatton, Esquire, by Lady Ann Duff, eldest daughter of William, 1st Earl of Fife, who died at Castle Grant on the 15th day of February, 1805, aged 59 years.

Sacred also to the memory of the following members of the family:—

Jane, the third daughter, who died at Grant Lodge on the 22nd day of May, 1819, aged 45 years.

Ann Margaret, their eldest daughter, who died at Grant Lodge on the 3rd day of November, 1827, aged 63 years.

James, eldest son of Colonel the Hon. Francis William Grant, second son of the said Sir James Grant of Grant, Bart., by the said Jane Duff; and of Mary Ann, only daughter of John Charles Duff, Esq., of Highham House, in the county of Sussex, his spouse, who died in London on the 15th day of March, 1815, aged 2 years and 11 months.

Mary Ann, above named, spouse of Colonel Grant (now 1841), 6th Earl of Seafield, who died in London, 27th February, 1840, aged 45.

Their eldest surviving son, Francis William Grant, M.P. for Inverness-shire, who died at Cullen House, 11th March, 1840, aged 26.

Lewis Alexander, 5th Earl of Seafield (eldest son of Sir

James and Lady Grant), who died at Cullen House, 26th October, 1840, aged 73.

On the lid of the coffin of the 7th Earl is a coronet and plate of silver, inscribed:—

John Charles Ogilvie Grant, 7th Earl of Seafield, 26th Laird of Grant, 1st Baron Strathspey, K.T. Born at Cullen House, 4th September, 1815; died at Cullen House, 18th February, 1881.

On the small slab in the south wall is inscribed:—

Sacred to the memory of Sir Ludovick Grant of Grant, Baronet. Born, 13th January, 1707; married, November 1735, to Lady Margaret Ogilvie, eldest daughter of James, Earl of Findlater and Seafield; and died at Castle Grant, 18th March, 1773.

One part of the enclosure is reserved for the Chief and his offspring, while the outer part belongs to collateral branches, as the families of Kinchurdy, Tullochgriban, and Balladirin.

The following inscription, upon a marble tablet within the Church, relates to a grandson of the under-mentioned minister of Abernethy, who was previously at Duthil:—

I. Capt. William Grant, 27th Regt. Bengal N.I., Assistant Adjutant General of Afghanistan, eldest son of the late Major Grant, Auchterblair, was killed in action at Gundermuck during the disastrous retreat of the British Army from Cabool on the 13 of January, 1842, aged 38 years.

Erected by his bereaved widow.

II. The next bears the names of the Uncle and Grandfather of the above Captain W. Grant:—

Erected by James Augustus Grant, Esq., of Viewfield, in memory of his ancestors of the family of Milton, who have had from a remote period their last resting place here, and where too are deposited the remains of his father, the Revd. John Grant, minister of Abernethy, who died 21 January, 1820.

It is told that the minister, having several sons in the army during the Peninsular war, was in the habit of reading the newspapers upon Sundays to his congregation, when anything of importance occurred regarding the progress of events.

III. The following is upon a stone within an enclosure:—

Alexander Grant of Tullochgorum died 28 February, 1828, aged 97, and Margaret Grant, his wife, died 15 April, 1850, aged 67.

Alexander Grant of Tullichgriban, Esq., died 22nd Feb., 1829, aged 98 years; and his widow, Margaret Grant, died 15 April, 1849. Erected by their only child, Isabella Elizabeth, wife of General Sir Lewis Grant.

John Grant and Elizabeth Lumsden, his spouse, both departed this life on the 9th Feb., 1806. Their son, Colonel Sir Maxwell Grant, K.C., died 22d Oct., 1823.

The above refers to one of the Muckroch family, the first of whom was the 4th son of Sir John Grant of Grant, who was knighted by James VI., and died soon after the year 1625. Muckroch Castle, the ruins of which still remain, is said to have been built in 1598; also, that the lands of Muckroch were excambed with the laird of Grant for those of Rothiemurchus.

IV. Margaret Cuming, died 20th June, 1790, aged 82, wife first of Robert Grant, farmer, Aangormack, next to Patrick Cuming, farmer at Easter Duthil. "Name what a Consort, a Parent, and a Friend, in her station, should be—and she was that."

V. A rough slab, upon which a hammer, square, chisel, and a gun are rudely carved, bears this brief inscription:—

Here lyes Donald Cuming, son of Patrick Cuming, Duthil. 1774.

VI. The next three inscriptions are from tombstones erected to certain of "*The Men*," as they are locally called:—

Duncan Cuming, merchant, Bridge of Endy, Coilum, Rothiemurchus, who died 21 Feb., 1839, aged 65, "was the last 26 years of his life effectually called to an enlightened mind to love and to believe the Holy Scripture."

VII. John M'Intosh, late farmer, Torspartan, died 27 Nov., 1843, aged 65. "A man distinguished for zeal, love, sweet communion, was, for the last 35 years of his life, called to repentance. He was gifted with a spirit of love, prayer, and charitable feelings to distressed souls, persuading them to fly from the wrath to come. This is erected by his affectionate neighbours as a token of their regards towards him."

VIII. George Cameron, farmer, Tullochgorum, died 5 Feb., 1848, aged 79. " For the last 28 years of his life he was brought to sharp repentance, to be a self-denying Christian, and to have love to the brethren."

The Men were those who professed to have been brought to a sense of their error by some miraculous means; after which they made it their business to go about and expound the Holy Scriptures to their neighbours. The appellation of *The Men of Ross* has been long given to laymen of that county who acted in the way indicated. *The Men* of Duthil had great faith. Not long ago, in the time of *The Men* above-named, when the Spey changed its course at a particular spot, *The Men* believed that Providence had made it do so in obedience to their prayers; and had the same recorded upon a stone, which they placed at the point where the river had diverged.

The district of Duthil appears to have been the property of the Earls of Strathearn prior to the time it fell into the hands of the Cumins, the old Lords of Badenoch. It was afterwards owned by Sir John (grandson of Gregory Grant of Grant), who is said to have married the heiress of Cumin, and thus acquired the lands. Duthil is still held by a descendant of Sir John, the Earl of Seafield, who is accounted chief of the Clan Grant. He married the youngest daughter of the late Lord Blantyre, and has issue, Viscount Reidhaven, born 1851.

On the west side of the burial ground, unmarked as yet by any monument, lie the remains of Ian Manndach, or Lom, the celebrated Jacobite poet; who, after the defeat of his party at Culloden, found, in his flight from the battlefield, an asylum in the farm house of Lochanhully, where he died after a brief illness, caused by fatigue and disappointment.

Although there are few objects of antiquity in the district, it can boast of many curious and interesting traditions, the more noteworthy of which have been preserved by Sir T. D. Lauder and by local writers, particularly by "Glenmore" in his "Legends of Strathspey."] (*Jervise's Epitaphs.*)

THE PARISH OF ROTHIEMURCHUS

Is in the Shire of Inverness. It lieth on the south-east of the river, and, including Glenmore in Kinchardine parish, it maketh a semicircle, whereof the river is the diameter, and high mountains the circumference.

The Church standeth on the river, a half mile below the south end of the parish, 6 miles south from Duthel; 6 miles south-west from Abernethie; 1½ mile south-east from Alvie.

Close by the church is the house of Downe,* the seat of Patrick Grant of Rothiemurchus, a baron in the county.

LOCH-AN-EILAN

[Signifies *Loch of the Island.* Dr. MacCulloch has beautifully described it thus:—A fir-lake, if I may use such a term, like Loch-an-eilan, is a rare occurrence; and indeed this is the only very perfect example in the country. No other tree is seen; yet, from the variety of the shores, there is not that monotony which might be expected from such limited materials. In some parts of it, the rocky precipices rise immediately from the dark water, crowned with the dark woods, that fling a profound shadow over it. In others, the solid masses of the trees advance to its edge; while elsewhere, open green shores, or low rocky points, or gravelly beaches, are seen; the scattered groups, or single trees, which, springing from some bank, wash their roots in the waves that curl against them, adding to the general variety of this wild and

---

* The present Mansion is a modern building without any architectural pretensions; but the site is most attractive on the banks of the Spey. The garden, situated in a deep dell among rich plantations, had its natural beauties much improved by the late Duke and Duchess of Bedford, who chose this charming spot as their summer retreat. (ED.)

singular scene. This lake is much embellished by an ancient Castle standing on an island within it, and even yet entire, though roofless. As a Highland castle it is of considerable dimensions; and the island being scarcely larger than its foundation, it appears in some places to rise immediately out of the water. Its ancient celebrity is considerable, since it was one of the strongholds of the Cumyns—the particular individual whose name is attached to it, being the ferocious personage known by the name of *the Wolf of Badenoch*. It has passed now to a tenant not more ferocious, who is an apt emblem of the red-handed Highland chief. The *eagle* has built his eyrie in the walls. I counted the sticks in his nest, but had too much respect for this worthy successor to an ancient Highland dynasty, even to displace one twig. His progeny, it must be admitted, have but a hard bed, but the Red Cumyn did not probably lie much more at his ease.

Sir Thomas Dick Lauder has availed himself of the romance attending Loch-an-eilan, and has described it well in his Lochandhu.] (ED.)

THE FAMILY OF GRANT OF ROTHIEMURCHUS.

The first of this family was (1) Patrick of Mukerach, son of John Grant, and Margaret Steuart, daughter of the Earl of Athole. Upon the forfeiting of Shaw of Rothiemurchus, Patrick got Rothiemurchus and Balnespick, in exchange for Mukerach. He was succeeded by his eldest son (2) Duncan, who, having no issue, was succeeded by his brother (3) John, father of (4) James, who had three sons, viz., Patrick, Colonel William, and Mr. John who died a bachelor. Colonel William purchased the lands of Ballendallach, and was father of Alexander, and of James, now of Ballendalach. (5) Patrick had three sons, viz., Patrick of Tullochgrue, Captain

John who died a bachelor, and (6) James the eldest son, father of (7) Patrick, now of Rothiemurchus [M.P.].

Rothiemurchus was by King Alexander II., anno 1226, granted to Andrew Bishop of Moray, for a forest, in exchange for other lands. And Bishop Andrew mortified it to the Cathedral of Elgin, for furnishing lights and candles. The Shaws and the Cummings had warm and bloody combats about this possession and Duchus of Rothiemurchus. The principal seat was a fort in a loch, called *Loch-an-elan*, the walls whereof do still remain. And this leads me to give some account of

THE FAMILY OF SHAW OF ROTHIEMURCHUS.

It is the general tradition that the SHAWS are descended of Macduff, Earl of Fife. Sir George MacKenzie, in his *Alphabetical manuscript of Genealogies*, says, " That *Sheach* or Shaw, son of MacDuff, was progenitor of this name." Sir Robert Sibbald dedicates his *Modern History of Fife* " To the Earl of Wemyss, Lord Elcho, and to the nobility and gentry of the name of Wemyss, Shaw, Toshean, Duff, Douglas, Lesley, and Abernethy, descended of the clan Macduff." Mr. Nisbet, in his *Marks of Cadency*, writeth, " That the Shaws are said to be descended of a younger son of MacDuff, Earl of Fife." The Bishop of Carlisle, in his *Scottish Historical Library*, says,

"I have seen a treatise of the origin and continuance of the Thanes and Earls of Fife sirnamed MacDuff, of whom the families of MacIntosh, Wemyss, Shaw, and Duff are descended." Let me add, that Dr. Abercrombie, in his *Martial Achievements*, observeth that King Malcolm Canmore rewarded those who had contributed to his restoration, from the names of which, or lands given to them, many ancient families have their sirnames, and particularly Gordon, Seaton, Lesley, Calder, Shaw, Strachan, Mar, &c.

These hints are sufficient to show the antiquity of this name, and their descent from MacDuff.

I see no reason to doubt, that the Shaws in the south and in the north were originally the same. But at what time they settled in the north I cannot determine. The Lord Lyon's records bear, that Farquhardson of Invercauld (descended of Shaw of Rothiemurchus) carries the Lyon of MacDuff as paternal arms; and a canton dexter, charged with a hand holding a dagger, point downwards; in memory of Shaw of Rothiemurchus assisting in cutting off the Cummines. Unvaried tradition likewise beareth, that Shaw Corshiaclach, *i.e. buck-toothed*, of Rothiemurchus, was Captain of the 30 Clan Chattan, in the memorable conflict against 30 Clan Cays, on the Inch of Perth, anno 1396, and that the Shaws possessed Rothiemurchus long before that time; and so I may call it probable, that they settled in the north in the beginning at least of the 14th century.

The lands of Rothiemurchus having been granted by King Alexander II. to Andrew Bishop of Moray, anno 1226, were held of the Bishops in lease, by the Shaws during a hundred years without disturbance. But, about the year 1350, Cummine of Strathdallas having a lease of these lands, and unwilling to yield to the Shaws, it came to be decided by the sword; and (1) James Shaw, chief of the clan, was killed in the conflict. James had married a daughter of Baron Ferguson in Athole, and his son (2) Shaw, called *Corfiachlach*, as soon as he came of age, with a body of men, attacked Cummine, and killed him, at a place called to this day *Lagna-Cuminach*. He purchased the freehold of Rothiemurchus and Balinespic; and by a daughter of Macpherson of Clunie, had seven sons, James the eldest, and Farquhar, ancestor of the Farquharsons, &c. Shaw commanded the 30 Clan Chattan on the Inch of Perth, anno 1396, and dying about 1405, his grave-stone is seen in the churchyard. (3) James brought a company of his name to the Battle of Hardlaw, anno 1411, where he was killed. His son, by a daughter of Inveretie, (4) Alexander Kiar, by a daughter of Stuart of Kinchardine, had four sons, of whom Dale, Tordarroch, and Delnafert, are descended; and (5) John, by a niece of MacIntosh, was father of (6) Allan, who, by a daughter of the Laird of MacIntosh, had (7) John, father of (8) Allan, who, having barbarously murdered his step-father Dallas of Cantray, was justly forfeited, and the Laird of Grant purchased the forfeiture about anno 1595.

The arms of Shaw are : Or, a lion rampant, Gule-armed and langued az; a fir-tree growing out of a mount prop. in base; and in a canton arg, a dexter-hand coup'd grasping a dagger, Gule.

FARQUHARSON OF INVERCAULD.

Farquhar, second son of Shaw of Rothiemurchus, was forester to the Earl of Mar, about anno 1440; and by a daughter of Robison of Lude, was father of (2) Donald, who, by a daughter of Calvene, had (3) Farquhar Beg, who married a daughter of Chisholm of Strathglass, and had (4) Donald, who married Isabel, only child of Stuart of Invercauld and Aberarder, and by her obtained these lands, anno 1520. His son (5) Finlay More (from whom they are called *Clan Fhinlay*) was killed in the Battle of Pinky, bearing the royal standard, 1547. By a daughter of Garden of Balchoric, he had seven sons, of whom several respectable families are descended. His eldest son (6) William had no issue, and was succeeded by his brother (7) Robert, who married a daughter of Inverchroskie, and had (8) John, who, by a daughter of Gartley, had a son (9) Robert, who married Anne, daughter of Erskine of Pittodrie, and had Robert and Alexander.

(10) Robert had no male issue, and was succeeded by his brother (11) Alexander, who married a daughter of Macintosh of that Ilk, and had William and John. (12) William died unmarried, and was succeeded by his brother (13) John, who died in 1756; by Margaret daughter of Lord James Moray of Douallie, brother to the Marquis of Athole: he had James, and Anne married to Æneas MacIntosh of that Ilk. (14) James married Emilia, daughter of Lord George Moray, son of John, Duke of Athole, and by her has issue.*

Invercauld bears quarterly. 1 and 4, Or, a lion rampant, Gule-armed and langued az. 2 and 3 arg; a fir-tree growing out of a mount in base seeded prop. And on a chief Gule the banner of Scotland displayed: and in a canton, a dexter-hand couped fessways, holding a dagger point downward. Crest, a lion issuant Gule, holding a sword in his dexter-paw, hilted and pomilled, Or, supporters, two cats saliant. Motto, FIDE ET FORTITUDINE.

[*Translation.*—By fidelity and fortitude.]

Having described the country of Strathspey, I go up the river Spey, and enter into

BADENOCH,

So called from *Badan*, a bush or thicket, be-

---

* The present representative is James Ross Farquharson, eldest son of the late James Farquharson, by Janet Hamilton. eldest daughter of General Francis Dundas; born 9 Jan. 1834; late Lieut.-Col. Scots Fusilier Guards; married 19 Nov. 1864, Elizabeth Louisa, eldest daughter of the late Alexander Haldane Oswald, of Auchincruive, and by her (who died 8 Aug, 1870) has issue. See Edward Walford's "County Families of the United Kingdom;" also Sir Bernard Burke's "Landed Gentry." (ED.)

cause it was anciently full of wood. I cannot trace the possessors of this country higher than to the Cummines, Lords of Badenoch, who, I doubt not, were lords of it in the 12th or beginning of the 13th century. Upon their being forfeited by King Robert Bruce, Badenoch made a part of the Earldom of Moray, granted to Sir Thomas Randolph, anno 1313. The earldom reverting to the Crown on the death of John Randolph, anno 1346, without issue male, George Dunbar, Earl of March, had, at least, the title of Earl of Moray, in right of his mother Agnes Randolph, sister and heir of Earl John Randolph. And when King Robert II. granted the Earldom of Moray to John Dunbar, he accepted Badenoch, Lochaber, and the Castle of Urquhart out of the grant. The said King Robert, anno regni 1 *mo* 1372, granted the sixty Davachs of Badenoch to his son Alexander and his heirs, which failing, to his brother David and his heirs (*Rot. Robert* II.). Lord Alexander died anno 1394, without lawful issue : David likewise left no son, and the Lordship of Badenoch remained in the Crown, till it was given to the Earl of Huntley, after the Battle of Brechin anno 1452, in whose family it continueth.

And because this country is mainly possessed by the MacIntoshes and MacPhersons, I shall here give a succinct account of these two families and clans.

MACINTOSH.

No one questions, that this is a branch of the MacDuffs, Thanes, and Earls of Fife. *Tosch* in Irish (from *Tus*, i. e., first or chief) signifies Thane, and *MacIntosh* is the Thane's son. (1) Shaw MacDuff, second son of Duncan, 5th Earl of Fife, who died anno 1154, is said to have had a command in the army of Malcolm IV. against the Moravienses about 1160, and that upon quelling that rebellion, the King made him Governor of Inverness, and granted him some lands near to it. This is highly probable; for when Prince Henry, only son of King David I., died anno 1152, and the king declared Malcolm the son of Henry successor to the Crown, he committed him to the foresaid Duncan Earl of Fife, to bring him through all the countries, and to have him proclaimed in all the burghs, heir of the Crown (*Chron. Melros.*). In this tour, Shaw MacDuff accompanied his father, and got into the favour of the young prince, who afterwards preferred him as said is. Shaw fixing his residence in the north, and being called, *Mac-an-toshich*, i. e., "the Thane's son," this became the sirname of the family. By Giles Montgomery he left issue (2) Shaw, who was 36 years governor of the Castle of Inverness, which he bravely defended against the Lord of the Isles. By a daughter of Sir Harry Sandyland, he had Ferquhar, William, and Edward, ancestor of Monivard, and died 1209. (3) Ferquhar had no issue, and was succeeded by (4) Shaw, son of William, and, by a daughter of the Thane of Calder, was father of (5) Ferquhar, who fought at the head of his clan against Haquin King of Norway, in the Battle of Largs, anno 1263. By Mora, daughter of Angus Oig Lord of the Isles, he had (6) Angus, who married Eva, the only child and heir of Dowal Dâl, chief of the Clan Chattan, 1292. By her he obtained the lands of Locharkeg, Glenluy, and Strathlochie, which remained with the family till they were sold to Lochiel in 1665. Argyle paid the purchase-money, and is Superior of those lands.

In consequence of this marriage, the Lairds of MacIntosh were (in royal charters, royal missives, indentures, contracts of amity, &c., of which I have perused many) designed " Captains of Clan Chattan." In a bond of man-rent, dated 4th April 1609, and granted by the MacPhersons to MacIntosh, they name him, " Our Chief, as it was of auld, according to the Kings of Scotland, their Gift of Chieftanry of the hail Clan Chattan" (*pen. MacIn.*). But if there were such a royal gift, it is now lost. Yet it cannot be doubted that the MacIntoshes, MacPhersons, MacBeans, Shaws, MacGilivraes, MacQueens, MacPhails, Smiths, MacInteers, &c., as one incorporated body, did own MacIntosh for their captain or leader, for about 300 years. In those times of barbarity and violence, small tribes or clans found it necessary; to come under the patronage of more powerful clans. Those incorporated tribes foresaid, went by the general name of Clan Chattan; yet every tribe retained its own sirname and chief.

Angus, by his wife Eva, had a numerous issue, and dying about 1346, his eldest son (7) William, married a daughter of Rory More MacLeod of Lewis, and had (8) Lachlan, who fought the Camerons at Invernahavon (See my "Military History"), and by a daughter of Fraser of Lovate, had (9) Ferquhar. This gentleman, being of a peaceable disposition, lived a private life, and resigned the chieftanry and fortune in favour of his uncle (10) Malcolm Beg, who brought a battalion to the Battle of Harlaw anno 1411, and for his conduct there obtained the lands of Braelohaber, in 1447. By a daughter of MacDonald of Moidart, he had Duncan, William of Thylachie, and Lachlan Badenach, and died 1457. (11) Duncan, by Florence, daughter of MacDonald Earl of Ross, had (12) Ferquhar, who died 1514, without male issue, and was succeeded by (13) William, son of Lachlan Badenoch, who married Isabel MacNivan, heiress of Dunachtin. He was murdered in Inverness, by one of his unruly clan, in 1515; of him came Strone. His brother (14) Lachlan Oig succeeded, and married Jean, heiress of line of Gordon of Lochinvar, and was barbarously murdered by some of his clan, in 1524. His son (15) William married a daughter of Findlater, and was treacherously murdered in Huntley Castle by that Earl's orders, anno 1550, for which Huntley paid a great assythment or compensation in lands. His son (16) Lachlan More was a gentleman greatly respected, for his behaviour in the Battle of Glenlivat, 1594 (See my "Military History"). He married a daughter of Lord Kintale, and died 1606. Of his sons are descended the families of Borlum, Aberarder, and Corrybrugh. His eldest son Angus went abroad to travel, and died in Padua anno 1593; by a daughter of the Earl of Argyle, he left a son (17), Sir Lachlan, who was, for some time, a gentleman of the bed-chamber to Prince Charles. He married a daughter of the Laird of Grant, and died in 1622, leaving two sons, William and Angus of Daviot. (18) William, by a daughter of Graeme of Fintrey, had a son, and dying in 1660, (19) Lachlan married the daughter of Lindsey of Edzel, and dying in 1704, his son (20) Lachlan died in 1731 without issue, and was succeeded by (21) William son of Lachlan of Daviot. This gentleman served some years in the army, and was finely accomplished, and dying in 1740 without issue, was succeeded by his brother (22) Angus, who married a daughter of John Farquharson of Invercauld, and died in

1770 without issue. He was succeeded by his nephew Æneas, son of Alexander third son of Lachlan of Daviot.

For arms, MacIntosh taketh quarterly. 1. Or, a lion rampant Gules for MacDuff. 2. Arg. a dexter-hand couped fessways, grasping a man's heart in pale Gules. 3. Az. a boar's head couped, Or, for Gordon of Lochinvar. 4. Or, a lymfad; her oars in saltire erected, sab. for Clan Chattan. Supporters, two wild cats proper. Crest, a cat saliant as the last. Motto, TOUCH NOT THE CAT BUT A GLOVE.

MACPHERSON.

An account of the original of the Clan Chattan and MacPhersons is published in the *Dictionaries of Collier, Moreri,* &c., too long to be transcribed here. I am sorry the author of it discovereth more vanity than historical knowledge. His fetching the Clan Chattan from Germany, because Tacitus mentions the Catti in that country, is a poor playing with the jingle of words. The marrying *Gillicatan-more* to the sister of Brute, King of the Picts, is mere vanity, without any foundation. The making the ancestor of the Keiths to have served King Kenneth II. in overthrowing the Picts is an unpardonable anachronism; for the Picts were overthrown by Kenneth about anno 842, and the ancestor of the Keiths was not heard of before the Battle of Barry, anno 1010. And the sending one of the clan on a pilgrimage through a great part of Europe and Asia, and then making him King of Leinster in Ireland, is such knight errantry as none but the

Irish should commit to writing, and yet not one of their historians mentioneth it.

It is to me probable, from the names Muiroch, Ewan, Colum, Gilicolum, &c., so frequent among the Clan Chattan, that they came originally from Ireland, and either took their name from or gave their name to *Catav*, now Sutherland, their ancient residence. Sutherland, in Irish *Catav*, and Caithness, *Gualav*, were anciently called *Catenesiacis et ultra montem, viz. Ord*. In Irish *Cad* is *altus*, high; and *Guael* is *humilis*, low, plain. And so *Catav* (from *Cad*, high, and *Taobb* or *Tav*, a side) is the high side of the Ord; and *Gaul av* is the low side of it. The very nature and figure of the country confirmeth the etymology—and the inhabitants might have taken their name, *Catach*, from the country. Or, if they were so called from Saint Catan or Cathain, an ancient Scottish Saint to whom the Priory of *Ardchattan* in Lorn was dedicated, and the Priory of Searinch in Lewis *ubi exuviæ Sancti Cattani asservantur*, " Where the remains of St. Cattan are preserved " (Keith's *Catal. of Scottish Bps.*), they might have given their name to the country. In this I shall not determine, and shall only add that their antiquity in Catav was such that I have not heard of any inhabitants in that country before them.

At what time, and upon what occasion, they removed from Caithness and Sutherland into

Lochaber I find not. The current tradition is that they were expelled, because Gillicattan, their chief, disobeyed a call to attend the royal standard, probably in the beginning of King Malcolm II.'s reign, which commenced anno 1004, and who then called his subjects into the field against the invading Danes. The conjecture seemeth to be favoured by this, that their chief was commonly called *Gillicatan-more o' Gualav*, i.e., "The Great Gillicattan from Caithness," implying that he came, or was driven, from Caithness.

From Gillicattan More some of them are called MacGillichattans. The general name is Catenach —from Muirach they are termed Clan Mhuirach, and from Gillicattan Clerach, Parson of Kingussie, they go now in Badenoch by the name of MacPherson. The MacBains, MacPhails, Catteighs, are branches of the old Clan Chattan; and the Keiths are likewise said to have descended from them. At what time they came from Lochaber into Badenoch I find not. Surely it was not all at one time, and probably the forfeiture of Cummine, Lord Badenoch, by King Robert Bruce, made room for them in that country.

It is the common tradition that Gili-Cattan-More lived in the reign of King Malcolm II., Cent. XI., and the most probable account I find of his descendants for about 200 years is as follows:—(1) Gili-Cattan More was father of (2)

Dougal, father of (3) Gili Cattan and David Dow ancestor of Invernahavon. Gili Cattan was father of (4) Muirach More, who had two sons, Kenneth and Gili-Cattan Clerach. (5) Kenneth had no issue, and was succeeded by his brother (6) Gili-Cattan Clerach, Parson of Kingussie, who resigned his pastoral charge, married, and became Chief of the Clan. He had two sons, Gili-Patrick and Ewan-Bane. (7) Gili-Patrick was father of (8) Doual Dâl, whose only child, Eva, married Angus MacIntosh of that ilk about anno 1292. - The direct male line failing thus, the chieftainry devolved to the descendants of Ewan-Bane, second son of Gili-Cattan Clerach. Ewan-Bane died about anno 1296, leaving three sons, viz., Kenneth, ancestor of Clunie; John, ancestor of Pitmean; and Gelis, the first of the family of Inveralbie. These, and their descendants, assumed the surname of MacPherson, from the said Parson of Kingussie; but the posterity of David Dow of Invernahavon were called *Clan Dabbi* in my time.

In the 14th century the Clan Chattan possessed the greatest part of the country of Badenoch, and lived happy and respected. But a fatal discord between two of the tribes broke their harmony, and occasioned the memorable combat on the North Inch of Perth in the year 1396. The Earls of Crawford and Moray, by commission, attempted to reconcile them, but without success;

wherefore they proposed that thirty on each side should decide the quarrel by the sword in presence of the King and nobility. (Who the combatants were, and what the difference between them was, see my *Military History*.) The parties, like the Roman Horatii and Curatii, accepted the motion; but when they were met on the day appointed one of the Clan Chattan had absented through fear, and a smith named Henry Wyne offered to supply his place for a crown of gold, about 7s. 6d. value. The conflict was fierce and desperate. Of the Clan Cay, 29 were killed, and the 30th escaped by swimming the Tay; and of the Clan Chattan, 19 were killed. The victory was much owing to Henry Wyne, which gave rise to the proverb, "He did very well for his own hand, as Henry Wyne did." His posterity (called *Sliochd a Gune Chruim*, the issue of the stooping smith) were incorporated with the Clan Chattan.

The family of Cluny, from Ewan-Bane, continued the succession, but I cannot pretend to give the names of the representatives before the last century. I know that in 1660 Andrew was laird of Cluny, whose son, Ewan, was father of Duncan, who died in 1722 without male issue. The direct line thus failing, the nearest collateral male was Lachlan MacPherson of Nuid (son of William, who was son of Donald, whose father, John, was brother to the foresaid Andrew of

Cluny). Lachlan, in 1722, had the designation of Cluny, and by Jean, daughter of Sir Ewan Cameron of Lochiel, was father of a numerous issue, of which the eldest son, Ewan of Cluny, rashly engaged in the Rebellion 1745, and was forfeited. He left a son by Janet, daughter of Simon, late Lord Lovat, called Duncan.

Cluny beareth for arms:—Parted per fess. Or and az. a lymphad, sails trussed and oars in action, of the first. In the dexter chief point, a hand couped fessways, grasping a dagger, point upwards, Gule. And in the sinister, a cross crosslet fitchie, of the last. Crest, a cat sejant proper. Motto, TOUCH NOT THE CAT GLOVELESS.

THE PARISH OF ALVIE,

That is, *rocky*, from *ail*, a rock. It lieth, a part on each side of Spey. On the west side, it extendeth from Craig Elachie 7 miles in length, and little above half a mile in breadth, from the river to the hills.

The Church standeth near to a mile from the north end of the parish, in a peninsula of a lake called Loch Alvie, 6 miles south of Duthil, 1½ miles west of Rothiemurchus, 2½ miles north of Inch, and 6 miles north of Kingussie.

In the north end is Lenevulg, the property of the Duke of Gordon.

Next southward is Delraddie, a part of the estate of MacPherson of Invereshie.

Below Delraddie on the side of the river, is Kinrara, for some generations the heritage of

MacIntosh of Kinrara and Balnespic, and now a wadset pertaining to Rothiemurchus.

South from Delraddie are Dillafoure, Pitcherin, and Pitaurie. The first, a feu-property of MacPherson of Dillafoure. The other two, the property of the Duke of Gordon.

Farther south is the barony of Dunachten, the property of the Laird of Macintosh, which came into his family, about anno 1500, by marrying the heiress. Here MacIntosh had a seat; but being burnt in 1689, it has not been rebuilt.

Next thereto are the lands of Rait, the seat of Shaw MacIntosh of Borlum, a feu-holding of the Duke of Gordon, as all Badenoch doth.

On the east side of the river, the parish extendeth $1\frac{1}{2}$ miles on the river, and about 3 miles into Glenfeshie south-east, all the property of the Lairds of MacIntosh and Invereshie.

ALVIE.

[*Situation, Soil, Climate.*—The parishes of Laggan and Kinguisie, with Alvie, comprise the whole district distinguished by the appellation of Badenaugh, extending from Corryarioch at the west to Craig Elachy at the east, upwards of 40 miles. The epithet *baden* is familiar in the names of places on the Continent, occurring twice in the cantons of Switzerland, and thrice in the circles of Germany, probably of similar import in their languages to that of the Gaelic, in which *baden* signifies bushy, and *augh*, level ground. On the north side of the Spey, the parish of Alvie is continued down the river from Kinguisie for 8 miles; and below this extent, it stretches down the river on both sides for two miles farther. The inhabited country, from the north bank of the river to the bottom of the mountain, is nearly 2 miles in breadth; and on the southern side, it stretches back into the Grampian hills, along a valley more than a mile in breadth, through which the river of Fessie winds its course, to the length of 6 miles of peopled country. The hills into which it extends, for many miles, beyond any habitation, are extremely barren, many of them rocky, and raised to such a height, that vegetation fails upon their summits. The interjacent valleys indeed produce a rich abundant pasturage in summer; but in winter they are generally inaccessible. The lower arable part of the country consists of a light dry soil, lying on a sandy gravel, and much encumbered with stone, producing weighty crops in a wet season, but exceedingly parched in dry weather. The climate is healthful and dry, and less snow falls than at the distance of a few miles to either hand, occasioned probably by its lying at an equal distance from the east and west seas; yet the mildews frequently injure the crops both of oats and bear. The early or late frosts generally hurt the potatoe to such a degree, as to be a great discouragement to the cultivation of that useful root; and it is seldom that more than a third part of the crop of pease, which are only raised on land that has been limed, can be saved. The people, however, attain to a good old age; several beyond 80 years: the last minister died at the age of 101, discharging the duties of his function, until within 6 months of his death.

State of Property.—The only family-seat in the parish is the elegant and spacious mansion of Belleville, lately built by the translator of the works of Ossian, the property now of his heir, James Macpherson, Esq., valued in the Cess Books at £384 Scots. The Duke of Gordon's estate amounts to the valuation of £525 13s. 4d. Kincraig and Dunaughton, the property of Mr. Mackintosh of Mackintosh, amounts to £350. Dalraddie, appertaining to William MacPherson, Esq., of Invereshie, amounts to £132 6s. 8d. And Sir James Grant of Grant, for the feu-duties of Dalefour, has a valuation of £2 Scots: making the whole parish equal to the valued rent of £1394 Scots.

The inferior tenants are poor, and their habitations wretchedly comfortless; their farms are small, from £2 to £6 sterling of yearly rent, and their land may be let from 5s. to 10s. the acre. The crops, consisting of oats, rye, barley, and potatoe, are in general sufficient for the subsistence of the inhabitants. The parish abounds with fir, birch, aller, and a few oaks; carried by the poorer people 40 miles to the nearest market towns, in small parcels, and sold to procure the few necessaries they desire. There is only one farm stocked wholly with sheep; the whole of that stock in the parish amounts to nearly 7000; the black cattle to 1104; the horses to 510; and there are 101 ploughs. The real rent does not exced £800 sterling; and £100 yearly may be obtained by the sale of the wood.

State Ecclesiastical.—The Church, manse, and greater part of the glebe, are situated in a green peninsula within a lake, which is half a mile in breadth, and a whole mile in length. It is a pleasant situation in summer; but so extremely cold in winter, that the name of the parish in the original Gaelic is supposed *elleibh*, the cold island; although, from the rocky mountain-brow skirting the north side of the valley, it is more likely to have been from *all*, a rock, similar to the parish of Alves in Moray, and Alva in Banffshire. The Church is so incommodiously placed in the eastern quarter of the parish, from which it is still farther detached by its peninsular situation, that public worship is frequently performed in the Church of the district of Inch, in the lower end of Kingussie, being much more contiguous to the greater part of the people of Alvie. Although the Church was placed in the peninsula during the times of Popery, yet this inconvenience could not be felt during that establishment, as there were three other chapels in the parish; that of St. Eata, at Kinrara, St. Drostan's, at Dunaughton, and the chapel of Macluach, at Belleville. As the Church in a short time must be rebuilt, perhaps the more central situation of St. Drostan's chapel ought then to be preferred.

The stipend, including the communion allowance, is £70, with a glebe nearly 2 acres arable, and summer-pasturage for one cow. The proprietors allow £15 for keeping the parsonage-buildings in repair. The right of patronage pertains to the family of Gordon. The salary of the parochial school is £10 sterling; and as session-clerk, the allowance is only the dues of the registration of baptisms, and the publication of the purposes of marriage; for the first, 1s. 6d., and 1s. for the last: the number of scholars about 30, with the customary fees. The Society for propagating Christian Knowledge maintains a school also in the parish, with an appointment of £9, to which is added, by a bequeathed endowment, the sum of £5, for discharging the office of catechist in the quarter of that establishment. The number of the poor is 25: and the contributions for their support about £3 yearly. The people are all of the national religion, and amount to the number of 1011 souls.

Miscellaneous Information.—The people have little idea of trade or manufacture, excepting a considerable quantity of a coarse kind of flannel called plaiding, or blankets, sold for about 10d. the ell of 39 inches. Although all disputes are settled by the justice of the peace, without recourse to the sheriff, or other judge, yet, from the difficulty experienced by the lower class in securing a subsistence, their honesty or veracity are not always to be depended on; they have no inclination to leave the spot of their nativity: and if they can obtain the smallest pendicle of a farm, they reject entering into any service; and are extremely averse to that of the military. They are fond of dram-drinking: and squabbles are not infrequent at burials or other meetings. Few of the older people can read: and they are rather ignorant of the principles of religion. There are 2 retail shops, 6 weavers, 4 tailors, 2 blacksmiths, and 2 who make the brogue-shoes worn by the poorer people.

The rivers and the lake afford trout, salmon, and pike: the salmon are killed by the spear, and caught by the rod of the angler. It is supposed the trout of the lake do not visit Spey by the brook which it discharges, as they are of a better quality than those of the river. The great road from Inverness to Edinburgh is conducted up the north side of the Spey for the whole length of the parish; it passes through a number of little heaps, or piles of stone and earth, opposite to the Church: the most conspicuous one was lately opened; the bones of a human body were found in their natural order, with two large hart-horns laid across.] (*Survey of the Province of Moray.*)

[The only lake is *Loch Alvie*, a beautiful sheet of water about a mile in length, and half a mile in breadth, which almost surrounds the glebe, manse, and Church, having a depth of 11 fathoms. Pike are found in it of from 1 lb. to 7 lb. weight. On the Tuesday morning of the floods of 1829, this loch rose to an unprecedented height, covering one half of the minister's garden. Being the Sacramental occasion, the ministers were confined prisoners within the manse, till the flood subsided on Wednesday forenoon.

A short way along the edge of *Loch Insh*, the railway plunges into the beautiful birch-clad knolls of Kincraig, whence it emerges on a high moorish plateau (James Evan Baillie, Esq., and Sir George MacPherson Grant), with a few trees scattered over its surface; from which a magnificent view is obtained of many of the highest of the Grampian mountains.

On the summit of *Tor Alvie*, a conspicuous mountain north west of Kinrara, George the last Duke of Gordon, erected a monument, or rather cairn, which bears an inscription on a brass plate commemorative of those officers of the 42nd and 92nd regiments belonging to this district, who fell at Waterloo.

Kinrara is the finest mansion in the parish, and is less than two miles from the Church. Jane Maxwell, the accomplished Duchess of Gordon, died 11th April, 1812, and lies interred in the grounds, at her own request, in a spot which she selected,—where a monument, erected by the Duke, constructed of hewn granite from the Grampians, marks the locality. In 1821, when Leopold, King of the Belgians was in Scotland, he remained ten days at Kinrara, the favourite residence of the above Duchess. There is a sprightly song and dance called "*Kinrara*," the latter of which may be found in Fraser's *Gaelic Airs;* commemorating the mirth and festivity that often enlivened the romantic retreat. Mrs. Allardyce of Cromarty composed the beautiful " Lament for the Duchess of Gordon."

Belleville, which gives its name to a district in this parish, was the property of James MacPherson, the author or translator of Ossian's poems, who died here on the 17th Feb., 1796, æt. 58; but was buried, at his own desire, in Westminster Abbey. The lands of Belleville were formerly the possession of MacIntosh of Borlum, the leader of a gang of robbers. The *barony of Dunauchton* came into possession of this family of MacIntosh by marriage in 1500, and the chief of the clan had a Castle which was burnt in 1689, and was never rebuilt. It is said that South Kinrara and Dalnavert, commonly called *Davochs of the Head*, the remaining portion of the MacIntoshes' property, formed part of the compensation given for the head of William 15th Laird of MacIntosh, beheaded by order of the Earl of Huntly in 1550, when on a friendly visit to Huntly Castle. On the meadow of Belleville, between the public road and the Spey, is the pond or lake of *Lochandhu*, formed by the river, and celebrated in a novel by Sir Thomas Dick Lauder.

The House of Lochandhu was said to have consisted of a plain and very low centre, hardly high enough for one storey, but appearing from its double row of small windows to be divided into two. On each side was a lower wing, running out to the front at right angles, dedicated to a variety of useful purposes. A birch-grove, which formerly engirt the pond, was the lair of the bandit Borlum. Here, it is said, Borlum murdered one of his own domestics, for refusing to cross the Spey with him and rob the house of a weaver in Killihuntly, who was known to possess some money; and here Borlum met his associates to plan their predatory excursions.

Belleville House occupies the site of *Raits Castle*, the chief ancient stronghold of the Comyns. It is an elegant mansion, after a design by the celebrated Adam, situated on a fine eminence sheltered on the north by an extensive plantation of Scottish fir and larch, and by *the rock of Craigbuie* covered with natural birch. By his literary labours, MacPherson raised himself from the humble profession of Parish Schoolmaster at Ruthven, where he was born, to a prominent position among the literary men of his time, and realized an ample fortune which enabled him to purchase the estate of Belleville. Among the many legacies and annuities which he left, his will directed that £300 should be expended in erecting a monument to his memory in some conspicuous situation at Belleville, which was done. Within a clump of larches, about half a mile south west of the mansion, and near the public road, there is a beautiful marble obelisk on which is fixed a medallion of MacPherson. On his death, Belleville passed into the possession of his son, who died in 1833, when it fell to his elder sister, the first spouse of Sir David Brewster, who lived here for some time.

There is a curious *artificial Cave* at Raits, near Belleville, the dimensions of which, when entire, was 145 solid yards, artificially built round with dry stones, and covered on the top with large grey flags. This cave was constructed by, and made the resort of a band of robbers, nine in number, who were designated by the unpronounceable name of *Clannrishicgillenaoidh*. Over the cave was erected a turf cottage, the inmates of which participated with the robbers in their spoils, chiefly carried on in revenge upon the MacPhersons, whose suspicions got excited. They, accordingly, sent one of their tribe, attired as a beggar-man, to seek quarters for the night in this dubious hut. Pretending to suffer from the gravel, the pauper was allowed to stay in another rude domicile hard by; who narrowly watched proceedings. By-and-bye a large flag-stone was raised within the hut, whence issued the entire band prepared for a sumptuous feast on the MacPhersons' mutton. By this stratagem the marauders were found out; and next night the MacPhersons massacred the whole.

About a mile to the west of the Parish Church at a place called *Delfour*, are the remains of a Druidical cairn, enclosed by a circle of large stones about 55 feet in diameter. In the vicinity of this cairn, rises an obelisk or Runic stone $8\frac{1}{2}$ feet high, 5 feet broad at the base, and diminishing gradually in breadth to the top, where it is only $6\frac{1}{2}$ inches. Both cairn and obelisk are in the middle of an arable field.

Several *tumuli* occur on the road to the manse, in one of which were found the bones of a human body entire, with two large harts' horns laid across.] (ED.)

Of the woods in this and the other parishes I speak elsewhere, and so go on to

THE PARISH OF KINGUSSIE AND INSH.

I begin with Insh, which is situated below Kingussie, on the east side of the river. Here the river passeth through a lake $1\frac{1}{2}$ mile long, and near to a mile broad, called Loch Insh. And when the river swelleth, a branch of it runneth on each side of a small hill on which the Church standeth, thereby making it an island; and hence is the name Insh.

The Church is $2\frac{1}{2}$ miles south of Alvie, and $3\frac{1}{2}$ miles north of Kingussie.

This parish extendeth near to 3 miles every way, betwixt the waters of Feshie and Tromie.

Feshie falleth from the Grampian hills, and being swelled by many brooks, after a course of about 15 miles, dischargeth into Spey below the Church, and it boundeth the parishes of Alvie and Insh. Tromie likewise runneth out of the Grampian hills a course of about 14 miles, and falleth into Spey, a mile north of Ruthven, and boundeth the parish of Insh to the south. All betwixt these two rivulets is the property of George MacPherson of Invereshie, chief of one of the principal tribes of that name.

Close by the Church of Insh are the lands of Balnespick, holding of Grant of Rothiemurchus, which had been the property of MacIntosh of Kinrara and Balnespick, but were sold to Invereshie about the year 1749.

An half mile up the water of Feshie, is the seat of the proprietor, who has a salmon-fishing on Loch Insh, and a passage-boat on Spey at the Church.

THE PARISH OF KINGUSSIE

On the east side of Spey, stretcheth about 6 miles from Tromie to Truim. The rivulet riseth in the hills of Drumochter, and running from south-west to north-east betwixt the parishes of Kingussie and Laggan, after a course of about 15 miles, falleth into Spey at Invernahaven.

Near the mouth of Tromie is Invertromie, the heritage, for several generations, of a branch of the MacPhersons of Pitmean, and in 1758 purchased by John MacPherson of the family of Invereshie. A mile up the river is Ruthven, a small village having a post-office. Close by it, is a green mount* jutting into a marshy plain; the mount about 20 yards high, and the area on the top of it about 120 yards long and 60 broad. Here Cummine Lord Badenoch had his seat and fort (See my "Military History"). The lands of Ruthven are the Duke of Gordon's property.

* The Mount of Ruthven, rising abruptly from the marshy plain south of Kingussie, has the ruins of an old Barrack on it, which have an imposing appearance, but which were much inferior in strength and size to the more ancient Castle which they displaced, which belonged to the wild Cummings, Earls of Badenoch. Queen Mary frequently visited this Castle, that she might enjoy the pleasures of the chase in the adjoining forests. The Barrack, built of stones in 1718, was defended against a whole Highland host by 12 men, under the command of a Serjeant Molloy, in Feb. 1746, when the rebels set it on fire. It was here that the chiefs re-assembled their forces, to the number of 8000, two days subsequent to the Battle of Culloden, in the hopes of Prince Charles again taking the field. (ED.)

Next up the river is Neid, a part of Clunie's estate now forfeited to the Duke of Gordon his superior, by the clan-act. At the mouth of Truim, is Invernahaven, the heritage of John MacPherson, Chief of the Clan Dabbi or Davidsons. And two miles up the side of Truim are Phoiness and Etterish, the property of a gentleman of the family of Invereshie. I pass to

The west side of the river, on which the parish extendeth 4½ miles.

The Church standeth near the north end, 6 miles south of Alvie, and near to 15 north of Laggan. The lands are Laggan, Ardbrylach, Kingussie, Pitmean, Strone, and Bealids; and are the property of the Duke of Gordon. Coulinlin is the heritage of Donald MacPherson, of the family of Clunie. Clunie is now the feu-hold of Andrew MacPherson, of Benchar, holding of MacIntosh as superior, and this gentleman holdeth Benchar in mortgage off MacIntosh of Borlum.

[The village of Kingussie occupies the precincts, and the Church the site of the ancient Priory dedicated to S. Columba, which was founded by George, Earl of Huntly, about 1490. The lands belonging to it were bestowed by the family of Huntly, and were resumed by them at *the Reformation.* Part of the ruined Chapel of the Monastery remains in a sequestered spot near the hotel. The Kingussie estate, on the death of the last Duke of Gordon, passed into the possession of James Evan Baillie, Esq., of Culduthel and Glenelg, formerly of Bristol. His territories now extend over a principal part of the "great lordship of Badenoch," *the country of clumps of wood,* as the word implies.] (ED.)

MACPHERSON THE FREEBOOTER AND VIOLINIST.

[James Macpherson was born of a beautiful gipsy, who at a great wedding attracted the notice of a half intoxicated Highland gentleman, one of the Macphersons of Invereshie. He acknowledged the child, and had him reared in his house, until he lost his life in bravely pursuing a hostile clan, to recover a spraith of cattle taken from Badenoch. The gipsy woman, hearing of this disaster in her rambles the following summer, came and took away her boy; but she often returned with him, to wait upon his relations and clansmen, who never failed to clothe him well, besides giving money to his mother. He grew up in strength, stature, and beauty, seldom equalled. His sword is still preserved at Duff House, a residence of the Earl of Fife, and few men could carry, far less wield it as a weapon of war; and if it must be owned, his prowess was debased by the exploits of a freebooter, it is certain no act of cruelty, no robbery of the widow, the fatherless, or distressed, and no murder was ever perpetrated under his command. He often gave the spoils of the rich to relieve the poor; and all his tribe was restrained from many atrocities of rapine by their awe of his mighty arm. Indeed, it is said that a dispute with an aspiring and savage man of his tribe, who wished to rob a gentleman's house while his wife and two children lay on the bier for interment, was the cause of his being betrayed to the vengeance of the law. The magistrates of Aberdeen were exasperated at Macpherson's escape, when they bribed a girl in that city to allure and delude him into their hands. There were a platform before the jail, at the top of a stair, and a door below. When Macpherson's capture was made known to his comrades by the frantic girl, who was so credulous as to believe that the magistrates only wanted to hear the wonderful performer on the violin, his cousin, Donald Macpherson, a gentleman of Herculean powers, did not disdain to come from Badenoch and to join a gipsy, Peter Brown, in liberating the prisoners. On a market-day they brought several assistants; and swift horses were stationed at a convenient distance. Donald Macpherson and Peter Brown forced the jail, and while Peter Brown went to help the heavily-fettered James Macpherson in moving away, Donald

Macpherson guarded the jail door with a drawn sword. Many persons assembled at the market had experienced James Macpherson's humanity, or had shared his bounty, and they crowded round the jail as in mere curiosity, but, in fact, to obstruct the civil authorities from preventing a rescue. A butcher, however, was resolved, if possible, to detain Macpherson, expecting a large recompense from the magistrates. He sprang up the stairs, and leaped from the platform upon Donald Macpherson, whom he dashed to the ground by the force and weight of his body. Donald Macpherson soon recovered to make a desperate resistance, and the combatants tore off each other's clothes. The butcher got a glimpse of his dog upon the platform, and called him to his aid; but Macpherson, with admirable presence of mind, snatched up his own plaid, which lay near, and threw it over the butcher, thus misleading the instinct of his canine adversary. The dog darted with fury upon the plaid, and terribly lacerated his master's thigh. In the meantime, James Macpherson had been carried out by Peter Brown, and was soon joined by Donald Macpherson, who was quickly covered by some friendly spectator with a hat and greatcoat. The magistrates ordered webs from the shops to be drawn across the Gallowgate; but Donald Macpherson cut them asunder with his sword, and James, the late prisoner, got off on horseback. He was some time after betrayed by a man of his own tribe, and was the last person executed at Banff, previous to the abolition of heritable jurisdiction. He was an admirable performer on the violin; and his talent for composition is still in evidence in "Macpherson's Rant," "Macpherson's Pibroch," and "Macpherson's Farewell." He performed those tunes at the foot of the fatal tree, and then asked if he had any friend in the crowd to whom a last gift of his instrument would be acceptable. No man had hardihood to claim friendship with a delinquent, in whose crimes the acknowledgment might implicate an avowed acquaintance. As no friend came forward, MacPherson said, that the companion of many gloomy hours should perish with him; and breaking the violin over his knee, he threw away the fragments. Donald Macpherson picked up the neck of the violin, which to this day is preserved, as a valuable memento by the family of Cluny, Chieftain of the Macphersons.] B. G.. (*The New Monthly Magazine*, I., 142. London, 1821. Also *The Book of the Chronicles of Keith*, &c., pp. 37, 43). (ED.)

KINGUISICH.

[*Situation, Soil, Climate.*—The Spey, on quitting the parish of Laggan, winds, in a variety of beautiful curves, through a level fertile meadow, intersecting the parish for its whole length, nearly 17 miles, to its extremity at the east. Its breadth from the banks of the river extends to either hand almost 10 miles; but of this extent the vicinity only of the river, and the valleys along its tributary streams, are inhabited, the rest being a wilderness of mountain pasturage, where a few huts are thinly scattered, for the accommodation of those tending cattle in summer. These mountains extend southward to the banks of the Tay, and northward by the sources of the Findern, in the parish of Moy and Dalarossie, to the lake and the river of Ness. The name in its literal import signifies the head of the fir-wood; but the firs have retired to such a distance that it has lost all right to that appellation. There are, however, several aller and willow trees interspersed on the banks of the Spey; and though parts of the rising grounds on the south are clothed in natural groves of birch and hazel, yet the country in general appears destitute of wood. The River Truim separates the south side of the parish from Laggan at the west; and the Feshie, holding a course nearly parallel for 15 miles through the Grampian Hills, forms its boundary on the east. The extent between these is divided by the Tromie nearly into equal parts; but holding a shorter course its stream is proportionally less, yet larger than the Gynag and Calder, considerable brooks sent into Spey from the north. From the windings of the river in the meadows of Kinguisie, it may be inferred that its noted rapidity takes place only in a lower part of its course. The alluvion of Feshie, therefore, in an era extremely remote, has deposited a bed of gravel at its influx, which has expanded the Spey into a lake called Loch Inch, about a mile in breadth, and almost two in length, which, with all the rivers that have been mentioned, contains trout and pike, salmon, and charr. Some years ago, the proprietors concerned in the lake laid out almost

£500 in making a cut through this bar, but through want of sufficient declivity in the ground the draining of the lake misgave, but the regurgitation at each swell of the river upon the meadows, about its western end, has been in a great measure by this means taken off. The soil in the meadows is sandy slime, the sediment of the water, incumbent on a light loam, which rests on a bed of clay; and in the higher grounds it is also in general a light loam, with a mixture of sand. This district, however, is but little adapted for the production of grain. Storms are frequent in every season, and frosts are uncommonly intense; they begin early in autumn and continue late in the spring; and heavy falls of rains are frequent in the harvest months, so that the crops are always uncertain. From the great elevation of the country above the level of the sea the climate is naturally cold, and though from this it might be regarded as healthy, yet the low meadow grounds have so little declivity that every flood overflows them; the stagnation of the water renders them swampy, and produces noxious vapours. Hence rheumatisms, consumptions, and their kindred complaints, are frequent.

State of Property.—The parish is possessed by 6 proprietors. The only family seat is that of William Macpherson, Esq., of Invereshie, pleasantly situated on a rising ground, near the skirt of a wood above Loch Inch, and, as its name imports, at the influx of the Feshie into the Spey. His valued rent in the parish, including Killyhuntly and Ballnespick, is £691.

Clunie, Benchar, and Invernahaven, on the banks of the Spey, with Phoiness and Eterish on those of the Truim, the estate of James Macpherson of Belville, Esq., amount to the valued rent of £461 13s. 4d. Scots. Land in the district of Inch appertaining to Mackintosh of Mackintosh, amounts to £160 Scots. Major George Gordon's estate of Invertromie is £80 Scots. Colonel Macpherson of Cluny has the lands of Noods and Bialledbeg, £273 6s. 8d. And the rest of the parish appertains to the Duke of Gordon, valued at £1,763; making the whole valuation of the parish equal to £3,929 Scots.

The cultivated farms are in general of inconsiderable extent, and the habitations mean, black, earthen hovels, darkened by smoke, and dripping upon every shower.

Barley, oats, rye, and potatoe are the produce of the cultivated ground, but the quantity obtained is not sufficient for the support of the inhabitants. Black cattle is their primary object, for the payment of their rents and for other necessaries. The whole number of sheep does not exceed 7,000 : part of them, and of their wool, with a few goats and horses reared in the hills, are also sold. Blacksmiths and weavers excepted, there are few mechanics of any kind; there being no village, they have no centre of traffic nor place of common resort, so that a variety of necessaries must be brought from the distance of more than forty miles. The wool which might be manufactured in the country must be sent by a long land-carriage to buyers invited from another kingdom; and flax, which might prove a source of wealth to both landlord and tenant, must be neglected, because people skilled in the various process of its manufacture are not collected into one neighbourhood.

State Ecclesiastical.—Upon the establishment of the Presbyterian government, the Presbyteries of Elgin, Aberlour, and Abernethy made only one. In the year 1707 Elgin was disjoined, and in two years thereafter the other two were also separated into their present independent jurisdictions; and, in the present arrangement, Kinguisich·makes the first parish in the Presbytery of Abernethy. The stipend, lately augmented, is £100 sterling. The rent of the glebe is £12, and as there is no manse the landlords pay £15 sterling for the hire of a house to the minister, who resides on a commodious farm at a little distance from the church, which has been lately rebuilt in a very neat and handsome fashion. The right of patronage appertains to the Duke of Gordon. The salary of the school is £11 6s. 8d. sterling and £2 as clerk of the session, with the concomitant fees, and the perquisites of that office; the number of scholars varies from 20 to 50. The poor on the parish roll amount to more than 50, and the only provision for their necessities is the contributions of the people in their assemblies for social worship. They are all of the national Church, amounting to the number of 1,803 souls.

Miscellaneous Information.—There are some Druid circles, which bear testimony of the many generations which have succeeded each other in this part of the country.

The remains of the Roman encampment, the green mount on which the ruins of the barrack remain, rises on a marshy plain to the height of 60 feet, the area of its summit measures 360 by 180 feet. It is supposed to be wholly artificial, and some of the old people mention that on sinking the well within the barrack, planks of wood were found laid across each other at equal distances from near the surface to the base. It was originally the situation of the Castle of Ruthven, the seat of the Cumings, Lords of Badenach. After the rebellion, in the year 1715, it was purchased by Government, and a spacious handsome barrack was erected, consisting of two buildings placed parallel, and two bastions in the diagonal angles, connected by the ramparts; it could have accommodated 2 companies of men and several horses. The party quartered here joined General Cope on his route to Inverness in August, 1745, leaving only Serjeant Molloy and a dozen men, who, in September thereafter, maintained the barrack against 200 rebels, for which gallant defence he was promoted to the rank of lieutenant. In February, 1746, being again besieged by 300, under General Gordon of Glenbucket, and some cannon, for 3 days he made such a good defence as procured the most honourable capitulation; the buildings were then destroyed by fire, and its desolated walls now only remain.

Several years ago a mine was opened, where some pieces of very rich silver ore were dug up, but no attempt has been made to ascertain whether it be worth working or not.

The people are in general distinguished by their moderation in religious opinions. Instances of theft are very uncommon, more flagrant crimes are now unknown. They are brave but quarrelsome, they are hospitable but addicted to drunkenness, they are polite but little to be depended on for the sincerity of their professions. Their genius is more inclined to martial enterprise than to the assiduous industry and diligent labour requisite to carry on the arts of civil life.] (*Survey of the Province of Moray.*)

THE PARISH OF LAGGAN,

Lieth on the head of the river Spey, and extendeth on both sides of the river, about 10 miles in length. In the north end it is about 4 miles broad, besides Delwhinny that is 2 miles in the hill of Drumochter.

On the west side of the river, 6 miles above Kingusie, stood the fine modern house of Clunie, which was burnt in 1746; and the estate of Clunie forfeited, by the Clan-Act, to the Duke of Gordon superior.

Six miles above Clunie is Garva, at the foot of the hill Coryerack, where the military road leadeth to Fort Augustus. At Garva there is a stone bridge over Spey, and beyond it there is no land inhabited on the west side of the river, which hath a course of about 8 miles further into the hills.

On the east side of the river, 6 miles above the water of Truim, is Strathmasie, the heritage of MacPherson of Strathmasie. And here the rivulet of Massie falleth into Spey.

Four miles farther south is Laggan, likewise Aberarder, and other lands pertaining to the Laird of Macintosh, and Galagie pertaining to the Laird of Grant.

All the rest of the parish is the property of the Duke of Gordon. The Church of Laggan standeth here at the north end of Loch Laggan. But as this is beyond the bounds of the Province of Moray, and the river of Spean issuing out of Loch Laggan runneth into Lochaber, I here break off.

LOCH LAGGAN

Is about 10 miles long, and apparently a mile in general breadth. It is embosomed among mountains, the declivities of which are for the most part covered to the water's edge with birch, intermingled with a large proportion of alder, rowan-tree, aspen, and hazel, the latter peculiarly remarkable for its uncommon size. All are grey with age. On the south side two small islands are seen, with ruins almost crumbled down to the water's edge. The one is called *Castle Fergus*, also *Eilean an Righ* (King's Island), which, though it may have been occupied by the Lairds of Cluny, has its erection ascribed to the first of our Scottish kings, Fergus, who used this as a hunting-seat. Several of these early monarchs are said to have been buried here. The adjacent isle, *Eielean nan con* (Dog's Island), is said to have been Fergus' dog-kennel; and the height to the south, in front of which the Marquis of Abercorn erected in 1836 a large and beautiful shooting-lodge, is called Ardverkie or *Fergus' hill*. Here Queen Victoria, and Prince Albert, and the Royal Family, quartered part of the autumn of 1847.

Lord Henry Bentinck, as assignee of the Marquis of Abercorn, rents these extensive wilds, including Loch Errocht side, as a deer-forest, from Cluny-Macpherson. A small lake intermediate between the loch just mentioned and Loch Laggan, and which throws into the latter, at its east end, the river Pattoch, is the true summit-level of the country. It thus stands above all the other lakes which contribute to the waters of the Tay, Spey, and Spean. While standing on any of the heights hereabouts, the traveller cannot but remark the evidences of the former submergence of the country under the sea; and also perceive how distinct the central chains of gneiss and mica-schist mountains are, from the group of higher and rougher Alps which bend away towards Ben Nevis and Glencoe. Fine white and blue granular limestone abounds all along Loch Laggan and the neighbouring ridges; and hence the fertility of which is gradually stealing over the brown wastes.

S. Killen's Church, The "little aul' Kirk of Laggan," is worth notice. Besides a very small altar-stone, it has two little side-altars, under rounded arches. At the south entrance is a large round granite baptismal font, capable of immersing the infants. In the oldest version of the ballad, of "Sir James the Rose," founded on fact, reference is made to the churchyard of Laggan. The doorway is not 3 ft. wide, and in both sides there is a grove, as if it had been closed in the manner of a portcullis, and a hole in each side may have been for the reception of a wooden bar. Near one side of the door is an *eyelit* or *oilet*, for reconnoitring.

Mrs. Grant, Laggan, a graceful authoress, favourably known to the public of last generation, by her "Letters from the mountains," and other captivating literature, and whose domicile in her widowhood was a favourite rendezvous for the *literati* of Edinburgh, was the wife of Rev. James Grant, minister of Laggan, 1775-1801. (ED.)

LAGGAN.

[*Situation, Soil, Climate.*—Although this parish be the highest in Scotland, in its elevation above the level of the sea, yet its Gaelic name, properly *na-lac*, signifies the hollow, expressing the appearance of the face of the country, composed of deep and narrow valleys. It is separated from the parish of Boleskin on the north, by a vast and lofty ridge of almost inaccessible rock, named *monuleie*, the grey mountain. From that quarter, therefore, it can only be approached by the military road from Fort Augustus to Stirling, which forms the continuation of the boundary of the province on the west. It is conducted over the mountain of Corryarioch to the inn of Garvamore, the farthest and most westerly habitation within the limits of the province. The road is formed along the western bank of the river Tarff, across its sources, to the summit of Corryarioch, towering far beyond, and above many an intermediate height. The road winds through stately trees in the deep groves of Inverisha, which are terminated, as the valley rises into the mountain, by lofty naked cliffs of picturesque and varied form. A number of torrents, streaming from the higher parts of the mountain, is poured with impetuosity over the precipice, and dashing down from shelve to shelve, broken with all the wild varieties of the rock, and foaming in their fall, exhibit some of the most romantic cascades that can be imagined. Some venerable pines wave among the rocks, seeming to watch over the incessant murmur of the torrents as they hasten their confluence to the central rivulet, the farthest branch of the deep-roaring Spey; while wreaths of birch adorn the more gentle declivities, where the foundation of the precipices have shot into the bottom of the glen. The summit of the mountain, attracting many heavy volumes of mist, is generally involved in clouds, which the Alpine blast rolls down in condensing fogs around the lower hills, with the chilling cold and penetrating damp of sleety rain, mingled with snow; deeply impressing all the terrors of this dreary, though elevated solitude. If the summit can be attained with an unclouded sky, the landscape is immense and transportingly sublime. The whole horizon around is an arrangement of distant mountains, far beyond all possible enumeration, immeasurably extended to the Western Isles, and to the eastern shore. Some tracts of country are generally conceived by intermediate clouds, through which the more lofty hills raise their dun heads like islands in the deep, giving a noble expression to the immense extent of the lower world around, exhibiting a scene of boundless magnificence, lighted up under an azure heaven, and basking in the blaze of meridian day, enchanting for a time the mind, while it shares in the sublimity of a prospect, partaking so much of infinitude, and impressing the admiring imagination with its relation to the universe, without boundary and without end. The descent is more immediately precipitous in 17 traverses cut across the eastern face of the mountain to its bottom: at which the Spey having collected its infant streams into a fair but inconsiderable lake, winds eastwards in growing majesty, progressive towards the German ocean; receiving from the Grampian mountains on the south, the river Masie, about the middle of the parish: which is bounded by the similar course of the Truim, from Drumuachter, at the east.

Parallel to the Masie, at the distance of 2 miles, the river Pattach holds an opposite course, towards the great lake of Lochlaggan; the environs of which form a separate district in the south-west extremity of the parish. The lake is of great depth, with bold rocky shores rising into rocky mountains. *Coill-more*, the great wood, the most considerable remain of the Caledonian forest, extends 5 miles along its southern side; the scene of many historical traditions: its waters, abounding with charr, and various kinds of trout, are discharged by the river Spean into the Atlantic ocean near Fort William. There are several smaller lakes: one bears the appellation of *loch-na-righ*, the king's lake; all of them stored with large black trout of the most delicate kind.

The air, though generally moist and cold, is, upon the whole, pure and healthful. The climate is extremely variable, exhibiting a difference strikingly perceptible at the distance of each 2 or 3 miles: it is often rain on one side of the river, while it is dry on the other.

The soil along the banks of the river, though rich, deep, and capable of producing as weighty crops as in the kingdom, is however but little productive, from the destructive influence of inundation, mildew, and frost. The higher lands on the declivities, although stony, produce more certain crops than the meadows on the plain, being ripened more early by the reflection of the sun from the rocks. The lands in the district of Lochlaggan, though higher, and in a climate still wetter than the banks of the Spey, are less liable to mildew and frost, from their being laid upon a bed of lime-stone rock.

State of Property.—The Duke of Gordon, and Colonel Macpherson of Cluny, possess the parish: the valued rent appertaining to his Grace is £1202 9d., and that to the Colonel is £599 Scots. The land is occupied partly by gentlemen, holding farms from £30 to £100 sterling of rent, and by shepherds, who hold sheep-farms of from £30 to £190 sterling of rent: the lower and most numerous class of tenants are the people, whose rents vary only from about £3 to £6 sterling. The rent of land, in general, seems to be on the rise: but the sheep-farms only seem capable of bearing any considerable advance; although the value of such farms depend so much on the seasons, and on the markets, yet a high idea of their value is in general entertained: in the space only of a dozen years, the rent of one has advanced from £30 to £190. The sheep-farms are all on the estate of Cluny, and exceed not the number of 5: they at present support about 12,000. The other farms, stocked with black cattle, sheep, and horses, support about 2000 sheep, 1600 cattle, and horses barely sufficient for labouring the ground. The best wedders sell at from 12s. to 16s.; those belonging to the poorer tenants, from 7s. to 9s.; wool unwashed sells about 8s. the stone; smeared wool, about 5s.; cows bring from £4 to £6; steers from £3 to £4; and horses of a small but hardy breed from £5 to £6. The mean quantity of meal produced in a temperate year is about 2450 bolls; but that is not sufficient for the support of the inhabitants. Only one-third of that quantity was produced by the crop of 1782. The advantage of enclosures, and the comfort of commodious habitations, are now perceived; and the tenants, at their removal, are allowed the value of the dykes and buildings on their respective farms. There are in the parish 7 tailors, 6 weavers, 3 carpenters, 3 masons, and 1 blacksmith, but no shoemaker regularly bred: the common people make their own shoes.

State Ecclesiastical.—The minister occupies a commodious farm, on the estate of the Duke of Gordon, near the Church, which was rebuilt in a central situation in the year 1785. The glebe is let for £12 of rent; and £20 is allowed by the proprietors for the parsonage buildings. The right of patronage appertains to the Duke of Gordon. The stipend, which is £70 sterling, is said to exhaust the tithes; but the proprietors of late, from personal regard to Mr. Grant, have promised to make it £100 during the remainder of his incumbency. The parochial school in the midst of the parish is an appointment of £16 13s. 4d. sterling, with the customary fees and perquisites of office: the number of scholars from 50 to 80. The Society for propagating Christian Knowledge maintain two schools in the western wings of the parish. The provision for the poor arises only from the contributions of the people when in Church. The members of the National Establishment are 1262; and 250 of the Church of Rome.

Miscellaneous Information.—In the midst of the Coillmore is a place distinguished by the name of the *ard merigie,* the height for rearing the standard. It has been held sacred from remote antiquity, as the burial-place of 7 Caledonian kings; who, according to tradition, lived about the period when the Scots, driven northward of the Tay by the Picts, held their seat of government at Dunkeld. It is likewise, by tradition, represented as a distinguished place for hunting: and it abounded in deer and roe till they were lately expelled by the introduction of sheep, with whom they never mingle. The kings, it is said, and their retinue, hunted on the banks of the lake for the greater part of almost every summer: which is rendered probable by its vicinity to the parallel roads of Glenroy which must have been formed solely for the purpose of betraying the game into an impassable recess, and could not have been executed but by the influence of some of the first consequence and power in the State.

In the lake are two neighbouring islands: on the largest, the walls remain of a very ancient building, composed of round stone laid in mortar, untouched by the mason's hammer. Here their Majesties rested from the chase secure, and feasted on the game. The other, named *ellan-na-kune*, the island of dogs, was appropriated for the accommodation of the hounds; and the walls of their kennel, of similar workmanship, also remain.

Near the midst of the parish is a rock 300 feet of perpendicular height: the area on the summit, 500 by 250 feet, is of very difficult access, exhibiting considerable remains of fortification; the wall, about 9 feet thick, built on both its sides with large flag-stones without mortar.

Near the eastern end of Lochlaggan, the venerable ruins of St. Kenneth's Chapel remain, in the midst of its own consecrated burying-ground, which is still devoutly preferred to the other.] (*Survey of the Province of Moray.*)

Having run over the valley of Spey that covereth the whole Province, I now return to the mouth of that river, to describe the Low Country: And begin with

THE PARISH OF SPEYMOUTH,

Extendeth in length, $4\frac{1}{2}$ miles from the sea southward on the bank of the river, and generally it is but half a mile broad, except the south end that is a mile in breadth.

The Church standeth near the river, over against the Church of Bellie, and about half a mile west from it; 3 miles east from Urquhart, and 3½ miles north from Dundurcos.

Till the year 1731 (*vid. Eccles. Hist.*) this made two parishes, viz., Essil and Dipple. Essil (*Iasal*, i.e. low) in the north end.

At the mouth of the river is the harbour and town of *Germagh*.

The harbour receiveth no ships of burden, being choked with sand and shut up by a bar.

The town of Germagh is a burgh of barony, consisting of about 60 dwelling-houses. It was long the property of the family of Innes, and now belongs to the Earl Fife, and feued out to small heritors.

South of the town are the lands of Essil, for several generations the heritage of Geddes of Essil, disponed in 1698 to Duff of Dipple, father of the late Earl Fife. Dipple (*Dubh* or *Du-pol*, i.e. the black or deep pool, viz., in the river) was church-land, for some time the heritage of the family of Innes, and now of Earl Fife. The Duke of Gordon has a farm or two in this parish, and for the space of about 4 miles above the mouth of the river is one of the best salmon fishings in the kingdom, belonging to the Duke of Gordon, the Earl of Moray and Earl Fife.

The Duke of Gordon's fishing is partly a perquisite of the Lordship of Urquhart, and partly purchased from Cumine of Ernside. The Earl of Moray's fishing formerly belonged to the

Bishop of Moray, and came to the Regent Earl of Moray with the lands of Dipple, about anno 1567, from Patrick Hepburn, the last R.C. Bishop. And when the lands of Dipple were sold, the fishing was retained, and the Earl Fife's fishing came to him with the lands of Germach, from the family of Innes; and with the lands of Essil, from Geddes of Essil.

SPEYMOUTH.

[*Situation, Soil, Climate.*—This parish lieth upon the northern bank of the river Spey, at its influx into the Moray Frith. Its length from north to south, along the course of the river, may be 6½ miles, its breadth 1½, partly terminated by the eastern end of the chain of mountain, ranging along the southern side of the champaign of Moray, and partly by the limits of the parish of Urquhart, which meets it on the plain. Where the post road approaches to the river, the country swells into a gentle eminence. Exclusive of this, and of the mountain side, it may be regarded as a plain, having one part sunk below the level of the other about 50 feet, having the river winding on its farther edge, which in the lower part of its course shifting at times its channel, and at times dividing its stream, with a considerable extent of fertile ground, much bare uncovered beach is also left. A great proportion of the plain above the bank is also uncultivated moor; but, with the application of lime, might be easily brought into productive cultivation. The arable field is partly a shallow gravelly soil, partly a light fertile loam of sufficient depth, and in some parts it is a sandy soil. The climate, comparatively temperate and mild, is scarcely subject to any other inconvenience besides parching easterly winds, which commonly prevail in April and May, often blasting the fruit in its blossom, and checking the growth of the grass. This part of the country is supposed to be the driest even in Moray, where it is said there are forty days more of fair weather, than in any other country in the north of Scotland. A drought

DERIVATION AND DESCRIPTION OF GARMOUTH. 303

frequently sets in during the month of July, prejudicial to the crop on the shallow soil. A showery summer is accounted favourable: and a quantity of rain, that would be very hurtful in most parts of the kingdom, is beneficial here. In the year 1782, when, from excessive rain, there was a general failure of the crop over Scotland, many persons here made more than common profit. The mean depth of rain-water falling in a year is about 24 inches.

State of Property.—Except the feuars of Garmach holding of the Duke of Gordon, his Grace is the proprietor of the whole parish, and also of seven-ninth parts of the fishery; the other two-ninth parts appertain to the Earl of Moray. Garmach, the only village in the parish, is a burgh of barony, containing 620 inhabitants: it has an annual fair on the 19th of June. The lands are occupied for the greater part by the proprietors, several of whom, by pursuits in other occupations, are in opulent circumstances. The name of this village is Gaelic; but its signification is not certainly ascertained: it may import the rough outlet, from the ripple of the tide at the influx of the river; but as it bore the same name when the mouth of the river was more than 3 miles distant, it may be rather a compound, corrupted of *var*, water, *augh*, a plain on the bank of a stream, and *na*, the Gaelic of the article the. The walls of the greater number of the houses in this village are composed entirely of clay, made into mortar with straw, in some cases having a foot or two in height from the foundation built in alternate courses of the same mortar and stone. In building this kind of wall, it is necessary to suspend the work a little, on the addition of every yard of height, that it may not warp from the perpendicular. With this precaution, it is frequently raised to the height of two stories, bears a slated roof, and is neatly finished within. If sufficiently covered on the top, it is found as durable, and more impervious to wind and damp, and appears as handsome, when daubed over on the outside with lime mortar, as walls of stone in the common fashion.

The parish is occupied in farms rather of small extent. A few rise to near 80 acres, some about 50, several about 30, and nearly the half of the whole number may be let from £4 to £10 of yearly rent. 10s. may be stated as the mean rent of the acre, varying from about 5s. to 15s.

Part of the lands which are let about Garmach bring from 20s. to 30s. the acre, and a small proportion rises to about £2 10s. the acre, making the average there about £1 5s.

The valued rent of the land of the parish is £2771 17s. 1d. Scots, to which is added, the valued rent of the fishery, £2541 17s 8d. Scots; total £5313 14s. 9d. Scots.

State Ecclesiastical.—In the year 1731 the parishes of Dipple and Essil, and the village of Garmach, originally appertaining to the parish of Urquhart, were, by the decreet of the Court of Teinds, erected into the parish, then named Speymouth. The glebes of the parishes of Dipple and Essil were exchanged with the family of Fife for the present glebe, which being then partly uncultivated moor, about 25 acres were found the equivalent. The Church and manse were built in a centrical situation; but the burying-grounds of the original parishes were continued: and their patrons, the Earl of Moray, and the proprietor of Gordonstown, use the right of patronage alternately. The stipend, including the allowance for the communion, is £53 6s. 8d. sterling; 77 bolls, 1 firlot, 2 pecks barley; and 32 bolls, 1½ peck oat-meal—at 8½ stone per boll of meal.

The parochial school was lately established at Garmach, though at one of the extremities, the most populous quarter of the parish : the salary is 8½ bolls meal, and 2⅛ bolls of bear: and as by Act of Parliament 1696, the salaries of schools "are declared to be by and attour the casualties, which formerly belonged to the readers and clerks of the kirk session," the schoolmaster is by this statute entitled to £2 sterling as session-clerk, paid from the parish funds under the management of the session. He is by the same statute likewise entitled to 1s. for the proclamation of the purpose of each marriage, and for every baptism entered on the record; and for every extract of such entry, and for every certificate granted by the session, 4d. He has moreover £5 11s. 1½d., the interest of an endowment by Mr. Pat. Gordon, watchmaker in Edinburgh, for the behoof of the Schoolmaster of his native place. The fees for teaching in parish schools are generally the same over the province; namely, for each scholar taught to read English, 4s. in the year; when writing is conjoined. 5s. 4d. yearly; for arithmetic,

6s. 8d.; 8s. for Latin; and for a course of book-keeping, half-a-guinea.

The Society for propagating Christian Knowledge have lately established a school, towards the other extremity of the parish, with an appointment of £10 yearly, to which the landlord adds a house, small garden, and £2 yearly; besides which, he has £1 7s. 9½d., the half of an endowment by the family of Fife, in a former generation, for the schools of the original parishes: a superannuated teacher at present has the other half. At this school, about 30 scholars generally attend; and about as many, the younger servants in the neighbourhood, attend the same master, for some hours during the evenings of the winter season. There are, besides, two or three poor women, who, in different parts of the parish, teach children to read: the poorest of the people have all their children taught to read, and most of the boys are taught also arithmetic, and to write.

Poor's rates are not known in this country; yet, with such labour as themselves are able for, all are by voluntary charity provided with the necessaries of life; very little is suffered by want, there is no abuse, and little temptation to idleness. The provision for the poor arises from donations, made by the people who attend the public worship of the Parish Church, collected immediately on its conclusion. These amount to about £20 sterling in the year, to which the hire of the pall at funerals is added, and £4 3s. 4d. bequeathed by the same ancestor of the family of Fife who made the endowment for the school, which are paid by his lordship. This fund, after discharging the fee of the session-clerk, and £1 as the wages of the session-officer, is divided half-yearly, generally among 40 persons, on the parish roll, in proportion to their respective necessities, besides occasional supplies in urgent cases. The number of the Established Church is 1302: there are 40 of the Church of Rome, and 5 of the Episcopalian profession.

Miscellaneous Information.—The people in general are honest, peaceable, and industrious, charitable also, and in cases of distress much disposed to acts of humanity. They are hardy and active, and rather above the middle size. Few go into the army; the greater part apply to husbandry, to the salmon-fishing; and the young men about the town of Garmach are disposed to a seafaring life, and become expert sailors. About 12 of the natives are at present the masters of vessels. The more wealthy wear English cloth, in which almost all are dressed on holidays. Most of the smaller tenants keep as many sheep as supply clothing for their families, and almost all raise flax, which they also manufacture into linen. Several families make a little both of woollen and linen cloth for sale. Moor turf is the fuel through the greater part of the parish. Sunderland coal, delivered from the ship at 2s. for a barrel of 13 stone, is mostly used about Garmach. The stone principally used is quarried from the rock that forms the bank of the river for a mile where the post road passes; it is limestone of a red colour; toward the top it is a stone marl, which, with intervening layers of clay, is used in the vicinity with great advantage as a manure. The stone becomes harder in proportion to the depth at which it is quarried.

The river Spey derives its remotest source from the mountain of Corryarioch, at the distance of almost 100 miles from its influx into the German Ocean. It is the most rapid river in Scotland; its fall for the last 3 miles of its course is 60 feet. It does not appear so large as the more gently rolling Tay; yet it is supposed to discharge an equal quantity of water in the year. In the middle and higher parts of its course, its branches stretch out to 15 miles on either side, and the extent of country which it drains is equal to 1600 square miles. Although its course is now directly into the sea, yet it is certain, that in ancient times, bending almost into a right angle when just upon the shore, it flowed westward nearly 3 miles, mostly parallel with the Firth, in a hollow marshy tract, called the Leen, now partly reduced into a state of imperfect cultivation. The tide flows up the river almost to Garmach, and, at neap-tides, the depth of water is 9 feet on the bar. The entrance into the harbour is sometimes shifted a little by the gravel washed down by the stream; but there being always skilful pilots, no detriment ensues. The expense of building a pier is supposed to exceed the value of the trade; but the shore on either side for 5 or 6 miles along the bay of Spey being smooth gravel, or soft sand (one little rock, the bear's head, half way between Garmach and Lossiemouth excepted), several vessels have in necessity been run ashore, with little damage.

At the harbour, there is a wood-trade, the most considerable, it is supposed, for home timber in Scotland. It is mostly fir, with some birch and oak. There are seven persons engaged in this trade; but for some years the greater part has been carried on by an English company, who, about the year 1784, contracted with the Duke of Gordon, for all the marketable timber of the forest of Glenmore, in the district of Strathspey, to be felled within the space of 26 years, at the sum of £10,000 sterling. When the timber of this, and of the other forests in Strathspey and Badenaugh, arrives at Garmach, after supplying a great extent of country, from Aberdeen to the Isle of Skye, it is carried in considerable quantities to Hull, and to the King's yards at Deptford and Woolwich. This company have also formed a dock-yard, and since the year 1736, besides a number of boats, they have built 24 vessels from 25 to 500 tons burthen, the greater number about 200 tons, amounting in all to more than 4000 tons, all of the fir-wood of Glenmore, both the plank and timbers. The greater part of this wood being of the best quality, these vessels are deemed equal to those of New England oak. The largest masts are 60 feet in length. Before the Commissioners of the Navy purchased any of this timber, they ascertained, by several experiments, that it is equal in quality to any imported from the Baltic. Several of these vessels have been purchased for the Baltic trade, one for the trade of the Bay of Campeachy, and several are employed in the trade of the company. Besides the vessels which they have built, several sloops have been also built at Speymouth by others, in the same time, and several have been repaired. The plank, deals, and masts, are floated from their native forests down the Spey in rafts, navigated by 2 men, at the rate of £1 10s. the raft. The logs and spars belonging to the English company are at times floated down in single pieces, to the number perhaps of 20,000 at a time, conducted by 50 or 80 men going along the sides of the river, to push them off by poles, as they stick upon the banks, hired at 1s. 2d. by the day, and a competent allowance of spirituous liquor. The medium price of logs, from 10 to 20 feet long, and from 12 to 18 inches diameter, is 1s. the solid foot; spar-wood of the same length, about 7 inches diameter, is sold at 7d. the solid foot; plank, 3 inches thick, and 10 in breadth, about 12 feet in length, are 3s. the piece—2 inches thick, 2s.; and deals, $1\frac{1}{4}$ inch thick, 8 inches in breadth, and 12 feet long, 1s. the piece.

The exports from Spey consist chiefly of wood and salmon, and 4 or 5 cargoes of grain, or meal, of 400 or 500 bolls each in a year.

From Oct. 1, 1791, to Oct. 1, 1792, vessels sailed from Spey with timber for different places, from 350 to 20 tons burden, average 50 tons, 82; touched at Spey, and took in salmon for London, having taken in part of the same cargo at other ports, 24; with oats and meal, 2; with yarn, 1 : number of vessels which sailed with cargoes, 109. Vessels arrived in Spey with coal, 11; with empty kits, staves, and hoops, 5; with iron and goods, 6; with salt, 1, 23.

The salmon-fishery, yielding a revenue of £1800 sterling yearly, begins on the 30th of November, and ends the 26th of August. It is seldom regular until the end of January. During the spring months, the greater part of the fish is sent fresh in ice to London—a late discovery, which adds greatly to the value of the fishery, as the highest price is in this way obtained : $4\frac{1}{2}$d. the lb. is the common price at the river-side. After the beginning of May, the greater part of the salmon is boiled, and sent to the London market. The fishery is carried on by nets and small boats, each navigated by 8 men, and an overseer, called the Kenner, from the Gaelic word for the head. The crew is changed every 12 hours : each man has £1 15s. of stated wages for the season, and 6d. each besides, when 6 fish are caught in the 12 hours, and 3d. only when they catch but 4. They have still a further allowance when they catch above a certain greater number, and may gain from £4 to £6 in the season. They have also as much bread and beer as necessary while at work, and a bottle of spirits to the crew for the 12 hours they are employed. They are accounted skilful in the business; and though wading in the water higher than the knee, and remaining the whole 12 hours in wet clothes, such is the power of habit, they feel no inconvenience from the cold even of the winter night. About 130 men may be the number generally employed.

This parish has a connection with the distinguished family of Chatham. Jane, spouse to Governor Pitt, the great grandmother of the present Chancellor of the Exchequer, was daughter to James Innes, Esq., of Redhall, on the bank of the Spey, directly opposite to Gordon Castle. The family of Redhall, represented now by Innes of Blackhills, are a branch of the family of Innes, Baronets of Coxtown. This circumstance has been always recognized in the country, and is ascertained by Edmonson's Peerage, "Family of Chatham."

The parish has been the scene of some actions in the history of the kingdom. Near the mouth of the river, the rebels of Moray, Ross, and Caithness, in the year 1078, made a stand, to oppose the passage of Malcolm III.; but, on seeing the resolution of the royal army in fording the river, their submission was offered, and received, at the intercession of the priests.

In the year 1110 an army of rebels halted at the mouth of the Spey, to dispute the passage with Alexander I. pursuing them. The King, forcing the passage, so terrified the rebels, that they were easily defeated by a detachment of the army, under the conduct of Alex. Scrimger.

In the year 1160 a rebellion, still more formidable, was quelled by Malcolm IV. in a battle that must have happened on the moors of this parish, wherein the Moray people were so completely routed, that the chief families of this turbulent province were removed to different parts of the kingdom, and others transplanted in their room.

In the year 1650 King Charles II. landed at Speymouth from Holland. A man of the name of Milne carried his Majesty on shore, and his descendants are yet distinguished from others of the same name in Garmach, by the appellation of King Milnes. His Majesty was received by the Knight of Innes, and other gentlemen, and dined with the steward of Lord Dunfermline, at that time the proprietor of the lordship of Urquhart, in a house of Garmach, built, as has been described, of mortar, and of late only taken down; and in this house it was, that his Majesty subscribed the Solemn League and Covenant.] *(Survey of the Province of Moray.)*

EPITAPHS IN THE CHURCHYARD OF SPEYMOUTH.

The old Churchyard is situated near the village of Garmouth close by the side of the Spey. It is particularly to be noticed not only for its fine situation but for the neatness with which it is kept; being an instance of the better feeling of late in manifestation. No remains of the old Church remain, although the foundations may be faintly traced.

I. Here Lyes Ane Honest Man. Called Walter Duncan And Alex. Duncan. Portioners in Germovth.

The above is round the edge of the slab. In the centre, as much as can be deciphered :—

. . . . lyffe . . . . 1640 . . . . and . . . . W. D. A .D. T. D. Here lays the body of . . . . Duncan feuar in Garmouth who Died 4 December 1777 aged . . . . Jean Galt Dyed Feb. 1774 aged 71.

The inscriptions are cut rudely, some of which are huddled into a corner of the stone.

II. Here. Lyes. Ane . . . . Religious Gentleman. James. James Pringle Who Dept^d. This Liffe The Last of Maye. 1641.
[In the centre.]
MEMENTO MORI.

III. Here Lyes . . . . Arnoch Who Departed This Lyfe 1678.

IV. Here Lyes. J   AMES Geddes and Margaret Shand His Spouse Who Deceast. in August. The. 7. 1680.

V. W. G.   J. M.   M. G.   E. G.   M. G.   M. G. 1682.
The initials are in separate lines.

VI. Here. Lyeth. George Gordon. Somtyme in Germouth Husband. to. Elizabeth. Johnston. Who. Died. the. 17th of November 1688. And their children James Margaret Anna and Margaret Gordon.

A Morthead is in the centre of the slab.

VII. Here. lyes. David. Clerk. Wakster. in. Garmoch. Who Departed. This. Life. The. 26. Day. of. February. 1703. yiers. And. John. Clerk. his. son. who. Departed. This life the 10th day of March 1691 yeirs.   David Clark . . . 1852.

EPITAPHS IN THE CHURCHYARD OF SPEYMOUTH. 311

VIII. . . . . John Archibald . . . . Children to Archibald. Geddes. of. Essil. Who. died in . . . .

IX. Here. Lyes . . . . Younge. An. Elder. Coppr. in. Garmoch. 1692. . . . A. A.

X. Here. Lyes. Barbara. . . . ES. Spovse. to. John. James. Sometime. Waker. in. Garmouth. Who. Deceast. March. 24. 1692. and six of his children who died in their young age.

XI. Here. Lyes. The. Body. of. James. Innes. Sometime. Duallar. in. Garmouth. He. Departed. 10. of. April. 1699. And. His Spouse Janet Duncan she and their son Andrew Innes.

XII. Here. Lyes. Alex. Ogilvie. lawful. son. to. Robert Ogilvie. in. Essil. who Died the 22 day of January 1715.

XIII. Here Lyes the body of Alexander Hossack sometime Fewer in Garmouth who died July 8. 1720 and his spouse . . . died . . . 9. 1733 and their son Robert Hossack sometime couper in Garmouth.

XIV. Here. Lyes. Master. George. Cuming. 47 years Minister of The Gospel At Essil. Who Departed this life the 20 Day of September 1723.

XV. Here lyes the body of Alex. Milne Fewer in Garmouth who dyed the 27 of April 1727 and Janet Dunbar his spouse who died the . . . . of . . . . And Robert Harie Milnes his children. Also Ann Filchet daughter of Alex. . . . .

XVI. Here. Lyes. The. Body. of. Agnes. Innes. Spouse to William Innes Couper in Garmouth who died the 23 of July 1732 . . . . years. Memento Mori.

XVII. Here lyes the body of James Robertson fuer in Garmouth who died Oct. 13. 1735 and his spouse Elspet Mitchal who died   (never filled in)

XVIII. This Stone is placed here by Alexander Gordon sometime fewer in Garmouth and his spouse Mariorie Winchester who died Octb. 4. 1740 and his 2d spouse Margaret Mill who died April 1750.

XIX. Here lyes the body of James Smith fewer in Garmouth who died 27 April 1746 and Barbara Marshall his spouse who died 26th June 1762.

XX. Here. Lyes. the. Body. of. Robt. Wilson. sometime. farmer. in. Spynie. who. departed this life March the 15 1746 and his spouse Katherine Ragg who departed . . . . and their

son James Wilson .... and his spouse Isabella Barry ....
and their children Katherine, Barbara, Robert, and Barbara
Wilson.

XXI. This Stone is placed here in memory of Isobel Braid
daughter to Alex. Braid late shoemaker in Garmouth. She
dyed March 10, 1763 aged 23.

XXII. Here lyes the body of Patrick Anderson dyer in
Elgin and lawful son of John Anderson of Mathiewell and
Grisel Stewart his spouse. He died July 27 MDCCLXVI in
the LIII year of his age.

XXIII. This Stone is placed here by John Rea Shipmaster
in . . . horn in memory of his father William Rea at Skippa
there aged 61 years, who departed this life the 14 September
1781 years. (*Rev. J. B. Craven's MSS.*)

West from Speymouth lieth

THE PARISH OF URQUHART.

This parish stretcheth upon the firth to the River Lossie 4 miles, and 2 miles in breadth.

The Church standeth near the south end, 3 miles west from Speymouth, 1 mile north from Langbryde, and 3 east from Elgin; the south and east parts are called the Lordship of Urquhart. They were a part of the lands of that priory, and were created into a temporal lordship in favour of the son of Lord Winton, Chancellor of Scotland and Earl of Dunfermline, anno 1591 (*Vid. Eccles. Hist.*), and were purchased by the Duke of Gordon about the year 1730.

North from the Church is the barony of Innes. The House of Innes is a fine modern building, surrounded with gardens, inclosures, and planting. In the year 1737 it was all consumed by lightning, but is now for the most part repaired and well finished.

West of Innes is the barony of Leuchars. This was anciently a part of the Earldom of Moray, and came to Sir Alexander Dunbar of Westfield as a part of his patrimonial estate. About the 1570 a daughter of Westfield married to Innes of Crombie, brought Leuchars and a half coble of fishing on the Spey into the family of Innes; and now it is the heritage of Captain John Innes, a branch of the family.

Here let me give some account of the name and family of Innes.

THE FAMILY OF INNES.

This is a local sirname. *Inis* in Irish signifieth an island, or a peninsula, such as a part of the lands of Innes very probably was. The antiquity of this family, possessed of the barony of Innes for 600 years, appeareth from the original charter. Beroaldus Flandrensis, who obtained this charter, either was a Flandrian, according to Sir James Dalrymple, or was one of the ancient Moravienses, and having been for some time in Flanders was called the Flandrian. Thus the ancestor of Fraser of Foyer, having been for some time in France, was called Hutcheon Francach. Many such instances are obvious. I incline the rather to this opinion because the Morays, Sutherlands, Innesses, and Brodies have all the same paternal arms, viz., stars differing only in the tincture; whence it is probable they were anciently Moravienses. The charter now mentioned was granted by King Malcolm IV. [in 1157], and though the original is lost there is extant a transcript of it under the subscription of Gavin Dunbar, clerk register in the reign of King James V. The form of this charter showeth it ancient. Our Kings had at that time (and not before King William) used the plural *Nos*, and ancient charters had no particular date, yet the date of this charter may be nearly fixed by observing that William, Bishop of Moray, was made Legate anno 1159, and died anno 1162 (*Chron. Melr.*), which bringeth the date within three years. King Alexander II. by his charter, 1st January, anno regni 12*mo*, 1226, confirmed the lands of Innes, Waltero filio Joannis filii Berwaldi * (*Pen. Inn.* [in the possession of Innes]). (4) Sir Alexander Innes succeeded his father Walter, whose son (5) William was the first of this family designed *Dominus de Innes* in an indenture betwixt him and Simon, prior of Pluscardine, in or before the year 1298. His son (6) William de Innes, is one of the witnesses to an agreement betwixt the town of Elgin and the monks of Pluscardine, dated the 4th of December, 1330. He is therein designed *Baro de Innes*. His son

---

* *Translation.*—To Walter, the son of John, the son of Berwald.

(7) Robert de Innes is designed *Dominus ejusdem* in a charter of King David the II. of the Forrestry of Boyne. This charter is without date, but it appears, by the other witnesses mentioned in it, to have been granted before the year 1360. His son (8) Alexander had three sons and a daughter: Sir Walter, the eldest son, died unmarried; John, third son, was, on January 23, 1406-7, consecrated Bishop of Moray, and died in April, 1414. He advanced the rebuilding of the Cathedral, and began the building of the great steeple. On his tomb is this inscription:—"𝕳ic jacet Reberendus in Christo Pater et D. D. Johannes de Innes, hujus ecclesiæ Episcopus, qui hoc notabile opus incæpit, et per septennium potenter ædificabit."* The daughter, Giles, was married to Ferquhard M'Intosh of that ilk. The second son (9), Sir Robert Innes, succeeded his brother. He married Dame Janet, daughter and heiress of Sir David Aberkerder, Thane of Aberkerder, now Marnoch, with whom he got a great accession to his estate. By this lady he had a son (10), Sir Walter Innes, who got a charter of confirmation of his mother's lands from King James the II. anno 1450. He married, 1st, Eupheme, daughter of Hugh, first Lord Lovat, by whom he had three sons and two daughters—Sir Robert, his heir;

* *Translation.*—" Here lieth the Reverend Father in Christ and Doctor of Divinity John of Innes, Bishop of this Church, who began this distinguished work and for seven years assiduously continued the building."

Beroaldus Innes of Hatton, from whom several of this name in Caithness are descended; his third son, John, was Bishop of Caithness; Isabel, eldest daughter, was married to James Dunbar, Earl of Moray; Margaret, the second to Patrick Maitland of Netherdale. Sir Walter, by his second lady, had a son, John Innes of Ardmilly, from whom several families of the name are descended. (11) Sir Robert Innes succeeded his father, and was infeft in all his father's lands anno 1456. He was a man of great personal bravery, and remarkably distinguished himself in the service of his King on many occasions, particularly at the battle of Brechin anno 1452. His lady was a daughter of the Baron of Drumlanrig, by whom he had three sons and two daughters—James, his heir; Walter, second son, ancestor of the families of Innermarkie, Balvenie, Coxtown, Innerbrakie, Ortown, Auchintoul, &c.; Robert, third son, progenitor of the Innesses of Drainie; his eldest daughter, Margaret, was married to Sir James Ogilvie, ancestor of the Earls of Findlater; the second was married to Barclay of Towie. (12) James Innes of that ilk succeeded his father, to whom he was retoured heir anno 1464. He married Lady Janet Gordon, daughter of Alexander, Earl of Huntly, and with her had a numerous issue. The male issue of Alexander, the eldest son, failed in the person of his grandson, John, who was succeeded by the grandson of (13) Robert Innes of Cromby, second son of James; which Robert was father of (14) James Innes of Rathmakenzie, who died fighting gallantly in the defence of his country at the Battle of Pinkie anno 1547, and was succeeded by his son (15) Alexander, who, by right of blood, as well as by mutual entail, succeeded to the representation and estate of this family. By his lady, Isabella, daughter of Arthur Forbes of Balfour, and niece of John, eighth Lord Forbes, he had a son (16) Robert Innes of that ilk, who succeeded him; and by Elizabeth, daughter of Robert, third Lord Elphinston, he had two sons —Sir Robert, his heir; and Sir John, father of Sir Robert Innes of Muirton. (17) Sir Robert Innes of Innes was a great favourite of King Charles I., who created him a Baronet of Nova Scotia, with destination to his heirs male whatever, by patent dated at Whitehall the 29th of May anno 1625. He afterwards sided with the Covenanters, and was appointed one of the Committee of Estates anno 1641. He married Lady Grizel Steuart, daughter of James, Earl of Moray, by whom he had three sons and five daughters— Sir Robert, his heir; James of Lichnet, second son; William, a Captain in the Guards; his eldest daughter, Elizabeth, was married to John Urquhart of Craigtown; the second daughter, Mary, was married to James Steuart of Rosyth; his third was married to Sir Robert Innes of

Muirton; his fourth, Barbara, to Robert Dunbar, Sheriff of Murray; his youngest daughter was married to Alexander, first Lord Duffus. He died before the Restoration, and was succeeded by his eldest son (18) Sir Robert Innes of Innes, who married Mary, daughter of James, fifth Lord Ross of Halkhead, by whom he had (19) Sir James Innes of Innes, who by his lady, Margaret, daughter of Henry Lord Kerr, apparent heir of Robert, Earl of Roxburgh, had his son and successor (20) Sir Henry Innes of Innes, Baronet, who married Jean, daughter of Duncan Forbes, of Culloden, Esq., by whom he had Sir Henry, his heir, and John Innes of Inchbroom, Esq., an officer in the army, and two daughters. (21) Sir Henry Innes of Innes, Baronet, married Anne, daughter of Sir James Grant of Grant, by whom he had James, his heir, and Robert, who went to the East Indies. He had also five daughters, Anne, Jean, Margaret, Sophia, and Ludovica. (22) Sir James Innes of Innes, Baronet, succeeded his father, Sir Henry. He is the sixth Baronet of this family, the 22nd generation in a direct male line from Beroaldus, and the second in precedency of the order of Baronets of Nova Scotia.

This family had for many years a very opulent estate. They were proprietors of the baronies of Innes, Luchars, Kelmalemnock, in Moray county; Crombie, Rothmakenzie, and Abercherder, in Banff county, and much land in the county of

Caithness. They early embraced the Reformation of Religion, and William, Laird of Innes, was a Member of the Parliament in 1560 which established that change.

Sir James Innes (son of Sir Harry, who died in 1762) sold the estate of Innes in 1767 to James, Earl Fife.

[In a few years thereafter, Sir James Innes, heir apparent by Lady Margaret Kerr, mentioned above, at 19, succeeded to the title and fortune of the Duke of Roxburgh. He had been previously married to the daughter of Captain Charlewood, the mother of his Grace—James Innes Kerr, yet a minor. The Balvenie Baronet is now represented by Sir John Innes of Edingight (pronounced Edinœith), the Baronet of Coxton by Sir Hugh Innes, and the Baronet of Orton by, it is said, Sir David Innes.] (*Grant's Edition.*)

The arms of Innes are, Argent, three stars, each of six points azure, with the badge of Nova Scotia in the centre. Crest, within an adder disposed circleways, a castle triple towered proper. Motto, PRUDENTIA ET VI.* Supporters, two grey hounds argent, each having a collar azure, charged with three stars of the first.

URQUHART.

[*Situation, Soil, and Climate.*—The parish of Urquhart may be understood to extend across the lowlands of Moray, from the sea upon the north to the mountain on the south, about 9 miles, though in this space one farm of the parish of Speymouth intervenes. So little of the cultivated ground lies on the southern side of the post road that it may be considered, in a general view, as forming its boundary as it passes from Elgin at the west to the River Spey at the east for the length of 4 miles,

* *Translation.*—By Prudence and Bravery.

parallel almost to the firth, at the distance of 3 miles on the north. The sea coast, which is about 6 miles in extent, is low and sandy, and as no brook or rivulet falls in between Spey and the water of Lossie there is no creek or landing place of any kind. Grain, which is the only article of exportation, is shipped in the harbours of Speymouth or Lossiemouth. Coal, the great article of importation, must be carried over-land from the same harbours, the former at the distance of 4 and the other of 6 miles. In addition to what has been already said of the climate, it is only to be observed that its superiority over that of the high country is most remarkable in the spring months. While all the operations of husbandry are going forward in the low parts of Moray they meet with a total interruption in the high country, distant only a few miles, by the intenseness of the frost or the depth of the snow. The winters likewise in general are so temperate that several plants, commonly ranked in the hot-house division, stand throughout that season in the gardens of Innes House, losing little of their verdure. It may likewise be observed, as another evidence of the excellence of this climate, that in the famine which prevailed over Scotland for 7 years in the end of the last century, owing to the cold and wet seasons, the land in Moray was all that time so productive as to spare considerable quantities of grain. It is well ascertained that in those years of dearth people came from the county of Angus to buy oat meal at the rate of £1 10s. the boll, to be carried across the Grampian Mountains, at the distance of about 100 miles. Towards the north-west part of the parish the land is low and flat, and a few feet only above the level of the sea, of which, at a remote period, it has been the bottom, as there are evident marks of the sea having receded from the coast. The soil here may be accounted loam. In the other quarters of the parish the ground is greatly more elevated, and of an unequal waving surface; and the soil, though in general sandy and light, is of a kindly and fertile nature, well adapted for turnip, potatoe, barley, and all kinds of artificial grasses, and a considerable part would be extremely fit for wheat, could manure in sufficient quantities be produced.

State of Property.—Four-fifths of this parish are the property of the Earl of Fife. About 26 years ago his

Lordship, being proprietor of considerable estates in the adjacent parishes, purchased the estate of Innes. He lately acquired the lordship of Urquhart, partly by an excambion with the family of Gordon, and partly by the purchase of several small feus, which had originally thereto appertained. He thus became possessed of so large a track of contiguous property, comprehending a great variety of ground, that he became enabled to complete plantations of a very large extent, which add much to the ornament and convenience of the country. Some moors and hills of great extent are planted, and a number of little rising grounds are covered with singular good taste, making their appearance with relation to each other extremely beautiful. In all these plantations the Scots fir at present predominates, but many of these are yearly cut down and the voids filled up with deciduous trees. Previous to the year 1779, when about one half of these plantations were formed, 3,000 Scots firs were planted on each acre, but since that time 1,200 only. Lord Fife has also enclosed many fields by hedges and hedge-rows, which are carried in part along the highways, affording considerable warmth and utility.

In a valley bending north and south stands his seat of Innes House,* in a park of considerable extent, diversified by groves of full grown lofty trees, young shooting plantations, verdant fields, and a small winding river, expanded in some places into a lengthened lake, and at others contracted into a neat cascade, decorated by a waving gravel path and several Chinese bridges. The approach to the house bends in a winding course through the grove, and terminates in an open lawn, having a very extensive but irregularly-formed garden on one side, in which are long reaches of fruit-wall, covered with the richest variety of fruitage—pears, cherries, plums, nectarines, and peaches. There are also many lofty forest trees, among which numbers of common fruit trees luxuriantly mingle. In the house are conjoined the magnificence of the Gothic castle to the elegance of the modern seat. It rises to the height of four stories. It makes two sides of a square, but of unequal length, having a square tower in the angle, which is occupied by the staircase within; it rises higher than the building, and is completed by a small round

* Innes House is in the parish of Lhanbryd. (ED.)

turret, opening into its level roof, which is surrounded by a secure stone ballustrade; and instead of the dead-wall heavy masonry, of which the chimney-stacks of modern buildings are composed, each vent springs lightly from the blue roof in its own separate airy column. The ground floor is occupied by the necessary household accommodations. The first floor contains a suite of three magnificently superb rooms, in which are a number of portrait pictures of Kings of England, Princes, and Queens, and of other personages of distinguished memory, many of them large as the life, and in the various dresses of their respective generations. There are also a few historical and other paintings, and several ancient historic prints of the largest size, in very costly frames, with plates of the most transparent mirror glass. The storeys above are occupied by the bed-chambers; among them is one splendid dressing-room, finished with paper richly painted in the Chinese manner, on which a variety of trees of exotic growth shoot from the floor to the ceiling, their branches animated by numbers of tropical birds, in various attitude, size, and form, each, however, of the most delicate plumage, and of the most vivid colours.

The only other heritor is John Innes of Leuchars, who has about one-fifth of the real rent of the parish, which he acquired about the year 1781 from another gentleman of the same name, who had built a handsome house and given some attention to the draining of the land. Since the present gentleman became the proprietor he has been attentive to raise hedges and stripes of plantation about the fields round his house, of the best kinds of deciduous trees, such as oak, ash, witch elm, and a great proportion of larix, besides several clumps of Scots fir, similar to those executed by Lord Fife. The farms are in general rather small for encouraging substantial improvements in agriculture—there are a few that may contain from 60 to 100 acres, but the common run is from 20 to 30. The rent of the land varies according to the nature of the soil —there are some fields let for 20s. the acre, while others are below 10s., the average may be from 10s. to 15s.

The valued rent is £5,567 15s. 3d. Scots, of which appertains to the estate of Leuchars £437 3s. 3d.

Ecclesiastical State.—The Earl of Fife acquired the

patronage from the family of Gordon in the excambion that has been already mentioned. The stipend, by decreet Feb. 1793, is 8 chalders victual, £40 sterling, including £5 for Communion elements, and a glebe consisting of 5 Scots acres. The schoolmaster's salary is 12 bolls of oatmeal and 6 bolls of barley, the other emoluments are similar to those of Speymouth. The funds for the support of the poor are some bequeathments, yielding £2 11s. 4d. sterling of yearly interest, and the donations collected from the congregation of the Parish Church, amounting to £10 yearly, which are divided among the poor enrolled in the parish list, being 20 in number at an average. The members of the Established Church are 1,030; the dissenters are 20, consisting chiefly of anti-burghers.

Miscellaneous Information.—The people are in general very sober and industrious in their several occupations, which are as well directed as their situation and circumstances will permit. Within these 20 years a great change to the better may be remarked in their clothing, their cleanliness, and every other circumstance that tends to make life more agreeable. There is one lake in the parish—the Loch of Cottes. Pike is the only fish it contains; in winter it is frequented by a considerable number of swans; in the spring and autumn by flocks of wild geese, ducks, and other water-fowls. In the upper part of the parish the Lake of Lochnaboe borders upon its limits at the west; the extensive plantations already mentioned are carried round its banks, and with the water, which is uncommonly limpid, forms a most delightful scene. These improvements have, however, been attended with one disadvantage. In some severe winters, several years ago, a few stags and hinds from the forests of Glenfiddich and Glenavon took up their residence in the plantations round Lochnaboe and never returned to their native forests, but increase in numbers every year, by breeding and by fresh emigrants. They make a fine appearance, and afford much amusement to the sportsman; but they are hurtful both to the plantations and agriculture. Throughout the summer, in the night, they pasture on the corns; in the winter, on the turnip; and as the crops of wheat and rye advance in the spring, they are particularly destructive to these; but the stem of the potatoe seems to be their favourite food, as they pass through fields of corn to browse upon them. Where the corn fields lie so near to their haunts on every hand, it will probably in a short time be found necessary to drive them back to their original habitation, or, after the example of the Earl of Moray in the west, to keep hounds for the purpose of their utter extirpation. Although these plantations have attracted the deer, they have not been favourable to the increase of partridges, and hares, owing to the protection which they afford to beasts and birds of prey. Were small premiums to be provided for the destruction of such vermin, it would prove more effectual for increasing the quantity of game than all the restrictive laws that ever were or ever will be enacted.] (*Survey of the Province of Moray.*)

PRIORY OF URQUHART.

[King David I. in 1125 founded the Priory of Urquhart. It was a cell of the Monastery of Dunfermline, and occupied by Benedictine Monks, called Black Friars, from the colour of their habit. It was liberally endowed with lands, now called the Lordship of Urquhart, the village of Fothopir, or Fochabers, with a fishing that belonged to the Thane of Fothopir, Penid, near Auldearn, the lands of Dalcross, &c., with all the rights that belonged in Moray to the Monks of Dunfermline. The Chartulary is lost, and there is no account of its revenues. The ruins of the buildings are to be discovered with difficulty in a hollow north-east of the present Church of Urquhart.] (See my *Monasticon*, vol. i., p. 325.)

CHURCHYARD EPITAPHS IN URQUHART.

The churchyard is kept in a very uninviting condition. Monteith gives the following in his "Theater of Mortality." not apparent now:—

I. Here lyes John, David, Gilbert, and David Marschells, the last died in December, 1627.

This about the sides of the stone, and within, as follows:—

> Here lies father and son,
> Goodsire and grand,
> Who liv'd and died
> Upon a poor twelfth-part of land.

The explanation whereof is this: the lands of Urquhart

are cast into 12 parts, every feuer has one or more of these 12 parts, each paying 30 bolls victual.

Mr. Alexander Gadderer, minister at Girvan, is the lineal successor by his mother, and now proprietor of that portion above mentioned. Here follows his epitaph:—

II. In spem resurrectionis Hic requiescit vir reverendus et eruditus Mr. Alex. Gadderer Parochiæ de Girvan qui præfuit ad annum 1688 ecclesiæ in regno Scotiæ. . . .

Translation.—In hope of resurrection, Here rests a reverend and learned man, Mr. Alex. Gadderer, who had the charge of the Church and parish of Girvan, in the kingdom of Scotland, in the year 1688. . . .

III. Here. lyes. Ane. Honest. man. called. John. Leslie. sme. Portioner. of. Mavirstoun. Who. Died. The 6 of February 1662. . . . . G. M.
      Memento Mori.
     [Small cross bones.]

IV. Here. Lyes. Elspet. Adam. spouse. to. Andrew. Newlands. sum. tim. Dueller. in. Glenach. Who. departed. this. lif. the. 28 Jun. 1674.

Death thou puts an hend unto wealth Beauty wit and Strenth until we appear before the Lord at Length.
A. N.   Blessed are the dead, &c.
E.*A.

V. Here. Lyes. Janet. Chalmers. Spouse. to. Robert. Chalmers. of. Tippertait. who. Died. the. Z. of. December. 1688.
With their children Margaret George and Mariore Chalmers.

VI. Here. Lyes. John. Amy in mauerstoune who died the 11th day of November 1689 . . . . spouse. . . . . Chester who departed the 20 day of May 1691.

VII. This Stone is placed here in memory of David Thomson who . . . . the * . . . . the * day of . . . . and his spouse Marjory Grant.
D. T.   M. G.   H. T.   I. T.

VIII. Here lyes the body of Lachlan Innes son to Robert Innes Portioner of Urquhart who died June 1695 and John Innes grandson to Robert Innes who died in October 1739 and his spouse Helen Chalmers who died in May 1752 and of William Innes let marchan Elgin who died the 30 August 1779 aged 70.

IX. Here lyes the body of James Simpson who sometime lived in Byres and died the 7 day of November 1713 and Margaret Innes his spouse who died the 14 of .... 1725.

X. Here lyes the body of Roderick Urquhart sometime dueller in Walkmill who died the 4th day of March 1732 and Mariorie Grant his spouse who dyed the 7 of Oct. 1715.

XI. This is the burial place of James Shank who lived in nether meaft who died December 20th 173- and his spouse Isobel Shank.

XII. This is the burial of William Russell farmer in Urquhart who died January 20 1748 and Ch^n Urquhart his spouse who died October the 7th 1750. Seven of their children who died young and William their only surviving child who died *   and Janet Casie his spouse who died *
W. R.   C. U.

XIII. This is the burial place of John Rob who lived in nether meft and died 6 July 1752 and of his spouse Christian Paul * ... and their children.

XIV. This Stone is placed here in memory of the deceased James Sinclair who died in the uper Bins Octr. 25 1794 and Jean Ogilvie his affectionate widow. (*Rev. J. B. Craven's MSS.*)

THE PARISH OF LHANBRIDE

Is so called either from the British *Lhan*, a church, and bride or brigida, *i.e.*, St. Brigida's Church; or (it being written in some ancient manuscripts *Lambnabride*) because a lamb, an emblem of meekness, was taken up and decorated with many ornaments on St. Bride's Day, as a memorial of her. This parish lieth south of Urquhart, and is a mile in length and as much in breadth.

The Church standeth a mile south of Urquhart, two and a half miles south-east of Elgin.

* Dates have never been filled in.

In the south end of the parish is Pitnaseir, a part of the lands of the preceptory of Maison Dieu, and now the heritage of Ogilvie of Pitnaseir, holding of the town of Elgin. In the south end is Cotts, for some generations the heritage of a branch of the family of Innes, and in 1757 sold to Alexander Bremner, merchant in Portsoy; holding of the Earl Fife.

Below Cotts is Cockstoun, a barony that had long been the property of a branch of the family of Innes of Invermarkie. Cockstoun was created a baronet in 1687, whose grandson, Sir Alexander, married the heiress of Barclay of Towie. The whole barony of Cockstoun now belongeth to the Earl Fife.

[*The Manor of Lhanbride* belonged to Robert and Matilda Hod [Hood] in 1225, and was in that year the subject of a dispute between them and Andrew, Bishop of Moray, who claimed it as the property of the Church. On the Pope appointing commissioners to try the question, King Alexander II. interfered, and insisted on its adjudication in his courts, as the estate was admitted to be a barony held of the Crown. The controversy was subsequently settled by arbitration, in arranging the terms of which the King appears to have taken a personal interest, as is shown by his having affixed his seal to the deed drawn up on that occasion. The Bishop resigned all claims to the barony, with the exception of his right to the Church of the manor and its glebe, while Robert Hod and his wife gave on their part, as a free gift, for the maintenance of the Bishop's table, a davach of Pitnasser and a piece of land, the boundaries of which were Lochlyn [Lochnabo] and the stream issuing from it, and another rivulet named Granuske. In detailing these boundaries allusion is made to dwelling-houses [*mansos*], a mill, a brew-house, and a workshop [*fabrica*], most probably a smithy or armourer's forge—all, doubtless, comprised in the village of the manor. This barony became subsequently the property of Sir Malcolm de Moravia of Tulybardyn. He transferred it in 1280 to his son, William de Moravia, who was most likely the proprietor of it when Edward I. passed through this part of the country.] (*Dr. Taylor's " Edward I. of England in the North of Scotland,"* pp. 107, 108.)

[Coxton Tower.—Not one fragment of history has been preserved relating to this small but picturesque Tower, which is within half a mile of Lhanbryd Railway Station. It is built of stone, roof and all, fire-proof throughout, even to the corner turrets. Excepting its two outer doors, which are backed by massive gates of cross-barred iron, no wood whatever is used in the whole building. It resembles many Border towers, having the lower room or vault for sheltering, or rather securing, the owner's cattle against marauders. Above this, was the dwelling of the laird, comprising the scanty accommodation of three rooms and several small closets, the latter being enclosed in the walls. To the lower dwelling-room there was no access from without, save by a ladder. A poor stone-stair has of recent years been erected. What is still more singular, there is no appearance on the exterior of any means of access to the upper rooms, although there is a circular newelled stair within the substance of the wall, in the angle between the cornered turrets. The sides of the tower, which were formerly protected by the walled court, have rather a cheerful expression; but the opposite angles are sufficiently dismal, and were rather to be avoided by the stranger in former times, for not a window nor opening appears in the walls, except so many port-holes for arrows or musketry. When we consider that every floor is a heavy semi-circular stone vault, the absence of external buttresses naturally forces itself upon our observation. No defect, however, has resulted from this; for, by an admirable contrivance, they are rendered unnecessary—the floors are vaulted at opposite angles. Thus, if the sides of the lower room arch stand east and west, those of the arch immediately above are north and south, and so they keep alternating. By this simple arrangement the weight of one floor or vault acts as a

counterpoise to the arch beneath; and the efficiency of this construction is evinced by the state of the building. Not a crack is visible, and we predict that, until the stone disintegrates, the Castle will stand. Within the rooms is a singular provision for communication, perfectly independent of the stair-case. In the centre of each floor is a square stone, fitted into a grove. These stones, when lifted up, show an opening from the summit to the base of the tower, and by the aid of a rope and pulley the requirements of its inmates might be attended to, and all the inconveniences of carriage up the narrow stair-case avoided. Over the only entrance, on the south front, is a large carved stone with armorial bearings, and the initials R.I.A.I. at the top, and I.R.K.G. at the bottom, with the date 1644. This has been inserted at a period considerably later (probably a century) than that of its erection.

There is a mound or hill on either side of the Tower, the one is named *Doohill*, and the other *Gallowhill*. The burly lairds of Coxton were sufficiently expert in vindicating their feudal rights of *pot* or *pit and gallows;* for, when the hill was being planted a number of skulls and human bones was found as palpable evidence in their favour. Choice engravings are given of the interesting Tower of Coxton in Billings' *Baronial Antiquities of Scotland*, from which has been borrowed the greater portion of the above letter-press.] (ED.)

[*Innes House* is about 4 miles from Elgin, is one of the baronial seats of the Earl of Fife, and is in the parish of St. Andrews-Lhanbryd. There are characteristics about Innes House which keep it entirely distinct from the other contemporaneous fortified mansions of the north. It is not so picturesque as many of them are. No one would think of comparing it with Fyvie or Caudor. Yet, though its meagreness throws it behind these buildings in fulness of effect, it belongs to a more ambitious class of architecture. It contains the same character of detail with that which imparts to Heriot's Hospital, Edinburgh, its beauty and oriental-looking richness. An elaborate account or account-book, in the possession of the Spalding Club, shows that the Laird of Innes contracted to build the House on the 6th May, 1640, with "Wm. Ross, Mr. Measoun." The items are particularized:—" Twa hameris and twa craneis maid be the commissar Smith in Elgin." Six score bolls of lime are, along with iron for "crookis and windowis," ordered from Leith, 250 miles distant. The account begins on 4th Sep., 1640, and ends on 13th June, 1653, amounting to £15,266 Scots, or £1,221 3s. 4d. sterling, no contemptible sum for a Morayshire laird to pay for his house in the middle of the 17th century.

The owner of Innes House was the representative of Innes of that ilk, occurring in charters of the 12th century, which ramified into various north country families of the name of Innes, and made repeated alliances with other neighbouring houses. The mother of Duncan Forbes, Lord President of the Court of Session, was Mary Innes, a daughter of the owner of this mansion. The name is of frequent occurrence in the feuds and other northern historical events of the 16th and 17th centuries. See Billings' *Baronial Antiquities of Scotland.*] (ED.)

ST. ANDREWS-LHANBRYD.

[*Situation, Soil, Climate.*—When Popery was the established religion in the Province of Moray, it was an article of faith, that the spirits of departed saints, though resident in heaven, beheld the transactions upon earth, continued to be concerned in mortal affairs, and had interest with the Almighty to obtain special favours for their friends below. Much prayer was therefore made to dead saints, and many honours were bestowed, in order to win the regard of such among them as were believed to have most credit in heaven, or were by accidental circumstances more affectionately attached to any particular district of this lower world. On this account, churches, chapels, and altars, were erected in honour of particular individual saints, even before the division of the kingdom into parishes took place. The apostle Andrew, it was believed, had appeared in a vision, promising to King Hungus the victory over the enemy; and his relics had been also miraculously employed in converting the nation to the faith of the gospel: being therefore in those ages a peculiar favourite, the church, which gave his name to the parish, was erected to the honour of his memory.

A Welch lass, also, of the name of Bridget, had acquired such distinguished reputation as a saint, that Dr. Macpherson of Slate, Diss. 15. shews cause to believe, that the whole of the Western Isles of Scotland were put under her particular protection, and so much appropriated to her, that Hebrides or Ey-Brides, being literally translated, mean the Islands of Bridget: and her Gaelic name of Bride is still recognised in the denomination of no fewer than 6 of the parishes of the Church of Scotland, there being 4 Killbryds, Panbryd, and Lhanbryd, all signifying Bridget's Church. For *killie* being originally the Erse word for servant, came to denote the Church where the servant of the Divinity officiated; and its signification was by degrees extended to imply also the burying-place, which, on account of the consecrated ground, became inseparably connected with the Church.

In the other denomination, the word *pan* is a corruption of the Latin *fanum*, or *phanum*, a temple, derived from a Greek word signifying light, because oracular illumination was there vouchsafed. Thus the lands, which were bestowed upon the canons of the Elgin cathedral, are still named the *Pans;* and the adjoining gate, which led through the college to the cathedral, still bears the appellation of the *Pans Port.*

The last denomination *lhan*, in the original British or Welch language, is a grove, and from the sacred places of the Druids, it has been in that tongue appropriated also for church.

This parish measures about 3 miles from E. to W. along the high way from Spey to Elgin. Its territory extends from the sea to the mountain, although the inhabited ground from N. to S. measures only about 4 miles, exclusive of an improvement one mile distant on the south, disjoined by an intervening skirt of the parish of Elgin, to which it pertains. It was originally the moor where the cattle were collected, for drawing part of the tithes of both parishes, before they were converted into money, from which it retains the name Teindland; and on account of its distance from Elgin, the inhabitants have in general ranked themselves in this parish. The general appearance of the country is a plain, interrupted however by several of those low intervening ridges, by which, as has been said, this country is diversified, all of them being covered with corn, or grass, or plantations of wood. The air is healthful and dry, and the soil in general sandy, yet fertile where it is low and damp.

State of Property.—The parish at present is shared among 8 proprietors. The Earl of Fife has the whole of what had been the parish of Lhanbryd, and the ancient barony of Kilnalemnoc, in St. Andrews, valued together in the Cess Books of the county at £1629 12s. 8d. Scots. The Hon. George Duff has Barmuckity, in the middle of the parish, of £462 5s. Scots of valued rent. The Earl of Findlater holds Linkwood and Linksfield in the west, with part of the lands of Newmill, amounting to the valuation of £674 2s. 3d. Scots. William King of Newmill, Esq., has the lands in the vicinity of Elgin, amounting to £203 Scots of valuation. Although there are several handsome houses in the parish, particularly at Linkwood, yet Pitgaveny, the property of John Brander, Esq., is the only family seat. It is a superb modern house, an oblong square of 4 stories, having a double-ridged roof, rising so far within a battlement, as to form a pleasant walk around. The front door is in the western side, between two lofty Doric columns, rising from the landing place of a spacious flight of steps, and supporting a massive pediment above: it opens into the principal floor, which, besides the hall and stairs, contains an ample parlour, breakfasting room, library, and bed-chamber; the great drawing room, and state bed-chambers, are in the third story. The stone of the walls is superior in whiteness and durability to the Portland stone, and more easily formed. The building stands on a gentle eminence, commanding Innes house rising through its groves, and the windings of the river Lossie, on the east; on the west, a stretch of the lake of Spynie, bending like a great river between its green banks, which rise to such a height as to conceal its termination at either end. On the nearest, stand the ruins of the Bishop's palace: an object perhaps more desirable in its present desolation, than when occupied by its lordly owners; who, if they attained that rank by their own merit, became in general craftily rapacious; or, if raised to it by mere interest, turned out to be absurdly arrogant. A wide extent of the richest cornfield lies everywhere around, enlivened with neat farmsteads, herds, and plantations: the neighbouring city of Elgin smokes behind an intervening green hill: at a distance, the blue mountains of Sutherland skirt the northern horizon, and the Moray Firth rolls its azure waves along their dusky bottoms. The domains of this house extend over large portions of the parishes of Drainy and of Duffus, on the other side of the lake. The valuation here is £341 2s. 8d. Scots.

[The estate of Pitgaveny was part of the lands belonging to the Bishopric of Moray, and some time pertained to a branch of the Brodies of Letheny. It was purchased about a century ago by James Brander, Esq., whose son and successor, John Brander, Esq., died in 1826, leaving a son and daughter—James, a Lieut.-Col. in the army, and Mary, who married the late Sir Archibald Dunbar, of Northfield, Bart. Lieut.-Colonel Brander, who succeeded his father as heir to the estate, served with the 42nd Highlanders in the Peninsular War and at Waterloo, where he was severely wounded. On his death, in 1854, his sister, the Lady Dowager Dunbar, succeeded to the estate, and assumed the additional surname of Brander. Her son and heir is Captain James Brander Dunbar of the Scots Greys. Besides Pitgaveny, the estate comprehends the ancient barony of Kineddar, on which the villages of Lossiemouth and Branderburgh, with their thriving sea-port are situated.] (*Morayshire Described.*) (See also Young's *Parish of Spynie*, page 223.—ED.)

The lands of Dunkinty and St. Andrews, separated by the river Lossie, appertain to John Innes, Esq., of Leuchars, and are valued at £802 0s. 6d. Scots; and there is the small estate of Scotstownhill, about 50 acres, valued at £88 14s. 6d. Scots, accounted a 40 shilling land of old extent, and the freehold of a branch of the family of Altyre.

There is, besides, a small property in the Barflat hills, a valuation of £24 5s. 1d. Scots, which in the last generation was bestowed by Gordon of Cairnfield, for the support of the Episcopalian Chapel in Elgin; making the valued rent of the whole parish, £4,222 1s. 8d. Scots. The farms in the parish amount to the number of 80; many of them containing from 100 to 200 acres; about 18 of them are occupied by people in the character of gentlemen, and about 12, being in the improvement of the Teindland ought to be accounted as belonging to the parish of Elgin.

The rent by the acre, on most of them, is varied every year by the variation of the price of grain, in which a portion of the rent is still generally paid. The mean rent may be stated at 17s. the acre, though a great proportion of most farms can be only valued at 5s. the acre, while some part of almost each, if separately let, would exceed a guinea by the acre of yearly rent.

Ecclesiastical State.—It has not been with precision ascertained, at what time the division of the kingdom into parishes took place. It is presumed this could not be carried at once into complete effect; alterations in the extent of parishes have from time to time been made, as the interest or convenience of parties concerned in the varying circumrotation of human affairs might suggest; and convenience in this respect in many cases, is still far from being yet attained.

In this parish, the Chapel of Kilnalemnock was probably an apartment consecrated within the Castle at Forrester seat, and upon its demolition would naturally fall into St. Andrews: and the Chapel of Inchbroom must have been disposed of in the same manner, upon the suppression of the priory of Urquhart, upon which it is supposed to have depended. It does not appear that there ever was a burial-place but at the last of these chapels.

In 1642 the parish of Oguestown, at present a part of he parish of Drainy, was united to St. Andrews. The bishop drew the great tithes of both; leaving, with the whole pastoral duties, the small tithes only to the vicar, which, valued at £6 11s. 1½d., are continued a part of the stipend of St. Andrews.

In 1780, the parish was formed into its present shape, by the annexation of St. Andrews to Lhanbryd. The stipend is 10 chalders, 4 bolls, and £26 13s. 9d., including the allowance for Communion elements. The former burying-grounds are continued; but the Parochial Church is erected in a situation more commodious for the people in general, than the old churches were for their present congregations. The right of patronage is now shared between the Crown and the Earl of Moray. The members of the Established Church are about 700; and the Dissenters, being Episcopalians, Seceders, and Methodists, are about 40.

In 1794, the schools which were at St. Andrews and Lhanbryd were, by the proprietors of the parish and the presbytery, conjoined into one parochial school, and the building erected contiguous to the Church. The salary is 14 bolls of bear, and £4 3s. sterling; the rest of the emoluments being similar to the other parochial schools in the country. The fund for the poor arises partly from 4 small bequeathments made in other times, and from the halfpence given by the people who attend the Parish Church, amounting in whole to about £16 sterling in the year; which, after the legal deduction to the session-clerk, and a small fee to the church-officer, is, without expense to the heritors, divided half-yearly among a roll of about 30 people, in proportion to the urgency of their respective needs.

Miscellaneous Information.—There is a mineral spring in the Tiendland, of a strong chalybeate kind. It has not yet acquired much celebrity, though it has given relief to all who have made proper trial of its effects. The river Lossie, entering the parish towards the north-west corner, divides it there from the town of Elgin, and continuing its course easterly through the parish for nearly two miles, turns round towards the north, until it reaches the sea at the village and harbour of Lossiemouth, having a corner of the parish of Urquhart crossing its channel, interjected between the estate of Pitgaveny and the Earl of Fife's property of Inchbroom.

There are three Lakes on the confines of the parish. That of Spynie is the largest, which though equally, rather more extensively connected with the parishes of Drainy and Duffus on its northern side, and that of Spynie itself lying along the greater part of its southern bank, yet the costly Drain, so advantageously made by Pitgaveny, naturally leads to its confederation here; and to make an entire connected account of it at once, may avoid repetition, and be more distinct, than to narrate the detached circumstances as they would occur in these parishes apart.

In the account of the parish of Urquhart, it is observed, that there are evident marks of the sea having receded from the coast; and there are satisfactory indications in the appearance of the ground, and particularly by the beds of oyster shells, which, though not now found on the coast, are frequently discovered on the banks of the river several feet below the surface of the earth, that at some other period, this lake must have been an arm or strait of the ocean, open in breadth at the east, nearly from the hill of Garmach to the head-land behind Lossiemouth, and stretching westward over the plain, till it again joined the Frith at the village of Burghhead. The general elevation of this tract does not yet exceed 4 feet above the level of the sea, save in one narrow space, across from the corner of the hill of Roseisle, where the eddy-wind accumulating the drifting sand, it has been raised to the height of 13 feet.

The irruption of the Goodwin Sands happened in the 10th century, in the reign of Malcolm III., and from Buchanan's History it might be inferred, that its effects were not limited to that quarter alone, but must have extended over all the eastern coast of Britain. "Among the prodigies of that period," says he, "may be reckoned an inundation of the German Ocean, so extraordinary, as not only to have overspread and overwhelmed the country with sand, but to have overturned also villages, towns, and castles." Another storm, extremely violent also, happened in the 13th century, upon the eastern coast of Scotland. In the year 1266, a great wind arose from the north, on the eve of the Feast of the 11,000 virgins; and the sea broke in, and many houses and villages were overwhelmed. "There never was such a deluge," says Fordun, lib. x. c. 22, "since the times of Noah, as appears from its traces at this day" (*sicut adhuc vestigia manifestant*).

To one or both of these irruptions may be ascribed, with some degree of probability, the separation of the Lake of Spynie from the sea, which is occasioned by a beach of pebbles, gravel, and sand, extending southward from Lossiemouth, for about 3 miles along the shore. In some places it is more than a mile in breadth, and covers an extent of about 560 acres: its general height is about 20 feet above the high water-mark; but it is cut out almost to the level of the sea in many channels, from 50 to 100 yards wide, waving parallel to the shore. Towards its southern end, it has acquired a thin surface of soil, producing dwarfish heath and juniper, and has been lately planted with Scots firs; but, in many places of great extent, it has yet acquired no sward, and the pebbles, gravel, and sand, are still as bare as when just left by the sea. It evidently appears to have been superinduced by the extreme violence of some dire commotion, which at once raising this immense mass of rounded stone and sandy gravel from the bottom of the ocean, poured it with an overflowing rapidity in the opening of the bay, penetrated farther upon either side, where the shallow water could give least resistance; but where its depth towards the middle must have given the greatest opposition, its progress seems to have been first checked, and a semi-circular mound of the largest pebbles has been raised, with a striking regularity, upon a bottom of sea-sand, now clothed with grass. The connection with the ocean being hereby cut off, the mechanical violence of the advancing surge, and the subsiding agitation of the retreating waves, would naturally form the alternate channels and ridges, which have been described upon this new shore, not then so cohesive as it is now, when consolidated by the long-continued influence of the power of gravity, hardly at the first exerted on the gravel, almost floating on the still intermingled water. The bottom of the lake, if at that time so deep as the sea, must have been gradually since then filled up, both by the winds and the waters sweeping down the sand and the mud, chiefly from the west, where the bottom of the lake has of course been first converted into dry productive land.

The communication with the sea at the west appears to have been gradually cut off. Until this was completely effectuated, it is evident that a passage would be again opened at the east, upon the subsiding of the storm. This appears to have been effected in the course of the present canal, and of the river Lossie, which at that time entered the lake upon the east side of the Castle of Spynie. These circumstances are ascertained by the Chartulary of Moray, fol. 93. in a protest taken in the year 1383 by the Lord Bishop Alexander Bar, against the noble Lord John Dunbar, Earl of Moray, and the burgesses of Elgin, respecting the right of the fishing and of the harbour.

"*Item*," says his Lordship, in the second article of this protest, " Because the port of Lossy, otherwise of Spynie, and the fishing grounds in dispute, are within the marches and limits, and within the extent of the said lands of Spynie and Kinnedar, and the island [probably Inchbroom], the extent of which along the banks is distinctly and universally known.

"*Item*,—Because the Bishops of Moray, our predecessors, with the knowledge and sufferance of the Earls, and of the burgesses of Elgin, had, and were in the use of having, the inhabitants of the village of Spynie, in the name and right of the Bishops of Moray, fishers of sea fish, sailing with their wives and families from Spynie to the sea, and returning in their boats with the fishes to the said harbour.

"*Item*,—Because our immediate predecessor, John Pilmore, of worthy memory, intending to improve and deepen the course of the said harbour, laboured therein, neither by force, nor secretly, nor dependently, but in his own right, as master of the said harbour, and turned the course of the water out of its ancient channel, by sinking little boats there; the Earl of Moray and the burgesses of Elgin, who were at that time, knowing and permitting it.

"*Item*,—Because we aver, and undertake to prove, that the said Bishops of Moray, each in his own time, had and were in the use of having, and we in our time have had, and now at present have fishers, with cobels and boats, for catching salmon, grilses, and finnacs, and other kinds of fish, with nets and hooks, singly and united, in the grounds in dispute, in name and right of the Table Episcopal of the Bishops of Moray, without impediment or opposition, the present dispute excepted, from the Earl of Moray, or from the burgesses of Elgin.

"*Item*,—Because our predecessors and ourselves, and others in their name and in ours, have exercised, and do at present exercise, those acts of navigation, in conducting boats to the sea, and bringing them back, in throwing nets and hooks, and catching fish alone and in companies."

It is not known whether Lossie was turned, clear of the lake, into its present course, by accident or design; but it is certain, that some time posterior to the age of Bishop Bar, the lake had been reduced to a less extent than its present bed; for when the ancient drain was improved into the present canal, the course of ridges wholly divested of sward, the formation of artificial roads, inclosures, and every token of ancient and unknown cultivation, most evidently and unexpectedly appeared. Among these, in a small island towards the western end of the lake, a quantity of peat-ashes was found, upon breaking up the ground, buried under the turf-wall of a cottage, that had been inhabited; and among the ashes was found a small number of coins, a little treasure that had been concealed under the hearth, upon some alarm of danger. A causeway also at that time emerged, formed of freestone from the quarry, quite across the lake, with openings for the passage of the water, each about 3 feet wide, covered with broad flag-stone. This revived the recollection of a circumstance then almost forgotten, that this causeway was called "the Bishop's Steps," and had been formed by his order, to allow his vicar to get from St. Andrews, after the service of the forenoon, to officiate at Oguestown in the evening of each Sunday. Near to the castle also, where the water was deepest, an artificial island was discovered, of an oval form, about 60 by 16 paces, appearing to be composed of stone from the quarry, bound together by crooked branches of oak, and as if the earth with which it was completed had been washed away during its submersion.

The limits of the lake, however, at this period of ancient cultivation, cannot now be accurately ascertained. Neglected most probably during the disastrous struggle between Episcopacy and Presbytery, it had spread out so as to extend to the length of 4 miles, and in no part of less breadth than one, covering the space of 2000 acres. Of these, Pitgaveny, by taking off 3 feet 4 inches of the depth of the lake, has, at his own expense, recovered 1162; of which there appertains to his own estate in the three parishes that have been already mentioned 800 acres; to the estate of Gordonstown, in the parish of Drainy, 104 acres; to the estate of Duffus, in the parish of Duffus, 132 acres; to the estate of the Earl of Fife, in the parish of Spynie, including "the Bishop's Precinct," belonging to the Crown, 72 acres; to the estate of Findrossie, in the parish of Spynie, 51 acres; and to the estate of Westfield in the same parish, 3 acres: 1162 acres. But the whole of this extent has not been so completely drained as to admit of proper cultivation. Various speculations concerning this object have been suggested; but as the level every way has been accurately ascertained, the most proper course for the drain may be readily and certainly determined.

The deepest part of the lake to the eastward of the castle, probably where the harbour had been deepened by Bishop Pilmore, being 10 feet, is found to be one lower than the channel of the river at low water in the harbour of Lossiemouth; but an immediate communication with the low water-mark of the sea, upon the west of the

Coulard hill, would at Spring tides give a fall of nearly 15 feet, and at ordinary tides of nearly 10, which would be sufficient to drain the lake: but as by much the greater part of its bottom is now only from 4 to 5 feet deep, every advantageous purpose of improvement would be obtained, by bringing the present canal down within the harbour. But as the river Lossie, opposite to the bridge on the canal, in the road from Elgin to Lossiemouth, is 5 inches higher than the canal, when both are in their ordinary state, and is often raised by floods to the height of 7 or 8 feet above the surface of the lake, and being distant from the canal only from 7 to 130 yards, it will be requisite in this course to raise a sufficient embankment along that side of the canal. This might be frugally accomplished, by disposing the earth that must be yet thrown out in completing the formation of the canal, in the form of a mound, as the banks are not yet shelving enough to stand in the gravelly soil through which its course is conducted. Were this effectuated, 600 or 700 acres of more land would be gained, and the whole laid more perfectly dry. The interest of the respective landlords in this acquisition may be readily inferred from what they have already obtained. It would be also practicable to have carriage by water, not only (as in the time of the Bishops) up to the castle of Spynie, but more than half a mile nearer to Elgin, along the course of the Sey Burn.

The Lake of Cottes is on the other side of Lossie, but in the neighbourhood and in the same level with that of Spynie, but considerably nearer to the sea, and, being quite unconnected with the river, might be drained at an expense proportionally inconsiderable; and besides its own extent, which is about 120 acres, a great part of the adjoining swampy plain would be thereby greatly improved, and the country about Innes and Leuchars rendered more healthful. This lake is supported by two brooks, each of such consideration as to work the machinery of a corn mill. This quantity of water united would be sufficient to keep the canal from filling up, and might probably create, at the out-fall, a salmon-fishery of some consideration.

The third Lake to be mentioned is Lochnaboe, in the south-east corner of the parish, described in the account of Urquhart. It is about 3 miles in circumference, containing a small island, prettily wooded. It is also surrounded by the forest which the deer now inhabit, and through which a road has been lately formed, offering an enchanting ride around the shaded margin of the placid lake. It might be drained at a small expense; but appearing to have been a moss, long since entirely dug up, the naked gravel of its bottom would hardly admit of cultivation.] (*Survey of the Province of Moray.*)

EPITAPHS IN THE CHURCHYARD OF LHANBRYDE.

The Church was dedicated, as the name implies, to 'S. Bride, or S. Bridget, Virgin. No vestige of the old Church remains.

In Bishop Bricius' great charter of the foundation of the canonries at Spynie (1208-15), mention is made of the assignation of the chantors of Lamnabride with a davoch of land. In 1225, when Bishop Andrew granted the Manor of Lamanbride, with its pertinents, and the davoch of Petnassare to Robert Hood and Matilda, his spouse, the manse and kirk davoch were reserved. The next mention of Lhanbryde is in 1280, when Malcolm of Moravia, knight, granted a charter of his whole lands of Lamabride to his son William. In 1529 (Douglas Peer), James Stewart, Earl of Moray, had charters of Cookstoun, Longbride, &c., from his father, James IV.

In 1574 the Churches of Llangbride and Urquhart were served by one minister, and each locality had its own reader.

[The old Churchyard of St. Andrews presents quite a contrast to the most of the churchyards in Moray, as it is situated in a secluded spot, a hollow by the side of the river. The day I visited I had some little difficulty in threading my way through the bushes up the narrow path and over the frail rustic bridge, which forms the only access from the Lhanbryd side. In the churchyard is a very rude Font, but in such a polluted condition that one is ashamed to write of it. So wrote, in 1869, the Rev. James Brown Craven, now Inct. of S. Olaf's, Kirkwall. Andrew Jervise says that "the old Font is broken in three pieces."]

The village of Lhanbryde is one of the loveliest hamlets in the north.

The Inneses of Coxton buried within the choir of the old kirk, and a recess tomb, which contains the recumbent and well-proportioned effigy of a knight in armour is still preserved at Lhanbryde. On the left is a freestone slab (adorned with the Innes arms, also a skull and cross bones), upon which is this inscription:—

I. Hic. Reqviescit. in. Dno. Alex. Innes. Cokstovns. ex. illvstri. Familia. Innermarkie. orivndvs. qvi. Fatis. Concessit. 5. Oct. 1612. sve. vero. ætatis. 80.

Translation.—Here rests in the Lord, Alex. Innes of Cokston, descended from the illustrious Innermarkie family, who died 5 Oct., 1612, in the 80th year of his age.

This old man was the father of John Innes of Haltoun, whose son James, against the "advyis" of his father and grandfather, "undeutifully coupled him selff in marriage with Mariory Innes, dochter to Alexr. Innes of Cotts," an act which so much offended his "guidsir and father" that they mutually bound themselves to "seclud the said James during all the dayes of the said Mariory's lyftyme, and the airs quhatsumever gotten, or to be gotten betwix them, for ever fra all benefit of inheritance that may appertein to them ather be birth richt, tailzie, succession, or ony other provysion quhatsumever." John Innes of Coxton appears to have died between August, 1634, and July, 1635. He was probably succeeded by Alexander, who married a daughter of Gight.

II. A slab (with the Innes and Gordon arms) is thus inscribed:—

Hic. Reqviescit. Maria. Gordon. Filia. Clarissimi. Eqvitis. De. Gight. qve. Fatis. concesit. 20. Avgvsti. Ano. . . . 1647. . . . . In. Piam. . . . . Memoriam. Hoc. Monvmentvm. constrvendvm. Alexandr. Innes. De. Coxton. Maritvs. Cvravit.

Translation.—Here rests Mary Gordon, daughter of the most illustrious Knight of Gight, who died 20 Aug., 1647, to whose pious memory her husband, Alex. Innes of Coxton, caused this monument to be erected.

It was in the time of the above-named Alexander of Coxton (c. 1635) that his brother, Innes of Leuchars, and other members of "the clan," were ordered to restore the property of the "umquhil, Mr. John Innes of Coxtoun," to his executors, also the charter kists of Coxton and

Balvenie, as well as to pay 1,000 merks for the "wrong and insolence committed in the taking of the place of Coxtoun."

There were Inneses of that ilk (a property in the adjoining parish of Urquhart) from the time of William the Lion, and from Walter of Innes, who died in the time of Alexander II., have descended the various branches of Invermarkie, Balvenie, Leuchars, &c. It was through the marriage of Sir James Innes of Innes, in 1666, with Margaret, third daughter of Harry, Lord Ker, that their great-grandson, Sir James Innes-Northcliffe, Bart., became, by decision of the House of Lords in 1812, fifth Duke of Roxburghe.

III. A flat stone, with carvings of the blacksmith's crown and hammer, bears :—

Heir lyes the . . . . honest man called David Russel, in Longbry, who died in yeir 1665.

IV. The following inscription contains the somewhat odd, but not unique, notice of a man erecting a monument to his own memory :—

This is the burial place of Patrick Paul, who lived in Darklin, and died 16 . . Jan, 17th, and his spouse, Grizel Maver, and their children, James Paul, who placed this stone in memory of his father and of himself, who died Nouer ii, 1756, and Elizabeth Miln, his spouse, who dyed the 29 of Septr., aged 66, the year 1771.

V. Here lys the body of Elizabeth Walton, first beloved spouse to William Tulloch, merchant in Elgin, who dyed Nov. 23, 1763, justlly lamented by all hir acquaintances.

In God I liv'd, in him I died,
I live with him, tho' dead I ly.

VI. In the area of the old kirk :—

This stone is placed here by Mrs. Ann Macfarlane to the memory of, and over the remains of her husband, the Rev. Thomas Macfarlane, late minister of Lhanbryde, who died November 1781; and of their son, the Rev. Thomas Macfarlane, late minister of Edinkillie, who died on the 7th August, 1827.

VII. Within an enclosure :—

Sacred to the memory of Elizabeth Tod, relict of the late Rev. James M'Lean, minister of Urquhart, who died in Elgin on the 20th day of Jan., 1851, aged 75 years.

This was the second wife of Mr. M'Lean ; his first wife, whose name was also Elizabeth Tod, died at Keith.

VIII. Near the south-west corner of burial ground:—
Sacred to the memory of John Sadler, who died on the 24th of Dec., 1858, in his 65th year. He was for many years the faithful servant of James, fifth Earl of Fife, by whom this stone was placed. St. John xi. 25, 26 verses.

IX. . . . . . Chalmer of Pedensir, some . . . . . Chalmer . . . . December 1713. And his spows, Mariore Watson, who died the 1 day of December, 1762, aged 81. And their children. Memento Mori.

X. . . . . of James Petrie, who lived in . . . . who . . . . of July, 1789 years, and his . . . . spouse, Agnes . . . . who departed the 15 of Aprile, 17 . 2 . . . . years.

XI. Here lyes the Body of Thomas Dick, Tacksman in Lonbrid. He died April the 15, 1726 ; and Janet Robertson, his spouse. She died April the 18th, 1730.

XII. Here Lyes the Body of Alexr. Phimister, son to William Phimister, in Trows. He Died May ye 14th, 1738, Aged 16 years. And George, William, John, and John Phimisters, his Brethren. And William Phimister, farmer in Trows, who Died November 11th, 1745, aged 63 years. And His Spouse, Margaret Shaiach, who died—(never inserted).

XIII. Here Lyes the body of Alexander Brown, sometime farmer in Darkland, who Died December 5, 1786, Aged 78. And his spouse, Jannet Achyndachie, who Died Nov. 25, 1754, aged 54. Erected by his sons.

XIV. Here Lyes the body of James Redoch, sometime farmer in Blackhills, who died March 2, 1775, aged 73 years. And his spouse, Margaret Paul, who died in the year . . . . . aged 61 years.

XV. In memory of James Shaw, late farmer in Hornbrae, who died . . . . 1779.

XVI. This stone is laid in memory of William Sheach, sometime farmer in the T . . . and who died February 1781, aged 42 years.

XVII. In affectionate memorial of William Campbell of the Excise this monument is erected by Margaret Peterkin, widow. He died Dec. . . . 1784, aged 63. Their daughter, Henrietta, died Feb. 20, 1779, and is here interred.

XVIII. Two enclosures, one at the east end of the kirk, the other near the south-west corner of the churchyard, built up on all sides, belonged to Inneses. The first, called the Leuchars Aisle, contains two slabs. One bears the Innes arms and this inscription:—

Heir. Lyes. Ane. Honorable. Man. Alexander. Innes. Mathi. Milne. Who. Departit. November. The. First. 1636.

This is probably the tombstone of Alexander Innes who witnesses a grant to his brother-german, John Innes of Leuchars, of the lands of Corskie, Mathie Mill, and three pairts of Germocht, in 1587. (See *Ane Account of the Familie of Innes*—Spalding Club.) It is from the Leuchars branch that the late Professor Cosmo Innes is descended, by whom the above Family history was edited, whose *forbearis* are buried in the romantic churchyard of Cowie, near Stonehaven, and in the Innes Aisle, Durris, Kincardineshire.

XIX. The second stone in the Leuchars Aisle also presents the family arms, with A. I. : I. K. in monogram, and the following:—

ALEX. INNES, IEAN KINNAIRD—1688.

These were Alexander Innes, son of George Innes of Calcots, and his wife, Jean Kinnaird, a daughter of Cowbin. They were married about 1655, when Innes received from his wife's mother a "present portion of 4,000 merks, with that part of the stell fishing callit the Eath stell."

XX. Formerly within the church, but now upon a marble slab, set in freestone, within the area of the old kirk:—

In this church lie interred Mr. John Paterson, once minr. of Dipple, and 47 years minr. of this parish, who died April 20, 1778, in the 81st year of his age and 51st of his ministry. And Helen Grant, his spouse, died Jan. 5, 1769, aged 76 years. Love to God and charity to men were their prevailing dispositions. He was fervent in the work of the Gospel, and she was a pious but humble Christian. This mont. is erected to their memory by their son, Mr. Robert Paterson, minr. of New Spynie.

XXI. Here. lyes. Iespar. Winchester. who. died. in. Spynie. 27. of. October. 1688. also. Iames. Sim. who. died. at. Pitgavnie.

May. 1658. William. Winchester. his. son. Worship. Him. that. made. the. heaven. the. earth. and. the. sea. and. the. fountain. of. water. Margaret. Sim. his. spouse. I.W : M.S.

XXII. Heir lyes Agnes Geddes, spous to Iohn Grant, in Kirkhill, who departed the 20 day of May, 1 . 81. I.G : A.G. (A Morthead is in the centre of the slab.)

XXIII. A table-shaped stone :—
Here lies interred the body of Andrew Gill, late schoolmaster at St. Andrews, who departed this life Sep. 5, 1791, aged 66 years. He was an affectionate husband, a tender parent, supported the noble character of an honest man, lived much respected, and died much lamented by his family and friends.

XXIV. Here. lyis. Ane. Honest. Man. called. George. Geddes. swmetime. Indweller. in. the. Wakmylne. who. departed. the. 12. of. Apryle. 1632. and. His. Spous. Margori. Simson. G. S.—MEMENTO MORI (round a Morthead).

XXV. Here. lyes. the. spous. .... the. .... who. dyed. in. Speynie. the. 17. of. October. ..... Also. James. Sim. who. died. in. Pitgavin. .... May. 1658.

A number of gravestones was used to floor the kitchen of the schoolmaster's house. Some of the linear divisions of the above epitaphs are comical. In many, the inscriptions are round the edge of the slabs, which, when filled, are continued in the centre. (See *Jervise's Epitaphs*.)

Next to Langbride is

THE PARISH AND ROYAL BURGH OF ELGIN.

The meaning of the word *Elgin* is uncertain. In British, *Hely*, i.e., to hunt, and *Fin.*, i.e., *Fair*, q. a pleasant forest or hunting place. Or, in Saxon, *Hely*, i.e., holy, and *Dun*, a hill. So *Helgun* (throwing out *d* to soften the sound) is a holy hill. In the repository of the town there is an old iron seal, with the inscription *Helgun*. And at the end of the town there is a green mount called *Our Lady's Hill*. Whether these hints may lead to the true etymology I determine not. Passing such curiosities,

The Town standeth on the south bank of the River Lossie, in the northern extremity of the parish, on a plain, and the ground sloppeth a little to the north. This situation is dry, pleasant, and well aired. The river has taken a winding turn northward from the centre of the town, whereas it anciently run by the foot of the gardens, and was the boundary of most part of the closses on that side. The town is one long street from south-west to north-east, crossed about the middle by the School Wynd or lane to the south, and by Lossie Wynd to the north.

The Cross standeth near to the middle, and near the east end standeth the Little Cross, from which the High Street divideth into two branches, whereof one runneth due east and the other leadeth north by east into the College.

The High Street is, for the most part, broad, beautiful, and well laid or causewayed.

On the middle of the street, near the Cross, standeth the High Church—a large and beautiful edifice, surpassed by few in the kingdom. It standeth on two rows of arched pillars, and is 60 feet broad, and above 80 long within the walls. No Church can be better furnished with seats and lofts of wainscot, and a pulpit of curious workmanship. It is lighted, besides several windows in the side walls, by a Venetian window of three arches in the western gavel, whereof the middle arch is about 15 feet high. It has four hearses of brass of curious work, each having 12 sockets, hung in the middle of the Church.

To the east end is joined the Little Church, where worship is performed on week days, and betwixt these two churches is the steeple, with bells and a clock.

The High Church, dedicated to St. Giles, stood on two rows of massy pillars, and was all vaulted and covered with thick and heavy hewed stone instead of slate. On the 22nd of June, being the Sabbath day, anno 1679 (the very day on which the Battle of Bothwell Bridge was fought), when the people had returned from worship in the forenoon, the whole fabric fell down, except the four pillars and vault that support the steeple. The re-building was finished in 1684 at the expense of the heritors of the parish, merchants, and tradesmen of the town, and some private contributors.*

* I have before me an account, charge and discharge, by James Winchester, some time treasurer of the town, of what money he received, and how it was applied. The charge amounts to £1,485 9s. 2d. Scots, and the discharge to £4,003 15s. 0d. Scots. The Laird of Grant, in payment of his stent, and by a voluntary contribution, furnished the whole timber necessary. The Laird of Muirton, besides his stent, contributed £266 13s. 4d. Scots. The Bishop contributed £133 6s. 8d. Scots, and Mr. Alexander Tod, minister at Elgin, £66 13s. 4d. Scots. The Kirk-Session paid out of the penalties £151 6s. 8d. Scots. Alexander Douglas of Spynie gave sixty bolls of victual, which, at £3 6s. 8d. per boll, amounted to £200 Scots. The building of the pulpit (besides the price

Westward of the Church standeth the Tolbooth, ornamented with a high steeple vaulted to the top, and with bells and a clock. The town is also accommodated with a large and well finished council chamber, a court house, and several strong prison rooms.

The houses in the town are all built of freestone, and many of them stand on pillars to the street. No town can be better accommodated with gardens, and there are few closses but have draw-wells. This town stood formerly farther to west than now it doth. For this see my *Military History*, and for the Cathedral, College, and religious houses, see my *Ecclesiastical History*.

The town standeth two miles north from the Church of Birnie, 1½ miles south-east of New Spynie, and 1½ miles west from St. Andrews. The parish to landward extendeth 8 miles from east to west, and 3 miles from north to south, and is situated on both sides of the river Lossie, which, rising in the hills betwixt Knockando and Edinkillie, runneth north 3 miles to the Church of Dallas, thence turneth east about 3 miles, and then running north-west, and watering the parishes of Birnie and Elgin, it passeth north, and after a course of about 15 miles falleth into the firth.

of the wainscot) cost £244, and the glazing of the windows and wire cost £400 Scots. I find nothing paid out of the common good of the town.

A half mile west from Elgin there is a bridge of one large arch, built anno 1636; on the east side of the river, a mile from the town to the south, are the lands of Maine, the property of David Brodie, M.D.

South-east from Maine are the lands of Langmorn, Whitewreath, and Thornhill, formerly a part of the estate of Cockstown, and now the property of the Earl Fife. Further east is Blackhills the heritage of Robert Innes of Blackhills.

On the west side of the river is the barony of Mosstowie, in the north-west end of the parish. The town of Elgin are superiors of it by the gift of King Alexander II., and now the Earl Fife has possession of it, by an adjudication against William Sutherland of Roscommon [third] son of [James, second] Lord Duffus, who held it in feu of the said town.

South-east of Mosstowie is the barony of Milntown, which, for about an hundred years, was the heritage of a branch of the family of Brodie, and by Joseph Brodie of Milntown sold to Lord Braco, about 42 years ago. It was Church land.

[Lord Braco, afterwards William, Earl of Fife, left this property, with other lands, to his 3rd son, Hon. George Duff, who long possessed them. He died in 1818, and was succeeded by his son, Major George Duff, at whose death they were disposed to Hon. George Skene Duff, who sold the subjects to his nephew, Alexander William George, Viscount M'Duff, only son of the present Earl of Fife. The estate in 1873 consisted of 14 farms and crofts, and was let at a yearly rent of £1,251 8s. sterling. The late Major George Duff enhanced the property by extensive plantations.] (R. Y.)

South and east of Milntown is the barony of Pittenrich and Monbein. Pittenrich was a part of the Earldom of Moray, and long the property of Douglas of Pittenrich, from whom the Earl of Moray purchased it in the end of the last century.

Monbein Upper and Nether, Bogside, the Haugh, &c., are the lands of the Preceptory of Maison Dieu, and hold of the town of Elgin. These baronies are now the property of Colonel Francis Stewart, uncle to the present Earl of Moray, except Upper Monbein, that pertaineth to Bailie John Laing of Elgin.

Westward lieth the Glen of Pluscarden, a valley extending three miles in length, and surrounded with hills, except to the east. It is (with the old mills near the town of Elgin) the property of the Earl Fife, except a few farms that Watson of Westerton holdeth of him in feu.

Elgin giveth title to Bruce, Lord Kinloss, and Earl of Elgin.

[*The lands of Maine* are a part of the ancient Earldom of Moray, and in 1471 were the property of Hays of Maine, of the Hays of Park and Lochloy, in which name they remained till some time after the 1621. I find Maine pertaining to the Laird of Innes in 1630, to Gordon of Maine in 1635, to Mr. Joseph Brodie, minister of Forres, in 1654, to Alexander Brodie (son of Mr. Joseph, and grandfather to Brodie of Muir House) in 1666. Then they came to Brodie of Letham, who conveyed them to his nephew, Thomas Brodie of Pitgaveny. His son, David, sold them to Dr. Brodie, writer, of Pitgaveny who died in 1703 without issue. Maine then fell to Dr. David Brodie, Inverness, son of Francis Brodie of Milton, born 1687, and died at Elgin, 1782. He married Margaret, daughter of Alexander Brodie, fourth of Lethen, by whom he had a son, Dr. Alexander Brodie, born about 1724, and died 1806, unmarried; and a daughter, Anne, married to the Rev. James Hay of Dallas, father of Colonel Alex. Hay of Westerton. Dr. Alex. Brodie sold the estate of Mayne towards the end of the last century to the Earl of Findlater, in whose family it continues. The estate of Mayne must have then been an exceedingly bare and barren spot, surrounded with sandy knolls. Plantations, after the lapse of half a century, have now reached maturity, not only embellishing the place, but handsomely remunerating the proprietor.

Whitewreath seems to have been acquired about the middle of the 17th century by the Rev. John Brodie of Auldearn, and Dean of Moray, third son of David Brodie of Brodie, who was served heir to his father in 1656. He was succeeded by his son William, advocate, Edinburgh, in 1712, and died unmarried in 1739. He is said to have been succeeded by his cousin, Sir William Dunbar of Durn. Early last century this large district was acquired by the Earl of Fife.

Blackhills at an early date was a part of the extensive estate of Innes, and held by one of the oldest cadets of that great house. It was much more extensive than at present. Running across the hills, it embraced some lands in the parish of Rothes, now belonging to the Earl of Seafield. The estate, as it now stands, was sold by Sir John Innes of Blackhills to Sir Archibald Dunbar of Northfield on the 23rd June, 1796, at the price of £7,000, who re-sold it on the 16th Aug., 1798, to Lachlan Cuming of Demerara, a descendant of Craigmill, in Dallas, for £7,353. Mr. Cuming made it his principal residence, and died there at an advanced age upwards of 30 years ago, when his trustees sold it to the Earl of Fife. It fitted in well to his Lordship's estates, being situated in the very heart of his property. The land lies high, and is somewhat cold and exposed, and the difference in the temperature between this and the lower part of the parish in the winter season is striking.

The Barony of Pittendrich contains 9 farms and crofts,

and has now a yearly rental of £1,808 5s. sterling. It is bounded on the east by the Aughteen Part Land of Elgin, part of the estate of Maine, and the River Lossie; on the west by the estate of Milton and the Earl of Fife; on the north by the lands of Inverlochty and the Elgin road; and on the south by the Buinach Hill. It has been acquired by the Earl of Moray at different times, but principally from the ancient family of Douglas of Pittendrich, who not only had a large estate in Morayshire, down to a late period, but were proprietors in 1472 of a third part of Duffus, Pitgaveny, Calcotts, Darkland, Sheriffston, and others. No trace of these Douglases now exists. The old trees probably define the spot where the mansion of the former proprietors once stood. A venerable dovecot still stands, having the bloody heart (the crest of the Douglas family), much obliterated, yet decipherable.

The Lands of Manbeen or *Monbein,* now part of the estate of Pittendrigh, formerly belonged to the Preceptory of Maison Dieu, but were early feued out and held by different vassals. They are now held in property by the Earl of Moray, but in superiority by the Magistrates of Elgin, as in room of the Preceptor of Maison Dieu, under the charter of King James VI. In 1567 the lands of Upper Manbeen belonged to Hieronymus Spens, as appears by a feu-charter granted in his favour by James Thornton, precentor of Moray, of church lands in Alves, with consent of the Bishop, dated 16 Aug., 1567. Probably they continued in the family of Spens, or Spence, up to the early part of last century. There is a curious old well on the property, with the initials H. S. and the date 1699 upon it, cut in stone, with the legend, *Ex dono Dei bibite gratis,* i.e., Drink freely from this gift of God. The initials are those of the then proprietor, Hieronymus Spence. There are other two wells higher up—the Earl's Well and the Green Well.

Upper Manbeen is a small farm, about 4 miles north-west of Elgin. A sculptured Stone there (a coarse mica slate) stands about 200 or 300 yards to the north-west of the farm-house. .There is no tradition of its having been on another site, nor is there any local history attached to it. (See plate xvii., vol. i., Stuart's *Sculptured Stones of Scotland.*)

On *the lands of Bogside* there formerly stood an

Hospital and Chapel dedicated to S. John the Baptist, but no date can be given. It is said that one of the tenants carried off the stones to construct "rumbling drains" on the farm, a general fate which befell ecclesiastical and castellated buildings.

At *Mains of Pittendrigh*, on the south side of a knoll, there was a hermitage or cell for an anchorite, which shared the like destiny as the above edifices at Bogside.

The pretty little estate of *Westertown* was a part of the Priory lands of Pluscarden, but for upward of 300 years it was separated from it. Alexander Dunbar, the last Prior, had several bastards, and, seeing that the Reformation was fast drawing nigh, he, on the 12th Sep., 1560, with consent of the Convent, granted a charter of the lands of Westerton in favour of "John Dunbar, brother of Patrick Dunbar of Sanquhar," two of his illegitimate sons. This John Dunbar conveyed the estate to Robert Dunbar of Inshallon and his spouse, by charter dated 29 May, 1576. This Robert Dunbar was succeeded by his son, also Robert, who conveyed the estate to Patrick Dunbar and Janet Cumming, his spouse, on 22 May and 9 June, 1615. On 1st June, 1643, Patrick Dunbar, son of the last Patrick, sold Westerton to John Watson of Coltfield, in which family it continued for generations. In 1768, John Watson, the then proprietor, who had been a merchant in Moscow, conveyed the estate to his sister, Margaret Watson, in life-rent, and after her death to Peter Rose-Watson, his nephew. He died insolvent in 1799. Westerton was saved from the wreck, and was disposed to his niece, Miss Margaret Rose, who sold it on the 26 Nov., 1813, to Lieut.-Col. Alexander Hay, son of the Rev. James Hay, minister of Dallas, by his wife, Ann Brodie, daughter of Dr. David Brodie of Mayne. Colonel Hay had for about 20 years been in India, and had there made a small fortune. He planted, drained, and took in lots of moorland, and built a handsome mansion in the modern castellated style, and laid off fine gardens, with lawn and fish-pond. He married a daughter of the late Captain Alex. Macleod of Dalvey, by whom he had three sons. His wife died in early life. He himself died in 1845, and his second son, David, heired the estate. He did not survive his father many years. In 1855 the property was sold to the Hon. George Skene

Duff of Milton, who, a few years afterwards, made an excambion of it for the estate of Ardgay, in the parish of Alves, with his brother James, Earl of Fife.] (See *Young's Annals of Elgin.*)

ELGIN.

[*Situation, Soil, Climate.*—It is by the chartulary of Moray established, that, prior to the year 1226, the name of the town, which is extended to that of the parish, was *Helgyn*, which it most probably obtained from one of those many Norwegian chiefs who bore the name of *Helgy;* and who, according to Torsæus, conquering Moray and the countries on the north, by the forces of Sigurd, Earl of Orkney, built this town, in its southern quarter, almost 900 years ago. The particle *en*, or *an*, marking the genitive case in the Celtic, make *Helgyn* to signify *of Helgy.* Sundry etymologies, however, have been also suggested from the Gaelic; the most specious among them is *el*, place, and *cean*, the head.

The town is placed in the north-east corner of the parish, Spynie lying close upon the north, and St. Andrews Lhanbryd on the east. The parish is stretched southerly from the town, over the widest part of the plain for 6 miles, towards the side of the mountain, which in this quarter, by a direct approximation to the firth, at once reduces the champaign of Moray to half the breadth to which it had gradually widened from its narrowest beginning on the bank of the Spey. Through this encroachment of the mountain upon the plain, a vale is opened, nearly parallel to the firth, along the course of the Lossie; and the lesser River of Lochty, winding through the deep dale of Pluscarden, extends the length of the parish westerly to the borders of Rafford, at the distance of 10 miles from the town.

The soil in general may be described as sandy, although in many places it is fertile loam, and in some a rich clay. The climate is warm, healthful, and serene.

State of Property.—The country district of the parish is shared among six proprietors. The Earl of Fife's property is valued in the Cess-Roll at £2,896 14s. 4d. Scots. The Earl of Moray has Pitnadriech, and Upper and Nether Monbean, at £1,274 8s. 4d. The Hon. George Duff, of the family of Fife, has Milltown, Inverlochty, and Bilbohall, at £1,189 9s. Sir Archibald Dunbar of Northfield, Bart., has Blackhills, on which there is a commodious mansion-house, spacious well-stocked gardens, and extensive plantations, valued at £208 2s. 2d. The Earl of Findlater has Main, at £203 16s. 8d., upon which are a spacious handsome house and gardens, with much ornamented ground, and a great extent and variety of plantations. Peter Rose Watsone of Cottfield has Westertown of Pluscarden, at £71 3s. 6d. The lands holding of the community, shared among the burgesses, with a part acquired by the Earls of Fife and Findlater, are valued at £486 7s. 4d., extending the valued rent of the whole parish to £6,330 1s. 4d.

The farms are of various extent—a few about 100 acres, a considerable number between 30 and 40, and some under 20. The mean rent of the land in the vicinity of the town is £2 sterling the acre, and from 15s. to 18s. in the country.

The town is well built; the houses in general are either new or of late improved, according to the modern ideas of handsome accommodation. It consists of one principal street, in a winding course, for little more than a mile, from east to west, widened to such breadth towards the middle of the town as to have the Church awkwardly placed upon it; and, at a little distance farther on, the town-house, a mean building adjoining to a clumsy square tower, almost without windows, which contains the hall where the courts and county meetings are held, and the common jail. Behind the houses which front the street, buildings are carried back on either side, in narrow lanes, for the length of 8 or 10 dwellings, in some cases separate properties, and containing for most part distinct families. Many of these lanes terminate in the gardens, affording a more immediate access to the country than the few public avenues offer. The water of the pit-wells in the town is a little brackish; a considerable quantity of this commodity must be therefore carried from the river, although distant from the town.

The oldest charter among the archives is granted by Alexander II. in the year 1234, giving and confirming to his burgesses of Elgyn a guild of merchants, with as ample privileges as any burgh in Scotland.

James II., by charter 1457, confirms the grants of his

predecessors, particularly the lands of Mosstowie, Dowalgreen, Grieveship, and Strathcant.

James VI., by charter 1620, grants the Hospital of Maison Dieu, with the patronage and teinds thereof, Upper and Nether Monbean, and Haugh, Upper and Nether Pitnasear, Upper and Nether Kirkdales in Knocando.

Charles I., by charter 1633, confirms the lands already mentioned, adding Glassgreen, Upper Barflathills, Bogside, with the mill lands and multures of Kirkdales, the Blackfriar Croft, and the lands and gardens belonging to the predicant brethren on the north side of the burgh; and all the ports and stations, bays and creeks of Spey and Lossie, and between Spey and Findhorn, where any ship or boat can be received; with power to hold the six great fairs and the weekly market, and that none else shall hold fairs or markets within 4 miles of town; and to hold courts, appoint officers, and enjoy all the privileges and immunities appertaining to royal burghs. In 1641, by a charter ratified in Parliament, March 8, 1645, the King adds the right of patronage of two ministers and one reader. It must, however, be presumed that the community at no time possessed the whole property which these charters convey; for in 60 years after the date of the last they made a bargain with the proprietor of Kinnedur for the only harbour which they ever possessed, and which might be rendered of little consequence by proper keys at the more secure and commodious stations of Burghhead, Covesea, and Stotfield; nor have they ever claimed any perquisite from the trade carried on at Spey; and a great annual fair has been always held at Lhanbryd, within half the distance from the town which the latest charter allows. The lands conveyed by these charters yield at present a revenue of nearly £1,200, while the income of the community, arising mostly from feu-duties, market tolls, and a few fields about town, does not exceed £200.

Their internal government was ratified by the Convention of Boroughs in 1706, by which the magistracy consists of the Provost, 4 Bailies, and 12 Councillors, annually elected by themselves, with the change only, of 5, but residenting burgesses only are eligible. The Council nominate a jury of other 15 to apportion the taxes affecting the trade; but no private tax can be imposed without the consent of a majority of burgesses assembled in the head court, which can only sit upon the 2d Tuesday of September, in which the state of the borough, and the expenditure of the revenue, may be investigated; and for the general satisfaction the books and accounts are ordered to be submitted to public inspection for the 20 preceding days.

State Ecclesiastical.—The parish is accommodated with two ministers of the Established Church, each with an appointment of £50 and 127 bolls of barley, including the expense of the Communion, which each of them celebrates once a year. They have a small glebe in common, a part of which was specially designed for a situation for their manses, but the Court of Session determined that the proprietors of the parish were not, as in common cases, bound to build houses for the ministers of Elgin, and the incalculable expense of civil justice in this kingdom deters them from suing for redress.

The Church appears a low, clumsy, misshapen building, at once deforming and encumbering the street. Its length is 80 feet and its breadth 60, but two rows of massy cylindric columns divide the floor into three compartments, nearly from one end to the other; the pulpit is placed in the middle space between the columns, and is wholly lighted by a Gothic window in the west gable; the steeple is upon the east end, and, being still unfinished, is only a very little higher than the church, of which its bottom is a part, while its top accommodates the clock and two well-toned bells; the steeple on each side is supported by an aisle, which was originally tombs, though in one of them the ecclesiastical courts occasionally meet.

On the east the steeple is also supported by a shapeless hulk of another church, almost in ruins now, though once the subject of an appeal from the High Court of Justiciary to the House of Peers, in a prosecution for ejecting the minister of the Episcopalian congregation. It is now a place of worship, in some respects on a similar establishment to that of Lady Glenorchy's Chapel in Edinburgh. The congregation is composed of people both of the town and country parishes around, who elude the law of patronage, though professing themselves of the National Church. They ordain or instal the preacher themselves, that is, a few who take the lead among them, without the moderation of a call, so requisite by Presbyterian principle, and without the smallest concurrence or approbation whatever of any ecclesiastical judicature, of whose jurisdiction, or regulations at least, he is independent. He possesses, however, all the countenance and almost every benefit arising from the National Church, unless it be a legal security for the stipend, without which, however, he must make his doctrine palatable, whether evangelical or not. He holds communion with the ministers of the town, and has the countenance also of several of the magistracy and eldership. His appointment is equal to £40 sterling yearly, arising from the rents of the seats, and from two endowments, each of £5 yearly, one bequeathed by a Dr. Gordon and the other by Mr. David Rintoul, one of the ministers of Elgin. Notwithstanding the charter granted by King Charles, and ratified as above by the Parliament, the Crown has always continued to exercise the right of patronage.

The Valley of Pluscarden is the only district of the country which seems to suffer by the substitution of the Reformed for the Roman Catholic Religion, by which they enjoyed the pompous establishment of the Priory in the midst of this sequestered vale. The minds of the people were cheered through the day and soothed during even the stillness of the midnight hour by the solemn sound of the consecrated bells, calling the venerable inmates to their statutory devotions; and they had access to the consolations of 16 holy men, in every season of distress, with the free and easy accommodation of the most splendid social worship. They had the means also of educating in the most commodious manner their little ones in a share of the literature of the times; and numberless important advantages beside must have accrued from the wealth of this establishment, expended among them, and from the resort of strangers of every rank, upon amusement, business, or devotion, to this magnificently sacred and hospitable abode. Now all is cold and silent, forlorn and melancholy desolation; everything pleasant and useful is vanished; no national establishment nor any private institution for their assistance in civil or religious erudition within the distance of 10 miles. By the royal bounty they once, indeed, had a missionary, but his appointment was gradually frittered down to insignificance, and for many years has been totally withdrawn. They were of late flattered with the expectation of a schoolmaster by the Society for Christian Knowledge, but the proprietors withheld the accommodations which the regulations of the Society require. Unless the children are taught to read the Bible, their parents believe they prove faithless to the vows they made when their little ones were baptised; and in the present times the profession of a tailor, or a blacksmith, requires the knowledge in some degree of writing and accounts. The people, therefore, of this district, consisting of about 100 families, support a schoolmaster wholly from their own funds, which must no doubt become ultimately a burden affecting the land rent.

They have, without a murmur, maintained also a Chapel of Ease among themselves for almost 40 years. Of late only they have been aided by a bequeathment of £5 yearly by the late Dr. Hay, one of the ministers of the town; the Earl of Fife also adds a donation of £3 yearly, which enables the incumbent to discharge the rent of a house and 2 or 3 acres of land, rented from his Lordship: the ministers of Elgin also are in the practice of giving each a guinea in the year: by all which means, the whole appointment extends to the yearly income of £20 sterling. Such, however, is the impression of the undiscerning zeal of reformation which still remains, and although several vaulted apartments within the Abbey are so entire as to have needed only windows and a door, yet the people built a homely Chapel, lest they should be polluted by this fabric of anti-christian idolatry. The Earl of Fife assists them in the repairs of the Chapel, and on that account enjoys the patronage of it.

Besides these congregations of the Established Church, there are in the town two Chapels of Episcopalians, one of Seceders, one of Methodists, and one of the Church of Rome: but all these dissenting Meetings have a considerable number of their members from the adjoining parishes: their number in this parish exceeds not 700, while the Establishment reckons nearly 3800.

There are two schools, chiefly supported by the revenues of the town. The grant of the property of the Roman Catholic Establishment of Maison Dieu by James VI. in

SCHOOLS; STATE OF PROVISION FOR THE POOR. 361

the year 1620, is destined, after maintaining a few poor, for the support of a teacher of "music, and the other liberal sciences;" for which, with the fees from scholars, and the perquisites of the office of session-clerk, he has moreover a salary of £15 sterling yearly.

The town has also established a master, in a separate edifice, for classical learning, with an appointment of £21, which arises in part from some small bequeathments in favour of this establishment, two of which have lately made a small addition to this endowment. The proprietors of the land bear no part of the expense of either of these schools, in which originally these rudimental parts of literature were conducted as it were in separate monopolies; the one having been interdicted from teaching Latin, and the other, the reading of English: but experience having shewn, that every kind of monopoly, the East India trade alone excepted, is disadvantageous to society, the number of scholars in both has for some time past been regulated only by the diligence or success of the masters, in neither of whom at present is superiority even by this trial manifested.

Experience has demonstrated, that, like the grave, the poor never say "it is enough:" that, however munificent the provision made for them may be, their wants are not supplied, their number is only increased. It is not yet 200 years since any public funds were destined for the poor. Before "the Reformation," all pious donations were made only to the Church, and the poor were wholly trusted to the care of Providence: but in the present times, perversely said to be so much degenerated, the collections made in the Church, about £45 sterling, are, by the yearly interest of a fund, extended to £53, under the management of the session, which, by bequeathments under the direction of the Magistrates, are still farther augmented to the sum of £71, for the annual support of the poor enlisted on the parish roll.

Besides which, Mr. Cumine of Pitullie, once Provost of the town, bequeathed a capital of about £336 sterling, for the maintenance of 4 disabled members of the Guild, nominated alternately by his heirs and the Magistrates, to the sum of £8 sterling yearly, with a house and garden to each; and by the royal endowment of Maison Dieu, other 4 disabled men are provided with a house, garden gown, and 4 bolls of barley in the year to each.

Besides these, the Guild of Elgin have a growing fund, by entries and a yearly contribution by each individual of 2s., amounting to a revenue of almost £80 sterling yearly, though as yet about £40 only is divided among their widows and impoverished members.

After their example, the 6 corporations, weavers, tailors, glovers, shoemakers, smiths, and wrights, have each their respective capital for widows and disabled members, arising from entry money and annual contributions.

There are also two Friendly Societies: the members of each contribute 7d. monthly.

There are also two Mason Lodges, the gentlemen having made a secession from the operative masons; but it is not ascertained, whether charity, or the amusement of sociality, be the chief end of their establishment.] (*Survey of the Province of Moray.*)

ST. GILES' CHURCH.

[For what reasons the Burgh of Elgin adopted St. Egidius, or Giles, as its patron, and erected a church in his honour, are unknown He was not a Scottish saint, and in no way connected with Britain, but of Eastern (Greek) origin. Edinburgh has paid him a similar mark of respect, by erecting its fine Cathedral Church to his memory; and England has dedicated many ecclesiastical buildings to St. Giles. The Church of St. Giles is first mentioned, in the Register of Moray, in 1226; but there is reason to believe that it was of more ancient origin, and that it is the Church referred to in a charter of William the Lion between 1189-99. Probably the cemetery around it was, in accordance with the practice which prevailed in the 13th century, the site of the Fairs of St. Giles, mentioned in 1389, and that it originally constituted the market place (*forum*), alluded to in the Register, in 1365. In its vicinity there were wooden booths, or *kraims*, which, like the Luckenbooths that stood near St. Giles', Edinburgh, were fixtures, where the free burgesses of the merchant-guild exposed their wares for sale. The sacred and the profane having thus become closely allied, the character of *festivals* (preceded by vigils or wakes) gradually degenerated, and eventually they were called *ferie* or *fairs*. It stood upon two rows of massive pillars, and the arches raised on them were of the First Pointed, or Early English style of architecture. It had a nave and side aisles, a central tower, and chancel. At the period of erection there was no intention to build a Cathedral in Elgin, and therefore St. Giles' Church was made suitable to the wants of the town. Its services were conducted by a Vicar appointed by the Bishop, assisted by various Priests, who said Masses at the Altars within the building. The Vicar of Elgin was appointed one of the Canons of the Cathedral. That there were various altarages is shown by a deed of donation dated on the Feast of the Nativity of the Blessed Virgin, in 1286, by which Hugh Herok, Burgess of Elgin, grants his lands of Daldeleyt (probably Dandaleith) for endowment of two chaplainries, one within the Church of the Holy Trinity (the Cathedral), at the Altar of St. Nicholas, and the other at the Altar of the Holy Cross in the Parish Church of Elgin (St. Giles), where prayers should be said for his own soul, and that of Margaret, his wife, and their parents and children; also, for the soul of Alexander III., the illustrious King of Scotland, and the souls of Archibald Bishop of Moray, and his successors. By another deed of donation, dated 20th October, 1363, granted by William de Soreys, Burgess of Elgin, he directs that a certain annual rent therein mentioned should be paid out of a particate of land on the south side of the Burgh of Elgin, for the benefit of the glorious Altar of the Blessed Virgin, Mother of God, within the Church of St. Giles, Elgin, for prayer for his own soul, those of his predecessors and successors, and all the faithful; and a foundation for a chaplain in St. Giles' Church, by Richard, the son of John, dated at the Feast of St. Gregory the Pope, 1365, for the souls of himself and Eliza, his spouse, John and Emma, his father and mother, and the souls of all the faithful departed. There were probably many other donations of a similar description. The Magistrates and Trades appear also to have had private Altars, with officiating Priests.

The Church of St. Giles, like the Cathedral, had to pass through severe trials. In 1390 it was burnt by "the Wolfe of Badenoch," in his ruthless attack upon the burgh. It does not appear to have been totally destroyed. The roof and all the wood work had been consumed, but the strong walls and massive pillars had resisted the flames, and no doubt the roof had soon been restored. The Church did not suffer in the raid of Alexander Macdonald, son of the Lord of the Isles, in 1402, nor in the conflagration of part of the burgh made by the Earl of Huntly in 1452; and at the Reformation, in 1560, it was entire. There is one of the name of Hervey mentioned as the Vicar, perhaps about the middle of the 15th century. He is referred to in a deed in the Register of Moray, unfortunately without date. In his time a glebe was designed to the vicar, and it is still known by the name of "Hervey's Haugh."

The Reformation brought about many changes in Scotland, and perhaps in no part more than in the City of Elgin, dependent very much on the bishop and clergy; and its prosperity must of course have suffered by their removal. There would be, therefore, perhaps few zealous Reformers in the burgh. Bishop Patrick Hepburn stuck hard to his benefice, and had sufficient influence to retain lands and revenues until his death in 1573. In the meantime, however, two Protestant ministers were appointed; and these had, no doubt, possession of St. Giles' Church, viz., Robert Pont, in 1563; and Alex. Winchester, in 1565. The latter continued in office until 1580. No church could be more inconvenient for Protestant worship than St. Giles. The various Altars, belonging to the different incorporated Trades, had to be removed. It had to be filled with pews and galleries, and the aisles, formerly so convenient for private devotion, had to be thrown into the body of the church. At the back of the pillars and arches the officiating clergyman could not be seen, and scarcely heard. Between 1563 and 1688 Episcopacy and Presbyterianism had a severe struggle for the ascendancy. From 1560 to 1573, Presbytery prevailed; from 1573 to 1590, Episcopacy; from 1590 to 1606, Presbytery; from 1606 to 1638, Episcopacy; from 1638 to 1661, Presbytery; from 1661 to 1688, Episcopacy; and from the latter date to the present time, Presbyterianism. During this period, however, the form of worship was never changed. There was no liturgy used. The Church was ruled by Kirk-Sessions, Presbyteries, and Synods; the only difference being that, in Episcopal times, the Bishop presided at the Synods; while, in the period of

THE FALLING OF THE ROOF OF ST. GILES' CHURCH. 365

Presbyterian government, there was a General Assembly. The Royal House of Stuart had an intense dislike to the Presbyterian party, believing them to be Republicans.

About 1621 the arch which connected the nave and chancel of St. Giles' Church was built up. This new place of worship was called "The Little Kirk." In Slezer's View of Elgin, which was taken as early as 1670, St. Giles' Church has a very different appearance from what it had in its later days, the tower being in the centre of the building, and the whole edifice presenting the appearance of a cross.

On 22d June, 1679, being Sunday, and the day on which the Battle of Bothwell Bridge took place, shortly after the forenoon service, the roof of St. Giles fell. It had been roofed with heavy freestone flags, and the timber work had become decayed—having probably had little repair for centuries. It was only the centre or nave that was destroyed. The side aisles, arches, and pillars, and the tower and choir escaped. This is proved from a minute of the Town Council, dated 21st January, 1680, in which it is stated that on the above day "the Provost, Bailies, and Counsell, with consent and advyse of the haill communitie, having met together in the South Yle of Saint Geilles' Church, their ordinar place of meeting, for considering the rebuilding of Saint Geilles' Church, within the said burgh, laittlie fallen; and, after due consideration, with consent foresaid, did appoint and ordain twentie months' cess to be stented upon and uplifted from each inhabitant within the said burgh, as their proportions for helping the rebuilding of the said Church."

The Church was repaired in 1684, at a cost of somewhat above £4,000 Scots. These repairs consisted of the upper part of the front being made new, and the whole interior being reseated. The pulpit, Magistrates' gallery, and many of the other galleries were of oak richly carved, and the Trades' Lofts had the emblems of their crafts engraved upon them. The roof of the Church was of open wood work, and there were four heavy beams across, attached to which were brass chandeliers of antique workmanship, each containing 12 sockets, hung by chains of twisted iron. The building was 80 feet long by 60 in breadth, and is said to have been capable of holding 2,000 persons, which would have been absolutely necessary when there was no other religious building in the town. The open roof having been found cold, the Town Council, on 13th August, 1753, resolved that it should be plastered, and a grant for doing so was voted out of the common good. A description of St. Giles is contained in William Hay's graphic verses, called the "Muckle Kirk of Elgin," composed for the Morayshire Society of Edinburgh at one of their annual festivals, in which the poet was entitled to some liberties.

The exterior of the Church did not possess many architectural beauties. The central tower was a square heavy mass, and its abrupt termination showed that the original intention must have been to erect a steeple. It has a bell and clock, and in the dial-plate was placed the moon, which, by a movement of the machinery, indicated the monthly changes of her phases. It was accompanied by the stars also. Two or more bells were sent to Turriff, in 1589, to be re-cast into one bell, which was rung until 1713, when it was cracked by a woman striking it violently with a heavy key, when a fire had broken out in the town during the night. It was again re-cast on 17 Aug., 1713, at the head of Bailie Forsyth's Close, by Albert Gely, founder in Aberdeen, the expenses being defrayed by the town. It is said that numbers of the rich citizens repaired to the spot and cast in guineas, crowns, half-crowns, while the poorer, also showing their zeal, threw in shillings and sixpences, while the metal was fused, in order to enrich the tone of St. Giles' Bell. It was again elevated to its former place, but it was again rent by the boys who rung it in loyalty on the King's birthday, upon the 6th June, 1785. It was taken down and refounded at London on the 17th October following, having the names of the then Magistrates cast on its body. Since then *Big St. Giles*' has sounded sweetly unmolested in the Established Church, which is now under the patronage of no Saint, dead or alive. The little bell, or prayer bell, called *the Minister's Bell*, was given to the town of Elgin by the Earl of Moray. It bears— THOMAS DE DUNBAR ME FECIT, 1402.

The roof and aisles of St. Giles were supported by five massive pillars and arches on each side. Four of these were square pillars, and the centre one was round. These were probably coeval with the original building of the

Church. The aisles were of the same date, also the western front door. The upper part of the front was new, and had a large modern window, called a Venetian window. Above the western front door stood a figure of St. Giles, the patron saint, dressed in his robes, with a pastoral staff in one hand and a Breviary in the other. The pulpit of the Church, now at Pluscarden Priory, was of oak, curiously carved, and bore the date 1684. It stood upon the fourth pillar, on the south side. It cost £244. Immediately to the west of it was the Magistrates' Gallery, of carved oak. There was a canopy of the same material over it, and the civic dignitaries sat there for successive generations in great state. On one side was a sand-glass, and on the other the usual dirty pewter baptismal bason of the period, with twisted iron holder. The water was always taken from the well, nigh hereunto, and a napkin was hung over the pulpit for *dichtin'* the minister's fingers afterwards. Farther west, on the same side, was the Shoemakers' Loft, which was always well filled by that numerous craft. In the front of the western gallery was the Blacksmiths' Loft. Next to them sat the Glovers, once a numerous body, but which gradually fell off until reduced to two in number—viz., James Elder and Robert Blencher. These also fulfilled their day, and were gathered to their fathers; and so the craft came to an end. Next to the Glovers was the seat of the Earl of Fife, the largest heritor of the parish, and then followed the Earl of Seafield and the Earl of Moray. These noblemen and their tenants and friends occupied nearly all the north galleries. On the east, adjoining the tower, was the gallery in which the merchants of the town sat, called the Guildry Loft, and behind them were the Tailors and Weavers, the latter almost involved in total darkness. The Carpenters had a Loft near the top of the Church, on the east end. It was erected about 1751, and was of inferior materials to most of the other sittings, and, from its extreme height, was a dangerous-looking situation.

The Church was only artificially lighted once a year— on the occasion of the winter Communion, the evening of the first Sunday of November. It then exhibited a wonderful spectacle. The four large chandeliers were filled with candles, and the pulpit and precentor's seat blazed with similar lights. The Magistrates and all master tradesmen had their own candlesticks, and each family and many private individuals had the same. The Church was illuminated with perhaps 500 candles.

Communion was celebrated on Sunday, the 1st October, 1826, and the last sermon was preached in it by the Rev. Richard Rose, of Drainie, on Monday, the 2nd.

The Church began to be demolished in the beginning of October, 1826, and was completely removed before the end of that year. The building itself, and the whole street around, were filled with the remains of the dead; this having been the cemetery of the burgh from the 12th till the 17th centuries. Large quantities of bones were carried away, showing that the churchyard here must have been large.

The street was thereafter levelled, and the foundation of the new Parish Church laid on 16th January, 1827, by Sir Archibald Dunbar of Northfield, Baronet, Convener of the County, formerly Provost of the burgh, in presence of a large concourse of spectators. The building was finished in August, 1828, and was opened for public worship on 28th October that year. It cost upwards of £9,000. It is of the Grecian Doric order, in the form of a Greek temple, being a copy of the monument of Lysicrates, planned by Archibald Simpson, architect, Aberdeen. It is seated for above 1,700 people.

Although St. Giles' Church had been the principal place of worship in the burgh for nearly six centuries, yet its removal had almost become a necessity. It had no beauty of exterior, being a most unseemly structure. The interior had some appearance of grandeur, but it was extremely ill-arranged, and quite unsuited for Presbyterian worship; many of the sitters not seeing the minister at all, and perhaps having difficulty in hearing him. In winter it was exceedingly cold; and there was no vestry, nor any accommodation for the ministers. While its architecture suited well enough with the old grey houses which then surrounded it, the fine modern buildings which have since been erected would have agreed very ill with the old fabric.

From the Town Council Minutes of 23rd July, 1795, *the Monument or Effigy of St. Giles* is ordered to be placed in the niche on the south side of the Tolbooth. This image previously was, as has been stated, above the chief entrance or western front door.

THE LITTLE KIRK.

"The Little Kirk" was the Chancel of old St. Giles' Church, and, as has been stated before, the connecting arch which joined the nave and chancel, was closed in the year 1621 and never opened again. This occurred during the incumbency of Bishop Alexander Douglas. A new door was made to open into the street, and the chancel set apart for week-day service. When the roof of the nave of St. Giles fell in 1679, the Chancel, or "Little Kirk," does not seem to have been in any way injured. In 1689, when Mr. Alexander Tod, the then minister of the second Charge, was deprived for not praying for King William and Queen Mary, it is probable that, through the influence of Lord Duffus, then paramount in the town, and of the Magistrates, who were almost all attached to Episcopacy, he was maintained in the "Little Kirk," and officiated there for a considerable time. Of the conclusion of Mr. Tod's life we know nothing. In 1704 the Magistrates of Elgin (Lord Duffus being then Provost) permitted Mr. Henderson, an Episcopal minister, to conduct Divine Service in the "Little Kirk," but the ministers having applied to the Privy Council an order was granted to the Sheriff to remove him. In 1713 the Magistrates permitted Mr. Blair, an Episcopal minister, to occupy the building. In consequence, a criminal action was raised against the Magistrates before the Court of Justiciary, which was remitted to the Court of Session, when, after proof, it was found that the "Little Kirk" was part of the Parish Church of St. Giles, and the Magistrates were ordained to restore it to the ministers, and were found liable in expenses, and ordained to pay a fine of £20. The Magistrates having appealed to the House of Lords, the decerniture of the Court of Session and Court of Justiciary was reversed, and it was ordered and adjudged that the appellants (the Magistrates) should have the possession of the "Little Kirk," it being no part of the Parish Church. The control of the building remained with the Magistrates in all time thereafter during its existence. "The Little Kirk," with consent of the Magistrates, appears to have been opened for public worship in connection with the Established Church in 1744; one of the ministers preaching a sermon on a week-day, which was probably continued for a long time.

In 1798, the "Little Kirk" having become ruinous, and the Magistrates, whose property it was, not being inclined to make any repairs upon it, the numerous congregation built a new and commodious church in Moss Street, and requested Mr. Bayne to continue as their minister in the new church, but he was interdicted by the Presbytery in 1799; which decision was confirmed by the Synod of Moray and General Assembly in 1800; so that the congregation was under the necessity, unwillingly, to give up their connection with the Established Church of Scotland and unite themselves to another denomination. "The Little Kirk" was demolished by the Magistrates about or previous to the year 1800, and all traces of it obliterated.

THE OLD JAIL AND COURT-HOUSE

Appear to have stood for many centuries in the centre of the High Street, on the site of the present water-fountain. They are mentioned in 1540. In 1572 they seem to have been undergoing repair; for on the 13 Oct. of that year the Burgh Court was held within the "Quhoir of the Parische Kirk." They probably were then thatched buildings; for about 1600 an entry occurs in the Burgh Records:—"Item, £3 6s. 8d. for fog to thack the Tolbooth." In 1602 they had become ruinous, and a contract was entered into on the 27 Jan. that year between the Bailies and Town Council, by which the contractors bound themselves "to big ane sufficient tolbeith, within the said burgh, quhair the auld tolbeith thereof presently stands, of threiscore futtis length, twenty futtis of braid and wideness." It was to have a sufficient prison-house, a Council-room, and other accommodation. The cost was to be 513 merkis, with other allowances. The work seems to have been completed about 1605. The stones of the wall enclosing St. Giles' churchyard were freely used in the building; and the roof was "sclaited wi' stanes frae Dolass."

Although a most incommodious building, according to modern ideas, it had a very picturesque appearance, with its stone steeple and high crow-stepped gables. It was erected in the year 1717, in room of the previous one, burnt in 1701 by Robert Gibson, proprietor of Linkwood, a lunatic confined in it. He married a sister of Anderson of Westerton, in the parish of Botriphnie, but was unhappy in his marriage, and his domestic troubles drove him mad. The cost of this building was £4,000 Scots, and 40 bolls of victual. The accommodation was not much. It consisted of the Sheriff's Court-House, and, immediately opposite to it, entering from the same passage, was a room for the imprisonment of debtors, above which was a room for criminals, and adjoining to it a horrible chamber called *the pit*, where delinquents of the worst description were placed for security. There was no fireplace in it. Light came through an open slit in the wall, in which there was no glass, and the poor criminal in a winter night was exposed in this stone chamber to the cold biting winds. It was truly *squalor carceris*. On the west end of the building was the Council Room, which, for the space of 125 years, was used as a place of meeting by the Magistrates, and where they held their quiet debates and elections; the old Council electing the new, without disturbance from the outward world, and not exposed to Newspaper reporters, like their less fortunate successors of the present day. On the north side, fronting the High Street, was a dungeon called *the Black Hole*, somewhat underground, where disturbers of the peace on market days, and petty delinquents, were confined for 12 or 24 hours, according to circumstances, often without light or food, in a very summary manner, much at the pleasure of the famous Police officer of the day, and frequently without any warrant. It was a very filthy place, without a ray of light, and no air except what came through the keyhole, and much infested with rats. The prisoners had therefore a miserable time of it, and were thankful to promise good conduct for the time to come, to be relieved from their wretched prison house. Within the Jail there was a winding turret stair on the south side, which led to a bartizan on the roof, the only airing place for the prisoners. The debtors seem to have been the only parties who enjoyed the privilege of walking here; the criminals had no such relaxation. In a summer evening the debtors (and in these days they were very numerous) were seen moving about, and breathing the cool evening air, after the confinement in their miserable apartment during the day, where they had their meals, and slept all together. In the steeple there were a clock and bell.

This bell was removed to the Grammar School, and probably is the same bell which is still used at the Academy. Historians write confusedly anent the jail and kirk bells. The clock had only one hand to indicate both hours and minutes. It is now in the Museum. The metal weathercock was placed on the top of the steeple in the year 1778. Its predecessor, which was made of wood, not answering the wind rightly, was sent to Inverness to be rectified on the 18th March, 1718. *He* fell down in 1778, when the one of metal succeeded.

There were several small shops under the prison, particularly one at the west end, long occupied by a cooper, who hammered and fired casks in the front of his shop, and made such disturbance by the heavy blows of his tools from dawn to dusk, as would not now be permitted for one hour by the more tender inhabitants of the present day. On the east end of the Jail, and attached to it, was a building of wood, but slated, called *the Meal House*, in which the Council sold meal to the inhabitants, it being then the duty of the Magistrates to furnish meal to the indwellers of the burgh at a very reasonable price, in particular during seasons of scarcity, which, in these days of free trade and more abundant supplies, is not required.

The Jail, Court-House, and other accommodation being found quite inadequate for modern requirements, were removed in 1843, and the old bell is now placed in the new Court-House, but its sounds are not so often heard as in former days. In conjunction with the bell of the Parish Church, it roused the inhabitants to the labours of the day at six o'clock in the morning, and it rang its curfew at eight in the evening. A very good though somewhat rough print of the Court-House and Jail is still preserved, published about 50 years ago, and a finer one is contained in Rhind's *Sketches of Moray* in 1839.

THE VICAR'S MANSE AND GARDEN

Were opposite St. Giles' Church, on the north side, and is said to have been accidentally burnt. The grounds extended from the High Street at the south to the stank of Burghbrigs at the north. The Burgh Records (19 Nov., 1650, till 4 April, 1659) evidence litigation hereanent. In the Process, 1765-69, the ministers Shaw and Rintoul against the heritors, a Proof was led as to there

having been a Manse; when John Rhind, a witness for
the ministers, deponed that there were 40 Manses in the
Town and College, or tofts and tails, which had belonged
to the Canons and Chaplains under the Catholic Establishment, although no houses now stood thereon; and
Mr. James Robertson of the College deponed that, although he owned six of these Manses, he could point to
one only, in which he dwelt himself. The Court of Session found in 1769, under this Process, that neither of the
ministers of Elgin was entitled to a manse.

In 1781, "the Vicar's manse, ground, and gardens"
belonged to Hay and Peterkin, ministers of Elgin; and,
with consent of the Presbytery and Magistrates, were by
them excambed with Dr. Thos. Stephen, in Elgin, for
croft-land of equal value, by contract of excambion dated
2nd, 4th, and 8th Jan., 1781. Dr. Stephen died in 1818,
and was succeeded by his son Dr. James Stephen, who, in
1823, disponed the western and largest portion of "the
manse, ground, and gardens" to John Forsyth, ironmonger; and the eastern or smaller portion, along with
some other ground, to Peter Nicholson, merchant. John
Forsyth built a handsome house and shop on the western
part, which he sold to the late Dr. John Paul, in 1841,
which now belongs to his son, Dr. John Liston Paul.
The eastern portion was built upon by Mr. Nicholson,
who shortly after sold the ground and building to the
British Linen Co., on which are now their branch-office
and agent's domicile.

Next and immediately adjoining *the Manse, Ground,
and Garden*, are the burgh subjects, formerly belonging
to Isaac Forsyth, the well-known publisher and bookseller, which after his death were sold by his trustees to
Dr. Mackay. The most prominent portion is the eastern
part, in which there is the old Tower, of which an engraving is given in Billing's *Antiquities*, vol. II., and Rhind's
Sketches of Moray, page 54. The ancient titles have
been lost.

Lower down the High Street, and in the immediate
proximity of Isaac Forsyth's Library and premises, stood
a venerable Mansion, formerly on a piazza, of which there
is a Plate in Billing's *Antiquities*, vol. II. The windowtops were highly ornamented, and bore the date 1680,
and the initials I. M. The titles do not go so far back as

the date of the building, and its original owner is now unknown. The existing titles bear that it belonged, in 1706, to James Cramond, merchant, who was a magistrate of the burgh; in 1718 to Alexander Mill, merchant; in 1761 to Capt. Peter Innes, R.A.; in 1768 to George Charles, merchant, in whose descendants' names it remained until 1826, when it was sold to Alexander Hay of Edintore, and by his trustees, some years ago, to John Anderson, merchant, who demolished it, and erected thereon a modern building.

A little east of the above, on the same side of High Street, there is a large House covered with grey slates. It may be a century and a half old. It has an extensive frontage to the street. Upwards of a century ago it was the property of Thomas Stephen, merchant, and Provost in 1770. The titles extend back to 1652, but the frontage may date a century later.

On the south side of High Street, and directly opposite St. Giles' Church, was erected, in 1776, the largest House ever built in the burgh. It had the Grant arms and the initials of the owner and his wife placed in the front. The builder was designed in the titles as James Grant of Logie. It entered from the street by a handsome gateway, which conducted into a paved court, within which was a large garden. There were two excellent shops fronting High Street, and the large building within the court was converted into two dwelling-houses, entering on each side of the gateway. It must have been a costly erection, and in a style to which the burgh was not then accustomed. Some 15 or 20 years after it was built, it was sold to James Milne, a native of Elgin, who made a considerable fortune in London. He succeeded his father-in-law, Provost Stephen, as agent of the Aberdeen Bank, who died, advanced in years, in 1828. He had a literary taste, and executed some fine pen-and-ink sketches, particularly heads of Roman Emperors. His son, Thomas Miller, who spent much of his early life in India and the Island of Java, succeeded and lived for the last 30 years of his life in Elgin and latterly in this property. He died on 7th May, 1870, and left the large House to his cousins, the Misses Stephen, who, after making many improvements, sold it in 1875 to the City of Glasgow Bank. Since the sale the building has been entirely renovated, and forms an immense improvement to High Street.

THE NORTH COLLEGE

Was the residence of the Dean of the See or Diocese, and was called *the Deanery*. From *the Criminal Letters*, as well as from *Ane Account of the Family of Innes*, page 128, we are informed that on the 1st Jan., 1554, a scene of strife and violence took place within the Cathedral during Vespers. Eighty of the family or clan of Innes, all armed, entered the Church, with the intent of murdering Alexander Dunbar, Prior of Pluscarden, David Dunbar, Dean of Moray, and other Dunbars who were laymen. The Dunbars had come for the same purpose, to slay William Innes of that ilk, with his servants. The feud did not prove fatal; but both families litigated for nearly 23 years, until the 18th Oct., 1577, when the animosity again burst out from seven of the Inneses, Geo. Douglas, Vicar of Aberchirder, and others. These came with arms to the manse of Alexander Dunbar, the Dean in the Canonry of Elgin, and beat and wounded Andrew Smyth, his servant and keeper of his horses, broke up the stable-door, and cut the halters of his horses, intending to steal them. The Dean, roused by the disturbance, came out in his habit, unarmed except with a dirk which he always carried. One of three John Inneses attacked the Dean with his sword, and wounded him severely on the head and both hands, and left him for dead. This John Innes, moreover, mortally stabbed in the breast Elizabeth Dunbar, a girl 13 years old, the Dean's eldest (natural) daughter. Also, in the silence of the night of the 29th May, 1578, the same set ransacked the Dean's house at Carsehillock, and carried away 40 sheep, wethers, ewes, and lambs. For these deeds the Inneses were put to the horn, which proved ineffectual; but a convention was held at the Cluny Hills, near Forres, on the 7th Nov., 1578, when the hostile parties were reconciled.

The Deanery was inherited by the Dunbars of Burgie for two centuries. Bad harvests succeeded from 1694 till nearly a century onwards. During the famine of 1742, the Lady Dunbar of Burgie, who then occupied *the North College* or *Deanery*, had a large pot of *Brochan* in daily use for the starving hordes. Tradition says that the lane which led to the Deanery was strewed with the dead bodies of those who were flocking thereto for relief, but whose last energies failed. In 1756 the Deanery, with grounds, was sold to James Robertson, Bishopmill, Provost of Elgin, who married Barbara Brodie, daughter of Joseph Brodie of Milltown, who procreated a family of sons and daughters. He married Barbara Brodie, daughter of the laird of Milton, or, as it is now called, Milton-Brodie, in the parish of Alves, formerly called Windyhills, which successively belonged to Dundases, Dunbars, and Brodies. He was succeeded by his eldest son, Joseph Robertson, by whose heirs *the North College* was conveyed to a younger brother, James Robertson, on the 29th March, 1784, who was long resident in Jamaica, where he had large estates. Latterly he resided in Elgin, the place of his nativity, where he died in 1816. He built the west wing of the present mansion, containing the dining-room, and planted the orchard, with many trees along the banks of the Lossie and upon the lawn. His son, Alexander, was born on the 13th December, 1803, and received his education at the Elgin Academy. He spent his first business years in London, in the lime trade. He took a great interest in the Parliamentary politics of the district, and did much to further the interests of Sir Andrew Leith Hay of Rannes and Leith-Hall. When the National Provincial Bank of England was started about 1835, Sir Andrew was one of the principal promoters; and through his influence Mr. Robertson was made Joint-Secretary and ultimately Managing Director. He was also a Director of various other Companies, such as the Commercial Union Insurance Company. He was well known in London as an authority in all matters of finance, and as one of sound judgment and foresight. He married Harriet B. Wemyss, daughter of Patrick Wemyss of Craighall, Aberdeenshire, by whom he had an only daughter, who is married to Dr. Wane, 20 Grafton Street, Berkeley Square, London, where he died unexpectedly of heart-disease and bronchitis on the 6th March, 1879, and whence his remains were taken for interment in the New Cemetery of Elgin.

The Deanery, in the 18 or 20 acres of which it consists, contains the foundations, not now visible, of other six of the old Manses connected with the Cathedral, with all their gardens and grounds. After Mr. Robertson was relieved from the active management of the Bank, he delighted in improving this Elgin residence. He built a new porter's lodge and a south wing to the house, containing kitchen and servants' accommodation, with several bed-rooms. For many years *The College* had been let to several tenants in succession; but latterly the proprietor was the sole occupant of one of the finest seats about the city of Elgin.

THE SOUTH COLLEGE

Embraces—1. The Archdeacon's Manse. 2. The Sub-Dean's Manse. 3. The Sub-Chanter's Croft. 4. A lot of ground acquired from Wm. King of Newmill. 5. Sanderson's land.

The Archdeacon was minister of Forres. The Manse was conveyed by Gavin Dunbar, then Archdeacon of Moray, to Patrick and Christian Pollock, by charter dated 14 Nov., 1574; and, after many steps of progress, fell to Alexander Cook, and was conveyed by James Cook and Janet Cook to the Hon. George Duff of Milton, fifth son of William, Earl of Fife, by disposition of date 18 May, 1768.

The Sub-Dean was minister of Dollas. The existing titles of the manse commence in 1689, when the subjects were in possession of   Stevenson, from whom they passed to Jonathan Forbes, father of William Forbes, Town-Clerk of Edinburgh. He was served heir to his father on 12 May, 1761, and conveyed the property to the above Mr. Duff by disposition of date 29 May, and 4 June, 1765.

The Sub-Chanter was minister of Rafford. The titles of this lot extend only to the middle of last century. John Wiseman sold them to Mr. Duff on 31 Aug., 1768.

The fourth lot was acquired by Mr. Duff from Wm. King of Newmill on the 27 Jan., 1768.

The fifth lot (Sanderson's land) was disponed by Margaret Sanderson and others to Mr. Duff on 25 May, 1794.

All these lots being enclosed in one park, it is impossible now to distinguish them. Part of the Mansion-house is probably as old as the time of the Archdeacon. Mr. Duff executed a deed of entail on 30 Dec., 1802, and died at an advanced age in 1818. In his time, the house was comparatively small; for then gentlemen of rank were content with moderate accommodation. He was succeeded by his only son, Major George Duff, who added largely to the house. On his death, the property descended to his cousin, the Hon. George Skene Duff, who never occupied the house himself. It was then let to tenants. For some years it was occupied by the great Naturalist, the late Charles St. John. In 1864 Mr. Duff sold the property to the late Archibald Inglis of Ceylon, who vastly improved the mansion and policies. It is to be regretted that he removed the old precinct-wall, using the materials for building purposes. Previous to his death he removed herefrom, when *the South College* was sold to Dr. Cooper of Old Deer.

GRANT LODGE

And its extensive grounds embrace the Houses of the Laird of Pluscarden, the Marquis of Huntly, the Bishop's town-residence, and Dunkinty House, with their parks and gardens, and forms an extensive domain. The entrance-gate stands at the junction of North College Street and King Street, on the south-east corner of the grounds, through which the approach winds gracefully, terminating in an oval space in front of the House. *Grant Lodge* is the jointure residence of the Countess of Seafield, and stands on the site formerly occupied by the Elgin residence of the Marquis of Huntly. It is a large handsome building of three storeys, with two conservatories, one on each end. The principal entrance is reached, a handsome *porte-cochere* supported on four massive pillars. The basement floor is occupied with the servants' accommodation. The first floor contains a large dining-room on the right, and a morning-room on the left, while the western wing contains the boudoir. On the second floor are the drawing-room and best bed-room, and a large suite of apartments. The grand staircase contains some fine valuable paintings by eminent masters, and several marble busts. No part of the House has the appearance of an older date than the middle of last century.

The Marquis of Huntly's House is referred to in the Burgh Records as far back as 1540, but it may have been much older. It stood on the north side of North College Street, and *the House of the Laird of Pluscarden* was near it. Both these Mansions are apparent in Slezer's *View of Elgin*, published in 1693. Probably *Pluscarden*

House was erected by the Mackenzies when they were proprietors of that estate.

Janet Brodie, wife of Ludovick Grant of Grant, bought the Estate of Pluscarden in 1677 for her son James, afterwards Sir James Grant, and perhaps at the same time the House in Elgin.

At what time the Grant family acquired the Marquis of Huntly's House cannot be ascertained.

In 1661, the Marchioness of Huntly lived in this House, and had a Roman Catholic Priest resident with her (the Rev. William Ballantyne), who died here, and was buried in St. Mary's Aisle in the Cathedral.

There is no record when Pluscarden and Huntly Houses were removed.

S. DUTHAC'S MANSE

Is now occupied by the house and premises on the south side of High Street belonging to Mr. Williamson, hatter. In Sir Robert Gordon's *Genealogy of the Earls of Sutherland*, page 32, it is stated that S. Duthac or Duffus was "a verie godly man, patron of Sanct Duffus his chappell, besyd the town of Tayn; into the which chapple a great confluence of people, yea some of our kings, did resort in pilgrimage in former ages." S. Duthac's Chapel in Tain, whose walls are yet considerably entire, being enclosed with a wall, and having a cemetery around it, was frequently visited by King James IV. on his many pilgrimages in the 15th and 16th centuries. Probably S. Duthac's Manse in Elgin was either a resting-place for pilgrims on their way to the shrine at Tain, or the residence of a chaplain. On the back of the present front house is the date 1707; but it may be doubted if it be so old, as the stone may belong either to an older building, or to the house further up the court, which is occupied as an inn, and seems older than the front building. The old titles are lost: but from *Abbreviatio Retornatorum Caput Elgin et Forres*, it appears that "Robert Innes, son of John Innes, burgess of Elgin, was served heir to his father in the rood of land and Manse of S. Duchat, a chaplainry founded within the Parish Church of Elgin, 9 Jan. 1629."

In 1782, *S. Duchat's Manse* belonged to the Earl of Findlater, who, on the 7th June that year, sold it, through Provost George Brown, to George Simpson, vintner in Elgin, from whose heirs it was adjudged by John Sime, of the Island of Antigua, on 7th July, 1795. His son, William Sime, tenant at Drummond, made up a title as heir to his father in 1808, which was confirmed to him by the heirs of George Simpson, by disposition dated the 15th and 17th Nov., 1808. He conveyed the subjects to the late William Gill on the 2nd July, 1812, whose trustees disponed the property to Mr. Williamson in 1867.

THE ORDEAL OR ORDER-POT

Was a deep pool in the hollow ground to the eastward of the Cathedral, and was long well-known to every schoolboy. Strange ideas of its awful depth and dark legends of its history haunted the minds of boyhood. So late as 1560, witches were publicly and legally drowned herein. It has been conjectured that, at a remote period, the channel of the Lossie may have passed through *the Order Pot;* for, whenever the Lossie was swelled by unusual floods, it made for its old haunts. There is an old prophecy, said to be Thomas the Rhymer's:—" The Order Pot, and Lossie gray, shall sweep the Chan'ry Kirk away." Many thousand carts of rubbish from the Cathedral grounds and elsewhere have been emptied into the "Pot." An etching of it is given in Rhind's *Sketches.* Herd-boys are represented in the act of drowning a dog or cat, while three cows are in contemplation as witnesses. The rushes seem to be of supernatural growth; and the foliage around the two western towers of the Cathedral are nondescript for abundance. He also gives the Trial for Witchcraft, from an old MS., of Marjory Bisset; who was dragged through the stour, in sore plight, with her grey hairs hanging loose, crying *Pity, pity.* A great multitude rushed through the *Paunis Port,* and surrounded the pool. The Friars repeated to Maister Wiseman, the clerk, who stood at her trial, that she had muttered her *Aves* or *Hail Marys* backwards; and others that the *maukin,* which was started at Bareflat, had been traced to her dwelling, and that the cattle had died by her connivance. But she, hearing this, cried the more, *Pity, pity, I am guiltless of the fause crimes, never so much as thocht of by me.* Then suddenly there was a motion in the crowd, and the people parting on every side, a leper came down from the House, and in the face of the people, bared his hand and arm, the which was withered and covered over with scurfs, most piteous to behold, he said,—At the day of Pentecost last past, this woman did give unto me a shell of ointment with which I anointed my hand, to cure an *imposthume* which had come over it, and behold from that day forth until this, it hath shrunk and withered as ye see it now. Whereupon, the crowd closed round and became clamorous: but the said Marjory Bisset cried piteously that God had forsaken her, that the ointment was the gift of her husband who had been beyond seas, and that she had meant good only and not evil, and had given it free of reward or hire; but that if *gude* was to be paid back with evil, *sorrow and gif Sathan mot not have his own*. Whereupon the people did press round and become clamorous, and they did take the woman and drag her, amid many tears and cries, to the pool and plunge her into the water: and when she went down in the water there was a great shout; but as she rose again and raised up her arms as if she would have come up, there was silence for a space, when again she went down with a bubbling noise, and they shouted finally *To Satan's kingdom she hath gone;* and forthwith went their ways.

THE FURLIN' YETTS

Was a narrow path between two dykes, leading from the back of the Tanworks eastward to the Dunkinty Road. Probably it derived its name from the *turnstiles* which were placed in this filthy lane to prevent the ingress of but one *genus* of animals.

Excerpt from the Town Council Minutes 1852, Feb. 23: —The Council having agreed to shut up the old footpath called "The Furlin' Yetts," in order that it might be incorporated with the grounds of Grant Lodge. They received in return about two acres of the land of Burghbriggs for a recreation ground to the inhabitants of the town, a Committee, consisting of the Provost, Magistrates, and others, was appointed to see that the rights and interests of the public were properly preserved.

THE GRAMMAR SCHOOL AND SANG SCHOOL.

Immediately after *the Reformation*, the schools were under the jurisdiction of the Town Council and Magistrates.

1585. *Thomas Moig* was Master of the Grammar School.

1594. By Charter dated 22 March this year, James VI. granted to the Provost, Bailies, Council, and Community of Elgin, and their successors, the Hospital and Preceptory of Maison Dieu, with all lands, tenements, annual rents, farms, profits, and emoluments belonging thereto, within the kingdom, under the burden of maintaining certain poor men called Beadmen, and for supporting a master for teaching music and other liberal arts within the burgh. This Charter was immediately acted upon, and a Music School was established.

1652. *Wm. Murray* was appointed Teacher at a salary of 200 merks yearly; for which he had also to "take up the Psalms in the Church."

1659. This same Music Master was also directed to teach English, Writing, and Arithmetic.

1683. *George Cumming*, Schoolmaster, was ordered to appear before the Council to answer for not going along with the children to the Loch of Spynie to pull bulrushes, in case of accidents.

1704. *Hugh Tod*, Master of the Grammar School, demitted.

Thomas Gordon, pedagogue to Patrick Barclay, of Towie, succeeded.

1717. *Alex. Roust*, appointed in 1717, resigned in 1748. He died about the middle of the century. His tombstone still exists in the Cathedral buryingground, but is almost illegible. It is said to have had the following lines upon it:—

The famous Rust is gone from us,
And mingled into dust;
But now it is hoped his soul's above,
Among the spirits just,
In vocal music, he excelled, &c.

He was Master of the Music School.

1727. *John Porteous* was Teacher of the Grammar School. Dismissed.

1730. *William Gordon*, Teacher of the Grammar School, was dismissed in 1739 "for frequently sitting up all night, drinking, and rioting in taverns."

1734. *Henry Innes* was also dismissed, because "he had lost authority over the boys, his scholars."

1744. *James Cruickshank*, Master of the Grammar School, "being under Church scandal, and had taken to merchandizing, was dismissed." This led to an Action in the Court of Session between the Magistrates and the Ministers as to jurisdiction, which was settled by agreement in 1748.
1746. *William Cruden* was appointed Master of the Music School.
1773. *Wm. Peterkin*, Master of the Grammar School, was presented to the Parish Church of Elgin.
1773. *William Farquhar*, Master of the Music School, was appointed to succeed the above in the Grammar School.
1773. *John Anderson*, Schoolmaster of Fyvie, was elected Master of the Music School.
1774. Brander, of Pitgaveny, presented two globes, celestial and terrestrial, for the use of the schools.
1781. *George Dann*, Teacher of the Grammar School. A dispute arose between him and the Magistrates, which became a lawsuit in the Court of Session, because he preached in Elgin and in the neighbouring Parish Churches. Resigned in 1782.
1782. *Alex. Wilson*, Teacher at Banff, succeeded. Resigned in 1802, having been appointed Minister of Aberlour. In 1799 the mean fabrics of the Sang School and Grammar School, having become unsafe and ruinous, were sold by public roup, and subscriptions (£500) were raised for *The Elgin Academy.*
1802. *John Anderson*, Master of the Latin School.
John Black, Teacher of Arithmetic and Mathematics.
—— *M'Combie*, Teacher of the English School.

THE LATIN SCHOOL.

1802–1815. *John Anderson*, above, died 1815.
1815–1825. *James Thomson.* Minister of Keith.
1825–1842. *William Duguid.* Minister of Glass.
1842–1844. *John Allan.* Minister of Peterculter.
1844–1859. *Donald Morrison*, LL.D., Glasgow Academy.
1859–1870. *Gavin Hamilton.* Retired.

MATHEMATICAL SCHOOL.

1803–1808. *James Thomson.* Minister of Pluscarden.
1809–1821. *John Waddel.* Died 1821.
1821–1857. *Peter Merson.* Resigned upon £50 annuity.
1856–1862. *William Macdonald.* Retired.
1862–1866. *John Garden.* Retired.
1867. *Robert Pattison.*

ENGLISH SCHOOL.

1803–1819. *Alexander Reid.*
1819–1827. *Alexander Brandsby.* Died 1827.
1827–1848. *James Jenkins.* Minister of Aboyne.
1848–1862. *James Macdonald.* Rector of Ayr Academy.
1862–1863. *Charles Anderson.*
1863–1866. *John Garden.*
1867. *John Mitchell.*

The Ettles Bursary.—Anna and Mary Ettles, Inverness, in 1863, bequeathed £500, which, being the amount of 50 shares in the Highland Railway Company, yield a Bursary of £21 annual value.

The Macandrew Prize.—James Macandrew, Elgin, in 1822 bequeathed £200 for Book-prizes in the Latin School.

"*Allan's Reward of Merit.*"—John Allan, M.D., a native of Elgin, in 1833, bequeathed £400 for three annual prizes in the Latin, Mathematical, and English Classes.

Dick's Mortification.—John Dick, London, in 1786, bequeathed £120, which yields about £5 yearly to the Classical Master.

At the east end of the Burgh is

THE ELGIN INSTITUTION FOR THE SUPPORT OF OLD AGE
AND EDUCATION OF YOUTH,

Founded by Major-General Anderson. It is a Grecian quadrangular edifice, two storeys high, with a circular dome for a clock and bell. The above Inscription is carved on the front. Fifty children and ten aged persons are accommodated—the children are admitted at the age of 8 or 9 and remain till 14, when they are apprenticed or sent to domestic service. There is also a public free school, on the Lancasterian principle, the average daily attendance of which is about 300. The house-governor and teacher of the School of Industry has a salary of £55 yearly, with board and house. The Trustees are the two Sheriffs, the two Parish Ministers, the Moderator of the Presbytery, and the Provost.

About the year 1730 there lived in the neighbouring parish of Drainie a worthy couple of the name of Gilzean or Gillan. They had a small croft and kept a cow, and "the gudeman" was occasionally employed at labouring work on the neighbouring farms. They had one daughter, an only child, who was universally acknowledged to be pretty and engaging, and who became attached to a youth named Andrew Anderson, belonging to the adjacent parish of Lhanbryd. The old couple thwarted their proposals, and Andrew, in a fit of despair, enlisted into a regiment then quartered in Elgin. May, or Marjory, determined to follow and share the fortune of her suitor. They were married in 1745. If rumour be true the match turned out ill, the husband ill-used his spouse. This, combined with the roughings which fell to the lot of a wandering life, bad health, and having now an infant in arms, she was necessitated to seek her native little cot in Drainie. Having once more reached the shores of Great Britain, but still far from Moray, the whole of the land journey from Deal was performed on foot, with the exception of what portions were passed in *lifts* from some countrymen's carts. By slow and fatiguing stages she reached her goal. In 1748 she came home, but the old dwelling was empty. John Gillan and his wife (as a labourer informed their daughter Marjory, who saw her peering in at the paneless window) were to be "socht in another place—baith lying aside ither in the kirkyard o' Kinethart." The shock was too great for the poor lonely young creature—the fatal news caused her to depart from the ruinous cottage a hopeless maniac. She, with her helpless babe (the future General Anderson) took up her abode in the Lavatory of Elgin Cathedral. This small chamber, about 5 feet square, at that time was in good repair and preservation, having a window and chimney, and the roof, as well as the walls, being of solid masonry. In this small cold crib, surrounded by melancholy ruins and the dread-inspiring precincts of a churchyard, did mother and son for years reside. The pauper-boy was soon taken notice of, and sent to the old Grammar and Sang School. Judging from his successful career in after life, he was an apt and persevering pupil, which resulted in the noble and high honour of General Major in the Honourable East India Company's Service. Prior to his enlistment he was apprenticed to an uncle in Lhanbryd, from whom he absconded for London. He was long in India and amassed £70,000, which he bequeathed to found and endow this Institution in 1832. He died in London in 1824; but for several years after his retirement from the army he lived in Elgin in the house which is now converted into the Commercial Bank. It was originally built by George Fenton, Esq., Sheriff-Substitute, who sold it to the General.

After her son had left to push his fortune, May Gillon, or Mrs. Andrew Anderson, wandered about as a beggar through the country a harmless imbecile, carrying with her a distaff, or "rock and spindle," commonly in use for spinning the finest lint or linen yarn. Spinning-wheels had not come into vogue. True and false traditions have come down about her peregrinations. At one period she left her abode in the Cathedral and appears to have exchanged it for some time in an old house in the vicinity of Ballindalloch; but another fatuous rival became so jealous of May and so annoyed her that she was fain to quit the debateable ground. Having returned to Elgin, she found shelter in a wooden shed which stood near to the Little Cross, and on the south side of South College Street. Some ill-disposed individuals, however, destroyed this frail tenement, and she was obliged to resort to her old quarters in the Cathedral. Old age was creeping on apace, and she began to look about her for a more comfortable home. A young woman who had been a servant in a family that May had frequented, and who had always shown her great kindness, having recently married a man of the name of Macleod, was now living in Stotfield. This hospitable pair gave her a permanent home under their roof. Wherever she went her gentleness and even religious cast of mind excited sympathy. One night, during the harvest of 1790, she came to Stotfield complaining of indisposition. Mrs. Macleod put her to bed and administered to her comforts. At her request a messenger was despatched for the minister, who could not be found; an "elder" was next thought of, but he had gone to the fishing as well as the others. Mrs. Macleod endeavoured to supply their place, and read suitable portions of Scripture, which greatly consoled her. During the night she grew worse, and next morning her spirit forsook its frail tenement, and all her trials and wanderings were over.

The substance of the above was given in *The Elgin Courier* of 28th Feb., 1851, upon the reading of which the Trustees of Anderson's Elgin Institution resolved to place a stone over Marjory Gillan's grave in the churchyard of Kinnedar, which was done shortly after, with the following Inscription:—

Sacred to the memory of Marjory Gilzean, or Anderson, who died at Stotfield in 1790, and whose remains lie here interred. This stone is erected by the Trustees of her son, General Anderson, the benevolent founder of the noble and useful Institution, which was opened at Elgin in 1832, for the education of youth and the support of old age.

EPITAPHS IN THE CHURCHYARD OF ELGIN CATHEDRAL.

I. Hic jacet Reverendus in Christo Pater D.D. Joannes de Innes, hujus Ecclesiæ quondam Episcopus Moraviensis, qui hoc notabile opus extruxit, et per septennium Episcopale munus tenuit.

Translation.—Here lies the Rev. Father in Christ John of Innes, Doctor of Divinity, formerly Bishop of this Church of Moray, who erected this remarkable work, and held the Episcopal gift for seven years.

Bp. Innes began the building of the great or centre steeple of the Cathedral, and was buried at the foot of the north-west pillar of it. Both the monument and the above inscription were destroyed by the fall of the steeple in 1711; but the latter has been preserved in Monteith's *Theater of Mortality,* 1794.

II. Hic jacet Wills de la Hay quonda. dns. de Lochloy qui obiit viii° die mensis Decebris anno doni mccccxxi.

Translation.—Here lies William Hay, formerly laird of Lochloy, who died the 8th day of the month of December, in the year of our Lord 1421.

The tomb is a sarcophagus in the middle of the choir,

with a knight recumbent on the top in full armour, with a lion couchant at his feet. The above was the second son of Sir John de Hay of Tillybothville, who married Margaret, niece of King Robert II., by whom he had three sons. The Hays resided at the Castle of Inshoch, protected by a morass, of which the ruins exist. The family flourished for centuries, and were connected by marriage with the Urquharts of Cromarty, Sutherlands of Duffus, Roses of Kilravock, Cumings of Altyre, &c. Colonel William Hay was the last proprietor, in 1704. Shortly after the lands of Lochloy and Park were sold to Alex. Brodie of Brodie, Lord Lyon, in which family they continue.

III. In the north transept of the Cathedral, called S. Thomas à Becket's Aisle, are monuments of several members of the Dunbar family:—

1. Bishop Columba Dunbar's tomb has a recumbent figure in vestments (1429-1435). Son of George, 10th Earl of March.

2. Sir Alexander Dunbar of Westfield, Knight, is represented by a recumbent figure in armour, with armorial bearings on his breast. He was the son of James Dunbar, 5th Earl of Moray. According to the Kalendar of Ferne, now at Dunrobin, he died on the 10th March, 1497. His widow, Dame Isabel Sutherland, daughter of Alexander Sutherland of Duffus, died on the 11th Nov., 1595.

Her name "Isabell" is usually latinised "Isabella," as it is in the Papal Dispensation for her marriage, and in the inquest which records her death as "Isabella, relict of the late Sir Alexander Dunbar, of Westfield, Knight." But occasionally it is latinised "Elizabeth," as in the Latin Charter of her son, Bishop Gavin, from which some translated extracts are given below.

The above monuments were much mutilated by the fall of the great steeple.

On the 2nd Sept., 1529, Gavin Dunbar, Bishop of Aberdeen, Sir Alexander's fourth son, founded and endowed, by charter, with consent of the King, two chaplaincies in the Cathedral Church of Moray.

"In honour of the Holy Trinity, and of St. Columba and of St. Thomas the Martyr, and for the salvation of the souls of the King and of his predecessors and successors, of Sir Alexander Dunbar of Westfield, Knight, and of Dame Isabell Sutherland, his spouse, parents of the Bishop . . . . Also for the salvation of the soul of the Bishop, the founder, and of other Christ's faithful."

The Charter ordained that the Chaplains were to celebrate Mass daily,

"The first in the aisle of St. Columba, for the soul of the Bishop, and for the other foresaid souls, and he shall be distinguished by the title of Dean's Chaplain. The second, however, at the Altar of St. Thomas, in the Cross of the Church, and he shall be called the Chaplain of Sir Alexander Dunbar, and shall pray for the soul of him, and of the said Isabell, his spouse, parents of the Bishop." . . . . "Moreover the said first Chaplain, entitled the Dean's Chaplain, shall make the Canons and Chaplains of the choir to celebrate yearly, with Gregorian chants, an anniversary, with a Mass of *requie placebo et dirige* for the soul of the Bishop on the day of his decease. . . . . . But the second Chaplain, called 'Sir Alexander Dunbar's,' shall in like manner cause to be celebrated by the same Canons and Chaplains of the choir another anniversary, with a Mass of *requie placebo et dirige*, for the souls of the said Sir Alexander, and of Isabell Sutherland, his spouse, parents of the Bishop, on the 10th day of the month of March."

(The above Charter is recorded in book 23, No. 79, in the Register of the Great Seal, and a copy of it is printed at pp. 417, 418 of the "Registrum Moraviense).

The subjoined extract is from page 223 of the British Museum copy of Monteith's "An Theater of Mortality," published in Edinburgh in 1713:—

"The Names of the Children of Sir Alexander Dunbar of Westfield, first Sheriff of Moray, as they are in the Dunbar's Burial-place, commonly called the Dunbars' Isle, in the Northside of the Cathedral Church of Morray, in Elgine—
1. Sir James Dunbar of Cumnock.
2. Sir John Dunbar of Mochrume.
3. Alexander Dunbar of Kilboyack.
4. Gavin Dunbar, Bishop of Aberdeen.
5. Janet Dunbar, Lady Innerugie.
6. David Dunbar, of Durrhs.
7. Mr. Patrick Dunbar, Chancellor of Aberdeen.
8. Leonard Dunbar, Student in Paris.
9. ——. Dunbar, who died young."

Of the above.

1. Sir James, of Cumnock and Westfield, heritable Sheriff of Moray, died on the 20th of April, 1504.

2. Sir John, of Mochrume, Stewart of Kircudbright, was killed in 1503 by Alexander Gordon, heir apparent of Lochinvar. (Sir John's second son, by his second wife, was Gavin Dunbar, Preceptor of King James V., Archbishop of Glasgow, and Lord High Chancellor of Scotland.)

3. Alexander, of Auldcash and Kilboyack, was killed in March, 1498, by Alexander Sutherland, of Daldred.

4. Gavin, Dean of Moray in 1487, Clerk of Register and of Council in 1503, Archdeacon of St. Andrews in 1506, was appointed Bishop of Aberdeen in 1519, and died on the 9th of March, 1531-2. His tomb may be seen outside the east end of the Cathedral of Aberdeen.

6. David, of Durris, died on the 23rd of February, 1521-2.

7. Mr. Patrick, Chancellor of Aberdeen and Caithness, died on the 8th of September, 1525.

The dates of the deaths of Sir Alexander, and of his sons, Gavin, David, and Patrick, are taken from the Kalendar of Ferne, now at Dunrobin.

Those of Dame Isabell Sutherland and of Sir James, are taken from two inquests recorded in the Sheriffs' Court Books at Aberdeen.

Unfortunately the upper part of the wall, on which the names were cut, has disappeared.

IV. On a slab with large cross filling almost the centre. Round the edge is:—

Hic. Jacet. Venerabilis. Vir. Magister. Gulielmus. Lyel. Quondam. Sub-decanatus. Eccles. Moravien. Obiit. Die. Men. 9 .... Anno. Dom. MCCCCCIIII.

Translation.—Here lies a venerable man, Mr. William Lyell, formerly Sub-Dean of the Church of Moray. He died the 9th day of the month .... in the year of our Lord 1504.

V. Hic. Jacet. Venerabilis. Thomas. Lesly. quondam. Rector de Kingusey, qui. obiit. Anno. Domini. MCCCCCXV.

Translation.—Here lies the venerable Thomas Lesly, formerly Rector of Kingussie, who died in the year of our Lord 1515.

VI. Hic. Jacet. Archibaldus. Lesly. quondam Rector de Rothes, qui obiit 3 Julii MCCCCCXX. Orate pro communi patria. (The rest effaced.)

Translation.—Here lies Archibald Lesly, formerly Rector of Rothes, who died 3 July, 1520. Pray for the common fatherland.

VII. Quiescit. in. Duo. M. Joannis Thorntoun ..... qui.

obiit. Anno. Domini. 1564. M. Jacobus. Thorntoun. Precentoris. Moravien. obiit. 1597. M. Henricus. Thorntoun. Judicens. obiit. 1593. Thomas .... Dedonanus et Elgine. obiit 1605. Margareta. Spalding. ejus sponsa M. Jacobi. sororis. filiæ. obiit. anno. domini. 1600 .... Hoc. Jacobus. Miln. filius. ....

VIII. On the west wall of the north Transept there is a tablet about 3 ft. square, with armorial shields, to the Dunbars of Bennagefield or Bennetsfield, in the parish of Avoch, Ross-shire. The inscription is curiously chiselled:—

Hic jacent M. John Dunbar de Bennethfield qui obiit 2 Decr., 1590, et Mar et Issob Dunbars ejus conjuges quæ obierunt 3 Nov., 1570, et 4 Decr., 1603, et Nicol Dunbar filius dicti M. Ion, quondam Balivus de Elgin, qui obiit 31 Janr¹, 1651, et Griss. Mavor, ejus spousa, que obiit 21 Juli, 1648, et Ione Dunbar, spousa Joni Dunbar filii dicti Nicol, que obiit 8 Septr., 1648; ideoque hoc instruendum curavit Joh. filius.

Translation.—Here lie Mr. John Dunbar of Bennetfield, who died 2nd Dec., 1590; and Margaret and Isabel Dunbars, his wives, who died 3rd Nov., 1570, and 4th Dec., 1603, and Nicol Dunbar, son of the said Mr. John, late Bailie of Elgin, who died 31st Jan., 1651, and Grace or Griswell Mavor, his wife, who died 21st July, 1648, and Joan Dunbar, wife of John Dunbar, son of the said Nicol, who died 8th Sep., 1648; and, therefore, John, the son, took care to have this to be erected.

IX. Requiescunt hic Robertus Innes ab eodem, et Elizabetha Elphinstone ejus conjux, qui fatis concesserunt 25 Septemb. et 26 Febr. anno sal. mun. 1597, et 1610. Ideoque in piam gratamque memoriam charissimorum parentum hoc monumentum extruendum curavit Robertus filius.

As a specimen of Mr. Monteith's translation the sequel is given:—

Here rests Robert Innes of that ilk and Elizabeth Elphinstone, his spouse, who died as above. And therefore Robert Innes, their son, caused this monument to be erected unto the pious and acceptable memory of his dearest parents.

X. Hic dormit in Domino Reverendus in Christo Pater M. Alexander Douglas, Præsul vigilantissimus Qui summa cum laude huic Urbi pastor, totique Moraviæ Episcopus profuit et præfuit 41 annos. Obiit ætatis suæ anno 62, et Christi, 1623, Maii 11. Relictis Alexandro et Maria liberis, uxoreque gravida femina, non minus vere religiosa quam generosa, cujus sumptibus hoc mausoleum structum est.

Semper vigila, ut si nescias quando veniat, paratum te inveniat, beati merientes in Domino, hæc corruptia induet incorruptionem.

B. M.   A. D. 1623.

O death, quhar is thy sting? O grave, quhar is thy victorie?

Bp. Douglas was buried in the south aisle of S. Giles' Church in a vault built by his widow and second wife, Mary Innes, daughter of Robert Innes of that ilk. Monteith says that, in 1706, the above was not legible. Then, how could he read it and publish it? When S. Giles' was demolished, in 1828, the monument was removed to the Cathedral. In 1851, June 30, Sheriff Cosmo Innes wrote to the Town Council, suggesting that it should again be removed from where it was (placed near the entrance gate) to some other more suitable spot, to where it now stands, in the north dyke or wall which encloses the Cathedral burying-ground.

XI. Here Lyes George Cummin of Lochtervandech, sometime Provost of Elgin, who died the 20 of September, 1689; and his spouse, Mariore Leslie, who died in September, the yeir of God 1656.

The above flat stone is in the south Transept, bearing the family arms. It was broken to pieces by the fall of the great steeple; when the debris was removed it was put together again. Provost Cumming's second wife is buried in S. Mary's Aisle, within the Duke of Gordon's tomb. Upon a slab, with the arms of the Gordons of Kinneddar:—

Here lyis the body of Lucretia Gordon, spouse to George Cuming, sometime Provost of Elgin, who died in September, 1668.

XII. Hic requiescunt exuviæ Margaretæ M'Aulay Murdochi miseratione divina Moraviensis quondam nunc Orcadum episcopi charissimæ conjugis, quæ fatis concessit mense Maio anno Dom. 1676. Necnon Davidis M'Kenzie prædicti episcopi filii natu minimi: ideoque in piam gratamque memoriam monumentum hoc extruendum curarunt superstites.

Translation by Monteith.—Here rests the corps of Margaret M'Aulay, dearest spouse to Murdoch by the mercy of God late Bishop of Morray, now Bishop of Orkney, who died as above. Also the body of David M'Kenzie, youngest son to the said Bishop. Therefore this monument is erected by the surviving to their pious and acceptable memory.

XIII. This monument, erected by Coline Falconer, minister of Forres, for himself and Lillias Rose, his spouse, and their posteritie, Jany. 13th, 1676. Job xix. 25, 26.

Near to the above in the same wall on a marble tablet:—

Sacred to the memory of Colin Falconer, son of William Falconer of Dounduff and Beatrix Dunbar, who was the daughter of J. Dunbar of Bogs, in the County of Moray, and grandson of Alexander Falconer of Halkerton and Elizabeth, daughter of Sir Archibald Douglas of Glenbervie. He was born in the year 1623, and was married in 1648 to a daughter of Rose of Clava. He was elected to the See of Argyle 1679, and in 1680 he was consecrated Bishop of Moray. He died 11th Nov., 1686, and was buried in the aisle of St. Giles' Church of Elgin.

This monument was erected by Hugh Innes, Esq. of Lochalsh, M.P. for the County of Ross, anno 1812, his great great-grandson.

XIV. Here lyes ane honest man called John Stronach, some tym of Mathie Miln, who departed this lyf 5 day of September, 1679, and Janet Leith, his spouse, who died the * day of *

Here we lye asleep
Till Christ the world surround,
This sepulcher we keep
Until the trumpet sound.

XV. Here. lyes. ane. honest. man. called. John. Geddes. Bvrgess. of. Elgin. who. died. Jvly. 1660.

XVI. Here. lyes. the. bodie. of. Lucretia. Gordon. spovs. to. George. Gordon. sometime. Provost. of. Elgin. who. died. in. September. 1668.

XVII. Monumentum D. Ro. Dunbar de Grangehill Durrsiorum triby Princeps 1675, in memoriam charissimæ conjuges [curravit] marits.

A holy virgin in her younger lyff,
And next a prudent and a faithful wyf,
A pious mother who with Christian care
Informed her children with the love and fear
Of God and vertuous acts, who can express
More (Reader) by a volum from the press?

XVIII. 1679.   Mind mortalitie
Concour eternalty.

* Never inserted.

Betwixt the cradle and the grave no rest we have.
Fear God, O mortal man what art thou doeing. Remember thy earant for thy glas is Runing.
It is no great matter whear the bodye be laied or whow it may be handled If it be well with the sowl.
This is the burial-place of James Young, glover burgess in Elgin, and his spovs, Agnes Stewart, and their children.

For the sepulchre of the Dukes of Gordon in St. Mary's Aisle, see pages 59, 60. The following appears in the "Theater of Mortality":

XIX. Hic jacet Joanna Gordon de Thomastoun, quæ obiit Elgini, 25 Julii, 1691. Ætatis 65. Matrona meritissima & honoroficæ parentelæ; seu virgo, seu nupta, seu orbata viro, supra sui sexus modum præclara; per 14 An. R. D. Geo. Chalmer, quondam de Raynie rectori matrimonio conjuncta: post cujus obitum per 31 An. perduravit fere vidua, erga Deum religiosa, semet sobria, liberorum & nepotum provida: quorum nonnulli defuncti, nominatim Margareta, uxor Jo. Grant, burg. de Elgin, quæ obiit 26 Decem. 1694. Hic secum sub spe beatæ resurrectionis requiescunt in pace.

Translation by Monteith.—Here lies Jean (?) Gordon of Thomastoun, who died as above. A most deserving matron and of honourable parentage. Virgin, wife, and widow, she was very famous, above the measure of her sex. For the space of 14 years she was married to the Reverend Mr. Geo. Chalmer, parson of Raynie, after whose death she continued a widow almost the space of 31 years, being religious towards God, sober towards her self, provident towards her children and grandchildren, whereof some are deceased, namely Margaret Chalmers, wife to John Grant, burgess of Elgine, who died 26 December, 1694, and rest here with her self, under the hope of a blessed resurrection.

XX. Here lyes James Laing, burgess of Elgin, who died the 8 of January, 1694, and Marin Lainge, his spovs, who died the 10 of August, 1682, and . . .

XXI. Here is the buril-place of Wm. Stevenson, som tyme gardner in the Colladge and burgess in Elgin, who liued vertuously and died under the sense of mercie in Christ the 4 day of February, 1684, and his spouse, Beatrix Bapley, who died the 4 day of Apl., 1717, and their chil Vileam, Alex., Besie, Isobel, Karen Stenson.

XXII. Grace me guid in hope I byde.
        Memento mori. 1687.

Heir is the burial-place appointed for John Geddis, glover burges in Elgin, and Issobell M'Kean, his spouse, and their relations.
This world is a cite full of streets,
And death is the mercab that all men meets.
If lyfe were a thing that money could buy,
The poor could not live, and the rich would not die.

XXIII. Sub hoc. cippo, conduntur exuviæ Annæ Cook, piæ modestæ ac charissimæ conjugis magistri Alexandri Gadderer, V. D. M. apud Girvanos Airenses, quæ obiit Januarii 17, 1698. Anno ætatis 25. Ibidem natorum ex iisdem nuptiis secundis paternis, viz. Jacobi Gadderer, qui obiit July 11, 1696, semestri exacto super annum infantiæ; Alexandri, qui obiit Maii 12, 1696, 4to a nativitate die.

Translation by Monteith.—Under this gravestone are reposed the bodies of Anna Cook, pious, modest, and most dear wife to Mr. Alexander Gadderar, minister at Girvan, Ayrshire, who died as above. And of James and Alexander Gadderars, children of the said second marriage, whereof James died as above, being above his infancy a year and a half old, and Alexander died as above, the 4th day after his birth.

XXIV. Memoriæ sacrum Elizabethæ Gadderar, filiae unicæ ex lectissima matre, Katharina Lammie, Angusiana. Pater utrique superstes Magister Alexander Gadderar, præco evangelii apud Girvanos Airenses posuit. Hæc obiit Aprilis 20, 1688. Ætatulæ suæ anno 8vo.
Unde sies, quid sis, quid futuris, hinc cognosce viator.

Translation by Monteith.—Consecrate to the memory of Elizabeth Gadderar, only daughter of a most choice mother, Katharine Lammie, an Angus gentlewoman. Mr. Alexander Gadderar, above designed father, yet surviving both (meaning this person and the above mother), placed this gravestone. She died as above. Passenger, learn hence where you are, what you are, and what you are to be.

XXV. Sub hoc cippo requiescunt Jacobus Innes, legitimus filius Magistri Joannis Innes, peritissimi medicinæ doctoris, fratris natu minoris Roberti Innes quondam domini de Drainie, & Maria Seton ejus uxor, legitima filia Davidis Seton, quondam domini de Menie, ; qui mortem obiere, ille pridie cal. Julii, anno 1685, & haec . . . . Extruendum curavit David Innes, filius superstes.

Translation by Monteith.—Under this gravestone rest James Innes, lawful son to Mr. John Innes, a most skilful doctor of medicine, younger brother to Robert Innes, sometime proprietor of Drainie; and Mary Seton, his wife, lawful daughter to David Seton, late of Meny, who died, he upon the last day of June, 1685, she . . . . David Innes, their surviving son, caused erect this monument.

XXVI. Hic jacet magister Thomas Paterson, filius legitimus quarto genitus Joannis, Episcopi Rossensis, qui obiit primo die Septembris, Anno Dom., 1674.

Translation.—Here lies Mr. Thomas Paterson, 4th lawful begotten son of John, Bishop of Ross, who died 1st Sep., 1674.

XXVII. Ps. xix. 7. John v. 28, 29.

    Corpore præstanti, vultuque animoque serena,
        Et bis nupta viro, hic suavis Eliza jacet;
    Fœmina labe vacans, piisque parentibus orta,
        Virtute & meritis, laude & honore nitens;
    Ter denos vixit sex & ferme insuper annos,
        Fida viris, mundo mortua, chara Deo.
        Decessit 12 die Augusti 1698. Ætatis 36.

Memoriæ charissimæ conjugis, Elizabethæ Paterson, dignissimis parentibus, ecclesiæ Scoticanæ ministris fidelissimis prognatæ; monumentum hoc extruendum curavit superstes maritus, dominus Jacobus Thomson, pastor Elginensis.

    Elizabeth here lyes, who led her life
    Unstained while virgin and twice-married wife;
    She was her parents' image—her did grace
    All the illustrious honours of the face;
    With eminent piety and complaisance
    All the decorments of exalted sense.
    David's swan song much in her mouth she had,
    More in her heart, on it established.
    Departing hence, it being her desire
    All and delight just when she did expire.
    By all bewailed, she in the flower of age,
    As Jacob's Rachel, was turned off the stage.
    One only child besides death by his sting
    Unto this urn within three days did bring.

XXVIII. This monument is erected by Major Hugh M'Ray, in remembrance of Margaret Sinclair, his spouse, lady of Kinloch, a daughter of the familie of Allister, who died at Elgin the 2nd day of March, 1690.

XXIX. Ach me. Am bvt gravel and dust, and to the grave returnin. I ·· most ·· o · painted pice · living glass. Man, be not

provd in thy shourt day. Hear lys the body of William
Sherar, . . . Elgin. . . .

XXX. Hic requiescit vir pius ac reverendus, dominus Robertus
Langlands, fulgentissimum quondam ecclesiæ sidus mellifluus
verbi præco, fidelis mysteriorum Dei œconomus, ecclesiæ Glas-
cuensis per annos aliquot pastor vigilantissimus; et ad Elginum,
paulo ante obitum, generalis hujus ecclesiæ synodi decreto
translatus ubi pie ac placide obiit pridie idus Augusti, anno
Dom. 1696. In cujus memoriam, monumentum hoc extruendum curarunt, amici et reverendus collega, dominus Jacobus
Thomson.

  Hac situs est humili clarus Langlandius urna,
  Flebilis heu cunctis occidit ille probis,
  Præco pius reserans sacri mysteria verbi,
  Et docuit populum sedulus usque; suum.
  Doctrinæ laudes variæ, prudentia rerum,
  Ornabant animum consiliumque; sagax;
  Et licet Elginum teneat, quem Glascua quondam
  Dilexit, proprium vendicat ipse polus.

Translation by Monteith.—Here rests a godly and reverend
man, Mr, Robert Langlands, lately a most bright star of the
Church, a most sweet preacher of the word, a faithful steward
of the mysteries of God, a most vigilant minister at Glasgow
for some years, and by an act of the General Assembly of this
Church translated to Elgine a little before his death, he died
piously and pleasantly 12 August 1696, to whose memory, his
friends and his reverend collegue, Mr. James Thomson, caused
this monument to be erected.

  In this small grave, the famous Langlands lies;
  All good men mourn for his sad obsequies;
  A faithful preacher, op'ning mysteries;
  Nor slothful, but was teaching ev'rywhere
  His people, with sedulity and care.
  His various learning and his counsel sound,
  With prudence great, adorned well his mind;
  Tho' Elgine holds, whom Glasgow lov'd before,
  Yet heav'n it self him claimeth for its glore.

In the North Aisle of St. Giles'.

XXXI*.—Robertus Lesly, comitus qui filius olim
  Rothusie fuerat, simul et suavissima conjux,
  Elpstonii soboles herois, conduntur in antro
  Hoc licet obscuro, celebres pietate supersunt.
  Hos quondam binos Hymenæus junxit in unum

Corpus, et his vivis semper suit una voluntas,
Unus amor, domus una fuit; nunc lumine cassos,
Una duos iterum condit libitina sepultos.

Translation by Monteith.

Tho' Robert Lesly, earl of Rothes son,
With his sweet wife, daughter of Elphinstone,
Heroick blood, lie in this grave obscure,
Their shining graces ever do endure.
Those, sometime two, did hymen join in one
Body and mind, in life's conjunction;
They had one love, one house; and now when dead,
Them here one grave and tomb has covered.

XXXIA. O death, where is thy sting? This is the burial place ordained for Arthur Chalmer, lister burgess in Elgin, and Jean Forbes, his spouse and their children.

Stay, passenger, consider well
That thou ere long in dost must dwell.
Endeavour then while thou hast health
Still to avoid the 2d death.
For on tymes minut doth depend
Torment and joy without all end.

O grave, where is thy victory?

XXXII. Here. lyes. ane. honest. man. called. Colin. Innes. glover Burgess in Elgin who departed this lyfe the 6 Febrie 1688.

XXXIII. Heir lyes. the corps of Janet M'Katn, spouse to William Nilson, sometime sedler burges in Elgin. She died the 15 day of April 1698.

XXXIV. This. is. nou. the. heritage. of. John. Cant. and. Jean. Forbes. his. spouse. indwellers. in. Bishopmilne. and. their. children.

Under. this. stone. lyes. the. bodie. of. ane. piovs. worthie. vertvois. gentle. woman. called. An. Forbes. spovs. to. Arthvr. Chalmer. lister. bvrgess. in. Elgin. who. departed. this. life. the. 15. day. of. September. 1695.

XXXV. Here. lyes. the. body. of. aine. piovs. and. vertvous. gentlewoman. Janet. Hephbvrn. spovs. to. Robert. Anderson. Commissar. Clerk. Mvray. who. dept. this. life. the. 10. day. of. March. 1692.

XXXVI. Here. lyes. the. children. of. Charles. Gordon. merchant. in. Elgin. Margt. Dvnbar. his. spous. to. vit. Robert

Alexander. Andrew. Margaret. Elspet. 9. who. died. in. the. nonage. (A verse of Scripture here.)

XXXVII. Here. lyes. . . . called. David. Petrie. . . . who. departed. the. 8. of. November. 1686 . . . and . . . my . . D . . . D . . . Chl.

XXXVIII. Here. lyes. the. bodie. of. Robert. Moray˙ glower. burgess. in. Elgin. who. died. the. 3. of. October. 1694˙ and his children James, Margaret, and Janet Moray.

✓ XXXIX. Here lyes the body of James Donaldson, merchant in Elgin, who died 13th day of November, 1698. I. D. and Jean M'Kean, his spouse, who died the 20 day of August, 1702.

XL. In piam gratamque memoriam reverendi admod. D.D. Alexandri King, celeberrimi nuper ecclesiastae fidelissimi suo gregi pastoris viri ornatissimi, qui Bonnills in Levinia annos X mituere suo sacro faeliciter functis et nationalis synodi theologorum Scotiae decreto Elginum translatus ibidem XV. circiter annis in eodem opere haud levi cum successu peroclis XXII mens Xoris an christogonias MDCCXV. Etat. suae LXIII—alitaber exuvias deposuit.

Memoriae suæ acer preclarae indolis & optimae spei juvenum Alexandri et Humphredi docti R. Dom. filiorum. Hic non. August. A.D. CI₀ Dec. VI, aetat. XI, ille XIII. calend. Jul. A.Æ. C.MDCCXI, aetat. XIX. vovam curii morte multarunt.

Puellae ibidem perpulchrae Isobellæ ejusdem R. D. filiae natu minimae quae XV. calend. sub An. ærae ante dictae 1703, ætat. suae iv, diem obiit.

XLI. Here lyes John Rind, gardener burgess in Elgin, who died the 28th of April, 1708.

XLII. 17   J. G.   K. B.   08.
[Cherub.]   [Cherub.]

This monument is erected by Katherin Brodie in remembrance of her deceast husband, James Gordon, merchant burgess of Elgin, who lieved Honestly, behaved discreetly, and at length, aged about 36 years, dyed Christianly the 3d December, 1708, and there children Margaret, Elizabeth, and Katherin Gordons.

Katherine Brodie died the 20 July, 1745, aged 67, and wife of the above James Gordon.

XLIII. Sub hoc cippo conduntur, in spem beatæ resurrectionis, exuviæ Robertii Innes filii lectissimi honorandi viri, Valteri Innes a Blackhills, qui morte abreptus in flore juventutis, animi vere generosi candore, vultus ingenui nitore, morum probitate, vitæ integritate, erga omnes charitate, veritatis ac pacis cultu semper conspicuus, magnum apud omnes sui desiderium reliquit, pie ac placide in Christo obdormivit Aprilis 23, 1705.

Translation by Monteith.—Under this gravestone are laid up, in hopes of a blessed resurrection, the corps of Robert Innes, most choice son of an honourable man, Walter Innes of Blackhills; who, being always notable for the candour of a truly generous mind, the brightness of an ingenuous countenance, for the probity of his manners, integrity of his life, his charity towards all persons, and for his respect to truth and peace, was taken away by death in the flower of his youth, and left a great desire of himself with all people, and fell asleep piously and pleasantly in the Lord as above.

XLIV. Memoriæ sacrum honorandi viri Valteri Innes, a Blackhills, qui obiit 6 die Februarii, 1708, & lectissimæ conjugis Isabellæ Kynnaird, quæ obiit . . . et posterorum.

Translation.—Sacred to the memory of an honoured man, Walter Innes of Blackhills, who died the 6th day of Feb., 1708; and of his most choice spouse, Isabella Kinnaird, who died . . . and their posterity. (See pages 404, 405.)

XLV. Sub spe beatæ resurrectionis reconduntur hic exuviæ Magistri Joannis Gilzean, filii Joannis Gilzean, municipis Elginensis; juvenis eximiæ sane indolis, ingenii acumine, bonarumque literarum cognitione, & pietate erga Deum assidua, parentes observantia, proximum benevolentia; morum denique, probitate in primis insignis: qui pie ac placide in Christo obdormivit, immatura morte fatisque abreptus acerbis, die 22 Jan. anno christogonias supra sesqui millesimum ducentesimo decimo, cum 20 annos & septem menses vixisset.

Translation by Monteith.—In hope of a blessed resurrection, here are laid up the spoils of Mr. John Gilzean, son to John Gilzean, burgess of Elgine; a youth of a truly notable engine, chiefly remarkable for his sharpness of wit, learning, constant piety towards God, obedience to his parents, good will to his neighbours, and lastly the probity of his conversation; who piously and pleasantly fell asleep in Christ, being pluckt away by untimely death and bitter fates in the year 1710, when he had lived 20 years and 7 months.

XLVI. Here lyes the body of Elizabeth Forbes, daughter to Robert Forbes, of . . . who departed this life at Elgin on the 12th of . . . 171 . . .

XLVII. This is the burial-place of John Innes, shoemaker burgess of Elgin, and his deceast spouse Janet Finlay, who died the 10 of Jany., 1722, and their children.

XLVIII. This is the burial-place of Anna Dunbar, spouse to Robt. Allan, senior, merchant in Elgin, who died 2 March, 1732, and James and Mary Allan, his children, and John Dunbar, late bayley in Elgin, and Janet Brodie, his sps. Job xiv. 1 and 2: "Man that is born of a woman is of few days and full of trouble. He cometh forth like a flower and is cut; he fleeth also as a shadow and continueth not." Job xix. 25, 26, 27. 1 Thes. iv. 14.

XLIX. Isobel Finlay, 1719.

L. This is the burial-place of Robert M'Kean, merchant burgess in Elgin, who departed this life the 14th day of April, 1722, and of age 55 years; and Agnes Pedder, his spouse, who * .✝.

LI. Hear lys the bodie of John Hall, weaver in Old . . . who dyed November the 8, 1725, and his son Joseph, who dyed . . . Benjamin James Hal.

LII. This is the burial-place of John Hay, merchant in Elgin, and Katherine Brodie, his spouse, with their children. Also here lyes the body of Katharine Russell, spouse to John Dunbar, merchant in Elgin, and grandmother to the said Katherine Brodie, who died the 25 of January, 1733.

LIII. This is the burial-place of Thomas Stephen, merchant in Elgin, who died the 19 of June, 1728, and of Elspet Dunbar, his spouse, who died the 20 of December, 1721, and of their son, Provost James Stephen, who died the 25 of February, 1779, aged 78, and his spouse, Ann Innes, daughter of Sir Harry Innes of Innes, who died the 7 of July, 1771, aged 69.

LIV. This is the burial-place of James M'Kean, merchant burgess in Elgin, who died the 12th Day of December, 1776, aged 72, and of his spouse, Elspet Ronald. J. F. B. Mc.

LV. This is the burial-place of Isobell M'Kean, lawful daughter to Robert M'Kean, late Bailie of Elgin, spouse to Mr. James Cruickshank, master of the Grammar School. She died the 12 of July, 1738. J. F. B. Mc.

LVI. To the memory of Katherine M'Andrew, a trusting, worthy Christian, who died Aug. 16, 1770, aged 43 years.

* Never inserted. ▲

This stone is placed by William and James M'Andrew of London, as a small token of true filial affection.

LVII. This is the burial-place of William Brander, merchant in Elgin, who died the 3 day of June, 1768, aged 24 years. "Thy dead men shall live together; with my dead body shall they arise."—Is. xxvi. 19.

> For man, it is manifest,
> Shall satisfy for man . . .
> And dying rise and rising with him saw
> His brother ransomed with his own dear life. . . .

LVIII. This stone was erected by James Sinclair, writer in Edinburgh, to the memory of John Sinclair, senior merchant in Elgin, and Rachel Jeffrey, his spouse, and of their children and grandchildren. 1772.

LIX. Here lies interred the body of James Miler, who died the 4th day of July, 1774, aged 66 years.

LX. Here lies William Stewart of Lesmurdie, who died the 12th day of May, 1771, and Barbara King, his spouse, who died the 8th day of December, 1794.

LXI. Here lyes the dust of the worthy and pious James Cramont, late bailie of Elgin, who dyed Feb. 12, 1737, aged 68, and of his spouse, Margaret Barrie, who died Jany. 17, 1746, and Mr. James, Alex., Elspet, Jean, Margaret, and Isobel Cramond, their children. Job xix. 23—"For I know that my Redeemer liveth," &c.

LXII. In sure and certain hope of a blessed and glorious resurrection, here lies the body of John Shaw, merchant and conveener of Elgin, who departed this life the 13 day of November, 1740 years. Also his spouse, An Baxter. Also their children.

LXIII. This is the burial-place of David Dickson, weaver and bleacher at Elgin, and Janet Cars, who died Jany. 7, 1748, aged 32, and their lawful son, Alex. Dickson.

LXIV. This is the burial-place of William M'Andrew, younger glover burgess in Elgin, who died the 9th of Feb., 1734, and Janet Chalmers, his spouse, who * . . . and their children.

LXV. This is the burial-place of John Stephen, merchant, senior burgess, who died the 16th of July, 1750, and Margaret Grant, his spouse, also * . . . and their children, Helen, Andrew, Wm., Mariore Stephens.

* Never inserted.

LXVI. Here lyes the body of James Grant, deacon of the Taylors, and burgess in Elgin, who died the 22 of Jany., 1760, aged 40 years, and his spouse, Margaret Morison.

LXVII. Here lies the body of John Scot, some time merchant burgess of Elgin, who departed this life June 7, 1766, aged 33. This stone was erected to perpetuate his memory by Isobell Anderson, his spouse.

LXVIII. This monument is erected by William Grant, in memory of Elizabeth Stephen, his spouse. She was born at Elgin 22 Feb., 1749, and died at Grantsgreen 3 July, 1768, in the day after the birth of her first and only child.

O what avail fair Beauty's fairest forms,
Harmonious features and attractive charms,
With modest wit, good nature, steady sense,
A heart of Kindness, Truth, and Innocence,
Which feels and shares a neighbour's joy and woe,
Nor knows a thought but all mankind might know.

When sweet Eliza meeting an early fall,
Just she was and lov'd, called off and mourned by all,
Alas no more our ravished breasts to move
With songs and smiles of innocence and love,
Why labour'd nature so profusely, say,
To form so fine a flower to last a day.

Yes she was form'd to teach our thoughts to rise
And call'd to draw and fix them to the skies,
Upright, approv'd to leave the stage
To shun infection in a wicked age,
And with blest Bands ever endless day employ
In scenes of beauty, virtue, love, and joy.

LXIX. This monument is erected by William Grant, in memory of Elizabeth Brodie, his second spouse. She was born at Elgin — Aprile, 1735, and died at Grantsgreen 18 August, 1779. She was remarkable for exact, prudent, genteel economy, ready, equal, good sense, a constant flow of cheerful spirits, an uncommon sweetness of natural temper, a great warmth of heart-affection, and an early and continued piety. Tho' these qualities displayed daily in her manner and actions could not fail of gaining esteem and affection, yet strict justice demanded this tribute to her memory.

LXX. On the south side of St. Mary's aisle, affixed to the wall with iron clasps, is a large Slab on which is inscribed the names of the Andersons of Linkwood for generations:—

This is the burial place of Thomas Anderson in Barmuckity, who died the 4th day of May, 1674; and of Robert Anderson, Commissary-Clerk of Murray, his son, who died the 17th Oct., 1715; and of Janet Hepburn, his spouse, who died the 10th March, 1692; and of James Anderson of Linkwood, Provost of Elgin, who died the 28th Aug., 1731, aged 51; and of Barbara King, his spouse, who died the 18th July, 1744, aged 56; and of William Anderson of Linkwood, Provost of Elgin, their son, who died the 13th June, 1745, aged 38. Likeways of Margaret Gordon, daughter of Alexr. Gordon of Cairnfield, spouse of Robert Anderson of Linkwood; also their son, who died the 6th April, 1777, aged 51; and of the said Robert Anderson, who died 4th March, 1797, aged 61; and of Charles Anderson, Manufacturer in Huntly, youngest son of Robert Anderson of Linkwood, who died 1st Nov., 1790, aged 30. Captain Alex. Anderson, of the 69th Regiment, eldest son of Robert Anderson of Linkwood, who died at Limerick, in Ireland, the 30th May, 1791, aged 38; and of James Anderson, Esq., second son of Robert Anderson of Linkwood, who died at Edinburgh the 20th May, 1808, aged 51; and of Clementina Gordon, daughter of Mr. Gordon in Newseat, spouse of the said Charles Anderson, who died 25th Oct., 1813, aged 52. Charles Anderson, their son, and Harriet Routh, his spouse, who both died and were buried at Aberdeen.

On another Slab, adjoining the above:—

In memory of Robert Anderson, Sheriff-Substitute and Commissary-Clerk of Moray, who died the 6th Dec., 1766; Elizabeth Mackintosh, daughter of William Mackintosh of Blervie, his first wife; Marjory Anderson, daughter of James Anderson of Linkwood, his second wife, who died 1761; Barbara Anderson, spouse of James Thurburn, in Drum, his daughter, who died 26th Feb., 1809; Lieutenant Robert Anderson, their son, who died at Bishopmill the 21st Aug., 1835, aged 80, and Isabella Thurburn, daughter of the above James Thurburn and Barbara Anderson, who died 7th Sep., 1845, aged 59.

On the above Stone is cut the Anderson arms:—Argent —a Saltier engailed sable, between four mullets, gules. Crest—A dexter hand, couped above the wrist, holding an arrow. Motto—REMEMBER THE END.

The Kings of Newmill were buried in the Greyfriars' Church. This family for about 120 years held a prominent position in Elgin. Two of them were Provosts. They were proprietors of the lands of Newmill and Panns, of part of the Auchteen Part Lands, and of houses and grounds within the Burgh. They were also for some time owners of a considerable portion of the Parish of Birnie. *The Kings* were benevolent and charitable for generations. Ample details of the family are given in Young's *Annals of Elgin*, p. 608, and in *Morayshire Described*, p. 203. They are buried in the Greyfriars' Church, where are the following Memorials:—

LXXI. In memory of THE REV. LACHLAN SHAW, Historian of the Province of Moray, And one of the Collegiate Ministers of Elgin, who died on the 23rd of February, 1777, in the 91st year of his age, and 61st of his ministry; And whose remains are interred within the walls of this Cathedral. This Monument is erected by a few Subscribers, admirers of Mr. Shaw's talents and worth. November, 1868.

The Fenton Tomb.

(1.) Sacred to the memory of Bailie John Fenton, sometime merchant in Elgin; Elspeth Young, his spouse, and their children; Christian Fenton, sister to the said John Fenton, who departed this life 1720.

(2.) This monument is erected by Provost George Fenton, in memory of Bailie Andrew Fenton, sometime merchant in Elgin, his father, who died 1st July, 1787, aged 75 years; and of Ann Sanders, his mother, who died 11th October, 1802, aged 74 years; and of James Fenton, his son, who died 21st January, 1796, aged 6 years.

(3.) Sacred to the memory of Mrs. Ann Fenton, spouse of Patrick Cameron, Esquire, writer in Elgin, who departed this life 16th November, 1824, aged 35 years. She was a dutiful daughter, an affectionate wife, and died much and justly regretted.

LXXII. Not far from the High Altar is a detached beautifully carved stone, bearing on the shield a Buck's head, and under it the sun shining, with the letters $M^B O M^L M$, and the Motto—" Cœlum fide cerno " (By faith I discern heaven). The stone refers to MURDO MACKENZIE BISHOP OF MORAY. See page 392, Epitaph XII., for his wife and son. Also Vol. III., pp. 344-346.

PROVOSTS OF THE BURGH OF ELGIN.

Thomas Wysman, Provost in	1261
Walter, the son of Ralph,	1343
John Young,	1540
William Hay of Mayne,	1549
William Gadderar,	1557
John Annand,	1567, 1568, & 1580
Alexander Seton, Earl of Dunfermline, about	1606
James Rutherford,	1618
John Hay,	1632
John Hay,	1643
John Douglas,	1657
George Cuming of Lochtervandich,	1663
Thomas Calder,	1666
George Cuming,	1670 to 1687
Sir Alexander Innes of Coxton,	1687 „ 1688
David Stewart,	1689
William Calder of Spynie,	1689 „ 1690
William King of Newmill,	1690 „ 1700
James, Lord Duffus,	1700 „ 1705
William Sutherland,	1705 „ 1709
William King of Newmill,	1709 „ 1711
George Innes of Dunkinty,	1711 „ 1714
Archibald Dunbar of Thunderton, M.A.,	1714 „ 1717
Robert Innes, Doctor of Medicine,	1717 „ 1720
James Innes, Doctor of Medicine,	1720 „ 1723
Robert Innes, M.D., from 1723 to 1726, when he died.	
James Innes, M.D.,	1726 „ 1729
James Anderson of Linkwood, from 1729 to 1731, when he died	
James Innes, Doctor of Medicine,	1731 to 1734
John Robertson, merchant,	1734 „ 1737
James Innes, Doctor of Medicine,	1737 „ 1740
William Anderson of Linkwood,	1740 „ 1743
James Stephen, merchant,	1743 „ 1746
John Duff, senior, merchant,	1746 „ 1749
Alexander Brodie of Windyhills,	1749 „ 1752
James Robertson of Bishopmill,	1752 „ 1755
Alexander Brodie of Windyhills,	1755 „ 1758
James Robertson of Bishopmill,	1758 „ 1761
Alexander Brodie of Windyhills,	1761 „ 1764
James Robertson of Bishopmill,	1764 „ 1767
Alexander Brodie of Windyhills,	1767 „ 1770
Thomas Stephen, merchant,	1770 „ 1771
John Duff, merchant,	1771 „ 1774
Alexander Brodie of Windyhills,	1774 „ 1775
John Duff, merchant,	1775 „ 1778
Alexander Brodie of Windyhills,	1778 „ 1779
John Duff, merchant,	1779 „ 1782

PROVOSTS AND BAILIES IN THE BURGH OF ELGIN. 407

George Brown, Linkwood, - - - - 1782 to 1785
John Duff, merchant, - - - - - 1785 „ 1788
George Brown, Linkwood, - - - - 1788 „ 1791
John Duff, merchant, - - - - - 1791 „ 1792
Alexander Brander, merchant, - - - 1792 „ 1795
George Brown, Linkwood, - - - 1795 „ 1798
Alexander Brander, merchant, - - - 1798 „ 1799
George Brown, Linkwood, - - - - 1799 „ 1801

PROVOSTS AND BAILIES FROM 1801 TO 1833.

1801.—George Brown, Provost; John Forteath, Francis Taylor. John Forsyth, junior, and Robert Joss, Bailies.
1802.—Joseph King of Newmill, Provost; John Forteath, Alexr. Innes, William Gauldie, and George Fenton, Bailies.
1803.—George Brown, Provost; Francis Taylor, Alexander Innes, Robert Joss, and William Gauldie, Bailies.
1804.—George Brown, Provost; Peter Nicholson, Francis Taylor, Robert Joss, and George Fenton, Bailies.
1805.—George Brown, Provost; William Dunbar, John Forsyth, jun., William Gauldie, and Peter Nicholson, Bailies.
1806.—Joseph King of Newmill, Provost; Francis Taylor, Wm. Gauldie, Robert Joss, and William Dunbar, Bailies.
1807.—Joseph King, Provost; Francis Taylor, Robert Joss, Peter Nicholson, and John Russell, Bailies.
1808.—Joseph King, Provost; William Gauldie, Joseph Collie, Peter Nicholson, and John Russell, Bailies.
1809.—George Brown, Provost; William Gauldie, Francis Taylor, Robert Joss, and Joseph Collie, Bailies.
1810.—George Brown, Provost; Francis Taylor, Robert Joss, Peter Nicholson, and John Russell, Bailies.
1811.—George Brown, Provost; William Gauldie, Joseph Collie, Peter Nicholson, and John Russell, Bailies.
1812.—George Fenton, Provost; William Gauldie, Joseph Collie, Francis Taylor, and Robert Joss, Bailies.
1813.—George Fenton, Provost; Francis Taylor, Robert Joss, Peter Nicholson, and John Russell, Bailies.
1814.—George Fenton, Provost; William Gauldie, Peter Nicholson, John Russell, and Joseph Collie, Bailies.
1815.—George Brown, Provost; Francis Taylor, Robert Joss, William Gauldie, and Joseph Collie, Bailies.
1816.—Colonel Francis William Grant, Provost; Francis Taylor, Robert Joss, Peter Nicholson, and John Russell, Bailies.
1817.—Colonel Francis William Grant, Provost; William Gauldie, Peter Nicholson, John Russell, and Joseph Collie, Bailies.
1818.—Colonel Francis William Grant, Provost; Alexander Innes, Robert Joss, William Gauldie, and Joseph Collie, Bailies.
1819.—Sir Archd. Dunbar of Northfield, Baronet, Provost; Francis Taylor, Alexander Innes, Robert Joss, and Peter Nicholson, Bailies.
1820.—Alexander Innes, Provost; John Forsyth, jun., Peter Nicholson, William Dunbar, and David Cormie, Bailies.
1821.—Alexander Innes, Provost; John Forsyth, jun., William Dunbar, David Cormie, and Lewis Anderson, Bailies.

1822.—Alexander Innes, Provost; Peter Nicholson, Lewis Anderson, James Henry, and James Petrie, Bailies.
1823.—Peter Nicholson, Provost; John Forsyth, jun., James Henry, James Petrie, and Francis Cruikshank, Bailies.
1824.—Peter Nicholson, Provost; John Forsyth, jun., David Cormie, Lewis Anderson, and Francis Cruikshank, Bailies.
1825.—Peter Nicholson, Provost; David Cormie, Lewis Anderson, James Petrie, and Harry Milne, Bailies.
1826.—Alexander Innes, Provost; James Petrie, Francis Cruikshank, Harry Milne, and John Johnston, Bailies.
1827.—Alexander Innes, Provost; Francis Cruikshank, Harry Milne, John Johnston, and Lewis Anderson, Bailies.
1828.—Alexander Innes, Provost; Lewis Anderson, David Cormie, Alexander Young, and George Robertson, Bailies.
1829.—John Lawson, junior, Provost; David Cormie, James Petrie, George Robertson, and Harry Milne, Bailies.
1830.—John Lawson, junior, Provost; Lewis Anderson, Harry Milne, John Johnston, and John M'Kimmie, Bailies.
1831.—John Lawson, junior, Provost; Lewis Anderson, John Johnston, John M'Kimmie, and Francis Cruikshank, Bailies.
1832.—James Petrie, Provost; Francis Cruikshank, Alexander Forteath, Alexander Young, and John Walker, Bailies.

This was the last election under the old system, the Reform Bill having come into operation at the election in November, 1833.

PROVOSTS FROM 1833 TO 1881.

William Gauldie, merchant,	1833 to 1835
John M'Kimmie, merchant,	1835 „ 1839
Alexander Young, banker,	1839 „ 1840
John M'Kimmie, merchant,	1840 „ 1842
James Wilson,	1842 „ 1848
James Grant, solicitor,	1848 „ 1851
James Grant,	1851 „ 1854
The same,	1854 „ 1857
The same,	1857 „ 1860
The same,	1860 „ 1863
Alexander Russell,	1863 „ 1866
The same,	1866 „ 1869
Alexander Cameron of Mainhouse,	1869 „ 1872
The same,	1872 „ 1875
William Culbard, merchant,	1875 „ 1878
The same,	1878 „ 1881
James Black, editor,	1881

END OF VOL. I.

www.ingramcontent.com/pod-product-compliance
Lightning Source LLC
Chambersburg PA
CBHW030549300426
44111CB00009B/914